CHASING 193

THE QUEST TO VISIT EVERY COUNTRY IN THE WORLD

BY

RYAN TRAPP
&
LEE ABBAMONTE

Table of Contents

Foreword

At 36-years-old, I feel like I've lived two completely different lives. My first 20 years of life were spent being a normal suburban American kid. I played sports, hung out with my friends, went to parties, chased girls, worked, graduated high school, and went to college. My first two years of college were spent in pretty much the same way, and then a funny thing happened. I studied abroad and everything changed.

I had never left the United States, and I had barely seen the northeastern U.S. for that matter except for a trip to Florida to visit family when I was a kid, and I hated that trip! Living in London in my junior year of college and traveling throughout Europe changed my life forever.

Before traveling, I only saw what was in front of me and never really veered from my goals. There's nothing wrong with that at all. However, now I like to veer off and see things from different angles and perspectives. I see things for how they are and not how they're said to be. I see things with an open mind. I've learned to look around a bit and take things in and look under the hood for things and experiences I didn't know existed.

Travel to me is a constant learning experience. It is the best education you can ever get. Travel teaches you about things you never dreamed about. Travel shows you there is so much good in the world, and travel can also show you the very worst of humanity. But the constant of travel is it's always changing. Travel is like golf. It's a hobby you can do your whole life and it's always different no matter how many times you play the same course.

Now I don't know what I'd do without travel. It's been such a big part of my adult life that it has actually become it. I have thus become a professional traveler. Not out of necessity or because it just happened accidentally. I consciously chose to do this because I love travel so much. It is a part of me.

I love to learn and I strive to have informed opinions on everything firsthand. Travel gives this to me, and no matter how many times you go to the same place it's always a different experience.

Travel is not about numbers and it's not about who did what or for how long. Travel is what you make of it. It is what you want it to be. Nobody travels like you and nobody takes what you take from it. Travel is yours. It is your freedom to do what you want; see what you want; meet who you want; go where you want; and be what you want. There is no end to travel — it will always be there.

That's what is so remarkable about this journey that I've been on the last 16 years. It's been a journey of self-discovery when I had already discovered myself long ago. I've never been running from anything, but I've always been running *to* something that's continually changing. Again, that's one of the beautiful things about travel and about exploring and discovery. You just have to take the steps to make it happen.

This book about remarkable travelers and their quests to see as much of the world as they can shows us how people from different walks of life came to this amazing but difficult hobby and lifestyle.

This book aims to find out what motivates them. In these interviews, extraordinary travelers are asked about themselves, their backgrounds, and the "why" behind their love of travel.

Only 98 people in history have (or claim to have) traveled to every country in the world. That's an amazingly small number considering how many people live and have lived on this planet since the advent of air travel. It's a remarkable number, and I feel honored to be a part of this elite fraternity.

Take it from me; traveling to every country in the world is not easy, nor is it cheap. What makes people want to sacrifice so much time, money — and potentially relationships — to visit every country? What makes people want to chase 193?

I think it's also important to distinguish how many countries there are in the world and where the number 193 comes from. 193 is the number of United Nations member states or countries. If you search around the Internet you will see other numbers as well for explaining how many countries there are in the world.

However, there are only 193 internationally recognized UN member states. The only other number I am willing to entertain as the number of countries is 196 if you count the Vatican, Taiwan, and Kosovo. The Vatican technically is a country, but it's not a UN member. Taiwan and Kosovo are not UN countries either, and are not counted for the purposes of this book.

There are many other lists and definitions of how many countries there are depending on who you ask. I've seen people conclude there are 206, 245, and other arbitrary numbers. Those are not accurate.

There are also travel clubs with lists like the Travelers Century Club, which currently lists the number of "countries" at 324. I quote the word countries because this word is loosely interpreted and includes places like Puerto Rico and Guam as being separate from the United States or French Guiana and French Polynesia as being separate from France. While I agree this is a more comprehensive travel list and a better indication of how widely traveled a person is, not all the countries listed are actually countries. Other lists range from 800+ to over 4000, where you get into the strange and obscure. So again, we focus on 193 countries.

Now, let's get started Chasing 193!

Lee Abbamonte

Markus Lundgren, Sweden

(Markus Lundgren at the South Pole, 2015)

Where did you grow up and what was your early life like?

I grew up in Piteå, in northern Sweden, and I still enjoy snow, although I can do without the darkness. Growing up I traveled a lot around Sweden, but my first trip abroad (not counting Finland and Norway) was to Cyprus when I was 14.

When did you go from casually traveling to making this a full-time goal, and what motivated you to travel to every country?

I did not have a goal to visit every country in the world until about eight years ago. After having spent a summer traveling around Europe and concluding that I had visited a total of 35 countries, I set a goal of 50, followed by 100, 150, and about eight years back a determination to visit all de facto independent countries. I have always been an "all-or-nothing" kind of person, so even if I did not start out with the goal to visit all, it came naturally after the first 100.

Do you remember the point where you said to yourself, "I can really accomplish this"?

After having visited about 100 countries I realized that it was possible. It helped that I at the time worked for the Swedish MFA and was posted to China. For my next post I applied for Nigeria to have easier access to the African nation states.

What have you done over your life to gain the freedom and finances to pursue as much travel as you have?

I have worked all summers since I was about 13, and always had a job on the side while studying. An advantage of working for the Swedish Ministry for Foreign Affairs is that, while being posted abroad, we have up to 46 days of vacation a year, in addition to official holidays. I also get to travel some for work, although not as much as some people would expect. I have perhaps visited five countries for the first time through my job.

Was there ever a time you felt like abandoning this goal?

Definitely. I have had ups and downs during my travels, and not all destinations are pleasant to visit and some are outright dangerous. Sometimes I have also felt it would be nice to have a family and spend time with them.

What were your worst travel experiences (i.e. detainment, bribes, car accidents, sickness, etc.) and why?

There have been many not so agreeable travel experiences. In Uzbekistan, I was taken into custody by the police four times in my two-week visit accused of various crimes like drug smuggling, and even of smuggling nuclear waste! The objective of all detainment was bribes, which made it difficult to plan day trips around the country. My trip from Tashkent to Samarkand ended up taking 16 hours instead of our planned two-three hours.

Other very unpleasant travel experiences were the two times I was strip searched. In Saint Petersburg's airport in 2001 I was accused of smuggling money. In the end the border police did not find any, even after looking everywhere. In December

2014, I was stopped on the road in southern Venezuela and accused of smuggling drugs. It was quite obvious that the two police officers only wanted a bribe and thought they could pressure me into giving them one, a tactic that failed miserably.

What do you consider one of the most adventurous trips you have taken?

One of my most adventurous trips was probably overland from Lagos, Nigeria to Tangier, Morocco in the summer of 2011. It was not adventurous because it was really dangerous (although I did fly from Abidjan to Monrovia to avoid rebel controlled areas), but more because I traveled on the same premises as locals in the poorest region of the world. That meant getting up with the sun to wait for a bush taxi or bus to fill up. That meant spending nights in old American school buses built for children, but now with added planks to fit even more people. That also meant being stopped every few kilometers by police or military, whose only objective was obtaining bribes from all passengers. In Guinea there was even a standard plastic bribe bag where passengers had to put in their bribe to get their identification documents back. It also meant staying in communal hostels without running water. Sights were quite limited, except for Ghana and Senegal, but I really enjoyed the arduous trip and getting to know the people I met. I must admit, though, that getting to Morocco was a relief, and I celebrated by getting my own room in a hostel.

What were your most challenging countries to visit and why?

The countries in Central Africa were definitely the most challenging, due to many areas of unrest and very poor infrastructure, especially the infrequent and expensive flights. The Democratic Republic of Congo (DRC) is, for example, a huge country but I have so far only been to the capital, Kinshasa. Some embassy colleagues told me that they often travel via third countries to reach other parts of the country due to the very poor safety record of the national air carriers.

What's the strangest thing you've seen/experienced while traveling?

I guess it is a coping mechanism, but I usually adapt quite quickly to local customs. In Equatorial Guinea, I stopped at a local restaurant and the only thing on offer was monkey and antelope meat, not the most common two choices. One thing I have never been able to accept is child beggars/miners/prostitutes/slaves, unfortunately all too common in some places, especially parts of West Africa. For example, when eating a meal in Niger on the roadside, ten small children waited patiently for me to finish, and then started fighting over my leftovers.

In Lagos, Nigeria I once almost stepped on a dead man lying on the sidewalk. No one around me seemed to react or think it was strange, everyone just walked around him or stepped over his corpse. I have several friends in Sweden that have never seen a dead person, but in many poor countries death is always present, and if you die on your way to work your corpse might be left in the street. I do not blame anyone for not doing anything about the man's corpse. After being stunned for a minute, I did what everyone else was doing and just walked around his body and continued with my day.

Which travel experiences stand out the most and why?

There are many memorable travel experiences, but the one that stands out for me is my first trip without my parents. When I was about to turn 16, I traveled to China for a month together with a few people I did not know. On the trip I learned that I can manage on my own. If I can get around in a country where I do not speak the language, and almost no one knows English, I can do anything. The airline lost my checked luggage, so I also realized that everything can be found almost anywhere, so there is no need for checked luggage when on the road. Traveling around the country by train, I got to meet interesting people and learn more about a fascinating culture. From this trip onwards, I have loved to travel — especially getting to know different cultures and visiting ancient sites. This, my first trip alone, is probably one of the main reasons I decided to learn Mandarin and live in China for three years.

What are the most overrated and underrated countries you've been to in your travels and why?

Iran is definitely the most underrated country I have ever visited. Watching the news one would expect people to be hostile against foreigners, but Iranians are the friendliest people I have ever encountered. I have traveled all over the country and practically everyone I met were curious, friendly, helpful, and willing to try to understand what I wanted to communicate. I never felt threatened in Iran and I walked in many cities there in the middle of the night without worrying about being robbed.

The most overrated country, in my view, is probably France. It is one of the most visited countries in the world, but its neighbors Italy and Spain have much more to offer with a population that is generally more accepting of strangers.

What are the best and worst meals you have ever had while traveling, and where were they?

I have a policy to try everything at least once, even (or perhaps especially) if it is gross. I have therefore tried delicacies like cockroaches, snails, snakes, bird's nest soup, live "drunk" shrimps, rat, starfish, scorpions, camels, crocodiles, guinea pigs, Kobe beef, blowfish, and some meats that are frowned upon in the West. The worst was probably a big fat white worm that tried to avoid me by wriggling. Since my hosts encouraged me to eat it, I swallowed it in one gulp. My best meal was definitely in a three-star restaurant in Tokyo with two chefs to every customer. The food was divine, even though it had no exotic meats or fish.

What country made you feel most out of your comfort zone and why?

I have never had any serious incidents. I have never been kidnapped, and when traveling in unsafe regions I always take precautions, one time I even hired armed bodyguards. I have been subject to a couple of robbery attempts, but never (yet) physically hurt. The most out of my comfort zone I probably felt was in Afghanistan, but that was mainly because I was visiting a friend that was working in Kabul and we always traveled in bulletproof cars with armed bodyguards wherever we went, never meeting any locals.

Do you speak any foreign languages? If so, which has been the most useful for you besides English?

In addition to English, I also speak Spanish, German, Swedish and Mandarin. Spanish has probably been the most useful since it is spoken in so many countries and I can make myself understood in countries where Portuguese, Italian, and African French are spoken. Traveling on the countryside in China, Mandarin has been very valuable. Swedish and German not so useful since most people here speak English. If I was to study another couple of languages it would be, in order of importance: French, Arabic and Russian.

Looking back from when you started traveling to where you are now, in what ways, if any, has travel changed you?

I am definitely more relaxed and open to other ways of doing things. I realize that there is not any country that is doing everything right, and that all cultures have advantages and disadvantages. I see the advantage of not being a minute late in Germany or China, but at the same time it is an advantage not needing to worry about being an hour late in Nigeria.

What is the longest continuous trip you have ever taken? When was it and where did you travel?

That depends on the definition of "trip." I have lived between six months and three years in six countries (Sweden, Switzerland, China, Nigeria, USA and Guatemala) and then traveled both nationally and regionally. Because I work, I usually cannot take more than seven to eight weeks off continually to travel. My last two seven week excursions were to Cuba, Mexico, the U.S., Canada, French Polynesia and Pitcairn, and then another recently to Isla Margarita in Venezuela, Brazil, Argentina, Antarctica (including the South Pole) and Juan Fernandez in Chile.

What is your favorite "off-the-beaten-path" destination and why?

I have really enjoyed visiting countries that are more or less cut off from the outside world. I therefore enjoyed North Korea and Bhutan very much, although I am very grateful I was not born there. I also enjoyed visiting Tristan da Cunha and the Faroe Islands because of the friendly people inhabiting the islands.

What are the best and worst places you have ever spent a night?

The best night would probably be in a private luxury resort on a private island in the Outer Seychelles. I normally travel on a budget, but since this was the most economical way of reaching the Outer Seychelles, I booked a night on Desroches Island and enjoyed the hotel's luxurious facilities.

I have spent countless nights sleeping on floors, on park benches, in buses, on trains, in airports, etc. One of the worst was in Adelaide, Australia, where I thought I would save money sleeping in the airport at night. I had not realized that they closed 01.00-04.00, and it was freezing cold outside. An Englishman and I tried walking for three hours to keep warm, but I was cold as an icicle when the airport finally opened at 4 a.m.

In your opinion, what country or place in the world feels the most authentic and untouched by tourism?

That would probably be the countries that receive no tourists and are mainly shut off from the rest of the world. Bhutan is a pristine and pleasant destination. North Korea, the Central African Republic (CAR), the Democratic Republic of Congo, Somalia and Yemen are a few destinations that receive few, if any, tourists. As a visitor I really enjoyed CAR, Yemen, and Somaliland because of the very friendly people. That authentic feeling is lost in mass tourist destinations like the Canary Islands, Bali and Morocco.

In your opinion, where is the most beautiful place on Earth?

I appreciate clean, simple, and uncluttered landscapes. So, to me, the most beautiful places on Earth would be the Arctic (e.g. Svalbard, western Greenland and Nunavut), the Sahel (e.g. northern Sudan, western Algeria, southern Niger) and mountainous landscapes (e.g. western Bolivia, eastern Peru, Bhutan,

Tibet, Nepal, Kashmir). While I often actively try to avoid the jungle, I eagerly try to include a few days in, for example, the Indian Himalayas when I visit India, to relax and just enjoy the normally slow-paced culture and beautiful landscape.

What do you enjoy most when traveling (cities, nature, people, cultural spots, etc.) and why?

I enjoy getting to know new cultures and people, especially the cultures in the Sahel, mountainous regions of the Himalayas and Andes, and the sub-Arctic regions. I am not a big fan of the sparsely populated countryside or the rainforest. I cannot say for certain why that is the case. I did grow up in the countryside. So perhaps I feel that I have seen enough of that. I am fascinated by different ways of viewing the world and try my utmost to make sense of different cultures and habits.

What travel accomplishments are you most proud of?

With time, lots of patience, and a little money, almost anything is possible. The travel-related accomplishment I am most proud of is visiting every UN member state, which I finished in 2013 with Canada. As for destinations, there have been several hard to reach places, but nothing impossible. I am very grateful, though, that I was able to combine Tristan da Cunha and Saint Helena in one three week trip with the RMS *St. Helena*, a luxurious and subsidized mail boat.

If you had just one personal travel story to share with someone what would it be?

That depends much on who I am talking to. When speaking to a group of high school students it turned out they were most interested in all the exotic things I had eaten, while someone that has spent much time in another country perhaps would be more interested in my experiences from that country.

A story I like to share, though, is my first — and probably only — jungle excursion. Together with a small group and a local guide I spent five days in the Amazon jungle. After a day by boat we arrived in the middle of nowhere. I looked for the guide every other minute, worried about being left alone as I estimated my chances of surviving on my own as very slim.

Everything we saw seemed poisonous, the plants, the trees, insects, birds, spiders, etc. We slept in tents, and one night I woke up and needed to use our homemade bathroom. Sitting down, I realized that two huge hairy spiders were on the ground in front of me and I just froze. I cannot even remember how I made it back to the tent. I did learn, however, that anacondas are not really dangerous after touching a few sleeping ones, and also that piranhas cannot eat a live cow in a couple of seconds after swimming with a school of them in a tributary of the Amazon River.

Besides your home country, where do you find yourself returning to over and over and why?

For work I travel to Brussels two or three times a month and privately I travel back to northern Sweden to visit my family about four times a year. Travel destinations I keep returning to are Italy and India. Both countries have much to offer. Italy in terms of ancient historical sites in every little town, and India in terms of both ancient remnants and very different subcultures. In terms of geographical destinations, I often return to the Sahel, mountains of the Himalayas and Andes, and the sub-Arctic and sub-Antarctic landscapes.

What is the ideal amount of time you prefer to travel on each trip before you are ready for home and a break?

Three to four weeks. I often travel longer for economies of scale when I am visiting destinations far away to save money, but I prefer shorter excursions since there is less risk of becoming exhausted by lack of sleep, unfriendly people, corrupt officials, or be subject to canceled flights that sometimes translate into a domino effect with subsequent missed flights.

If you had an unlimited budget and space and time was no object, what would your perfect travel day look like? (for example: start your morning in Bora Bora; afternoon on a safari in Kenya; night in Australia, etc.)

I am not a big fan of beach destinations. I prefer historical sites, especially ancient historical sites. I would probably use my unlimited budget to make quick stops in hard to reach places, either because of cost limitations or due to security issues.

I would start the morning on the South Pole, continue to the North Pole, spend some time before lunch in Thule, Greenland, eat lunch on the shrinking Aral Lake and then in the afternoon visit Najaf and Karbala in Iraq, before finishing with a night under the starry skies of Timbuktu, Mali.

For those looking to travel to every country, what is the best piece of advice you could offer them?

Not to rush. When I first started traveling I was a bit stressed about how much there was to see and how little time I had. Because of that stress I missed many interesting sights and have spent time going back to places I feel I never did justice to. A far more economical way of traveling would have been not to rush, although rushing did have the added advantage of not having to spend much time in places that turned out to have less to offer than expected.

For someone that has been almost everywhere, what still gets you excited about packing your bags again?

There are still many new places to visit, new cultures to understand, and new experiences to have. I have also started going back to places I really enjoyed. Since my first visit is often done on a tight schedule, a second or third trip is often needed to really appreciate and understand the culture of a place. Many countries are also very diverse. This is why I find myself going back to see more of, for example, India, China, and Ethiopia.

Do you ever feel you have missed out on certain aspects of life being away from home so much?

Sometimes, yes. My sister has chosen a completely different lifestyle. She stayed in the town where we grew up, got married, had four children, and spends most holidays with family and friends. I sometimes wish I had that option, but at the same time I know that after just a few weeks at home I would start to long for a new adventure, even if only a weekend trip to Norway.

Looking ahead, what travel plans and goals are you still pursuing, and what is on your "Bucket List"?

I do not think I will ever completely stop traveling, although I now focus more on places I like. Still on my bucket list are my remaining TCC (Travelers' Century Club) destinations: British Indian Ocean Territory, Wake Island, and Midway Island, as well as some of the more remote corners of Russia.

Steve Newcomer, U.S.A.

(Steve Newcomer in Madagascar)

Where did you grow up and what was your early life like?

On the eastern plains of Colorado, surrounded by cattle feed lots and alfalfa fields and within sight (on a clear day) of Pike's Peak. Even as a kid I'd get up early, before the rest of the family, and take walks around town. I wanted to know what was around the next corner or over the next hill. And I day-dreamed, at that time, of visiting "far off" Denver or Colorado Springs. I was a stamp collector as a kid. I'd order those "bags of stamps" that were advertised in magazines and it gave me such pleasure to come across one from a country I'd never heard of. I figured the stamps were as close to all those countries as I'd ever get! Then when I was in high school I did a class report on the United Nations and I dreamed of visiting all those fantastic countries I read about. Little did I know at that time that I actually would! My family took summer road trips each year, which no doubt had an influence on my love of travel. But deep down, I think there's a genetic component to my wanderlust. Even now, nearly six decades later, I still can't bear to sit still for too long.

When did you go from casually traveling to making this a full-time goal, and what motivated you to travel to every country?

My goal was simply to travel — to see as much of the world as possible. To witness, firsthand, what I'd read about in *National Geographic* magazines or seen on television. It wasn't to visit each country. It was simply to see "the world", to have an adventure, to observe the lifestyles of people different from myself, to encounter wildlife and vistas which were unknown to me, to broaden my horizons. I never had a checklist of places to visit because the checklist would have been endless. So I just journeyed to the places I could afford at the time. Because of limited resources, travel has never been a "full-time" goal, though it's something I've relished wholeheartedly for the few weeks each year that I could get off work to pursue. It's a matter of putting your resources where your heart is. I live as simply as possible so I can travel as much as possible.

Do you remember the point where you said to yourself, "I can really accomplish this"?

I never had a "goal" of visiting all of the world's countries until an unexpected turn of events in 2003 when a flight I was on with Herb Goebels (a prolific world traveler) unexpectedly terminated its services at the K50 Airport near Mogadishu, Somalia. I always said I could not consider myself to have visited a country unless I had legally entered the country, passed through immigration, and spent at least one night there. And I had always figured that would be impossible in such a dangerous place as Somalia was at that time. But here we found ourselves in Mogadishu, being looked after by a dozen machinegun toting men and a friendly warlord. For three days, we stayed at a downtown Mogadishu hotel and were driven around the city in pickup trucks with an ample supply of armed body-guards. We then managed to secure space on a flight to Sharjah leaving from the Wanlaweyn airport some 100 kilometers north of Mogadishu. After that adventure, in what was without a doubt the most difficult and dangerous place on Earth at the time, and after talking with Herb, who was visiting all the countries on Earth, it only then dawned on me that visiting the remaining UN countries would be obtainable.

What have you done over your life to gain the freedom and finances to pursue as much travel as you have?

I'm a librarian. That's hardly a career to amass wealth! And before being a librarian I volunteered as an English teacher, a refugee camp worker, and church worker in various countries of Latin America. Because of my passion for travel, I have drastically reduced other expenses in my life. I live frugally in a small studio apartment. I have no car, no house, and very few possessions. I eat macaroni and cheese out of a box and breakfast cereal twice a day! My priority is travel, so that's where most of my resources go. You have to decide what's important to you and live accordingly to meet your goals, no matter your income. Much of my travel has been by public buses with many nights spent sleeping in bus stations, train stations, homes of people I have met along the journey, and in hostels.

I consider myself one of the luckiest people on Earth. I realize that because of when and where I was born, the education I obtained, and the opportunities I have had, that I am one of a fortunate few in this world to have the freedom and financial capacity to see so much of the world. And I believe I have a responsibility to give back to others I meet on my journey. I impose a "luxury tax" on myself with the money going to local charities or development programs I encounter in the places I visit.

Was there ever a time you felt like abandoning this goal?

I'm convinced there's a genetic component to my wanderlust. It's hard to "give up" when it's in your genes!

What were your worst travel experiences (i.e. detainment, bribes, car accidents, sickness, etc.) and why?

A mugging at knife-point by a gang of thugs in Montego Bay, Jamaica in 1985; my backpack, money, passport — everything but the clothes on my back — was taken from me. Standing bruised, scratched, and penniless in another country is both terrifying and energizing. I was just happy to be alive. It reminds one how precious life is and that the material things are replaceable.

What do you consider one of the most adventurous trips you have taken?

Some of my overland journeys stand out as my most adventurous. Taking buses, boats, trains, and hitchhiking to reach a destination and relying on the kindness of strangers to get me there. One of the fun ones was back in the 1980's when I hitchhiked and traveled by public bus from Venezuela to the southern tip of Argentina, across the Amazonas region of Brazil. "Roads" in Amazonas were nothing but muddy tracks back then. The bus from Manaus to Porto Velho spent several days and nights slip-sliding its way through the jungle, getting stuck and sliding off the road numerous times. The bus driver repeatedly ordered all of us to get off and "push" — so often that we were joking that we would have been better off walking to Porto Velho! By the time we reached Porto Velho, the bus and all of its occupants were covered completely in mud and mosquito bites.

What were your most challenging countries to visit and why?

Visa issues and civil strife are the usual reasons for making visits so challenging. Angola was the most difficult for obtaining a visa. The country, in 2003, was just emerging from decades of civil war. I had to solicit the visa in Namibia and pay an exorbitant sum to get it. The visa for Sudan took the longest to obtain (nearly 5 months), but was well worth the wait. Libya was off limits to American tourists for decades, but when it finally opened in 2004, I joined the first tour group (from Canada) that was granted entry.

What's the strangest thing you've seen/experienced while traveling?

There have been many. While in Uganda I was invited to attend the circumcision ceremony for a teenage boy. He was covered in ashes and was part of a large procession jumping, dancing, singing and chanting through the village and the countryside for about an hour to become exhausted. When he arrived back at his home the local "doctor", using no anesthesia, circumcised him in front of the whole village and one foreigner (me). If he did not cry or scream he was considered a man (he passed the test). I was then invited to his home to congratulate him on his entrance to manhood.

Which travel experiences stand out the most and why?

Volunteer organizations provide great opportunities to see the world, even for those of us with little money in our pockets. The six months I spent with Brethren Volunteer Service working in refugee camps on the El Salvador/Honduras border were without a doubt the most educational, memorable and life-changing months of my life. When one immerses oneself in a totally different environment, language, culture, and lifestyle, one cannot help but be changed. Living with war refugees for six months, sleeping in hammocks, eating tortillas and beans, and witnessing the human tragedy of people being uprooted from their villages and suffering from the brutalities of war is life-changing. Spending a few months or years immersing oneself in another culture is far superior experience than rushing through a checklist of places to visit.

What are the most overrated and underrated countries you've been to in your travels and why?

Everyone is different. What I find attractive in a destination may be abhorrent to others. And what I find terribly unsatisfying is a highlight for others. I like mountainous landscapes, encounters with different languages and cultures, off the beaten track destinations with few tourists, and places with abundant wildlife. I don't like crowds of tourists, fine dining, shopping, or sunbathing. So a vacation at a crowded resort on a sun-drenched island isn't my cup of tea. On the other hand, it'd be hard to pass up an opportunity to visit Antarctica, Rwanda, Madagascar, or Papua New Guinea.

What are the best and worst meals you have ever had traveling and where were they?

I only eat because it keeps me alive. I find little pleasure in it. I'm a man of simple tastes. Give me a banana and I'm a happy camper. With that in mind…

Best food: Whether in a roadside diner or a hotel restaurant, the rice in Iran was consistently flavorful. The spaghetti in Mogadishu was the best I've had. And the pork shashlik in Georgia was to die for.

Worst: I'm not fond of mare's milk (Central Asia), camel cheese (Mongolia), monkey stew (Gabon) or Brussels sprouts (USA).

What country made you feel most out of your comfort zone and why?

As a gay man, my most ill-at-ease moments are those when I am amongst people who are speaking unkindly about the LGBT (lesbian, gay, bisexual, transgender) community or any other minority group, regardless of the country I'm in. Some of my most uncomfortable moments have been right here in the good ol' USA among fellow citizens who unknowingly hurt or insult me without getting to know me. On a recent Amtrak trip across the U.S., I was seated at a dining table with a couple from Colorado who, not knowing I am gay, began speaking about the "menace" that gay people have wrought on the country and that gays should be locked up to protect society from our "depraved" ways. Needless to say it made my cross-country train trip an unsettling experience as we found ourselves together on several occasions during the trip. I try to use such experiences as opportunities to better understand why others believe as they do and to sometimes introduce myself, as a gay man, to them. In some instances, we hold views as a result of never having personally known someone of the group we are insulting. It reminds me that words are powerful tools which can unite and divide people and I am responsible for choosing my words carefully, especially when I am among people of a culture who may hold very different views than my own. When we travel we are ambassadors of goodwill and our words can build bridges or tear them down.

Do you speak any foreign languages? If so, which has been the most useful for you besides English?

While living in Central America, the Caribbean, and Brazil I learned Spanish and Portuguese. I wish I had also learned French, Mandarin, Arabic, and Russian.

Looking back from when you started traveling to where you are now, in what ways, if any, has travel changed you?

My world view has evolved. When newsworthy events occur anywhere in the world, my thoughts turn to the people I have known and still know in those countries. Travel makes news much more personal. Issues are seldom "black" or "white" anymore — there's a lot of gray as we grow to understand differing viewpoints. Travel enriches one's life and broadens one's perspectives. It teaches patience — a lesson I have yet to fully learn.

What is the longest continuous trip you have ever taken? When was it, where did you travel?

When I was in-between jobs in 1986, I took a four-month backpacking trip around the world: New Zealand, Australia, Nepal, and India.

What is your favorite "off-the-beaten-path" destination and why?

I love the solitude of Antarctica. The sound of crackling ice. The curiosity of the penguins. The absence of human beings. The 24-hour daylight in summer.

What are the best and worst places you have ever spent a night?

Best: In a hammock suspended between two palm trees listening to the waves roll in on a Brazilian beach. It doesn't get better than that. Oh wait. Yes it does. Add in a couple of Brazil's famously handsome men, please!

Worst: The rat crawling across my face at night on the ferry from Wadi Halfa, Sudan to Aswan, Egypt in a cabin the size of a coffin built for two. Better to sleep on deck than in a cabin, and be sure to do your "business" before boarding and hold it until you arrive. The communal squatter runneth over — way, way, WAY over!

In your opinion, what country or place in the world feels the most authentic and untouched by tourism?

Myanmar. But change is coming quickly.

In your opinion, where is the most beautiful place on Earth?

The most beautiful spot on Earth is the place where you are loved.

What do you enjoy most when traveling (cities, nature, people, cultural spots, etc.) and why?

I enjoy them all, but nature and wildlife are especially inspiring for me. There's nothing quite like being surrounded by ice-covered mountain slopes and thousands of penguins in Antarctica; or being covered in the mist coming off of Iguazu Falls on the Argentina/Brazil border; or hiking a lonely trail in the Himalayas; or nursing a baby orangutan in Malaysia; or snorkeling with whales in the Austral Islands.

What travel accomplishments are you most proud of?

A few things might set me apart from some other travelers:

First is my penchant for traveling light. I don't like being burdened with luggage and unnecessary "stuff." It detracts from the journey if one has to be concerned about lugging things around all the time. So whether for a weekend getaway or a several months-long adventure, I travel only with a very little backpack. If it doesn't fit underneath the seat in front of me, it doesn't go on the trip.

Secondly, I travel solo most of the time and use public transportation as much as possible. Overland journeys from Prudhoe Bay, Alaska to Panama City, Panama; from Uribia, Colombia to Ushuaia, Argentina; from Singapore to Scotland;

and from Cape Town to Cairo are a few of my most enjoyable adventures. Of course, because of the limited vacation time I've had each year, I've had to do each of these journeys in segments over many years.

And lastly, I've been able to accomplish my travels on a librarian's salary.

If you had just one personal travel story to share with someone, what would that be?

The same as my most memorable one (see above). In a nutshell, don't be afraid to volunteer. Don't be in a rush to get to the next destination. The best travel memories are those acquired by immersing yourself in the place you visit.

Besides your home country, where do you find yourself returning to over and over and why?

Brazil. It's my favorite. I lived there for a few years and grew to love it. Brazil exudes sensuality. From its people to its landscapes, cities, and natural resources, it is top of my list.

What is the ideal amount of time you prefer to travel on each trip before you are ready for home and a break?

365 days a year. No breaks!

If you had an unlimited budget and space and time was no object, what would your perfect travel day look like? (for example: start your morning in Bora Bora; afternoon on a safari in Kenya; night in Australia, etc.)

It's an issue of "time." There simply aren't enough days in one's lifespan to witness and relish all that this planet has to offer. To understand a place, you have to live there for some time, and there are just too many places deserving a visit.

My perfect travel day would be to be blindfolded and taken to some unknown corner of the world and dropped off to fend for myself — preferably in a place where I don't understand the language. The most exhilarating travel days are the ones when my senses are bombarded by new sights, sounds, smells and experiences and my brain runs in overdrive to make sense of it all. And if time were no object, I'd visit every national park, every UNESCO site and attend every festival each country has to offer.

For those looking to travel to every country, what is the best piece of advice you could offer them?

Let it happen naturally over your lifetime, as a result of your innate wanderlust and curiosity. Better to know a few places well than to have rushed through all of them. Visiting every country and not having memories to share makes the journey nearly meaningless.

For someone that has been almost everywhere, what still gets you excited about packing your bags again?

It's the same thing that excited me as a kid: experiencing something which soothes my restless soul.

Do you ever feel you have missed out on certain aspects of life being away from home so much?

Away from home? "Home" is wherever I am at the moment.

Looking ahead, what travel plans and goals are you still pursuing and what is on your "Bucket List"?

I'd love to visit all the world's national parks and all of the UNESCO World Heritage Sites, both the ones on the official list and the ones on the tentative lists. There are over 2500 of them! For me travel is not about crossing borders, but about experiencing the beauty, culture, people, events, and wildlife of our planet. And doing what I can to preserve them for future generations. UNESCO sites, while by no means exhaustive, at least provide a basis for cultural exploration.

Nina Sedano, Germany

(Nina Sedano)

Where did you grow up and what was your early life like?

I was born in February 1966 in Frankfurt am Main in Germany and grew up with my mother as an only child. My grandmother living nearby took care of me as well. I had a great-aunt far away then in Munich, a great-cousin with husband and daughter even further away in Oklahoma City, USA. That was my family.

My father left when I was about three years old, hardly being interested in family. Our paths crossed our last time in life when I was 10 years old. At an early age, I felt more without roots than belonging to a real family. Today I may say, "My mother could not give me roots — but instead, she gave me wings."

I was cross-eyed; had spectacles at seven months old. Before I walked, I talked. Though always a little shy, I cared for communicating and had a big heart for animals. We didn't have much. Nevertheless, I was happy.

Visiting friends, pen-pals, horseback riding, books, languages and England (where I spent three weeks as a language student when I was 13, 15, and 18) became important as a teenager. Only school was a disaster after the first four years. Science gave me a hard time — or were it the teachers not explaining it clearly? I felt helpless my entire school-life, so I never felt like studying at university. I wanted to be independent and earn money. During summer holidays in Paris, I worked in a restaurant at age 19. I also learned French by talking to people. On the way home from Paris, I visited a pen-pal in northern Italy that I knew from the previous year in England. Back in Germany I started a vocational training (going to school and working in an office) in Wiesbaden.

When did you go from casually traveling to making this a full-time goal, and what motivated you to travel to every country?

To see the whole world was neither a childhood dream of mine nor a teenager's wish. Traveling with my mother as a child and attending language courses abroad in my youth gave me interesting experiences.

Straight after my vocational training, back in Frankfurt, I found a proper job in a credit card company. Finally, I earned enough money to afford traveling further away from Europe. On my first trip overseas in 1988, I went to the USA and I visited my great-aunt in Oklahoma and a friend working as an au-pair in Florida.

Every employee at my company had 30 days of holiday time off a year. We could take an additional day off per month from any extra hours worked too. As wisely as the money was earned, I used the free days to make the most out of them. Be assured, leading a normal working life, I was stretching each holiday as cleverly as possible. Weekends and bank holidays were used in order to have 70-80 days a year away from home. Being married for a while, my husband and I both did the same.

In my twenties, I took to travel and getting to know the world seriously. At 20, I had traveled to 10 countries, at 30, to 47 countries. I only started counting them when men wanted to know how many I'd been to when I was in my early thirties. I, for myself, wouldn't have thought about it. Later on some colleagues in my office, not understanding my passion for traveling, made my life at work every day more miserable, while at the same time I felt desperate with loneliness. My friends had their own families and I was alone.

Something about this situation had to be done, so I changed my life drastically. In May 2002, by now having traveled in 92 countries, I left my job and unhappy life behind for my biggest adventure — the world.

My motivation is, and always will be, our Planet Earth. It is the wonder of the Universe and home to all living things. Humankind has found nothing like it. It will forever not be near, but be mind-blowingly far away. I longed to discover more of our wonderful world, to have experiences with all my senses and lead a self-determined life. Traveling, still with a child's curiosity, gives me positive energy. I'm trying to make the best out of my time around.

Do you remember the point where you said to yourself, "I can really accomplish this"?

Actually, no. I was aware there was at least one country which does not let women in on their own (Saudi Arabia), and I knew there would be other nations to make gender an issue, and I was right…

But there was a special moment inspiring the following thought: I could at least *try* to accomplish it.

It was a warm sunny day with a blue autumn sky in Frankfurt in 2006 when I visited a friend at home with another friend. We were cozily sitting at a table, munching on a tomato-mozzarella salad while talking about different topics, which had neither to do with traveling nor the near and far away world. Suddenly, as if the bright shining sun was hiding behind dark clouds, our chatting took a strange turn when our host said to me in an unnerved tone, "Nina, you cannot visit every village in the world."

Her hands lying on the table were formed into fists, her knuckles white. Her lips were a thin line. No muscle in her face moved. It reminded me of a mask. Only her gaze penetrated me. My jaw almost dropped and my eyes widened like they do in my travels, when I had seen something astoundingly beautiful. My face felt as hot as a stove to fry an egg on and my thoughts went out of control wandering and then thinking to myself, "Nina, just keep calm and say something!"

I managed a bittersweet smile and looked straight into her cold eyes. The mozzarella-tomato salad rumbled in my stomach, wanting to add something to the conversation. I took a deep breath before my words poured out, "Of course, I cannot see every village in the world. That's impossible and not my intention! Who would do something that crazy? I wouldn't, I can assure you." My reply seemed to soften her. The subject was quickly changed again. My other friend didn't seem to have noticed.

In any case, at the very same time a thought struck me like a flash, "Not every village, but every recognized country of the United Nations!" I kept the thought to myself, not wanting to be provocative.

This kind of inspiration felt like a revelation, and came even as a surprise to a passionate globetrotter like me with 132 countries traveled. Never had I considered such a goal before. All I ever wanted was to get out into the world to see, dream and wonder...

When I finally landed in Frankfurt from Turkmenistan on September 30, 2011, I had accomplished it — hard to believe for me, even now!

What have you done over your life to gain the freedom and finances to pursue as much travel as you have?

Nothing special really. We were rather poor as opposed to rich growing up. I was use to being modest, not wanting or needing a lot. I did not smoke or drink. Nor indulge in luxury items such as fashionable clothes. I had an old car for nine months which gave me nothing but trouble. I'd rather walk, cycle, or get on public transport and always was careful not to waste resources, learning early to recycle and avoid using one-way products like plastic, foam, etc. I'd rather bring my own bag, cup, or box to refill.

At the age of 22, my mum and granny helped me to buy a small apartment with a living room, bedroom, separate kitchen, and bathroom. From then on I had to pay off a debt, while I always managed to save money for traveling. For the past 26 years it has served as a home base I love, long for and come back to after another journey.

Nowadays, I talk, read to, and show photos to audiences. In May 2014, my book, Die Ländersammlerin (literally translated as *The Female Country Collector*) was published by Eden Books in Germany, wherein I share my experiences in more than 40 countries and tell how and why I became what I am today. Four weeks later, the book hit the bestsellers list and is still among the first three on it at the time of this interview. The book was declined by many publishers initially.

Never give up believing in yourself, despite people putting stones and rocks in your way, if you really want to achieve something.

Was there ever a time you felt like abandoning this goal?

I'm glad I never considered giving up my travel plans, although some countries made a visit difficult.

For Saudi Arabia, there is no way for women to travel on their own, only in a group.

For Iran, I needed to make five visa attempts in Central Asia and was even thrown out of the embassy thanks to my gender in Bishkek, Kyrgyzstan.

In Cameroon, I was sitting around for three hours among other people in the waiting room of the embassy of Equatorial Guinea, only to be sent home to get the tourist visa in Berlin.

My last country, Turkmenistan, granted me only seven days of entry instead of the original ten days requested. Outside the capital of Ashgabat I had to travel with a guide — only to be left alone in the hotel room and at breakfast.

The more difficult the men behind bureaucracy made it, the more I wanted to go there. In the end, I did get in to every country — thank you!

What were your worst travel experiences (i.e. detainment, bribes, car accidents, sickness, etc.) and why?

I am lucky so far to have traveled without accidents or being detained — touch wood.

My worst experience was food poisoning. Not only were the stomach cramps awful, but also the fact I was on my own feeling more alone than ever. One of the few times I was traveling when I wished to be in bed at home.

Towards the end of eight months traveling through Asia, I got really sick in Varanasi, India. That day I had eaten a Samosa, drunk the usual cola, but at night I was shivering with a fever. The restroom was another floor downstairs — a blue toilet bowl placed around a hole in the ground without means to flush it. There was nothing to hold on to while I was hovering over it. I survived the night. Still weak, but feeling better, I moved on with an empty stomach and left town. Months later, in a hostel in Pakistan, I learned of some Spaniards who got so sick in Varanasi that they had to be put on a drip in hospital. I faintly remember reading in my guidebook some kind of warning that foreigners were poisoned deliberately by restaurants to share the patients expenses at the doctor. Unbelievable.

What do you consider the most adventurous trip you have taken?

One of my most exciting trips was in December 2001. I started in Kigali, Rwanda. From there I left by bus on a road (which was considered dangerous by locals because of occasional fights in the mountain region) to Bujumbura, Burundi. At the border I got a three-day visa and had a friendly chat with the official. Arriving at the capital I met someone by coincidence to show me around town, attending several weddings. Back in Rwanda, I managed to see the mountain gorillas without having booked it in advance, which was worth every cent of the $250 US I paid then for this once-in-a-lifetime adventure — it was the highlight of this trip. The next day I crossed the border to Goma into the Democratic Republic of Congo (DRC) for the day, curious to see the town at Lake Kivu. Several weeks later the volcano of Mount Nyiragongo erupted, blowing its top off in the Parc National de Virunga, which is the world's second oldest national park. From Rwanda, I went by road to Uganda to see Murchison Falls on a boat trip on the Nile, among other places, ending this great trip in Nairobi, Kenya shopping for great handicraft souvenirs of wood and soapstone.

What were your most challenging countries to visit and why?

Many countries are for the long-legged, long-haired blonde woman more of a challenge than for men, (e.g., Afghanistan). Getting to places in Kabul without public transport, not using taxis which are unsafe for lone women, but asking foreigners with a bulletproof vehicle for help is really something, as is leaving the country by bus through the spectacular Khyber Pass and upon arrival at the Pakistani border to be then accompanied until Peshawar by a bodyguard.

Traveling by local transport from N'Djamena, Chad and hitting a region of rebels after crossing the border on the way to Bangui, Central African Republic was another challenging trip. Had I been aware beforehand, I would have taken a plane. It was dangerous, far from what I had expected and known from crossing borders on the Black Continent.

Some African nations are more of a challenge before, during, and after elections. Better to be avoided. Shit happens and I was right there or on my way there not taking them into consideration. Lots more stories to tell...

What is the strangest thing you've seen/experienced while traveling?

North Korea in general, and in particular the eerie worship of the body of Kim Il Sung in his palace by masses of people dressed in their best attire. It was an odyssey through brightly lit tunnels, with soft-sounding music for the mourners, and longer walking-escalators than at any airport in the world, to a special cleaning station for people fully dressed where powerful air machines are blown on people to knock off any debris or dust. Then leaving our bags and cameras, we were shown around the museum before we reached the Hall of Tears, where we had to bow several times from different angles to the "Eternal Leader" while he lay in state. It was a creepy experience not to be missed. Talking about it now still gives me goose pimples.

Which travel experiences stand out the most and why?

People's hospitality and being a part of their everyday lives for a couple of days. I consider myself very lucky when I get the chance to stay in people's homes. In Brunei I visited a Canadian family. Knowing me through emails only. The husband picked me up from the harbor 70 miles away and they took me in. When the family was invited to a private home for the Chinese New Year, I was welcomed as well. Something I would have never experienced staying in a hostel or hotel.

In The Bahamas, I stayed with an English guy. Arriving from Germany via the Dominican Republic and Miami after 24 hours traveling, I was invited to a dancing class at his friend's house. Though dead tired, I was too curious to decline and came along. While sitting in a cozy chair, I dozed off. We all had a good laugh.

Laughing with people, no matter where in this world, is also very important to me. I can't live without it. An honest smile is always the best weapon.

What are the most overrated and underrated countries you've been to in your travels and why?

Overrated for me is India. Underrated are the neighbors Pakistan and Bangladesh.

India was trouble from the very beginning when I was at the consulate in Frankfurt. I contended with stubborn employees unable to read the visa form properly and charging me for their mistake. At the Indian land border, I was sent back to Bangladesh. I needed a new visa, paying again for their faults. Much more hassle came during traveling for six weeks through the country.

On the contrary, in Bangladesh, there is a great infrastructure with good roads shaded by trees, and in Pakistan the people were so much more welcoming and helpful. Thanks to people's curiosity, I had interesting experiences also staying with locals. Both countries have great natural and interesting cultural sights to offer.

What are the best and worst meals you have ever had traveling and where were they?

To make your mouth water, and your stomach rumble — to die for:

1) Thai green curry with shrimps, beef or chicken at the stalls of Khao San Road in Bangkok or anywhere else on this planet.

2) Fish with fresh vanilla sauce, rice, and vegetables in a small restaurant in Hell-Ville on the island of Nosy Be, Madagascar.

3) Down the road from home in Frankfurt, the best Italian food in the restaurant 'Fontana di Trevi'.

To make you want to die:

1) Grilled mutton, which smelt like an old ram, at a private home in Quba, Azerbaijan. Within less than an hour, I went running for the toilet — which was an outhouse with a hole in the ground. A couple of hours later, I started shivering and the rest of the night I had the highest fever ever to show on a thermometer since childhood.

What country made you feel most out of your comfort zone and why?

Equatorial Guinea, because of a tourist visa problem. Obtaining it in Berlin at the embassy, I had to provide a certificate of no criminal record and proof of being HIV-negative. In Malabo, I was not allowed to travel outside the capital without a special permit. I paid for it on the day of arrival, but had to go to another office a mile away for a signature. So I did, but the person in charge never showed up while I was waiting for hours. Nobody knew why or was willing to help.

Do you speak any foreign languages? If so, which one has been the most useful for you besides English?

At an early age, I was fascinated by communicating and languages while playing with children of different nationalities. Learning Latin and ancient Greek at school were tedious. Lively English was more fun. With German as mother-tongue, after school I learned French, Spanish, and Italian fluently. Portuguese well enough, and some basic knowledge of Arabic, Greek and Russian — being able to read them. Besides English, Spanish and French, a sensibility for body language was the most helpful. The last saved me a couple of times.

Looking back from when you started traveling to where you are now, in what ways, if any, have travel changed you?

I have been rewarded with so many positive experiences that will stay with me forever. Leaving to travel the world has made some negative thoughts or problems at home become unimportant, disappear, or become null and void. It has made my life worth living. Traveling has opened my eyes, my heart, and given me unconditional love for the beauty of variety on our fascinating planet.

What is the longest continuous trip you have ever taken? When was it and where did you travel?

In 2002, the euros first year, at the end of September, my longest journey started in South Korea. Then by boat to Japan, and from there by plane to the Philippines, Taiwan, and Vietnam. My trip continued via an unpaved road to Cambodia, spending Christmas at Angkor Wat. I then traveled further on by boat up the Mekong River and by road, where I spent New Year's Eve in Laos, and then later on to Thailand. From Bangkok, I had no alternative but to fly to Myanmar and later to Bangladesh, and on to Nepal (including a road trip to Lhasa, Tibet and back again) and flying from Kathmandu to Bhutan, then crossing the land border into India, and at the end of May 2003, coming back home.

What is your favorite "off-the-beaten-path" destination and why?

The Orkney Islands. Small with a lot to offer. Friendly people, curious cows, rough nature, fresh fish and chips, and enchanting mystical sites left by a prehistorical culture, which disappeared about 4000 years ago. Skara Brae, a settlement with probably the world's first toilets some 5000 years back showing ditches from the houses under the earth to the fields; the Neolithic grave of Maes Howe with its different chambers; the Stones of Stenness and Ring of Brodgar, which are two ceremonial stone circles on the UNESCO World Heritage list and worth seeing.

What are the best and worst places you have ever spent a night?

Worst places are rooms with mosquitoes, cockroaches or rats, no running water in the bathroom and bad/no light in the bedroom in general. And in particular, I spent my worst nights in the Central African Republic, three of them in a village at the border to Chad, sleeping on the concrete floor in a store room using my backpack as a pillow. Then I spent another night sleeping on an pick-up truck loaded with luggage and things at a roadside near the capital of Bangui some days later. At least at the last location two friendly military accompanied the group of locals and me.

One of the best nights was on a safari. Sitting with others on a bench most of the night watching wild animals come to the waterhole outside the camp, while the cheeky jackals were already inside behind us. They would look for food in the rubbish bins and drop the lid with a 'clang'. I thought, 'Who are those noisy people disturbing the silence of the savanna?' I finally realized those hungry little carnivores, who had found their way to get in the camp, were making the noise.

In your opinion, what country or place in the world feels the most authentic and untouched by tourism?

I would say Madagascar and its national parks. The country is not in easy reach; it is difficult to get to many of the national parks; most of the national parks are only accessible on foot, and I think that's great; in those vast forests you may get really lucky to see some lemurs and other animals.

In your opinion, where is the most beautiful place on Earth?

The most stunningly beautiful place on Earth is the Ngorongoro Crater in Tanzania where nature, wildlife, and humans meet. To be precise, the spot where you cross the crater rim on an unpaved road. You see the entire rim before you with the crater below, the perfect little ecosystem seeming to have existed forever — here time stops and becomes eternal. The view is mindblowing, making your eyes water and wanting to return to it again and again — if only in your thoughts.

What do you enjoy most when traveling (cities, nature, people, cultural spots, etc.) and why?

All of the above mentioned, plus animals (best watching them in their natural habitat from horseback) plus arts and food. I also enjoy different types of fruits and spicy meals. I like the variety of the world. One doesn't exclude the other. I learned languages for a better understanding of people and their cultures. I could not live without music and books anywhere. Bungee jumping, skydiving, and ballooning are among other exciting activities not to be missed.

What travel accomplishments are you most proud of?

As I'm not healthy enough to climb high mountains, dive the deep sea, or do other things like it, I'm grateful to have seen the mountain gorillas in Rwanda, the migration of the herds in the Serengeti of Tanzania and the Moai of Easter Island.

Now I'm so happy to have the chance to share my travel experiences in my book with others in hope of making women, men, travelers and couch potatoes curious to go out and see more of our wonderful world.

If you had just one personal travel story to share with someone, what would that be?

Far away from everywhere in the Pacific Ocean, on the volcanic Easter Island (an awesome place to go to), I took a tour around the island in a car with two other ladies. In a certain area along a slightly downhill road, our driver stopped the vehicle, disengaged the gear, and shut down the engine. Slowly, the car would move backwards up the hill all on its own. What a feeling! Was it magnetism?!

Besides your home country, where do you find yourself returning to over and over and why?

For seeing friends and being happy to speak the languages, I used to return a lot to England, Spain, Italy and France in former times, when I did not have the other goal of going to every country. Getting to travel the rest of the world made this quite difficult. Now that I am finished with that, I will go back to those countries more often, adding in Portugal. I love Europe.

What is the ideal amount of time you prefer to travel each trip before you are ready for home and a break?

When I had seen less of the world, I just wanted to spend more time traveling. Several months away from home at a time were great. These days I'm happy to be back home after four weeks. Doing a lot each day while away, and exhausting myself with many new impressions, I can take in less than I used to. Getting older, my home is becoming more important as well. The success of my book kept me busy in 2014, so I stayed in Germany for seven months without going abroad — a long time for me.

If you had an unlimited budget, and space and time was no object, what would your perfect travel day look like? (for example: start your morning in Bora Bora: afternoon on a safari in Kenya: night in Australia, etc.)

The perfect travel day would be extremely short and something I have never done before in life, and surely will never do.

I'd like to orbit around the Earth in the International Space Station, where the sun goes up and down several times in 24 hours. I do not have any idea how that day (and those hours) would really look like. I'll leave it for the benefit of my imagination...

For those looking to travel to every country, what is the best piece of advice you could offer them?

I have heard so many people saying, "I will do it when I have more time, money, when I'm older, retired…" etc. Stop it! No excuses! Do it now! Start while you're young and healthy. Don't postpone it for later. You have a long way to go and make sure you take your time to enjoy it.

For someone that has been almost everywhere, what still gets you excited about packing your bags again?

There are lots of places on Earth I haven't seen with my own eyes yet. It is always an adventure to get out of everyday life for a while, unwind, use your positive energy, focus on different aspects, and then come back home full of new impressions and experiences. As long as I'm healthy, I want to go on traveling. Not as much as I used to, as my hunger for the world is stilled, but I always have some appetite for more.

Do you ever feel you have missed out on certain aspects of life being away from home so much?

It is quite the other way around. My plan A in life — to find a partner and have children — did not come true. My marriage without offspring ended in divorce after a few years. While still working, I didn't meet a man who wanted to have children with me or join me traveling just for a bit. Not being able to force love one or the other way, I needed a plan B. It turned out to be quitting my job at the age of 36 to travel the world. It was the best decision to make under those circumstances — never to regret it.

Looking ahead, what travel plans and goals are you still pursuing, and what is on your "Bucket List"?

I would like to see the current 1012 UNESCO World Heritage Sites. Of course, I will never get to see them all. Every year, there are more added. I have seen the ones in Germany, but not enough in Europe. That's where I intend to travel more in the near future. Life will continue to be interesting no matter where I am.

It would be marvelous to get my best-selling book translated into different languages to inspire others to travel our wonderful planet and make the best out of their lives.

Dan Walker, Costa Rica

(Dan Walker with his Rolls-Royce)

Where did you grow up and what was your early life like?

I was born in Comox, on Vancouver Island in Canada. It seemed wandering was in my system, as the only way my mother could keep me around was put me in a harness and attach it to the clothes line. My grandparents and mother moved to Victoria, British Columbia when I was still very young. When I got a tricycle my mother put dog tags around my neck with my name and phone number on it as I was always gone. She would get calls from strangers many miles away where I had stopped to ask directions. I've never been homesick — I was on a train across Canada to join the Air Force two days after I graduated from high school.

When did you go from casually traveling to making this a full-time goal, and what motivated you to travel to every country?

My first serious trip was in 1964 when a friend of mine and I decided to quit our jobs and go around the world. We had $30 between us when we left Victoria, and from then on hitchhiking until we ran out of money then worked until we had enough money to hitchhike again. After over a year on the road in Canada, U.S., and Mexico I got engaged in Halifax when on my way to Europe. That ended travel for many years. After I sold everything I owned in Canada in 1991 and moved to Costa Rica, travel became a full-time goal. I joined the TCC (Travelers' Century Club) as an aspiring member with about 70 countries, and decided I wanted to complete the list.

Do you remember the point where you said I can really accomplish this?

After traveling through a number of war zones in Africa with Tim Carlson, we both knew we could handle anything that came our way. He went on to complete the TCC list. I still haven't. There are a couple of parts of Antarctica and BIOT (British Indian Ocean Territories) still to go.

What have you done over your life to gain the freedom and finances to pursue as much travel as you have?

From the time I got married I worked very long hours, started my own business, reinvested everything I could, and made the right decision more than half the time. For over 30 years work dominated my life — very little travel.

Was there ever a time you felt like abandoning this goal?

Not once I started. There was no thought of turning back.

What were your worst travel experiences (i.e. detainment, bribes, car accidents, sickness, etc.) and why?

I've been violently ill. The last time was in a remote area of Afghanistan when some wonderfully hospitable farm people invited my wife and I to their house, where they served delicious fresh bread, butter, yogurt, and milk. I knew we might be in trouble, but also knew it would be very discourteous to say no. My wife had diarrhea for over a month and I was throwing up for a couple of days. There have also been plane flights where the plane turned back after a long while for one reason or another, but I think those go with the territory. It is necessary to get at it and salvage what is possible for connecting flights.

What do you consider the most adventurous trip you have taken?

There have been some pretty amazing trips. One of the trips to Africa with Tim Carlson in 1999 was quite interesting. We met in Paris, then flew to Nouakchott, Mauritania. On the flight we met the vice-dean of the University of Nouakchott, whose family took us from the airport to their house for tea and snacks.

We spent the next couple of nights on the flat roof of his house, although without much sleep, due to the extreme heat. He showed us around the area, then rented an old Mercedes to drive us to our next stop, Dakar, Senegal. The ride was exciting — he would slow to 100 kph to go through villages, but on the two lane roads he did around 130. He was an incredible negotiator in 5 languages — no police checkpoint or border was a problem, and when police demanded a video tape I took of a coastal village, he called his uncle who was chief of police and the problem disappeared.

After a couple of days in Dakar, Tim and I carried on to Ziguinchor in Casamance Province, which was ending a civil war where 600-700 people were killed. There were army checkpoints, some with tanks, all over the place. They were tearing cars apart, including taking the seats out, when driven by locals, but they just waved us through.

We had tried to get a visa for Guinea-Bissau, but almost all their embassies had closed and foreign embassies in the country had been evacuated due to the war, so no airlines would fly there. They had an embassy in Dakar, where they were delighted to give us a visa immediately — probably the only one issued for a while! One of their staff even drove us back to our hotel after the visa was provided.

We hired a car to drive us to São Domingos in Guinea-Bissau. The only excitement was when I left my travel vest containing documents and money on the back of a chair in a makeshift outdoor bar. A hole had been cut in a 20 foot container through which booze was sold, and seating was at tables and chairs scattered around a field in front of the container. We had walked to a river to watch fishing before I discovered I forgot it, but on our return it was not only where I left it, no one was even sitting nearby. It was a major relief to see the thousands of dollars all still there, so I bought rounds for the whole bar. There was a lot of hand shaking when we left!

A Mercedes and driver cost about $50 per day, and we had him take us all around, including the beach areas. Another fellow named Bas took to us so he rode along — his local knowledge and language skills were a big help, including when we drove to The Gambia over unbelievably horrible roads that cost the driver a tire. The Gambia was very relaxed, with super friendly English-speaking people.

From there, we flew in the old Russian Antonov used by Air Ghana to Conakry, Guinea. There wasn't a lot of war damage, but the presidential palace was abandoned after being hit by a missile and the street lights hadn't worked for a couple of years. We did most exploring out of the city, where there are beautiful waterfalls and lakes.

Our next flight was to Freetown-Lungi International Airport in Sierra Leone, the airport for the capital city, Freetown, but we found there was no way to get from airport to the capital. The ferry across the wide river had been sunk by the rebels while transporting tanks. We bribed our way onto a Russian helicopter hauling medical supplies.

The press has been calling Guinea-Bissau, Sierra Leone, and Liberia the 'triangle of death'. A travel company laid on a Mercedes to give us a tour of the city, where many buildings were destroyed. The city changed hands three times, and it shows. There were heavily-armed troops manning roadblocks everywhere. The UN sent peace keeping forces the following week, but when they arrived they were taken hostage by the rebels. We had no serious problems. After hanging around for a couple of hours we got back to the airport on the same Russian helicopter.

On arrival at Monrovia Airport in Liberia, there were three hopeful taxi drivers, but the first two got into a fight over who would take us, so while they were rolling around on the ground fighting we took the third taxi. He drove us for the next couple of days. Monrovia was once very prosperous, the center of shipping registration for the world, but after 10 years of war, three years of which was centered in the city, there is little left. There were two hotels operating with generators and trucked water, but no working infrastructure, including electric, telephone, and water.

The hotel bar was packed with people in formal gowns and tuxedos that night. Tim and I had come earlier and had a table on the balcony, but as there were no seats left elsewhere, a formally dressed fellow asked if he could join us. He turned out to be the assistant to the speaker in parliament, so the next day we met him for a tour of parliament, and to meet many of the ministers. We were quite the celebrities, likely being the first tourists in 10 years. The civil servants here didn't even pretend to work — most had their heads on their arms, asleep at their desks.

Our driver took us to the refugee camp outside of town, where he lived. Here houses and small shops were made of twigs, cardboard, tin, or whatever people could find. Everyone was friendly and welcoming, and the dirt streets were relatively clean.

When we left, our political friend insisted on accompanying us to the airport, where he had the president's personal building laid on for us. It was welcome, as our flight was over two hours late. People ran around getting our passports stamped, etc., while we watched big screen satellite TV in air-conditioned comfort. When some officials made a move to inspect our baggage some sharp words from our friend had them scurrying away.

Ivory Coast was a low point, unbelievably corrupt and everyone seemed to have a surly attitude. The main city, Abidjan, seemed prosperous, with four lane highways and modern buildings, but nothing worked. No Internet or faxes were possible. Fortunately, we stopped by the Canadian Embassy to say hello, so I had their business cards. Standard procedure at the airport is to take a passport, put it in the drawer, and ask again for the passport, extorting a bribe to get it back. When I refused to pay I was taken into a small room and threatened with charges of currency infractions. I demanded to see the airport manager, and to make a phone to call the Canadian Embassy, whose card I showed. It got ugly, so another guy was sent in to turn up the heat, which heated me up further. Apparently I could be heard out in the parking lot. They eventually said get out of here, and pointing to Tim said, "Is he with you?" And when I said yes they told him to get out as well. In the waiting area, we found everyone else had paid $50 or more to keep from missing their flight.

The next stop was Ghana, a real breath of fresh air. It is English-speaking, most things worked, people were friendly, and there is lots to see and do. There is a beautiful university that looks like a resort, done in Mediterranean architecture.

We drove from there to Lome, Togo, where we were informed that our flight to Niamey, Niger, was canceled. The next day we drove to Cotonou, Benin where we arranged another ticket to Niamey, but it left from Lome. Knowing how unreliable Air Afrique is, we phoned and found it too was canceled, but that we could fly back to Abidjan, overnight, and hope for a flight to Niamey the next day. Ivory Coast was the last place we wanted to go, so we bought tickets for a hot, dusty, bumpy 10 hour train ride to Parakou, Benin. The next day we hired a car and driver to go to Niamey.

Niamey, the capital of Niger, is really different. During the uranium boom many huge modern office buildings and hotels were built, but when the market collapsed so did the city, leaving a virtual shack town spotted with super modern steel and glass buildings. It is normal to see camel caravans strolling down a main road in the city. When we were there, one in three children died before age five and life expectancy was 43 years old and the literacy rate was 17% in spite of supposedly free compulsory education.

The next flight was to Bamako, Mali, where we caught a riverboat for the five night trip to Timbuktu. We became friends with the army officer in charge of the region of Mali bordering Niger, a very useful friend as in each city the chief of police was either his cousin or uncle. We left the boat well-connected!

The boat was a floating village, with pigs, chickens, and goats. The lowest class passengers slept on top of the freight, drank river water, and killed a chicken for dinner which was cooked over a small brazier. I had one of the two deluxe class cabins, meaning I had air-conditioning, which worked occasionally. I also had a shower, sink, and toilet, but no toilet paper, towel, or soap. This turned out to be unimportant as there was no water. When I wanted water, I asked for a "seau de l'eau" and they would throw my bucket overboard to refill it with filthy water to flush the toilet. I bought bottled water to wash with. (The locals use the river for sewer, washing, and drinking.) Also included was a large menagerie of wildlife — bugs of all sizes, shapes, and descriptions — the floor swarmed with them. Walking barefoot was not an option.

There is not a lot in Timbuktu except the odd salt caravan. Flights out had been canceled for a week, so the airport was filled with people desperate to leave, and we were told our ticket didn't have the right stamp. We hired a big Bedouin guy to negotiate for us, so money changed hands and our ticket was stamped. When boarding was announced, the mob of people in the one room terminal stormed the check in counter, which stretched across the width of the room, climbing over it and jamming the one exit door. Guards and ticket agents stopped those who had mere tickets, allowing only those who had "authorized" tickets to board the aircraft.

Once in Mopti, a tour operator took us to visit the very interesting Dogon Country where people live in stone houses high in the mountains. They retreated there when Muslims were forcibly converting the rest of the area. They are high on education for their young, and are very hard workers.

We drove to Bamako, where I caught a flight to Paris. My flight out of Paris was two hours late leaving, which was causing me some worry, as I had a two-hour connection in Miami; however, it proved to not be a problem as 3 1/2 hours out into the Atlantic a guy about four rows ahead of me went nuts and started yelling profanities at the people behind him, threatening to kill them, etc., etc. I didn't notice the turn, but when we had been in the air for about six hours the plane was descending — a bit disconcerting, as I thought we should be only about two-thirds of the way across the Atlantic. The guy beside me looked out the window and said, "That's land! That's France!"

All I could come up with was, "Oh, shit!"

Six uniformed gendarmes boarded and made off with the fellow. When the crew said they were going to take an hour to fuel and then head for Miami, I explained that I had already been travelling for 36-hours and that there was no way I could make my Miami to Costa Rica connection, and asked them for a hotel. They gave me dinner, breakfast, hotel, and transfer vouchers, and then took me to the terminal by van. The plane was not near the ramps (I guess for the police vehicle) and I was the only one who got off. The next day Air France was late again, but I made it to the gate in Miami for my Costa Rica flight with 15 minutes to spare.

What were your most challenging countries to visit and why?

The most challenging countries usually have to do with politics, like North Korea, Myanmar under the military government, Equatorial Guinea, and so on. I've managed them all, but none were easy. There is a saying that the less desirable a place is to visit the harder it is to get into.

What is the strangest thing you've seen/experienced while traveling?

I saw a full-sized water buffalo being driven down the road between two young men on a motor bike outside of Hanoi, Vietnam. It was on its back crossways. Legs tied above and the rear guy was on the back fender.

Which travel experiences stand out the most and why?

I think driving my 1957 Rolls-Royce around the world in 2007, particularly the Russian part. We were hosted by the Russian Automobile Society — they used the trip to promote better roads. It was called "Across Russia in Comfort and Safety." We dined (and drank vodka) every night with the local society officials, and there was media interviews every day. The China portion was also amazing — it was the people that made it such a great adventure.

What are the most overrated and underrated countries you've been to in your travels and why?

I think the Galapagos Islands were the biggest disappointment, due to all the TV and films I had seen featuring it. We arrived in a bad El Niño year, and the warm water had killed off a lot of wildlife — there were dead marine iguanas all over the place. Even so, although it is no doubt an amazing place, the build-up led to too high expectations.

Afghanistan would be the most underrated, largely due to their continual conflicts, I suppose. The people and scenery were both amazing and it is very worth visiting as a tourist.

What are the best and worst meals you have ever had traveling and where were they?

We have had too many absolutely amazing meals to single one out. The worst would definitely be when driving across Tibet. It was October — cold, no heat in the hotels, and buffet meals would come out with no heat under them. In five minutes, they would be stone cold with about half an inch of hard white grease on top. It was a great weight loss program.

What country made you feel most out of your comfort zone and why?

I think the Mogadishu part of Somalia. There was no government to speak of (I don't think anyone even investigated killings), and it was the most downright dangerous place I've seen. People were not friendly; they seemed to look at everyone with suspicion and distrust.

Do you speak any foreign languages? If so, which has been the most useful for you besides English?

I've been living in Costa Rica for 24 years, so I speak Spanish and English. I have enough German, French, and various other languages to get lodging, food and beer (not necessarily in that order of importance). Any bit of language is useful and helps break the ice with people who don't speak your language.

Looking back from when you started traveling to where you are now, in what ways, if any, has travel changed you?

It has given me an enormous understanding and respect for other cultures; a great realization that different is not bad or wrong. It has made me much more accepting of others.

What is the longest continuous trip you have ever taken? When was it and where did you travel?

It would be from Costa Rica to Argentina and Antarctica by ship, back to Buenos Aires for a flight to South Africa, on to Kuala Lumpur to explore Malaysia and all the other Southeast Asia countries, ending by traveling to all the principal Indonesian islands, including the Dani country in Irian Jaya. It took a little over five months. On the other hand, my first hitchhiking trip was almost a year and a half, but I stopped to work when I had no money.

What is your favorite "off-the-beaten-path" destination and why?

Iceland ranks high due to scenery, friendly people, and ease of travel. I also have a favorite R & R place called Alam Indah, near Ubud in Bali, but that likely doesn't count as off-the-beaten-path. My favorite non-mainstream journey would be following the Chinese portion of the old caravan tea route in China. This was in use before India had tea and the old cities along the way have been kept much as they were. They still are vibrant and alive.

What are the best and worst places you have ever spent a night?

The worst would be when I strung my string hammock between two tall cactus and the rope broke during the night, landing me on a shorter but very prickly barrel cactus. The discomfort lasted several days! I think Alam Indah, Bali, would count among the best.

In your opinion, what country or place in the world feels the most authentic and untouched by tourism?

Certainly the least desirable countries of Africa would qualify, and the back country of Tibet.

In your opinion, where is the most beautiful place on Earth?

That is really difficult to answer; it is such a beautiful and varied world with so many dazzling wonders. Beauty is in the eye of the beholder, but where I live in Costa Rica, would certainly be a contender with gorgeous beaches, mountains, forests, rivers, lots of sunshine, wildlife, and a year-round great climate.

What do you enjoy most when traveling (cities, nature, people, cultural spots, etc.) and why?

People and their cultures, including history, because I like to learn. Natural beauty is also a big attraction, because it is pleasing to the senses immediately. It fits in well with a philosophy I heard and have adopted — "Live like you are going to die tomorrow. Learn like you are going to live forever."

What travel accomplishments are you most proud of?

We have a number of grandchildren, and starting at the age of 10 my wife and I have taken them anywhere in the world they want to go for two or three weeks. It makes me very proud to see them learning other cultures, learning a bit of language, understanding why doing things differently is sometimes better for other people, learning the history and getting to know the people. There is not one of them who does not want to travel again to learn more. We are proud to have opened their eyes and minds to the world.

If you had just one personal travel story to share with someone, what would it be?

Likely the Rolls-Royce trip around the world. It took over a year to put together, and was amazing.

Besides your home country, where do you find yourself returning to over and over, and why?

We like England, as we have made many friends there. The history is amazing for a North American and there is a lot to do. It is a good place for very soft adventure between some of the tougher places to travel, especially if English is your first language.

What is the ideal amount of time you prefer to travel on each trip before you are ready for home and a break?

Two and a half to three months, although we have had a number of trips that were longer. I just got back from a three month trip, will be home for a week, and then off on another trip of about two and a half months.

If you had an unlimited budget and space and time was no object, what would your perfect travel day look like? (for example: start your morning in Bora Bora; afternoon on a safari in Kenya; night in Australia, etc.)

It would be totally comprised of places I have not been, and I'd want more time in each place.

For those looking to travel to every country, what is the best piece of advice you could offer them?

Pack only a carry on suitcase, never check luggage. This has saved me trouble on many occasions. Smile a lot at people, and meet them if possible. Don't worry if you don't speak the language — communication is always possible. Learn a few basic operative words of the language in each country. Keep a note on your computer or iPad of the phrases you learn in each country so you have them if you return. Don't drink the water, but try different food. It'll build your immune system.

For someone that has been almost everywhere, what still gets you excited about packing your bags?

The idea of finding somewhere different than anywhere I've seen is always exciting. I'm really looking forward to both my next trips. One is for a Costa Rican granddaughter who has turned 10, and thus gets to go anywhere in the world she wants with my wife and I. After watching the movie *Frozen*, she decided she wants reindeer, dog sleds, northern lights, snow, and an ice palace, so we are taking her to the Murmansk area of Russia. Besides her list, she will learn about cold, the culture, and see how life is without daylight.

The other is an expedition cruise to Antarctic islands I've not visited before. Both have me excited about packing my bag — no plural — anything more than one carry on is excess baggage!

Do you ever feel you have missed out on certain aspects of life being away from home so much?

No, never. I've gained far more than I could possibly have missed.

Looking ahead, what travel plans and goals are you still pursuing, and what is on your "Bucket List"?

I'm working on visiting all the states, provinces, or whatever they are named in every country. I won't make it — I'll be making the final great trip before then — however it is nice to have a goal and see as much as I can.

Larry Leventhal, U.S.A.

(Larry Leventhal)

Where did you grow up and what was your early life like?

I was born in Vinogradov in Ukraine, which was at that time in Hungary and called Nagyszolos until the time of the Holocaust. I am Jewish so it was a very difficult period. We left Hungary because of the German invasion. The family of my mother was rich and in the diamond business and she managed to hide some diamonds — which were then used to cross borders because we had no passports — and we managed to get to Switzerland, where we lived in Vevey in the French-speaking part of the country.

When did you go from casually traveling to making this a full-time goal, and what motivated you to travel to every country?

I was on the terrace of a hotel in the north of Haiti and some people told me about the Travelers' Century Club (TCC), so I joined. I think it was 1981. I still have not been to every country (missing Syria and South Sudan). I do not think I will ever get to Syria or to places only reachable by boat like Tristan da Cunha, Tokelau, or Pitcairn Island. The reason I do not travel by ship is seasickness. Even if I do not get seasick, I am nervous about it and that spoils the enjoyment of the trip.

Do you remember the point where you said "I can really accomplish this?"

Not really, but I feel that I have still not accomplished my ultimate goal.

What have you done over your life to gain the freedom and finances to pursue as much travel as you have?

I worked in the school system and also in the travel industry (I had a travel agency here in Brooklyn). In the school system I had long summer vacations, so there was always time to travel.

Was there ever a time you felt like abandoning this goal?

I do not think so.

What were your worst travel experiences (i.e. detainment, bribes, car accidents, sickness, etc.) and why?

1) I was on a plane that was shot at while attempting to land in Santo Domingo during a revolution.

2) Waiting in Buenos Aires for my mother, who was coming from New York via Bolivia and who, along with the other passengers, was kidnapped and held for a short time in Santa Cruz.

3) I was in Papua New Guinea in the 1980s with my mother. We had flown to Port Moresby from Cairns, Australia. After a day or so we flew to Lae and then to a town in the highlands (the name of which I do not remember) to see a festival called the sing-sing. The locals were dressed in nothing — that is they

were totally naked. My mother at that time was already elderly but that did not stop a chieftain from deciding that he wanted to make her his fourteenth wife. We found out at the hotel that he would not take no for an answer, so his men were coming to the hotel to take her by force. We were taken immediately to the airport and got the next flight out of Papua New Guinea.

What do you consider one of the most adventurous trips you have taken?

I would qualify my visits to the Dogon Country and Timbuktu as adventurous for me because the way of life there is so very different from what I am accustomed to. They wear a minimum amount of clothing and eat gruesome things like rats, snakes, and bugs. Some still live in caves with no modern conveniences.

What were your most challenging countries to visit and why?

Probably Saudi Arabia or North Korea because of the difficulty in getting visas.

What's the strangest thing you've seen/experienced while traveling?

The bizarre customs of some groups in Africa like the eating of all sorts of things like bugs and snakes. Among the Islamic people in eastern India and Bangladesh there is a festival in which the main feature is skinning cows alive. I do not remember the name of the festival, but it was gruesome but also fascinating to watch. When they finish skinning the animal they hang the hides on the walls and eat the meat because, of course, the animals die when they are skinned. They don't look at it as gruesome, but I guess everything is in your background and perspective. For example, I was brought up to think of eating pigs as sinful and disgusting, but Christians do not think of it that way. So people who eat bugs or rats or snakes or cats or dogs have been raised to think of it as acceptable.

In the 1980s I spent five days driving the Nullarbor Highway from Perth to Adelaide. There are long stretches of absolute nothingness with no population. At some places there are roadhouses with motels, restaurants, and gas stations. The staff of those places live there because it would be too far for them to commute. Reservations for stays along the way are made through an Australian agency. It is very important to drive only during daylight hours because of the kangaroos. They are very stupid creatures and they sleep during the day. At night they search for food. They are attracted by light and run into the headlights of vehicles. Long trucks called 'road trains' travel all night. They are big and heavy enough that hitting kangaroos is no problem for them. For a regular car such a collision would cause great damage and even fatality. In driving along I saw no living kangaroos, but the road was littered with hundreds of dead ones — I think I counted 789. The drive was very interesting to do once, but it is not something to be repeated.

Which travel experiences stand out the most and why?

I have had so many wonderful experiences that I cannot really choose one. But one of my favorite memories was when I was traveling with my mother and we were in a very expensive hotel near the Amalfi Coast in Italy and we had no reservation for dinner even though the price of our room included dinner. While arguing with the doorkeeper, Sophia Loren arrived and invited us to share her table, so we had the experience of having dinner with her.

What are the most overrated and underrated countries you've been to in your travels and why?

Every country is interesting in its own way, but my very favorite destination is, and has always been, Israel.

There are only three countries of all those I have visited that I would never go back to. One was Jamaica, where I got mugged but managed to run away. Another was Zaire (the former Belgian Congo) and the third was Nigeria.

In the '80s I flew from London to Lagos, Nigeria on British Airways. The plane was full, but I immediately noticed that, except for the crew, I was the only white person. A member of the crew asked me why I was going there and where I was staying. It turned out that the crew was staying at the same hotel. They then asked me how I was going from the airport to the hotel, which I think was the Hilton. I said I would take a taxi and they said that was definitely not a good idea. After some discussion, the captain offered that I could go on the crew bus guarded by soldiers with rifles and I accepted their kind offer. After checking into the hotel, which was very nice, I asked at the reception what there was to do in Lagos and they told me about the hotel pool and garden. When I said that I was interested in sightseeing in the city they advised me that I must not leave the hotel grounds because of high crime rates. I asked if I might be mugged or robbed and they said that I definitely would be mugged and robbed. So I arranged at the British Airways office (which was in the hotel) to get a flight back to London the next day and went to the airport on the crew bus.

What are the best and worst meals you have ever had traveling and where were they?

I do not like Oriental food and find the food in India to be much too spicy. Hungarian food in general is, in my opinion, marvelous.

One interesting story was going to Tonga by plane from Apia, Samoa. I had a hotel reservation at the International Dateline Hotel in Nuku'alofa and was staying for three nights until the next flight. I had no other plans. At the airport (it was late afternoon) I took a taxi to go to the hotel. The driver was pleasant and spoke fairly good English, so I asked him if he would drive me around and show me the places of interest on the island for the next three days. He agreed and we set a price. He dropped me at the hotel and said he would come back the next morning. He arrived punctually. He was young and told me that he was recently married and his wife had just given birth to a baby boy. When he told his wife about me, she said she would like to meet me. She was happy because now he had a job for the next three days and did not have to look for a customer at the airport. I was not particularly interested in meeting her but I thought it would be interesting to see where a taxi driver lived, so I agreed. When we got to his house, she was very excited. It seems that after he left to go to the hotel a truck had passed the house and hit and killed a dog. She ran out and got the dead dog and was planning to roast it for their dinner that night. She felt that I had brought them good luck and invited me to share the dinner. This was a problem because I definitely was not going to eat the dead dog.

There were three possibilities:

The first was to accept it and eat dead dog. This was out of the question. The second was to say that eating a dead dog was disgusting, but if I did that I would be insulting them and they meant well. So I lied and said that I had been sick in Samoa and went to a doctor and he said that I should not eat meat for the next three days so my stomach would get better. This, of course, was not true, but it did save me from eating dead dog, and they were not insulted.

What country made you feel most out of your comfort zone and why?

In certain ways North Korea may be the most "exotic" place I have visited with so many restrictions. When I arrived at Pyongyang by plane on Air Koryo from Beijing, they took my passport at the plane exit at the top of the steps. I did not see it again until entering the plane on departure. The crew did not sit down or fasten their seat belts during takeoff or landing. We were informed that we could not under any circumstances leave the hotel without our guides and there were guards posted at the exits to make sure that we did not do so. When we were out of the hotel the guides (male or female) went with us into the bathrooms and stood in front of the stalls. We were not permitted to change money. We could use any currency for small purchases and got change in the same currency. The trip was fully-inclusive except for small souvenirs and postcards. Even the road we used to go from Pyongyang to Panmunjom was segregated. There were parallel roads for North Koreans and foreigners. When we went to see the Mass Games at the May Day Stadium, the thousands of North Koreans were already there and we were seated in a separate walled-off section. At the end of the performance they remained in their seats until our bus departed. The only North Koreans we had any contact with were those who worked in the hotels, restaurants, and shops that we visited and they were probably very thoroughly checked. We were given bizarre political explanations such as that the border had to be carefully guarded because the entire population of South Korea would like to escape to the north. When we boarded the metro train the guide yelled something in Korean and all of the occupants of the train immediately got up and exited. We were well-fed with food of good quality and the people we observed from the bus window did not appear to be hungry. But then again, we had no choice of where we were taken. Our guides were pleasant and spoke languages well but they had definitely never been outside the country. People may or may not have been curious about foreigners but they never attempted to approach our group. We saw no evidence of private ownership of cars except by high government officials. So there was not even the most superficial contact between us and private citizens. They ask foreigners if the Korean language is spoken and they will not give you a visa if you admit that you speak Korean. In any case, you could not contact ordinary citizens even if you did speak Korean fluently. Getting North Korean money is not allowed. The guide gave me one small coin for a souvenir. The explanation given to us is that foreigners have dirty hands and so are not permitted to touch the money. Obviously this is ridiculous. I asked if we could view the home of the guide, but this request was politely declined.

Do you speak any foreign languages? If so, which has been the most useful for you besides English?

In addition to Yiddish and French, which I speak fluently, I can speak some Hebrew, Hungarian, Russian, and Latvian. Yiddish is useful to meet Jewish people especially in Eastern Europe. French is very useful in Africa.

Looking back from when you started traveling to where you are now, in what ways, if any, has travel changed you?

I feel that I now have a much better understanding of the world.

What was the longest continuous trip you have ever taken, when was it, where did you travel?

I took a 90-day bus trip from London to Kathmandu in 1978 during a sabbatical. It went through Europe to Turkey and then via Iran, Afghanistan, Pakistan, and India to Nepal. On this trip, we were deported from Iran and got to visit the Buddhist statues at Bamiyan in Afghanistan, which the Taliban later destroyed.

What is your favorite "off-the-beaten-path" destination and why?

I don't know if the Russian Federation is "off-the-beaten-path" but I am trying to complete visiting all of the oblasts there. I also liked São Tomé and Príncipe very much. People there were friendly and few people visit these islands. Nauru is also extremely interesting and bizarre. It is not easy to go there because a visa is needed and there are very few Nauru embassies. The entire country was one big phosphate mine and because of this it was very rich, so they had no need for tourists. It was someplace to see, but I have no desire to go back there.

What are the best and worst places you have ever spent a night?

I stayed in a wonderful place in Ravello high above the Amalfi Coast. The worst place I ever stayed in was in a filthy dump in Rwanda. We arrived in Kigali, Rwanda during a festival and had to stay in an absolutely terrible "hotel".

In your opinion, what country or place in the world feels the most authentic and untouched by tourism?

Untouched by tourism would definitely be North Korea. Saudi Arabia is definitely authentic, but not in a desirable way. Even though the facilities are modern and comfortable, Saudi Arabia is abhorrent because of its medieval customs, especially in its treatment of women. Very few people visit Ascension Island. When I went it was necessary to have an invitation from the governor.

In your opinion, where is the most beautiful place on Earth?

This is really an impossible question to answer. Some places that come to mind are the old city walls of Jerusalem; the canals of Venice; the cliffs of Moher in Ireland; the Great Wall of China; the North Cape in Norway; the Bosphorus in Istanbul; the area inside the walls of Dubrovnik; the Alpine passes in

Switzerland; Mont Saint-Michel in France; Ayers Rock in Australia; Iguassu Falls in Brazil; the Taj Mahal in India; the tulip fields in bloom in Holland; Mount Fuji in Japan; the Norwegian fjords; the Shwe Dagon pagoda in Burma; Red Square in Moscow; the old parts of Prague; the Danube in Budapest; Table Mountain in Cape Town. The list could go on and on because there are so many beautiful places in this wonderful world.

What do you enjoy most when traveling (cities, nature, people, cultural spots, etc.) and why?

Meeting and talking to local people is very interesting to me and I like small towns to get the authentic atmosphere of a country.

What travel accomplishments are you most proud of?

Going by plane to Antarctica from the south of Chile was great because I do not travel by ship; also, getting to every UN member country except two.

If you had just one personal travel story to share with someone, what would it be?

Once I was in a small hotel near the Djoudj National Bird Sanctuary in northern Senegal, not far from the Mauritanian border. The room I was staying in had a ceiling fan, which was on because the climate there is hot. I got up to use the bathroom and while I was in there I heard a big noise. The fan had somehow become detached from the ceiling and came crashing down on the bed in which I had been just a few minutes before. I was incredibly lucky because if I had been in the bed I would have been very seriously injured. The management of the hotel was very unsympathetic and even wanted to charge me for repairs to the fan and the ceiling.

Besides your home country, where do you find yourself returning to over and over and why?

I go to Israel very frequently because I think of it as a second home. It is my favorite country in the world and I have been there about 35 times over the years. Many Jewish people, such as myself, feel very comfortable there because it is the only Jewish country in the world. Birobidzhan (in the Russian Far East) may be called the Jewish Autonomous Oblast, but only a very tiny portion of the population is Jewish and not too many people can speak Yiddish there. I have been to almost every corner of Israel from Rosh Hanikra and Ramat Hagolan in the far north to Eilat on the Red Sea (Gulf of Aqaba) in the extreme south. I have crossed the Jordanian and Egyptian borders and approached the Syrian and Lebanese borders, which are not open. I even crossed unofficially into Lebanon to attend the wedding of a chambermaid who worked in the small hotel in Metulla where I was staying with my mother. We crossed in an Israeli military vehicle and came back the same way.

What is the ideal amount of time you prefer to travel on each trip before you are ready for home and a break?

My ideal trip is two months long.

If you had an unlimited budget and space and time was no object, what would your perfect travel day look like? (for example: start your morning in Bora Bora; afternoon on a safari in Kenya; night in Australia, etc.)

Going to the South Pole, which I have not yet done, or ballooning over the Cappadocian countryside, being invited to have dinner with the Queen of England, and traveling into outer space.

For those looking to travel to every country, what is the best piece of advice you could offer them?

Try to go to different regions on different trips and try to have an open mind and look for the good points of each place you visit.

For someone that has been almost everywhere, what still gets you excited about packing your bags again?

I may have been to most countries, but there are many places within countries which I have not yet seen. I am trying to visit every oblast, krai, okrug, and republic of Russia. This is not easy because of the vast size of the country. Some of the zones in the Caucasus I have not visited may not be safe. Chukotka in the very far east near Alaska is not easy to reach, but maybe I can go there in 2017 with my Russian friend from Ulyanovsk. I will visit the remaining oblasts in central Siberia on my forth-coming trip. The other big countries I would like to revisit are Argentina and Brazil. Then there is Saint Helena and I am looking forward to the opening of the new airport there early next year. Except for South Sudan, which is the only African country I have never visited, I have no desire to go back to Africa except to see the migration of the wildebeest in Kenya and The Garden Route in the Western Cape province of South Africa.

Do you ever feel you have missed out on certain aspects of life being away from home so much?

No.

Looking ahead, what travel plans and goals are you still pursuing, and what is on your "Bucket List"?

My next trip is in May 2015 for two months and over that time I will visit numerous oblasts and republics in Russia including Orenburg, Kurgan, Omsk, Altai krai, Novosibirsk, Altai Republic, Kemerovo, Khakassia, and Tomsk. I am also going to revisit the Kaliningrad region, Belarus, and Kazakhstan. On the way I will stop in England, Finland, Sweden, Latvia, and Lithuania. I would also like to visit every one of the departments of France, which is one of my favorite countries. Going to Bogota, Colombia is also on my bucket list as I have only been to Cartagena on the coast and to the San Andres and Providencia islands.

Seth Sherman, U.S.A.

(Seth Sherman, Yemen, 2014)

Where did you grow up and what was your early life like?

I grew up around New Orleans and New York City with parents who were a geneticist (father) and a clinical social worker (mother). When I was very young, my parents got into an automobile accident and I had to live with my grandparents, who were frequent travelers, although to the more common international destinations.

When did you go from casually traveling to making this a full-time goal, and what motivated you to travel to every country?

I only traveled with my family until I graduated high school and began college prematurely. I was partying way too much and dropped out after three months, at which time my parents and I agreed that a long solo trip was in order. I started and ended in Rome, going clockwise around the Mediterranean for nine months, spending time in Italy, Greece, Turkey, Lebanon, Jordan, Israel, Egypt, Morocco, and Spain before I returned home and resumed my studies. I was backpacking with friends in East Africa in the 90s, when we met an elderly couple who were members of the TCC (Travelers' Century Club), which I researched when I got home. It seemed to be a challenging goal and I have never looked back.

Do you remember the point where you said to yourself, "I can really accomplish this"?

I think that I've always seen TCC as something that I could accomplish. In the mid-00's, I heard of MTP (Most Traveled People) and decided to selectively add some of the additional destinations, although I'm not willing to spend $10,000 for the privilege of stepping on and off an uninhabited atoll in the Pacific. With 324 destinations on TCC, I can spend some time in each, getting to know a little bit about the people and place. With nearly 900 on MTP, I would not learn anything which, for me, would be an empty experience.

What have you done over your life to gain the freedom and finances to pursue as much travel as you have?

I'm a physician and stock trader, which helps pay for this expensive hobby.

Was there ever a time you felt like abandoning this goal?

Not really. Like all of us, there have been times of frustration and loneliness but, overall, I wouldn't trade it for the world (pardon the pun).

What were your worst travel experiences (i.e. detainment, bribes, car accidents, sickness, etc.) and why?

For detainment, I think that I've been luckier than some of your other travelers. My worst was being held for six hours during an overland border crossing between Uzbekistan and Turkmenistan. Although I had a multiple entry visa for Uzbekistan, I didn't have an entry stamp for my crossing from Tajikistan. Nobody spoke English and I don't speak Russian or Uzbek, so they held me until some enlightened soul in Tashkent alerted them to the low probability of my sneaking into a country when I could have entered legally.

As for bribes, I was traveling with a girlfriend from Moldova into Transnistria by bus. The guards wouldn't let us pass without a $100 bribe each, which we didn't want to pay. The problem was exacerbated by the same English-Russian language problem as above. Finally, the other passengers on the bus started screaming at the border guards in Russian to let us pass, which they eventually did.

My worst experience with sickness was traveler's diarrhea, on a public bus in northern India with a different girlfriend. She got the driver to stop in a small town where there was only a small, dark and dirty outhouse complete with assorted spiders. I had a similar experience in the Ngorongoro Crater, where my driver was trying to keep his jeep between me and a pack of pachyderms.

What do you consider the most adventurous trip you have taken?

I've done mission trips with my father to the Nicobar Islands, Africa, and New Guinea. One time, we spent two months on Wuvulu, a small island in the Ninigo Group, northwest of Wewak, New Guinea, in the Bismarck Sea. There was not any electricity, running water, or accommodations for visitors, so we slept on the floor of our host's living room. We ate what they did (mostly fish and fruit), took rainwater showers and bathed in the lagoon (excellent snorkeling). Before we left, they served us their local delicacy: coconut crab.

What were your most challenging countries to visit and why?

For me, the most challenging countries are those that just don't want you there, such as Angola, Libya, and Belarus. I'm fairly easygoing and adaptable and can usually make the best out of a bad situation.

What is the strangest thing you've seen/experienced while traveling?

Maybe pre-pubescent children getting married in rural India, although that was 25 years ago.

Which travel experiences stand out the most and why?

For me, it's usually the people, the occasion where you befriend a local, get invited into their home, and cross the line between tourist and guest. I also love wildlife, so my first African safari and visit to South Georgia were amazing, getting so close to nature.

What are the most overrated and underrated countries you've been to in your travels and why?

This is a hard question because the best rated countries (like Italy, France and Ireland) are excellent destinations, but just very crowded and commercialized, unless you visit off-season. The most underrated countries are those that have just become relatively safe (even if just momentarily), but before they're discovered by the masses.

What are the best and worst meals you have ever had traveling and where were they?

My worst was in Armenia (which may have been excellent for others). The granddaughter of our host brought out what looked like an incredibly appealing big frothy vanilla milkshake. Taking my first sip, I discovered that it was yogurt, which I despise. My girlfriend finished hers and the hosts went to get us some cookies, I bribed her into letting me swap glasses and finishing mine. The best may have been the coconut crab in Wuvulu, which was accentuated by spending time with my father and bonding with our hosts.

What country made you feel most out of your comfort zone and why?

I was staying with the pygmies of the Central African Republic with my driver. We were told to bring rice, in exchange for hospitality. Well, when the rice ran out, so did their hospitality and they chased us off, throwing stones at our jeep.

Do you speak any foreign languages? If so, which have been the most useful for you besides English?

I'm conversant in Spanish and French and have started studying Arabic. If I can ever master that one, I'll start on Russian. I think that's all my small head can handle. I used to speak a little Dutch as I was dating a Netherlander after I graduated. One day, while eating with her extended family, the mother asked me in Dutch how I liked their meal, to which I replied, "licker shtuk, licker ding" (pardon the spelling), which means delicious. What I didn't know, but immediately realized when all heads turned to my girlfriend, was that it is only used in a sexual context.

Looking back from when you started traveling to where you are now, in what ways, if any, have travel changed you.

I think that I've got a broader experience compared to those who don't travel. I realize that some things are better abroad and some are better here (which I appreciate more when I return). I love the quote from T.S. Eliot's *Little Gidding*:

"We shall not cease from exploration, and the end of all our exploring will be to arrive where we started and know the place for the first time."

What is the longest continuous trip you have ever taken? When was it and where did you travel?

The nine month trip that I took when I dropped out of college. I've had several two month trips, but it's hard for me to get off more consecutive time than that.

What is your favorite "off-the-beaten-path" destination and why?

The trip to Wuvulu with my father would be my favorite (see above).

Another was a few years ago when I traveled with several friends on the *Hanse Explorer*, to be the first set of people to climb the peak on Bouvet Island. The expedition lasted 35 days. Thirty-three days were in exquisite luxury (this was the boat that Bill Gates used to bring his family to Antarctica) and two days were spent slogging through guano, climbing ice peaks and falling into crevasses. I would never do it again, but I made some new friends and would not have wanted to miss it.

What are the best and worst places you have ever spent a night?

A great night was on a train with a girlfriend in India. Although we were in a car with about 50 other people, at 0300, everyone else was asleep (I hope) and we had a great romantic interlude. I'm glad this was before the days of YouTube. Another great night was with my father in the Chumbe Eco Lodge, off the coast of Zanzibar.

The worst nights were in airports, waiting for a 0400 flight.

In your opinion, what country or place in the world feels the most authentic and untouched by tourism?

I think that some of the remoter parts of Central Africa and inhabited islands of the South Pacific without runways are still relatively pristine, although most of those locations are now overpopulated and dependent on Western packaged goods. It's disheartening to see beautiful islands filled with litter. On the other hand, you can't fault people for wanting what we have. Also, the more remote Shetland Islands are not very touristy.

In your opinion, where is the most beautiful place on Earth?

Several years ago, on the ship *Klebnikov*'s last voyage, we stopped at Larsemann Hills, one of the more pristine Emperor penguin rookeries, a helicopter excursion. All you could see were these beautiful, white, mountains and the snowy bases on which they stood. Then, after about a mile's trek, was this large rookery of Emperor penguins, sheltered from the winds on four sides. I was one of the last to leave and was able to spend time with these magnificent birds and their chicks, almost alone in this amazingly beautiful wonder-world.

Maybe my greatest pleasure in traveling is meeting and be-friending people of different cultures and learning as much as I can about their lives and world.

In the late '80's, I got a permit to visit Tibet. Driving with my guide/driver, the car broke down as the weather started getting worse. We made a temporary fix and found a settlement of several houses where we could stay and try to make a more permanent fix. We were there for about 2 days before we could fix the radiator, but the Buddhist hospitality was so genuine that it was sad to leave. We all exchanged presents with what we had at hand, but the memories, at least for me, will last a lifetime.

Maybe the most beautiful place on Earth is a brilliant and clear night sky, from which we can cast our gaze upon what is an extremely small part of the universe and realize just how small our world is but to give us the perspective that the challenge at hand — to explore the far reaches of our small planet — may not be as daunting as it first seems.

What do you enjoy most when traveling (cities, nature, people, cultural spots, etc.) and why?

For me, it's meeting and interacting with people and nature. I'm not very into attractions (well seen on Google Earth) or information museums (more data on Wikipedia). But the personal and nature interactions that cannot be obtained elsewhere. On my first solo trip, I spent the weekend with a family from Rome when I offered to help the grandmother carry her packages. I've never (and never will) gotten over the feeling of being a guest, rather than a tourist or traveler; or the thrill of befriending a tortoise on Aldabra, or baby penguins on South Georgia Island.

What travel accomplishments are you most proud of?

On a trip to New Britain with my father, we witnessed the consecutive natural disasters of an earthquake, volcano, torrential rains, and flood. As they had more planes than pilots, I got to use my piloting skills to help evacuate people and bring in supplies.

If you had just one personal travel story to share with someone, what would that be?

I was recently in Yemen and heard gun shots outside of my hotel. The next morning, as the lobby was empty, I wandered outside and met some of the freedom fighters who were defending Sana'a from the Islamic State. Spending time with them, I realized just how lucky I am not to have to fight for every freedom that I have. All of us contributing to this book have had the luck to be born in the times and places where we were and to have the means and capability to do what we're doing. I believe that I'm more humble and appreciative from traveling.

Besides your home country, where do you find yourself returning to over and over and why?

I love the quiet beauty of the Shetland Islands and rural France, the crowds of India and the wide open savannas of Africa (which is where my family originally comes from).

What is the ideal amount of time you prefer to travel each trip before you are ready for home and a break?

Maybe three or four weeks. I'm close to my family and puppies and miss them when I'm away too long. Then after a few weeks home, I'm ready to leave again.

If you had an unlimited budget and space and time was no object, what would your perfect travel day look like? (for example: start your morning in Bora Bora; afternoon on a safari in Kenya; night in Australia, etc.)

As much as I love the destinations, I hate the packing, unpacking, and airport security, so I think this scenario is not for me.

For those looking to travel to every country, what is the best piece of advice you could offer them?

Plan on making a lifetime project out of it and not trying to get it done in five years. For each big trip, choose five (or so) countries that are reasonably close together and spend enough time in each to get to know a bit about the place. I have friends trying to finish the MTP list who will land in a country, province or state, get off for a moment and back on the plane and take off again, checking off another destination. That would not be a fulfilling experience for me.

For someone that has been almost everywhere, what still gets you excited about packing your bags again?

Blue water sailing with friends. I'm starting to get the itch to buy another sailboat and to do a circumnavigation or two, visiting destinations that are difficult or impossible to otherwise reach.

Do you feel you have missed out on certain aspects of life being away from home so much?

I have. As you can't be in two places at the same time, my traveling has kept me away from events in the lives of family and friends. It's also been hard on my social life as not many people like to travel like we do (I'm currently single).

Looking ahead, what travel plans and goals are you still pursuing, and what is on your "Bucket List"?

As I believe that a meaningful trip to outer space is beyond my reach, obtaining a smaller sailboat than the one I had and sailing it around the world sounds interesting, exciting and obtainable. I would also like to finish the TCC list (I'm up to 310) but could live with myself if I didn't.

Jeff Shea, U.S.A.

(Jeff Shea completes the 'Seven Summits' atop Mount Vinson in 1997)

Where did you grow up and what was your early life like?

San Francisco and Millbrae, California. My father told us funny bedtime stories about fictional characters that traveled all over the world getting into mischief. He took us to parks and museums and had expansive thinking.

When did you go from casually traveling to making this a full-time goal, and what motivated you to travel to every country?

I decided at 19 that I wanted to go to every country on Earth. I was motivated by curiosity to know everywhere.

Do you remember the point where you said to yourself, "I can really accomplish this"?

When I had traveled enough as a pauper, backpacker, and hitchhiker, then saw I had enough cash to see it through to completion.

What have you done over your life to gain the freedom and finances to pursue as much travel as you have?

It all began with a decision, and it had nothing to do with having money. I just decided to do it. The money came later. The travel began immediately. Initially I slept under bushes and had a budget of $1 a day for everything.

Was there ever a time you felt like abandoning this goal?

No.

What were your worst travel experiences (i.e. detainment, bribes, car accidents, sickness, etc.) and why?

There is a thin line between worst and most vital, worst being a bad thing, but vital meaning living to the fullest. If an experience is painful, it is also memorable. So, my thoughts go to the time when I was on a 50' sloop sailing to Wallis from Orona Atoll near Canton Island in Kiribati (in the middle of nowhere), and I began to get very sick. After five days of suffering in sweltering heat at sea, we landed in Wallis Island, where I found I had malaria (again). The whole experience was very painful, staying in the hospital there, feeling like my stomach was going to explode, feeling like I was dying (which I was, as I had Falciprium malaria). I had to cut my trip short.

What do you consider the most adventurous trip you have taken?

Without a doubt, it was my 2014 return to the Meseta de Ichum (aka Ichun), an ancient tepui in the deep Amazon of southern Venezuela. No human being had ever been deep into the interior of the Meseta. In 2013, I led an attempt to do so. We cut through the forest at a rate of one kilometer a day. We didn't get very far, only about 10 kilometers. In 2014, I led another expedition into the Meseta's interior. We established 20 camps along the Ichum River in an attempt to reach its source, using two boats made from PVC and inner tubes. These lightweight boats were made this way so that we could disassemble them when we reached rapids and waterfalls. We started off with a group of nine — five Shiriana Indians, three men from Caracas, and myself. After fifteen camps, four of the Shiriana staged a mutiny and left. Instead of going back, I convinced the remaining Shirina and one other companion to forge deeper south. At Camp 21, we discovered an insect that has never been seen before in Venezuela and of which only six specimens were ever found in history. We were the first to ever visit Jaguar Falls on foot, so named because a jaguar walked right in front of me, only five meters away, as I approached the falls. The journey took us through areas of great beauty. It was psychologically and physically very challenging. It was an effort to maintain our sanity as we battled upriver for a month. This was more adventurous than my summit of the North Ridge of Everest in 1995.

What were your most challenging countries to visit and why?

Bouvet Island, because of the logistics of getting there and landing on its shore; Iraq, in 2002, because of the political difficulty of getting a visa (but a great trip!); Iran, in 1984, when the Ayatollah was in power, and because Americans were the enemy; Saudi Arabia — I was able to go to Mecca because I had taken on the Muslim faith (in order to marry my wife); North Greenland and East Greenland because in both places I had to join an expedition to explore them. Solomon Islands because I sailed there from San Francisco in 1982; and Niger in 1988 because I traveled across the Sahara on the back of a date truck to get there.

What is the strangest thing you've seen/experienced while traveling?

Seeing the "Pulsating Stone of Sulawesi." Seeing this mysterious white stone pulsate all the colors of the spectrum when dropped in water and stopping immediately when taken out was the most inexplicable thing I have ever seen. The stone pulsated as if it had its own energy. It was not a trick, but a natural object. It was said that it was brought by the *nenek moyang* (ancestral spirits) in order to help a woman find a husband. The stone was dropped in water, and she drank the water. Later, I tried the same thing. That evening, a beautiful young woman came into my life.

Which travel experiences stand out the most and why?

1. Exploring the unexplored Meseta de Ichum (aka Ichun) in Venezuela. (To go to a place that has never been seen by human eyes was extraordinary, because we didn't know what we would find. I had always wanted to see a jaguar, leopard or panther, but never had. As we approached the magnificent falls deep within the Meseta above Camp 14, the awesomely beautiful animal walked right by me and leaped up into the forest.)

2. Standing on the top of Mount Everest, having summited it by the hair-raising North Ridge. (You can see Kanchenjunga in Sikkim. The cliffs are 10,000 feet high.)… as well as…

3. Completing the Seven Summits by climbing Mount Vinson in Antarctica. (Standing looking out over the vast sea of ice, bitterly cold.)

4. Walking by myself across the Altiplano of South America. (Sheer isolation, high up in the Andes, pulling my water cart 500 kilometers through a waterless area. Difficult, but inspiring.)

5. Walking across the Atacama Desert in Chile. (Again, sheer isolation and magnificent night skies. The thrill of setting out without certainty what would come next.)

6. Walking out of the Highlands of New Guinea, a 39-day epic that found me lost in the rainforest. (Being transformed by understanding the majestic beauty of the forest and the importance of preserving natural areas.)

7. Seeing the Aurora Borealis from our first-ever survey of Warming Island, the world's newest island, discovered by our team leader Dennis Schmitt. (A vividly cold place of great beauty, with three sawtooth peaks to the north and the new canal separating us from Greenland below us.)

8. Being part of Schmitt's discovery of one of the most northerly features of land in the world, Stray Dog West, off the coast of northern Greenland. (The thrill of discovery, reaching it by walking on the sea ice, the awesome, austere beauty of Greenland.)

9. Sailing across the Pacific Ocean in a 40' yacht in 1982. (A dream to sail the high seas, the sense of freedom and to be where there are no countries at all.)

10. Walking alone across Transylvania by compass point in 1997. (A novel idea to go in a single direction, through villages, across streams and forests — a feeling of freedom.)

What are the most overrated and underrated countries you've been to in your travels and why?

I don't think of countries as "overrated." Places, yes. There are hundreds of overrated places. But countries, there is always something interesting, unknown, or hidden wonders in any place. Overrated places would include Boracay, a white beach area in the Philippines — there are thousands of other islands there. Why join the tourist crowd?

What are the best and worst meals you have ever had traveling and where were they?

Among the best:

Punta Arenas, Chile — Pure de palta (avocado) and Tierra del Fuego King Crab.

San Francisco, California — Original Joe's.

Among the oddest:

Termites in Nigeria. One I did not eat was deep-fried tarantulas in Cambodia. In New Guinea, a goat's tongue was offered. I only took one bite. In Zaire (now the Democratic Republic of Congo), I ate monkey.

What country made you feel most out of your comfort zone and why?

Honestly, the country that makes me most uncomfortable is my own: the U.S.A. This is because I find the people too opinionated and militantly intolerant of different life perspectives. I was also not very comfortable in Iran in 1984. I am not comfortable in any place where it is illegal to walk down the street with my shirt off.

Do you speak any foreign languages? If so, which have been the most useful for you besides English?

Spanish, conversational (most useful)

Bahasa Indonesia, conversational

French, rudimentary

At one time, a smattering of Pidgin English.

Looking back from when you started traveling to where you are now, in what ways, if any, have travel changed you.

It taught me that the way I was brought up was backwards. I had placed importance on monetary wealth and I believed in the merit of economic development. Travel has humbled me immensely. I grew to deeply respect the simplest of lifestyles, particularly tribal, and I became very skeptical of the concept of wanton human infrastructural development of the world.

What is the longest continuous trip you have ever taken? When was it and where did you travel?

Twenty-six months. I departed by sailing in a 40' ketch under San Francisco's Golden Gate Bridge on Halloween Night in 1982. Five of us sailed to Hawaii, Kiribati, the Solomon Islands, and finally to Papua New Guinea. There I got off and traveled to Lake Kopiago, and then I walked out of the highlands. I later went by ship from Irian Jaya to Jakarta, then to Singapore. I went overland from there to Thailand, flew to Nepal, and backtracked to Bangladesh, then overland to Africa through Iran. I later flew to Holland then home to the U.S., finishing December 1984.

What is your favorite "off-the-beaten-path" destination and why?

Meseta de Ichum, in the southern Venezuelan Amazon. It was a privilege and significant for me to see a completely untouched place.

What are the best and worst places you have ever spent a night?

Best: On top of the Great Pyramid of Cheops.

Worst: Sitting under a tarp in the rain all night, lost in the forests of New Guinea. On this portion of the journey out of the highlands, my female companion was walking slowly and the villagers that were showing us the way to the next settlement, which was days away, left us behind. They had our food pack. We survived on honey until we could find our way back to the previous village (Wabia).

In your opinion, what country or place in the world feels the most authentic and untouched by tourism?

Bhutan, Myanmar, Mongolia, Papua New Guinea. And, of course, North Korea.

In your opinion, where is the most beautiful place on Earth?

If I had to say it in a nutshell, I would say, the Himalayas. That is no doubt, because I have an affinity for high places. Why? For several reasons: The quiet and the grandeur; the clean air, the views; the atmosphere is different. But this also translates in an interesting way to the people. Mountain people tend to be different — rugged, outgoing, natural.

It is not surprising to me that native people often attribute spirits to the high mountains, and this is probably not truer than in the Himalayas. In fact, when you spend time there, you can understand why this is so — The mountains seem to actually have a spirit. They are inspiring.

I believe this also influenced the religions. An example is the festival of Mani Rimdu, which is celebrated every year with splendor at Tengboche Monastery in the Solo Khumbu. The mountains visible from Tengboche — Everest, Lhotse, Nuptse, Ama Dablam, Kantega — are mesmerizing.

So, not only are the Himalayas visually inspiring, but spiritually as well.

What do you enjoy most when traveling (cities, nature, people, cultural spots, etc.) and why?

In general it is being out far from the cities, adventuring in little-traveled places, seeking solitude, and quiet and mystery. I like doing unusual things, like creating my own expeditionary journeys (e.g., walking across the South American Altiplano, etc.). Doing things on foot, like climbing mountains. And, of course, to be complete, highlights of my travels often involved romantic encounters with beautiful foreign women.

What travel accomplishments are you most proud of?

(Most of these were previously mentioned.)

1) Leading the first expeditions into the Meseta de Ichum in Venezuela.

2) Climbing the Seven Summits (including Mount Everest via the North Ridge).

3) Traveling (so far) to 2313 of the world's 3978 provinces, including visiting all 358 provinces in Southeast Asia.

4) Walking across the South American Altiplano.

5) Walking across the Atacama Desert.

6) Being part of the discovery of Stray Dog West.

If you had just one personal travel story to share with someone, what would that be?

That would be my experience running away from a rhinoceros… I excerpt my journal from that day…

March 19, 1984 — Chitwan National Park, Nepal

9 a.m. Well, I wanted to see an Indian One-Horned Rhinoceros, but this morning I had a physical confrontation with one!! There I was, running across the field of elephant grass with mamma rhino (and baby following) coming after me.

We'd gotten up 'late' at 6 a.m. Gabrielle, Ed, and I walked upriver, but after a 'ways' decided it was fruitless and headed to the machan. Way out in the field was a rhino. I got out my camera. Just then, Ed pointed out a rhino just below us walking away from the machan! I snapped a photo, then went down to get closer but could not find it. Back in the machan, I decide to go to the other out in the field, I was looking back at Ed and Gabrielle in the machan but their hand signal became confusing so I came back. They said I almost walked on top of it.

I was heading out again when they called out that there was a baby rhino with it and I shouldn't go. I thought they were bull-shitting me, so I crept up to it. I had it in sight the whole way. I was silent, then stepped on a twig. The menacing beast looked around. I moved slowly about while she continued to graze. She rambled slowly towards me. I saw the baby rhino and I became afraid.

When I snapped a good photo, the she-rhino heard the shutter and took notice of me. I began to back off and she made for me. I ran, looking back. The rhino stopped, looked, and corrected her direction twice in pursuit and I leaped through the dry grass barefoot, being pursued by two tons of meat with a horn! I felt for the first time in my life, afraid for my life, afraid for my life because of a wild beast. As I reached the jungle cover, I made for the machan while the beast and her baby took off in the other direction. Gabrielle waited for me with a hug. Unfortunately, Ed didn't get a picture of me with the rhino in pursuit. I took one last photo of the running rhino before reaching the machan.

Besides your home country, where do you find yourself returning to over and over and why?

South America, because there are many wide open and little traveled and/or undiscovered places. Asia, for business and personal reasons.

What is the ideal amount of time you prefer to travel each trip before you are ready for home and a break?

No limit. I would prefer unlimited. The feeling of freedom usually beats staying in one place.

If you had an unlimited budget and space and time was no object, what would your perfect travel day look like? (for example: start your morning in Bora Bora; afternoon on a safari in Kenya; night in Australia, etc.)

I suppose the answer to that would be personal! On another level, a perfect travel day would be to meet an undiscovered tribe and photograph them.

For those looking to travel to every country, what is the best piece of advice you could offer them?

Just do it. Don't let yourself be discouraged by money or lack thereof.

I have two favorite sayings in this regard, both from Shakespeare:

1) "Rather… see the wonders of the world abroad than living dully sluggarized at home, wear out thy youth with shapeless idleness."

2) "Our doubts are traitors. And make us lose the good we oft might win. By fearing to attempt."

For someone that has been almost everywhere, what still gets you excited about packing your bags again?

Going on an expedition to an unfamiliar place that involves risk and the reward of accomplishment and unusual experience.

Do you feel you have missed out on certain aspects of life being away from home so much?

Yes, but not as much as one might think. When it is a big part of your life, your life will revolve around it and people around you can come with you. Also, new experiences have a surprising quality of rejuvenation and added personal power; this makes up for a lot of what is lost by leaving home.

Looking ahead, what travel plans and goals are you still pursuing, and what is on your "Bucket List"?

1) Go to every province on Earth. (I still have over 1600 left to see!)

2) Explore the unexplored areas remaining on Earth.

3) Finish my journey by natural means (on foot, raft, etc.) across South America. (I've completed part of it already by walking across the Atacama and Altiplano.)

4) Wrangel Island.

There are more things than I can count, but the above items are some of the big ones.

Ed Reynolds, U.S.A.

Mount Yasur Volcano
on Tanna Island,
Vanuatu,
January 24, 2014

(Ed Reynolds)

Where did you grow up and what was your early life like?

I grew up in Connecticut. During World War II, I lived with my brother year-round at a boy's camp with locations in Connecticut, New York and New Hampshire. Early travels were between the camp's locations. After the war, in 1947, my stepfather had a lot of vacation time and he took my mother, brother, and I on a long trip across Canada and then down through the western national parks to San Diego. After a short venture into Baja California we continued back to Connecticut via Texas. My stepfather was then transferred to Dallas, Texas and I spent several years traveling back and forth from Connecticut to Texas. I attended Southern Methodist University in Dallas and continued to travel back and forth to Connecticut, purposely varying the route so I visited almost all the states east of the Mississippi.

In 1957, I enlisted in the USAF (United States Air Force) and earned a commission and navigator rating in Texas. My first operational unit was in Bangor, Maine, where I volunteered for every mission to a new location I could. From Maine, I was transferred to Bermuda and then Southern California where I flew missions throughout the Pacific spending time in Alaska, Hawaii, Wake, Guam, Japan, the Philippines, and Thailand.

The USAF then transferred me to New Hampshire. I took a long route there via the northwest and northern states completing my traveling through all 50 states. Then I was sent to Okinawa for four months where I flew numerous missions to every USAF base in Thailand and the Philippines.

Eventually I was assigned to Vietnam where I flew extensively around the country and left the country almost every weekend on trips to Hong Kong, Korea, Japan, Taiwan, the Philippines, Singapore, Malaysia, and Diego Garcia. I also unofficially spent time in Laos and Cambodia.

When did you go from casually traveling to making this a full-time goal, and what motivated you to travel to every country?

I started taking cruises in 1999, and in 2006, on my first visit to the east coast of Africa, I met Cathy and Bob Prada, of Advantage Travel and Tours. They introduced me to the Travelers' Century Club (TCC) list and the International Travel News (ITN). I found that I had already visited 100 of the TCC destinations and that Advantage Travel could schedule me on tours to unusual destinations. I then started taking their trips and my number of TCC destinations started to increase. Many of the travelers in the group I traveled with were on the quest to visit every country in the world. They introduced me to the Most Traveled People (MTP) list which provided me with destinations in addition to the TCC list. Since the average person is not familiar with the TCC or the MTP, I focused first on visiting the 193 UN Member States, which people could relate to. After I accomplished visiting the 193 UN Member States, I was motivated to visit as many of the TCC and MTP destinations that I could arrange.

Do you remember the point where you said to yourself, "I can really accomplish this"?

When I met Klaus Billep of Universal Travel System (UTS), I realized he could schedule me for the really difficult places to visit and with a combination of Advantage Travel and UTS I could visit every country in the UN.

What have you done over your life to gain the freedom and finances to pursue as much travel as you have?

Serving 22 years in the USAF provided a pension to support my wife and home expenses. My travel funds have come from selling a house I inherited from my mother and my 401k from my post-USAF career as an Information Management Consultant. I stopped working full-time in 2011, but still work several months a year to fund my travel.

Was there ever a time you felt like abandoning this goal?

No.

What have been your worst travel experiences (such as detainment, bribes, car accidents, sicknesses, etc.) and why?

In 2008, I was on a Holland America World War II Battlefield cruise from New Zealand to Japan. On a port call in Rabaul, New Britain, Papua New Guinea, I was touring a cave containing 12 Japanese tenders. The cave had a cat walk above the tenders and I was on a section that collapsed two stories above the floor. I landed on top of seven other passengers, spraining a wrist and cutting my leg on the edge of a rusty tender. Five of the group were flown home but I completed the cruise with my wrist in a cast and my leg swelling from rust poisoning. Several months later I was on a tour of some South Pacific islands when I suffered from a high fever and my leg swelled up. I cut the tour short and flew back to L.A. and was hospitalized for two weeks suffering from cellulitis.

The second worst travel experience was having my passport stolen in Paris's Charles de Gaulle Airport as I was on my way to join a tour of eight West African countries in November 2010. I was able to get a new passport the next day, but I couldn't replace the visas, so I rented a car and visited every province in France and the countries of Andorra, Monaco, Italy, and San Marino.

Another travel experience occurred in 2013 when I was on the Oceanwide Expeditions, M/V *Plancius*, that suffered engine failure on an Antarctic cruise and we had to spend eight days at King Edward Point, Grytviken, South Georgia Island, before we were rescued.

What do you consider one of the most adventurous trips you have taken?

1) My first long trip in 1947 touring Canada and the United States. It started my love of travel and opened my eyes to the adventure and beauty of visiting different areas.

2) Holland America *Prinsendam* Explorer Cruise in October and November 2006 from Athens to Cape Town, South Africa, followed by safari in Botswana and a visit to Victoria Falls. It was my first visit to Egypt and the West African countries. The first safari and the beauty of the falls were very memorable.

3) My tour of Iraq, Jordon, Syria, and Lebanon in 2009 with Advantage Travel & Tours. We were the first American tourists to tour Iraq after the war.

What were your most challenging countries to visit and why?

The most challenging country for me to visit was Libya. During my USAF career I attempted to visit it on several occasions and was not able to arrange it. When I started to cruise, I twice obtained a visa for a scheduled port call only to have Gaddafi at the last minute deny Americans from going ashore. Finally, in 2013, Klaus Billep at Universal Travel Systems told me he thought he could arrange through his agent in Tripoli my visa. The visa was not granted before I left the U.S. to visit other countries in Africa. Klaus was then informed by his agent in Libya that tourist visas were not being granted but the agent could get me a work visa. I had to divert from my schedule to visit the African countries and fly to Madrid to wait for the visa to be sent from the U.S. I spent a weekend visiting San Sebastian before the visa arrived enabling me to visit Libya, tour the coastal UNESCO World Heritage Sites, and then continue back on my schedule of visiting an African country that I had not visited on previous trips.

Another challenging country for me to visit was Eritrea. I was scheduled to visit the country in 2012 with a group of eight. We all submitted our visa applications at the same time, but two of us from California were either not approved or were denied. The Eritrea Embassy just sat on our request until we had to get our passports back to start our trip. One explanation, but not confirmed, was the Eritrea government was mad at the United States for forcing them to close their consulate in Oakland, CA because a number people joining terrorist groups in Asia had traveled from the U.S. on Eritrea visas.

What's the strangest thing you've seen/experienced while traveling?

I was very surprised by The Basilica of Our Lady of Peace of Yamoussoukro, Côte d'Ivoire. The size and the beauty of the basilica totally surprised me.

Which travel experiences stand out the most and why?

1) Visiting and climbing to the top of Angkor Wat. For eighteen months in Vietnam, a large aerial picture of Angkor Wat hung in my office and on my monthly flights (in a C-47) from Saigon to Bangkok we used to fly low over the site. It took me 35 years to finally visit it.

2) Visiting the biblical sites of Israel and floating in the Dead Sea, because of their biblical significance.

3) Visiting Petra, Jordan, because of the beautiful buildings and the fact it was undiscovered by the western world for centuries.

4) The Grand Canyon was an unbelievable experience to see for a 12-year-old boy from Connecticut. Later, when I was stationed in Southern California, our air refueling missions used to fly east and west over the canyon. We could look down on its beauty from the 'Boom Operations' window. On clear days, it was always an amazing sight.

Each trip and each destination on my travels have had standout experiences. The world is a beautiful and exciting place. I never get tired of the experiences.

What are the most overrated and underrated countries you've been to in your travels and why?

Every country I have visited has had some interesting aspect. I don't rate them because they all have their good and bad and I don't pay much attention to other people or travel publication's ratings. Therefore I can't judge a country as overrated or underrated.

What are the best and worst meals you have ever had traveling and where were they?

One of my best was at the Tivoli Restaurant in Copenhagen in 1960 and recently in Fernando de Noronha. I can't recall a "worst" meal.

What country made you feel most out of your comfort zone and why?

I have never felt out of my comfort zone. My visit to Bangui, Central African Republic was the closest because I wasn't met by a guide at the airport and the taxi I took to the hotel did not take a direct route and wanted to overcharge me. Fortunately the staff at the hotel and a VIP guest convinced the taxi driver to accept a fair rate.

Do you speak any foreign languages? If so, which has been the most useful for you besides English?

I don't speak any foreign languages. I suffer from dyslexia and have trouble reading, spelling, and pronouncing English words. I think I hold a record for flunking college English nine times at five different colleges and universities before I discovered that I had dyslexia and was able to compensate for it.

Looking back from when you started traveling to where you are now, in what ways, if any, has travel changed you?

Since I have traveled since I was six years old, I can't say it has "changed" me. It has been "me" all my life.

What was the longest continuous trip you have ever taken, when was it where did you travel?

My first long trip was across Canada, Mexico, and the United States, which took two months in 1947. I also took a trip on the Holland America *Prinsendam* Explorer Cruise over October/November 2006, which took 46 days while visiting 15 countries en route from Athens, Greece to Cape Town, South Africa, and a post-cruise safari to Botswana, Victoria Falls, and Swaziland.

What is your favorite "off-the-beaten-path" destination and why?

Socotra Island off of Yemen, because it had few tourists (I met only two ladies from USAID), beautiful beaches, caves, and beautiful umbrella trees (which are not really trees).

What are the best and worst places you have spent a night?

The best was at the Four Seasons in Cairo, Egypt.

The worst was in Erbil, Iraq because a convention required we change hotels. Second worst was in Laga, East Timor — again a last minute foul-up in our reservation.

In your opinion, what country or place in the world feels the most authentic and untouched by tourism?

Kiribati is a country that is almost untouched since World War II. It certainly has not set itself up for tourism. Nauru is another island nation that has not set itself up for tourism and is what it is. The same can be said for Somalia, including Somaliland.

In your opinion, where is the most beautiful place on Earth?

Beauty is in the eye of the beholder. Each destination has some beauty in it. The weather plays a big part in determining if there is beauty in visiting a specific place. I am so amazed by Earth and its variety I can't say that one place in the globe is the most beautiful.

What do you enjoy most when traveling (cities, nature, people, cultural spots, etc.) and why?

I primarily enjoy the look, feel, and people of the countries and places I visit. If I can understand how the people live and conduct their day to day life, I feel it has been an enjoyable visit.

What travel accomplishments are you most proud of?

My tours of: Iraq in 2009, North Korea in 2012, South Sudan in 2012, Libya in 2013, and Yemen in 2013.

The tour I took in 2009 with Advantage Travel & Tours to Iraq is the travel accomplishment I am most proud of because very few tourists have visited the central areas of Iraq since the second Gulf War. If they travel to Iraq they usually fly into the relatively safe city of Erbil and tour the Kurdish areas. Our tour group flew into Baghdad and, after spending eight hours in the airport getting visas applied to our passports, spent several days in Baghdad touring the city and surrounding areas. We then rode by bus north to Erbil, stopping at archaeological sites along the way. After touring the archaeological sites in the Kurdish region and Mosul areas, we returned to Baghdad and toured Babylon and other archaeological sites. We were proud of taking the tour because American forces stationed in Iraq told us they never got to see all the sites we toured during our time in the country.

My unaccompanied tour of Libya in 2013 on a "work" visa was another proud travel accomplishment. I had a great local guide but I was on my own when not with him on daily tours.

Also, I am proud of having the guts in 2013 to tour Yemen unaccompanied except by local guides and to fly into Mogadishu without a local guide.

If you had just one personal travel story to share with someone, what would it be?

I vary my stories by determining what I think people are most interested in. I have several stories I often share with people.

1) Crossing the border by foot at a border crossing in the mountains between Turkmenistan and Iran. The border staff

didn't know how to process Americans. They contacted their headquarters and were told to fingerprint us because the U.S. fingerprints Iranians when they visit the U.S. The staff had no experience or equipment to fingerprint us so they used their stamp ink and rolled each finger to the right and then back resulting in ten smudges that were unreadable.

2) Spending the night in a bus stuck in the mud in North Korea. As the driver and the guides tried to dig the bus out we were able to walk around the farmland on our own. A team of twelve mine workers with lighted helmets finally dug us out after midnight.

3) As an ardent Boston Red Sox baseball fan, watching them win the pennant and World Series on a cruise ship TV with other Red Sox fans in 2004. (I also watched them on a hotel computer when they won in 2007.)

4) Becoming stuck on a bed of sea shells in Guinea-Bissau and being rescued by eighteen naked natives that rowed out to our boat and lifted it up and put it back in the channel.

5) Being marooned at King Edward Point, Grytviken, South Georgia Island for eight days when our ship's engine failed.

6) Touring Iraq in 2009 with a private tour of Babylon conducted by the curator of the site.

7) Touring Libya on a work visa in 2013 where I was able to have private one-on-one tours of the archaeological sites of Sabratha and Leptis Magna and then hearing two gun battles in Tripoli the night before I left the city.

As you can tell, I have many stories, which are one of the big joys of world travel. Every trip is an adventure with stories fit to please the listener.

Besides your home country, where do you find yourself returning to over and over and why?

Hong Kong — because my wife loves to shop and we spend her birthday there every five years since 1972.

What is the ideal amount of time you prefer to travel on each trip before you are ready for home and a break?

Two to six weeks. It is somewhat determined by the mode of travel. Cruises can be the longest if they frequently stop at interesting ports. I am not a fan of long periods of days at sea.

If you had an unlimited budget and space and time was no object, what would your perfect travel day look like? (for example: start your morning in Bora Bora; afternoon on a safari in Kenya; night in Australia, etc.)

It would be to travel in First Class on a B-787 or A-380 to a site I hadn't visited before, preferably a UNESCO World Heritage Site. Then have a local lunch with a local guide that I could engage in conversation about the country. In the afternoon, I would then like to swim and snorkel in warm water with beautiful coral and colorful fish to observe. In the evening I would have a great local dinner in a five-star hotel with excellent Internet so I could check email and record my journal, followed by a walk around the neighborhood and then a nice bed to rest in before a new adventure the next day.

For those looking to travel to every country, what is the best piece of advice you could offer them?

Subscribe to the International Travel News, and use travel agencies that have experience in the countries you want to visit and can supply experienced escorts that hookup with experienced local guides.

For someone that has been almost everywhere, what still gets you excited about packing your bags again?

The adventure and new experiences I am sure to have on my next trip.

Do you ever feel you have missed out on certain aspects of life being away from home so much?

Since I have traveled all my life either for work or pleasure, I get antsy if I am home very long. Remember, I traveled annually while growing up and commuted halfway across the country while attending college in Texas to my home in Connecticut. I joined the USAF where I was on a flight crew. Worked as an International Consultant for twenty years flying as much as 52 times a year (I have flown 3,000 flights since I retired from the USAF and worked in over thirty countries), so it has been my life.

Looking ahead, what travel plans and goals are you still pursuing, and what is on your "Bucket List"?

I would like to complete visiting all the destinations on the TCC list; take the Trans-Siberian railway across Russia; and visit all of Italy and Switzerland by auto or bus.

Ted Cookson, U.S.A.

(Ted Cookson in Australia)

Where did you grow up and what was your early life like?

I grew up in the small town of Coos Bay on the southern Oregon coast. Several activities from my childhood influenced my desire to travel. My parents put a framed *National Geographic* map of the world on my bedroom wall early on, and they also gave me a Motorola shortwave receiver. I recall keeping a log of all the stations and countries to which I had listened on shortwave. At age 12, I began collecting stamps, eventually specializing in those of the Pitcairn Islands and Norfolk Island. My early habit of reading *Time* magazine also spurred an interest in world affairs at the expense of U. S. affairs.

When did you go from casually traveling to making this a full-time goal, and what motivated you to travel to every country?

I began traveling frequently in early 1998. In one five-year period, I made it to 97 new Travelers' Century Club (TCC) destinations.

Do you remember the point where you said to yourself, "I can really accomplish this"?

I thought I could probably accomplish my goal of visiting all of the non-Antarctic destinations on the TCC list when I began to travel regularly in early 1998.

What have you done over your life to gain the freedom and finances to pursue as much travel as you have?

I was able to bank some savings while working as a commercial banker in Riyadh, Saudi Arabia, between 1981 and 1985. After that, I morphed into an entrepreneur, dabbling in travel while I was in Cairo and eventually opening a travel agency there in 1988. I did that for 25 years before leaving amid the turmoil of 2013. Being in the travel field for so long helped me in planning, and Cairo turned out to be a good base from which to travel.

Was there ever a time you felt like abandoning this goal?

No, there was never a time when I felt like abandoning my travel goal.

What have been your worst travel experiences (such as detainment, bribes, car accidents, sicknesses, etc.) and why?

My worst travel experience was suffering from food poisoning some fifteen years ago in Asuncion, Paraguay, the night before I was to fly Asuncion - Buenos Aires - Miami. Unfortunately, I was still sick when I flew and had to make frequent trips to the little room at the back of both planes.

What do you consider one of the most adventurous trips you have taken?

In June 1987, a girlfriend and I were among the first Westerners to cross over the 16,002-foot Khunjerab Pass from Pakistan's Hunza region to China's Xinjiang region via public bus. This was only the second summer that this mountain pass had been open to travelers who were not citizens of either Pakistan or China. We accomplished the bus journey from Gilgit to fabled Kashgar in five days, passing grazing yaks as we approached the stone markers at the summit. While the Chinese had already paved the highway in Pakistan right up to the border, at that time, they were only beginning to improve the gravel road from the border to Kashgar. After our Gilgit to Kashgar bus trip, we flew to Urumchi and then rode the train from there to Chengdu before flying up to Lhasa. We also traveled overland across Tibet and down to Kathmandu. During an amazing seven-week adventure we covered northern Pakistan, Xinjiang, Tibet, Nepal, and northern India.

What were your most challenging countries to visit and why?

Organizing my visit to Tokelau probably involved the biggest logistical challenge of any of the Travelers' Century Club destinations. Since access is normally only via public ferry, one must coordinate flights into and out of Apia, Samoa, and then hope for no surprises at sea. However, as the vessel which was normally employed as a ferry was out of commission while undergoing repairs in New Zealand during my visit, I wound up sleeping in a container from Apia to Tokelau aboard the substitute cargo ship. Luckily, the ship didn't arrive back in Apia too late for me to make my onward air connection. A woman in Apia was kind enough to loan me a sheet sack in which to sleep.

What's the strangest thing you've seen/experienced while traveling?

I could respond that the eerie sight of Plymouth, the former capital of Montserrat now covered by lava, appeared very strange to me after arriving on the island from Antigua by helicopter. I could also respond that the mysterious pinnacle called Ball's Pyramid off Australia's Lord Howe Island appeared strange as I glanced across at it through the window of an aging prop plane just prior to landing on the Lord Howe air strip. But perhaps it'd be most appropriate for me to respond that spying the very substantial remnants of the *Bounty* at the Fiji Museum in Suva seemed very strange as I hadn't expected to see that there. In fact, this incident and a couple of others — of happening across Pitcairn Island- and *Bounty*-related artifacts in out-of-the-way locations all over the world — inspired me to compile Pitcairn Island and the Bounty Saga - Institutions and Monuments: A Worldwide List of Related Archives, Churches, Gardens, Houses, Libraries, Monuments, Museums and Ships. I published this title as my second Amazon.com e-book in 2012. (As an aside, the title of my first monograph, also published as an Amazon.com e-book, is A Diary of the Final Cruise of the RMS St. Helena to Tristan da Cunha, January 15-28, 2004.)

What stand out as your most memorable travel experiences and why?

In 1973 I wrote a 50-page senior thesis in college on the medieval history of Darfur, so some of my most memorable travel experiences involve the Sudan. In 1974 I visited Darfur, and I also sailed on a public ferry for eight days from Juba north through the Sudd to the port of Kosti, south of Khartoum.

What is the most overrated and underrated country you've been to in your travels and why?

Perhaps it was just a matter of my not being prepared, but I felt that the Galapagos was underrated. After traveling through West Africa, I thought that many of the countries there were overrated. Senegal and The Gambia are two countries which come to mind.

What is the best and worst meals you have ever had traveling and where were they?

As a vegetarian who enjoys making a meal out of a loaf of bread, perhaps the worst meal I ever had was a loaf of bread full of baked weevils that I consumed for lunch in Bissau in

1986. At the same time, probably the best meals I ever had were the fresh baguettes on which I lunched in a host of West African countries in 1978.

What country made you feel most out of your comfort zone and why?

I was out of my comfort zone while traveling solo in Rhodesia (now Zimbabwe) during the hostilities there in 1978. A number of vehicles were attacked along highways in the countryside. Luckily mine wasn't one of them.

Do you speak any foreign languages? If so, which has been the most useful for you besides English?

I studied Arabic in university for five years. That language has of course been useful in North Africa and the Middle East. But the "travel French" I acquired during my solo travel in West Africa in 1978 has also been extremely helpful.

Looking back from when you started traveling to where you are now, in what ways, if any, has travel changed you?

I have learned that, while all of mankind has the same basic needs, people are a product of their environment. I also learned that kindness will usually be repaid with kindness, and I have been the recipient of some amazing hospitality during my many travels.

What was the longest continuous trip you have ever taken, when was it, where did you travel?

My longest continuous trip was a 14-week marathon during the summer of 1978 by air (and, in South Africa and Zimbabwe-Rhodesia, mainly by train) from Dakar to Cape Town to Cairo. Since then, I have taken 85 cruises (as of late 2014), including four world cruises. So far, the longest of these was 94 days. However, there is a 108-day world cruise in my future in early 2015.

What is your favorite "off-the-beaten-path" destination and why?

Norfolk Island is my favorite "off-the-beaten-path" destination. Since reading Nordhoff and Hall's *Bounty* trilogy as a young teenager, I have been fascinated by Pitcairn Island and the *Bounty* saga. I like Norfolk Island for its enduring beauty and for its historical and cultural connections with Pitcairn.

What is the best and worst place you have spent a night?

The best place I have ever spent the night was Begawan Giri Villas near Ubud in Bali. The likes of Barbra Streisand and Sting have enjoyed those luxurious digs.

On the other hand, the worst place I ever spent the night was a small, $2-a-night hole in the wall in a small burg near Doguba-yazit in eastern Turkey, not far from the border with Iran.

In your opinion, what country or place in the world feels the most authentic and untouched by tourism?

In 1984 Bhutan felt rather authentic and was still untouched by tourism. In 2014 Angola felt the same way to me. Almost no one spoke English in Luanda, and no postcards were available for sale in Luanda or in Cabinda. Until recently tourist visas for Angola were very difficult to obtain as well.

In your opinion, where is the most beautiful place on Earth?

I suppose that I consider Norfolk Island to be the most beautiful location on the planet. I love the view of Phillip Island from Mt. Pitt, and I also like picturesque Emily Bay. Some of the cliff-side views, from Anson Bay and Captain Cook Monument, remind me of similar Pacific Ocean coastal views near my hometown of Coos Bay, Oregon.

What do you enjoy most when traveling (cities, nature, people, cultural spots, etc.) and why?

I enjoy visiting cities with their many museums. But I also like to travel to cultural and natural monuments.

What travel accomplishments are you most proud of?

I adopted the Travelers' Century Club list in 1985 and then began to try to finish the list in 1998. A five-year concentrated effort to reach nearly 100 countries was followed by eight more years of traveling to pick up newly-added countries and other odds and ends around the world. So at this point I am proud of having visited all 324 destinations except the French, Norwegian, Australian, and New Zealand Antarctic territories. After a ten-year effort, I am equally proud of having visited 54 of the 59 U. S. national parks and 104 of 109 U. S. national monuments. I have visited all of the U. S. national parks and national monuments in the Lower 48 states (as of late 2014). The ten parks and monuments I have yet to see are in St. Croix, Alaska, and American Samoa.

If you had just one personal travel story to share with someone, what would it be?

In 1997, divorced for over a decade but still friends with my first wife, I invited her to room with me on a travel agents' trip to Iran. However, because her British Airways aircraft had to set down in Larnaca, Cyprus for a lengthy period to await spare parts, she arrived in Tehran two days late, after our tour had already departed from Tehran. As a consequence of her late arrival, I happened to sit in the back of the tour bus near Barbara, the woman with whom I have been captivated for the past seventeen years!

Besides your home country, where do you find yourself returning to over and over, and why?

Through the years, I have found myself returning to Egypt over and over again. I spent a junior year abroad at The American University in Cairo in 1971-72 and then spent a graduate year studying Arabic there at the Center for Arabic Study Abroad in 1973-74. After many annual visits, I moved back in 1985 and remained until 2013. In all, I have lived in Egypt for 30 years. Although I may never live in Egypt again, I look forward to visiting it many more times. I have found truth in the adage, "He who drinks from the Nile is bound to return."

What is the ideal amount of time you prefer to travel on each trip before you are ready for home and a break?

While I still take journeys of many different lengths, I prefer to travel for a minimum of three weeks up to three months or so.

If you had an unlimited budget and space and time was no object, what would your perfect travel day look like? (for example: start your morning in Bora Bora; afternoon on a safari in Kenya; night in Australia, etc.)

If budget, time and space were not an issue, then I would like to spend the morning at Camp Sherman on the Metolius River west of Bend in central Oregon, the afternoon on Pitcairn Island, and the evening enjoying a dinner and show in London.

For those looking to travel to every country, what is the best piece of advice you could offer them?

My advice to those looking to visit every country is to conserve your resources and organize your travel geographically to the extent possible.

For someone who has been almost everywhere, what still gets you excited about packing your bags again?

Like many travelers, I enjoy researching and planning the itineraries of trips almost as much as taking the journey itself. The packing of my bags usually brings on a rush of anticipation.

Do you ever feel you have missed out on certain aspects of life being away from home so much?

No, I don't feel that in being away so much I have missed out on certain aspects of life back home. On the contrary, I feel like wherever Barbara and I are at the moment is home.

Looking ahead, what travel plans and goals are you still pursuing, and what is on your "Bucket List"?

I am still pursuing the remaining U. S. national parks and national monuments outside the Lower 48 states — that is, those located in St. Croix, Alaska and American Samoa. I am also giving thought to trying to visit the largest cities in the U. S. and/or the world.

Veikko Huhtala, Finland

(Veikko Huhtala with his wife, Oili)

Where did you grow up and what was your early life like?

I was born in Urjala, a small village 50km from Tampere, Finland. I joined the UN Peace Keeping Forces at age 23, where I served for more than five years.

When did you go from casually traveling to making this a full-time goal, and what motivated you to travel to every country?

I first traveled to European countries and then Africa after making money with the UN. When I had 100 countries visited I thought, "Why not try to visit all the remaining countries as well?" Now I am almost done.

Do you remember the point where you said to yourself, "I can really accomplish this"?

When I traveled to N'Djamena, Chad. In my opinion, Chad is one of the most terrible countries in the world. So when I visited what I consider the worst one, I realized I can easily travel to all remaining countries as well.

What have you done over your life to gain the freedom and finances to pursue as much travel as you have?

Working for seven years abroad and making money through that for traveling. Also, I'm always traveling in the cheapest way possible and I use the cheapest hotels also. By doing that I can save a lot of money for other trips.

Was there ever a time you felt like abandoning this goal?

No. Most countries leave good memories for me when I visit, but there are many countries where I do not want to be ever again, such as Cuba, Nicaragua, Haiti, Bangladesh, and many African countries. But when I visited these "bad" countries, I'm happy that I did it.

What have been your worst travel experiences (such as detainment, bribes, car accidents, sicknesses, etc.) and why?

In Equatorial Guinea my wife broke her ankle and we had to stay three days in the country before there was a flight back to Europe. Those three days were the most horrific days in my traveling life. But everything eventually went well and my wife's ankle is good again and we can continue on traveling.

What do you consider one of the most adventurous trips you have taken?

The two voyages I made to the Pitcairn Islands in 2009 and 2010. Sailing by small ship in the very stormy Pacific was not very comfortable, but these islands — Oeno, Pitcairn, Henderson and Ducie — were something miraculous. Before those trips, I was always thinking that I'd never have the possibly go to Pitcairn. Now I have been there twice!

What were your most challenging countries to visit and why?

Somalia. Everybody knows what kind of town Mogadishu is. Even the plane flying in from Djibouti was terrible — a very old Russian one with Russian pilots. However, I was very happy when I got the Mogadishu stamp in my passport.

What's the strangest thing you've seen/experienced while traveling?

The nice buildings in Turkmenistan. When I went to Ashgabat, I was thinking that there would be nothing. It was a very big surprise when I saw they had many nice buildings all over.

Which travel experiences stand out the most and why?

Traveling to Easter Island. I had read stories about these stone heads and when I saw them it was the most amazing thing in my life. Also the Seychelles in 1984, after working for half a year in the Nubian Desert in the Sudan. I planned to spend my first holiday over there and it was like paradise to me. I still consider it the best independent country in the world.

What are the most overrated and underrated countries you've been to in your travels and why?

I did not like Cuba at all, or Mongolia in 1986. I know many people who think of Cuba as the best country in the world. I do not understand why. Ulaanbaatar in Mongolia is now a very big and nice city, but when I was there the first time 25 years ago there was absolutely nothing.

What are the best and worst meals you have ever had traveling, and where were they?

Best: Shark beef in the Solomon Islands in the early 1980's.

Worst: Rice with chicken in Nauru in 2000 — the chicken was raw and bloody.

Normally I always want to eat local food. European food I can eat at home.

What country made you feel most out of your comfort zone and why?

One country I did not like at all was Somalia, of course. Mogadishu was the most terrible place I have been, but I did not stay there overnight. The flight from Djibouti was most terrible I've been on, too. But it was one more travel experience in my life and I am still alive.

Do you speak any foreign languages? If so, which has been the most useful for you besides English?

Besides Finnish, only English. I never studied English at the school, but I manage with the language when traveling. And normally I need only two words: taxi and hotel. People understand these words in every country.

Looking back from when you started traveling to where you are now, in what ways, if any, has travel changed you?

I'm very happy now that I have visited almost everywhere. Now I can spend more time at home. I'm not traveling as much anymore, but I still hold it very close to my heart.

What was the longest continuous trip you have ever taken? When was it, where did you travel?

Three and half months. Falklands, Ascension, Saint Helena, South Africa, and then all the other neighboring countries in southern Africa.

What is your favorite "off-the-beaten-path" destination and why?

Henderson and Ducie Islands. Both islands were far from everything and the landings were not easy. In Ducie, I nearly died when a big wave hit our rubber boat far from the coral reef. I still have coral pieces stuck in my legs.

What are the best and worst places you have spent a night?

The Circus Circus Hotel in Las Vegas was the best. The worst was in Tahiti at a guesthouse near the Fa'a'☐ International Airport. Millions of mosquitoes and these mosquitoes were also very poisonous and they gave me very big lumps everywhere on my skin.

In your opinion, what country or place in the world feels the most authentic and untouched by tourism?

Comoros Islands — or at least it was in 1987. I don't know what the Comoros are like today, but when I flew in from Johannesburg to Moroni it felt like another planet.

In your opinion, where is the most beautiful place on Earth?

I think the most beautiful place on Earth is near Mt. Cook in New Zealand. I stayed there Christmas night with my wife, Oili. Just the two of us without any other people. There were flowers and snow on the mountain at the same time. I'll never forget this landscape. In my opinion, New Zealand is the most beautiful country in the world.

What do you enjoy most when traveling (cities, nature, people, cultural spots, etc.) and why?

Nature. I do not like buildings, expect Egyptian pyramids. For example, in the USA, I have visited the Everglades, Yosemite, Sequoia, Yellowstone, Niagara, etc. Nature parks are my hobby, not buildings.

What travel accomplishments are you most proud of?

I'm very proud that I am one of the most traveled people in Finland.

If you had just one personal travel story to share with someone, what would it be?

My UN Service in Egypt 1973-1974. I was guarding Moshe Dayan when he was negotiating with Finnish General Ensio Siilasvuo. The UN life was a nice experience.

Besides your home country, where do you find yourself returning to over and over, and why?

Today it is to Tallinn and Stockholm. Cruises are virtually free for Club members. Usually I make 10 voyages to Tallinn and five voyages to Stockholm every year.

What is the ideal amount of time you prefer to travel on each trip before you are ready for home and a break?

If I'm going to the Pacific, it lasts from three to five weeks. If I am only going around Europe, I will stay only one week maximum.

If you had an unlimited budget and space and time was no object, what would your perfect travel day look like? (for example: start your morning in Bora Bora; afternoon on a safari in Kenya; night in Australia, etc.)

I'd like to one day go to the South Pole by plane. I haven't been to Antarctica yet, because I do not want to visit only one place there. In that area (flying to the South Pole), I can get to much more regions in the same time. Now I just have to save money for the trip.

For those looking to travel to every country, what is the best piece of advice you could offer them?

Do not go to only one country at a time per trip, otherwise you will die before they are all completed. It is very easy to travel to the neighboring countries for every trip you take. In this way, traveling becomes much cheaper as well.

For someone that has been almost everywhere, what still gets you excited about packing your bags again?

New locations are always fascinating. But it all depends on money; without it, travel is very difficult (obviously).

Do you ever feel you have missed out on certain aspects of life being away from home so much?

Only once. My brother died and I missed his funeral while I was traveling in Alaska. I was ashamed of this, but I did not want to lose my money because all my flights were already paid for.

Looking ahead, what travel plans and goals are you still pursuing, and what is on your "Bucket List"?

I still want to visit the "Ebola countries" — Guinea, Sierra Leone and Liberia. My next trip is to Eritrea and perhaps to South Sudan also. And eventually: SOUTH POLE! After that I will celebrate with a beer!

Bill Altaffer, U.S.A.

(Bill Altaffer in Star City, Russia, July 2014)

Where did you grow up and what was your early life like?

In L.A. in the 50's at a time of hot rods and surfing. I graduated from the University of Southern California (USC) with a B.A. and M.S. in History.

My travels would never have happened if my father from an Iowa farm hadn't become a dentist and moved to L.A. He promised my mother he would show her the world. She was from Kansas and I think she just went along with the idea. So, with the stress of being a dentist, my father would take roughly six weeks off from his practice a year to relax. Starting in 1949 with a trip to Alaska, we traveled every year (usually by ship) to various parts of the world. In the early sixties, in order to see Africa, we started to fly places.

For years, I was dragged along with a feeling I was missing ordinary Little League experiences. But when I started to combine my enthusiasm for surfing into our trips, the travel bug kicked in and I couldn't get enough. I went surfing in Australia, Peru, Tahiti, Japan, South Africa, etc. Then I was hired as a tour manager for Travelworld and Hemphill Harris and my travels began to increase and expand. Right place, right time — Luck.

When did you go from casually traveling to making this a full-time goal, and what motivated you to travel to every country?

I was in Mammoth Lakes (California) teaching World History in high school and took a school break to go past 100 countries to become a member of the Travelers' Century Club (TCC). I finally became a member in 1972.

Do you remember the point where you said I can really accomplish this?

I was in my thirties, and it became apparent it was doable. I knew it was a lifestyle of tour till you drop.

In 1972, when I first started working in the travel world, I was at the office in Hollywood and I saw this guy in a neck brace. I found out he was a tour manager who had just gotten back from Afghanistan. His plane had flipped over with his group aboard due to a wind gust and it killed half the people in it, but he survived, and here he was in the office. I thought, "Hmm, what am I getting myself into?" Anyways, I started out a couple days later going to Egypt. At that time the Russian's had just left after they had rebuilt the Aswan Dam. So we left from Cairo to Abu Simbel, which we never made, but we stopped in Aswan and they told us at lunch that the plane was having trouble, so the group got a little uptight thinking, "What's wrong with the plane?" At the end of the day they got the plane running and we went out to the airport at Aswan to go back to Cairo. My people asked, "Is this safe?" and I said, "Well, yeah, the FAA checks all the airports and airplanes in the world and all that stuff." So we get on the plane and start down the runway and just before liftoff the EgyptAir plane hits the brakes and skids to a stop and now I'm thinking, "Wait a minute, maybe there is another way back to Cairo?" The train would take two-three days, and I even thought maybe a camel at that point. So we went back and started down the runway and the same thing happened again when they hit the brakes, so now I'm thinking, "My people are really getting upset." So the plane comes back and this happens again — three times in a row! Then this mechanic in an Arab robe with hand tools starts messing with the jet engine and the captain of the plane makes him come on board the plane, so I am thinking, "This is like *The Flight of the Phoenix*. If we crash out in the desert he gets to fix it again, or you're guaranteeing your work so you're riding with us." So we flew back to Cairo at a 45 degree angle and I was pressed against the bulkhead, and there was no explanation or service on the flight, but we survived.

I was at Starbucks recently having coffee and talking to a pilot and she said, "You were probably flying on one engine, which is why you took off and flew at an angle." Which is pretty damn dangerous.

What have you done over your life to gain the freedom and finances to pursue as much travel as you have?

At first I traveled to over 80 countries with my family and on my own surfing trips. Later I chose teaching (I got summers off to travel) and then leading work tours for companies like Travelworld and then Hemphill Harris (where I got that job after teaching the owner, Ron Harris, how to ski) that allowed the pursuit. I also worked with a company called Marine Expeditions where I put together trips like Antarctica to England and a multi-segment trip from Santiago, Chile to Port Moresby via a lot of the world's most obscure islands, like Juan Fernandez, Niue, Wallis Island, etc. After some tours I was leading ended, I would travel on my own to nearby countries to maximize my time and money. Now I travel with my own company, Expedition Photo Travel (no, you don't need a camera), and I am still a tour manager for companies like UTS (Universal Travel System) as well as putting together tours for a couple other companies which I guide to places in Eastern Europe, Central Asia, Siberia, and to North Korea.

I have a small, elite group that I plan exotic trips for and we feel that after visiting a place, something bad always happens and we don't want this to get out or they will stop us from traveling:

- Valley of the Geysers blows up after our visit to Kamchatka.

- Islamabad Marriott blows up after our lunch there.

- The flag ceremony outside of Lahore was blown up last week by terrorists.

- Our ship *Indian Ocean Explorer* was hijacked and burned after our Chagos expedition.

- Our Kabul hotel, the Intercontinental, was bombed.

- Hotels in Jakarta blew up.

- Towns along the Pamir Highway were attacked.

Was there ever a time you felt like abandoning this goal?

Never. Once you have the addiction, it's permanent, and I've given that to some of my students and children.

What have been your worst travel experiences (such as detainment, bribes, car accidents, sicknesses, etc.) and why?

Normally I see the above as an opportunity to personalize and color my trips and I see travel problems as a chance to laugh and increase my expertise.

One of my scariest moments was in 1962 when I was 18 and had just arrived in Sydney on a 42-day family cruise. I had my 9'10" Dewey Webber surfboard with me to ride some South Pacific waves. I knew I wanted to go first to Manly Beach. My ship, SS *Monterey* of the Matson Lines, was docked on the Bondi side of the harbor. So with my board I took the Manly ferry north across the inside of the bay. Halfway across the 30 minute ride, I looked out the window to the east and saw a giant wall of green water. The waves were so tall I couldn't see the sky! It hit us. Our 3/4 story ferry tipped ninety degrees to where I was standing on the bulkhead. The giant wave put out our engine and we were now drifting towards the Heads, or cliff wall. It took a long five minutes before the engines came back to life and we continued on to Manly Beach.

What do you consider one of the most adventurous trips you have taken?

One interesting story is about a trip I put together to Pamir Highway with Mir Corp and the tour manager I used — and have used for probably a dozen trips — was Paul Schwartz from Washington State.

We were at the Tajikistan border from Kyrgyzstan and we're headed up to the 18,000 foot Pamir Highway. We get to the border and there is the army there and Paul goes in to do the paperwork because we had to get all this permission to go into Tajikistan. All of a sudden I notice our van backing up and the gate coming down in front of it and there are eight or so of us milling around, and I go, "That doesn't look good." So then Paul comes back with a white face and he's just really embarrassed and he tells us they won't let us go 20 miles into Tajikistan because we don't have the right permits. Obviously it's a pay-off situation, so it comes down to we can pay them and they'll let us go but we'd have to take an officer and a soldier in one of those small, little Russian jeeps that are made for four people. There was no roof rack and there was a spare tire in the back so there was no place to put the luggage. So we end up putting eight or nine of us, plus all our luggage, plus the officer and the soldier into the little Russian jeep, and I just started laughing — it was the funniest thing! These are the things that I travel for. These are the things I'm going to repeat dozens of times over the next decades because it is so absurdly humorous. Nobody thought it was funny at the time, but it's funny later. I had just had my knee replaced and I figured it would come loose with 200-300 pound guys on top of me, and we're all getting pressed down and squeezed in like sardines with the luggage, and we're bouncing up the Pamir Highway until we reached the guys waiting for us at the other checkpoint. Totally hilarious. Dust, dirt, the jeep can only go about five miles per hour, there's potholes everywhere, it's bleak as hell — there's like one piece of foliage living, no trees, nothing. Just terrain.

I also used to travel to surf. Way back in the early 60's, when I was in Hawaii for two months surfing the South Shore of Wai-kiki in Oahu, I saw a travel agent advertising going to all the Hawaiian Islands in one day, and I barely had the money for this — it was like, $186. So I talk to my buddy, who I am still friends with today and he lives in Thailand and I used to visit him all the time and play tennis with him, and say, "Let's do this." So we left Oahu at 5 a.m. and we ended up going to Kau-ai, which was the first time I had been there, and we do the whole island tour there. Then we were on the Big Island, on Maui, and then on Molokai. It was like a 14-15 hour day, but it was cool.

What were your most challenging countries to visit and why?

I first went to Russia 1964. I was in the first tourist group to China 1979, and one of the first American tourists in North Korea. I was an early visitor to Tuva and Tibet when it opened to travelers. I visited Albania just after independence. Also in Iraq, Afghanistan and Kuwait after the first Gulf War; Cuba in the 80s; and Libya in the early 90s. Not too long ago I also vis-ited Dagestan and Chechnya. They were all difficult at various times.

What's the strangest thing you've seen/experienced while traveling?

Fifteen years ago, I was one of the first Americans to visit So-cotra, flying there on Yemenia Airways out of Sana'a. I had put a small group together for the trip. While on takeoff, the plane's left engine catches fire and we have to abort. For half an hour people disembark and then return. The pilot then says, "This is not a restaurant — you can't get on and off!" He then says he doesn't know what the problem is, but we are going to take off in five minutes. We never do and later the flight was canceled. We ended up getting there the next day.

On a flight out of Angola to São Tomé, I was on another plane that had a right engine catch fire. Herb Goebels (an accom-plished world traveler who has been to every country in the world himself) looks at me and says with his heavy German accent, "You know as much as we travel it's only a matter of time…"

Leading a "Circle Pacific" tour in the seventies, I was in New Guinea when the Australians were about to leave. There was a time when the Aussies were not that friendly to Americans. So, when an Aussie local guide in Mt. Hagen purposely sent my tour group's luggage to the wrong place, I ended up chartering a DC-3-type paratrooper plane to fly back to Port Moresby to continue our voyage. We were sitting in metal seats facing each other from the bulkhead as we flew unpressurized at tree-top level, seeing old ladies wrapped in blankets. It was a sight. Next day our plane blew up on takeoff and caught fire. Choices I had to make on the fly in order to get our luggage back.

I would like to thank the hundreds of people all over the world that helped me get on planes that were overbooked, and hotels that had no rooms left. The people I met had no idea I was trying to see as much of the world as possible, but just helped me out of their own kindness.

Which travel experiences stand out the most and why?

1) Surfing Three's surf break at Waikiki with overhead waves.

2) Skiing hoarfrost snow in Canada in the Selkirk Mountains from a snow cat.

3) My trip on the *Aranui* (which is what the license plate on my car says because I am so impressed with the ship and where it goes in the Marquesas). I was on this 16 day cruise to the Marquesas, and on Tuamotu they have this hike you can go on for ten or twelve miles. So I sign up for it and we're going to hike to the other side of the island where the ship is going to be in the evening. They had told us when we started that if you hear the ship's horn go three times, "We will see you next month." Which means you're on your own for a month on whatever island you're on. So we start the hike and it starts to rain like mad and I have my camera. I go under a tree to protect it and it get squared away and then I start back, and the girl, who was our guide from the ship, stopped counting properly and they had made an extreme right turn into the jungle. So I just kept proceeding down this path alone and I went on for about an

hour and hadn't seen anybody. Then I see what looks like a group of people up somewhere ahead so I pick up the pace, but it wasn't people, it was trash, where this little village had put it all, but it looked like people from a distance. So I kept going and I came to an abrupt cliff, like an overhang on the Na Pali Coast, where it dropped down 1000 or more feet to the ocean, and I realized I was lost. So I turn around and I start jogging back in the mud and I'm going as fast as I can for an hour and I finally look down on the village and I can see that the *Aranui* was still in the bay and there was a whaleboat (which the *Aranui* uses for boarding and offloading things instead of zodiacs) in the middle of the bay headed towards the *Aranui* and I start running down the path and one of the natives at the village by the pier sees me and starts yelling to the whaleboat to turn around. I later find out the only reason the ship was still there was in the whaleboat was this seamstress that takes measurements for clothes that she makes back in Tahiti. She comes in every so often to the Marquesas and takes the orders and measurements, etc. She was late getting all the measurements that the natives had wanted — but thank God they wanted enough pants and shirts or whatever they had made that day. So they finally plucked me up and I got back on the ship and I didn't do that again on the next island. Otherwise I'd still be there. So that was luck — otherwise I would have a different story to tell!

What are the most overrated and underrated countries you've been to in your travels and why?

None are overrated — they are what they are. The third world is underrated and the State Department's "Do Not Go" list — for the most part — is a "Go To" list for many of us.

What are the best and worst meals you have ever had traveling, and where were they?

Some of the best have been The Carnivore outside of Nairobi, which has just about every meat dish and variety of animal in Africa. You eat looking out on Nairobi National Park — it is not for vegetarians. Best lobster I ever had was on the rooftop of the Meridian Hotel in Luanda.

My worst meal was cutting into a steak in Kathmandu in the sixties and having a roach crawl out of it.

What country made you feel most out of your comfort zone and why?

I was in Djibouti, and I was there with a couple other TCC members. One was elderly and he wanted me to get him some stamps. We were staying at the Sheraton there and he stayed back at the hotel and I went down with this Catholic priest, Bob Ippolito, and he's a TCC member too. So anyway, it's noon and we're down in the town square in Djibouti, and this was about the start of my trip through Central Africa, so I had all my tickets, credit cards, and money and everything in my backpack. So we're in the square and Bob says he's going to go over to the bookstore and buy something. So he goes and this guy comes up to me selling postcards, so I pick up some for Bernie, my elderly friend who stayed back at the hotel. Then this guy who is selling the cards has his friend behind me start getting into my backpack, and this instant switch comes on me thinking, if I lose that stuff — Djibouti at the time had no relations with America — I'm fucked. There is no way I'll get out of here, there will be no way for me to pay my hotel bill, there will be no way I can eat, no way I can get on a plane. You know who's going to give me the money to get home? Maybe there is a Swiss Embassy, I don't know. So I swing around and I give him a two-knuckle strike right to this guy's chest and I fucking nail him, man. And the other guy with the postcards was right there and I knock them both down. There was this instant I reacted without thinking — which I learned from my basic karate training — and it really paid off seeing the big shock on their faces... I didn't hate the guys, but the inconvenience they would have made for me would have been miserable.

I was also in Zanzibar during a malaria epidemic and passed through Asia twice during the SARS outbreak.

Do you speak any foreign languages? If so, which has been the most useful for you besides English?

Japanese and some Spanish. It's always a good idea to try to speak a native tongue, even if you butcher it.

Looking back from when you started traveling to where you are now, in what ways, if any, has travel changed you?

It started when I was seven years old with the SS *Princess Kathleen* sinking in Glacier Bay in Alaska. All the travel didn't change me — it made me. It is who I am. I also feel that I was lucky to make 90 percent of my travel in the last century when the world was more diverse.

What was the longest continuous trip you have ever taken? When was it, where did you travel?

I spent a year during a sabbatical with half in Asia and half in Africa. I used to think if you didn't travel for a year you weren't free.

What is your favorite "off-the-beaten-path" destination and why?

Places in Siberia. My favorite would be Pevek in Chukotka.

What are the best and worst places you have spent a night?

Worst was 30 hours on the floor in Libreville, Gabon waiting for a plane.

Best was the Presidential suite at Nusa Dua Hotel in Bali.

In your opinion, what country or place in the world feels the most authentic and untouched by tourism?

Tannu Tuva (Tuvan People's Republic, Russia).

In your opinion, where is the most beautiful place on Earth?

Yosemite National Park; Aldabra for the beautiful water; Mexico for the people; St Anton am Arlberg in Austria for the skiing; Ethiopia for the Danakil Depression; San Diego because it is the nation's finest city.

What do you enjoy most when traveling (cities, nature, people, cultural spots, etc.) and why?

All of the above as they relate to all past history and current affairs.

What travel accomplishments are you most proud of?

I've been to the home country of every person on Earth.

If you had just one personal travel story to share with someone what would it be?

About 20 years ago, I had visited 10 of the 13 countries in South America, but I needed the Guiana's. It took about six months to get the visas — it was very difficult at the time because nobody was ever in the offices in Washington, D.C. Eventually I flew down there out of Miami. Suriname is pretty interesting. Guyana was pretty good. French Guiana is pretty sterile. So when we were in French Guiana the only thing to do is see Devil's Island, and then there's nothing else except what keeps the country afloat, which is Kourou, where all the satellites are set off because its closer to the equator then, say, Cape Canaveral, and it's less expensive. So, after Devil's Island and all that stuff, we came back and I have a rental car and I am driving around and I see Kourou up on the jungle road. I pull in there and I'm going down the road with my buddy, Kevin, and I see the guard tower and the AK-47's, and I say, "Kevin, give me your Costco card, you got one right?" He gives me his and we go up to the guard and I pull mine out and I hand him the two Costco cards. And the guard goes, "Costco?" and I say, "Yes, we're both members of Costco." — which is the truth. And he looked at us and checks the faces and the photographs on them, both matched, and he hands it back to us and says, "Go on in." So we went in and gave ourselves a self-guided tour of the space facility — they weren't setting anything off that day — and went to the museum and the launch pad and saw everything.

So that's my idea. You gotta always have something in your hand — anything — because a lot of people can't read overseas. So if you lose your passport and you're going up to the border you damn well better have something to show them, even if it's your third-grade math test.

Besides your home country, where do you find yourself returning to over and over and why?

Russia, because of the people and the changes since the Cold War — it used to be my least favorite.

What is the ideal amount of time you prefer to travel on each trip before you are ready for home and a break?

Three weeks is my usually the shortest time out of my home country, but I like two month trips.

If you had an unlimited budget and space and time was no object, what would your perfect travel day look like? (for example: start your morning in Bora Bora; afternoon on a safari in Kenya; night in Australia, etc.)

I would like a private jet that I could point everywhere.

For those looking to travel to every country, what is the best piece of advice you could offer them?

Have kids later in life and then take them on trips right away.

For someone that has been almost everywhere, what still gets you excited about packing your bags again?

I think that by continuing to plan trips in advance, you can't die. So, just keep booking and planning ahead. Jet lag seems to get worse, though.

Someone asked me recently when I will stop exotic travel, I said, "*NEVER.*" I'll probably just fall over somewhere, but not at home.

Do you ever feel you have missed out on certain aspects of life being away from home so much?

When I was a kid, it was Little League I felt I missed, but that has since passed.

Looking ahead, what travel plans and goals are you still pursuing, and what is on your "Bucket List"?

In the spring, it's an expedition cruise to the Kermadec Islands. In early July, I will make my sixth trip to North Korea, and in late August I'll lead a tour around arctic and western Russia.

Nuno Lobito, Portugal

(Nuno Lobito)

Where did you grow up and what was your early life like?

I grew up in Lisbon, in a small section of the city, in 1965. The dictator, António de Oliveira Salazar, didn't accept people writing with their left hand. In school, when I was five or six years old, I remember everybody saying to me, "You need to change to the right hand." This made me a little bit confused because I am left-handed. This was one of my first real memories. I grew up with my grandfather and grandmother, because my parents worked in Lisbon and only came back in the evenings. It was an amazing experience because my grandfather played guitar, and I'd sit with him and learn a little bit about music.

When did you go from casually traveling to making this a full-time goal, and what motivated you to travel to every country?

I have a thirst to learn about the world. For me, traveling is the most interesting school in the world. When you're traveling, you feel freedom. You learn about many different cultures… This is my way of life. I never imagined in my wildest dreams I'd visit all the countries of the world when I was young. Back then, I never thought of the tribes living in the Amazon. From 2000 to 2005, I lived five years there. My son is from the Amazon. My ex-wife is from the Amazon.

I don't accept society and its rules, and I don't accept many concepts society embraces either. People love materialism; people love to show off and all this. I try to learn about different cultures, for a better understanding.

On the 11th of November, in 2011, I finished all the countries of the world. When this was finished, for me, it was a miracle. It was a magical day, because I had realized my dream. When you're traveling, you learn a lot about different cultures. 99% of my travels, it's alone, because I want to share it only with myself. I don't want to stay with other Portuguese or speak Portuguese, for example, while in China; it's not my concept of traveling.

Do you remember the point where you said to yourself, "I can really accomplish this"?

When I had visited 35 or 45 countries in Europe, I said to myself, "No, this is impossible!" This was about '86, when I finished with photography school. My first big trip after this was in India, Nepal, Bhutan, etc. When I arrived at 100 countries, it was in Madagascar in '96. I was in a marriage with an Italian woman, and I said, "Now with this marriage, I'll stop traveling." Eventually, I finished the first marriage and I started traveling again and continued on. I kept on traveling and eventually I had visited 186 countries, leaving the most difficult. This is probably 2008 or 2009. I had just come back from a trip to Yemen, Somalia, and Djibouti, and I thought, "Oh my God this is possible. I can do this."

On 11/11/11, I finished my last country, Iceland.

What have you done over your life to gain the freedom and finances to pursue as much travel as you have?

When I was young, I worked doing photography in an advertising studio. It was good for making money, and it was enough money for traveling. In the '90s, I was an editor for a VIP magazine. The name was *Looks*. It's a famous magazine and made me a lot of money. I was also editing photography, and that made me a lot of money, and I was also traveling a lot. Later, I was teaching in Restart, which is a journalism school, and I was also doing my own workshops. I also have written six books already. I'm the editor and author for the books. I produced the books with my own money, and then I sold them myself. I'm not selling in any bookshops. This means I'm making an investment. For example, I paid €5,000 to produce these books and sold 5,000 books for €45,000. Also, I have a television program that has been going since 2011, when I finished traveling to every country in the world. I now have about 500 television programs already taped, and I have two more contracts for three or four years to continue that and I make enough money from that too. I have an old car, a Land Rover. I have very good, expensive cameras like a Leica. I have sponsors like Air France and the KLM group which sometimes offer me free airline tickets when I put them in advertisements, and I make enough money for traveling with that, too.

I stopped traveling in 2014 for a little bit, because I had a second divorce. When you're traveling, not many women want to stay with you, because you're always traveling and I now need to take care of my boy, Angel, who lives with me. In 2015, I will start traveling again because I want visit more beautiful places.

In the end, the money for traveling comes from books, school, television, advertising, and also public and private workshops.

Was there ever a time you felt like abandoning this goal?

In 2011, my second ex-wife told me, "You need to stop the traveling because I want to stay with you." I was traveling nine months out of the year. We started a big discussion, and I explained, "Carol, I'm not going to stop the traveling. This is my life. This is my drug and it's impossible. If you like, I can do six months of staying here, and six months I'm out traveling." She tells me, "OK, then I want a divorce."

It's OK, I say. "Go. Get the divorce, but I'm not going to stop traveling."

For me, traveling, it's the best part of my life. For 30 years, I'm traveling around the world. It's an easy feat now that everybody has access to low cost everything. When I started I needed to change money even for Spain. I needed a visa for France — No European Union, no Internet, no low-cost airlines. But I never stopped traveling. For me, traveling is the best part of my life. I'm addicted. I live to learn, and traveling for me is the best school in life for learning. I'll never, ever stop. One day I will, when I die. But, in my opinion, I will continue many, many years because I am 49 years old — I'll be strong for a couple of years more.

What have been your worst travel experiences (such as detainment, bribes, car accidents, sicknesses, etc.) and why?

I'll start with the last one when I was in Gaza last May. I was shooting photos in a cemetery and turned around and looked straight at two guns in front of my face. I put up my hands and say, "Man, I don't speak Arab." But I said it in English, and the people did not understand me. Later, I met someone in the streets to help me and lead me away from this place.

Another was when I was in the war in '96 or '95 in Serbia in the ex-Yugoslavia. I remember being in the bunkers four, five days with no food except bread and water.

I'm a photographer and I'm a traveler. And when you mix those together, you have a double sensation. When you're traveling without a camera, it's OK, but when you use the camera in Somalia, in Iraq, and those kind of countries, it's so dangerous.

The biggest adventure in my life was five years in the Amazon. In the Amazon, I lived for two years in a pirogue. A pirogue is a small wooden boat. I traveled around inside small rivers. In the Amazon and other rivers — alone. Can you imagine two years, without proper food, without hotels or restaurants?

Of course, in Somalia, I needed two bodyguards. In Iraq, it was so easy for me, because I was living with a family. Afghanistan was easy. Chad, it was difficult. But the strongest sensation, for me, it's in Gaza, in Serbia, and the Amazon... I don't know where I keep my energy for the Amazon — I have had malaria twice.

What stand out as your most memorable travel experiences and why?

I started with my jeep, a Land Rover Discovery from '92, from Portugal and stopped later in Lagos, Nigeria. One month by road, through Liberia, Guinea, Senegal, etc... This was very powerful. Also in Gaza. When you're traveling alone there, inside of the bunkers and tunnels, it is so difficult. I was traveling alone. I got the permit for Gaza in Egypt, because I entered in Rafah. It was a very difficult trip.

The best ever in my life was the Amazon. Why? Because I had malaria in Madagascar, where I lived for three years; and when I was sick, I had a vision that said, "Leave Madagascar." I watched my vision when I had falciparum malaria — Indian people, tribes, a young boy crying, a beautiful woman from the Amazon, and a book. All these flashing lights, and I had 45 degree fever... I said to my family I need to go to the Amazon and my family said, "Amazon? But the Amazon has a lot of malaria." I have written the book *Amazon Hidden*. It's my second book. When you follow your vision, you can catch your dreams. This is exactly what I feel. It's my most memorable travel experience.

From all the places I have been, those that awed me most were Tibet, Laos, Vanuatu, India, and the Amazon. The Amazon rainforest was perhaps the most interesting paradise I have visited up to now.

What is the most overrated and underrated country you've been to in your travels and why?

I have two different countries where I feel most comfortable. When I think of a culture, it's Denmark or Sweden. In Scandinavia in general, the people are so friendly and open minded. Everything is easy. The people don't like war, don't like complication, don't like the trouble. Only problem is the weather. It's terrible.

Where I feel the most uncomfortable, it's in Israel, because the people can be rude. I don't want war (I'm Buddhist). They harass me, check my body and all my things and interrogate me and make me feel uncomfortable. It's terrible for me when I travel there.

What is the best and worst meals you have ever had traveling and where were they?

The best food of my life, it's in Japan. I'm completely crazy for sushi and sashimi, and all this Japanese and South Korean food. It's amazing.

The worst was in the Amazon. After three or four weeks of being there, I was with the tribes, the Papuan tribes. We ate this strange kind of meat. I ate all the organs, all the intestines, and all the stuff from the mouth of the animal. This killed me — it was so terrible. But if you don't accept and receive this food, it's the same as if you inviting me to your house and offered me a lobster and I say, "No, no, I don't eat lobster." You have to accept the rules of the tribe.

What country made you feel most out of your comfort zone and why?

Probably Somalia. Somalia is a country where white people are not welcome. I remember when I entered Somalia I needed to stay with two bodyguards. If you need to go to the bathroom, the bodyguards are outside of the door. This is not a movie. Somalia is a very dangerous country for a white man. I would like to go back and stay there a month. So, the most uncomfortable country and the most dangerous, it's Somalia, in my point of view. I think it's the most difficult.

Do you speak any foreign languages? If so, which has been the most useful for you besides English?

I speak Portuguese and Spanish, because it's my neighbor. I also speak Italian because it came through my first marriage. I speak French because of my time living in Madagascar. I also speak Malgache from Madagascar after living there for three years, and I understand some words in Thai and Arab. With Thai, it was from living in a temple eight months, a Buddhist temple, and I also know some words for traveling around Arab countries.

Looking back from when you started traveling to where you are now, in what ways, if any, has travel changed you?

The world has changed a lot since I start traveling in the '80s. It was so difficult to prepare a trip. For example, I traveled in India in 1988 and the information at the time was not a lot. Now we go on Google, and you find a lot of information, discussion forums, and everything.

I'm a photographer. When I started shooting photos in the beginning it was black and white in film. I had to go to the laboratory for printing. Today, it's different. Today, you can shoot the photo, pin it in the computer, and then in five minutes, you're editing it with your Photoshop.

Traveling between then and now, everything has changed. Now, in five minutes, you can buy a flight, or you can rent or book a place in a hostel. In my early days, we needed to go walk in the streets and find a hostel by going door by door. In the '80s, the technology we have today didn't exist. So what we have today is a concept of '90s and 2000's. Travel life, for me, has changed for the better.

What was the longest continuous trip you have ever taken, when was it, where did you travel?

My longest trip was in the Amazon. I lived for five years in the Amazon. I have had many different long trips. But normally, it was nine to ten months out of the year, but after finishing all of the world countries on 11-11-11, I'm more relaxed. Now I am traveling about three months a year.

What is your favorite "off-the-beaten-path" destination and why?

My best destination, it's always the next, where I don't know what will happen. Iran, it's a very, very cultural country. I know many people think the people from Iran are Arab, but they are Muslim, not Arab, and the culture is very rich. It's a Persian culture with a long history. Of course, I don't speak about politics, because with political people, it's always shit. Sorry, but I hate politics. From United States to Europe to China to North Korea, always it's the same. It's business and money, etc. But the first place I think of, it's Iran. The second one is Indonesia. Indonesia is lovely, because it has many different cultures, Buddhist people, Hindu people, Catholic people, Muslim people, good waves, cheap, good food, lovely weather, and I think it's one of the most interesting countries. Third is Portugal. Not because I'm Portuguese, and I know people are thinking, "Oh, because you are Portuguese?" No, no, no. Portugal doesn't have wars and Portugal has a lovely, good culture. Portugal has ten months of sun, it's two hours to London, six or seven hours to northern Brazil, one hour to Morocco, and six or so hours to New York. For me, this is incredible position in the world. Also, we have a very strong history, with our sailors and the discoverers. Portugal is the best — good wine, good food, good waves. It's amazing.

What is the best and worst place you have spent a night?

The best night of my life, it was in the Amazon, when I was sleeping up in a tree in the jungle. The tree is probably 25 meters high, and it's incredible, with amazing, big clouds. Also, I have had lovely nights in very, very good resorts and everything there was free to my employers and for myself in a five or six star hotels in Jamaica. That was just an amazing sensation.

The most difficult, and the hardest night of my life, is when I crossed Turkmenistan. It's a long trip, six days by jeep. The second day, when I arrived completely tired, I didn't have a room. In Turkmenistan, if you don't have local money and also have a paper receipt of the money you changed in a bank, you are not allowed to rent the hotel. I arrived and they asked me for the money. I had the money, but I changed it in the black market in Turkmenistan, because banks were too high. The people asked me, "Where is the receipt from the bank?" I didn't have one. "Well, you cannot sleep in this hotel." I ended up sleeping in a very, very bad house with more than 14 Greek men, which was so hot and stuffy, and I had just had more than 11 hours in my jeep, and next day in the morning, 11 more hours to go. We didn't eat anything. This night was so terrible. I will always remember that. I slept on the floor with no mattress, no nothing.

In your opinion, what country or place in the world feels the most authentic and untouched by tourism?

The Amazon. It's divided by six countries. It's not only Brazil. It's Brazil, Colombia, Ecuador, Bolivia, Venezuela, and also Peru. This makes the area amazing. Because in the Amazon, you can breathe nature, you breathe life, and you learn a lot about yourself. You need to be strong to survive or you're dead. The last one, probably, is Madagascar. It's the second biggest island world and they have the exact same amount of people as in Portugal, nine million. Imagine, it's a very long island with nine million people and you can, driving by car and jeep, enjoy every bit of it.

In your opinion, where is the most beautiful place on Earth?

The Gili Islands in Indonesia and the Amazon.

What do you enjoy most when traveling (cities, nature, people, cultural spots, etc.) and why?

When I'm traveling, I like people, a lot of people. It's the most powerful and interesting thing for me. The culture, the rituals, the tribes and all the energies they exude. I am not a person for big towns. I prefer always the small villages. I also like nature. But people, it's exactly what I live for — communication, talk, sharing experiences. This is amazing to me.

What travel accomplishments are you most proud of?

I married twice on the road, the first in Italy and the second one in the Amazon of Peru. When you follow your dreams, and if you trust yourself, we are what we believe. When I'm traveling, I never imagined marriage in the Amazon. The ceremony we had with the Indian tribes. This is what happens when people follow their dreams and always trust themselves. Not over thinking a lot with your brain. Not thinking a lot with your heart. Make a mix of half and half, always following your sensations. Thinking everything is possible. The most interesting history, for me, it's following my dreams. When I had this vision in Madagascar, and said, "I can follow this dream and go to the Amazon. Write a book, find marriage, and have my son." This was for me the most interesting thing. There is more to life than travel, but my life, it's all about traveling. It all stays together.

If you had just one personal travel story to share with someone, what would it be?

Two years in a pirogue in the Amazon. I traveled two years in the Amazon in the jungle, on the river. For me, it was an amazing experience. Sometimes, the songs of nature give you a lot of energy for you to continue with your soul searching on the road. For me, it was my best trip so far.

Besides your home country, where do you find yourself returning to over and over and why?

Indonesia is the place where I feel the most comfortable when I return again and again. I always discover myself and discover a new area of the country, and because it's cheap, the travel is easy. It's multicultural. It has Hindu people; it has Muslim people, Buddhist people, and Catholic people. Everybody living in synchrony and together… And I think it is one of the main places I go back to besides my own country. I feel comfortable there.

What is the ideal amount of time you prefer to travel on each trip before you are ready for home and a break?

I'm living alone with my son, so it's three months maximum now. But the perfect time is six months home, then six months traveling. This is perfect. From October to March, I think it's an amazing time to travel, because all over Europe it's a little bit cold, so you can head out to the sunny countries.

If you had an unlimited budget and space and time was no object, what would your perfect travel day look like? (for example: start your morning in Bora Bora; afternoon on a safari in Kenya; night in Australia, etc.)

I'd wake up in Bali, Indonesia or the Gili Islands. Have a very good breakfast and then two hours of surfing. Afterward, I'll fly to Papua New Guinea. Have an amazing day shooting photos with the Indian tribes. Then fly to L.A. and have a lovely night with amazing nightlife.

Another would be I'll have breakfast in Paris at Café de Flore. It has culture, coffee, and exhibitions. Then, fly to Morocco, have a lunch, and then on to Madagascar for the sunset and surfing and then end with the nightlife in L.A. I very much like the nightlife in L.A.

For those looking to travel to every country, what is the best piece of advice you could offer them?

When I started, I was on a budget. I was always couch surfing. Now you have a lot of different couch surfing sites such as Hospitality Club and Couchsurfing. You can work, for example, in Europe. You can work in September by picking oranges, October grapes for wine, November tulips in Holland, or in France at a pizzeria in Milan all the year. You can pick kiwis, oranges and bananas in Australia. You can be doing many things and there are many different sites for people to find seasonal work. You can work, for example, in Darwin with bananas for two months on a farm. With the money made you can spend three months traveling in Asia, because life in Cambodia, Indonesia, India, and other countries there is very, very cheap. You are close because AirAsia flies all over Asia and to Australia. But the way I travel now, it's different, because I'm a photographer and I always sell my reports and photos. But for young people, in my opinion, it is to find good work and work six months and then travel six months. I think this is the best.

For young people starting now at 20-25 years old, they need to be doing it step by step. Try doing all this with discipline, because if you don't have discipline in your life, you don't have anything. I think discipline is very important. You may create targets, such as traveling in a certain area where you'll visit ten countries, then visit seven in another, twenty in yet another, and making it year by year. I think in 20 years, you can visit all of the countries in the world. After you finish with the countries of the world, you go for smaller targets. For example, small islands, small provinces and republics — because the world is now divided into departments. Some spots, you cannot do now, so first do big countries. While doing these targets year by year, never, ever surrender. Sometimes life is hard. You may need to change your marriage or change your work. Always keep on the target very clearly, and never follow the other roads. If your road is this road, don't change the road. Please, young people, please listen to me. I lost two marriages. I lost many, many friends. I lost many opportunities for work, but I never, ever lost the road I was following.

Do you ever feel you have missed out on certain aspects of life being away from home so much?

I try to give all the best for my son, like the best college. I think I'm doing exactly what I promised for myself, but nothing is perfect. But that's why I always give my best compassion to people, like by helping any person who asks me about travel or photography. I'm happy with my decisions and I'm comfortable when I'm doing what I love.

Looking ahead, what travel plans and goals are you still pursuing, and what is on your "Bucket List"?

I would like to return to many, many places. For instance, I would like to make another visit to India, another visit to Papua New Guinea (because they have a lot of small islands). The Amazon I would like to go back to… I have ten spots, but the most powerful, to me, is the Pacific Ocean. There are a lot of small islands that are interesting.

In Asia, I would like to go back to Tibet again. I would like to go to the Mai Temple in Thailand, where I lived. But always, when you return, you have a different view. For example, the Nicobar's in the Andaman Islands. I visited the first time in '86 or '87 and I went back in 2011. Everything changed. Also, the many different Indonesian islands I would like to visit more and more of — Greenland too. I wait and wait. I keep waiting for the correct time for Aurora Borealis lights there.

As for my objectives, and my target for the next five years, it's arriving at the fourth or fifth ranking in the world on MTP (Most Traveled People)... Now, I am eighth in the world. Over the next five years, probably, if my travels continue, I can arrive at fifth or sixth. Step by step, for the next five years. That is my plan. One day, I don't know, but probably in 10 years, I will make first in the world.

One thing I know 100% is that I will continue traveling everywhere. Like when new countries such as South Sudan come into being. I was in South Sudan one month after it became a country, and I can promise to continue traveling when those things happen. Because traveling, it's 65% or 75% of my life, and it makes no sense to stop it.

Mike Spencer Bown, Canada

(Mike Spencer Bown in Mogadishu, Somalia, December 2010)

Where did you grow up and what was your early life like?

I went all across Canada. My family liked to take long road trips. We'd look where the sun was shining and drive in that direction, sometimes transcontinental journeys would result from this simple plan, through the United States or Canada. I did a lot of my schooling in Calgary, with the Rocky Mountains near to hand. When I was still rather young and not traveling full-time, I used to go live in the bush, my longest is 86 days without seeing another human or speaking, as part of a six month stint, but I've done a couple more entire summers living off the land, and several three month or shorter sessions, some in tropical wilderness or different continents.

The wilderness used to be my favorite non-travel related pastime, but it is mind-bending to go so deep into bush-mode, which is one and the same as aboriginal dream-time: it takes months to return to a civilized mode of thought, if you are skilled making the transition. I shifted over to doing full-time travel as a way to ease out of the rigors of living off the land. Bush time is much more dangerous than even the most dangerous countries. I've had dozens of quite serious run-ins with bears, and have developed my bush-craft enough that I've accompanied expeditions, such as one retracing of an old fur and gun trading route through the Rockies, as the official bear-barger. A mountain lion once made a pretty serious effort at killing me, and I've almost starved a few times — once I lost over twenty kilos due to giardia and bad luck in an extended wilderness stay, hundreds of kilometers from the nearest town. After that time, I was always sure to stock an emergency food supply of tinned tuna and beans.

When did you go from casually traveling to making this a full-time goal, and what motivated you to travel to every country?

In my early twenties, I wanted to transition out of living alone in the wilderness to something more social: I'd decided that I'd learned what the wilderness could teach me, and was eager to learn more about this big planet of ours. At the time, I'd only done a bit of Europe and North America pretty well, and Central America too, plus or minus. I picked up a new girlfriend who made a living by trading between countries, and buying silver jewelry to sell at music festivals across Canada. We backpacked a lot of Asia together, just by taking risks on various trade goods, and trying out products to have manufactured, shipped by container, and then wholesaled in North America. The Asian economic crisis was very good to us, as most importers thought that Indonesia would collapse, and pulled out.

We ramped up and shipped despite the inability to get insurance on the containers as they were passing through riot-prone cities. This sort of business was stressful, and required a certain tolerance for risk, but it took up almost no time, and was hugely profitable. Mostly we just backpacked around and stopped in to check up on manufacturing every so often, and then backpacked as our goods crossed the Pacific, then quickly flew back to sell them. Eventually we parted ways, and she moved to settle in Bali, but I had enough money that I didn't have to do more than the occasional bit of trading to support myself from then on, as long as I lived without possessions, as a full-time traveler. I was well set up for travel at the time, a rolling stone who had gathered no moss… I lived out of the same old backpack for what turned out to be 23 years. 24 now, I suppose, as I'm still going. Everything I've ever owned has been on my back in this bag, and I have no home or even home base. My backpack looks shabby and old, which is excellent, as it means no thief tries to steal it, what with other people's shiny new packs on offer.

So, I did not move from casual traveling to less casual: the trend for me was a move from extreme wilderness, to a more relaxed backpacking with an eye for easy business and trade opportunities, and finally, to a casual sort of roaming around the Earth. Also, I never had in mind visiting every country, I wanted to keep going, and, after 23 years, I found that I had a good feel for every country, but only as a side effect of trying to see everything that interested me in terms of nature and history and culture.

Do you remember the point where you said to yourself, "I can really accomplish this"?

I used to wonder sometimes if I'd stop and settle down, but it never happened. Feeling tired of travel was for me a medical symptom. Over the years I discovered that if I started to feel like that, it meant I was about to come down with either malaria or giardia, so I'd start to attend to other symptoms to sort out which of the two it was… The feeling of looking at a map of unexplored regions and thinking, "Meh…" was something requiring a pill, either Coartem or Flagyl.

What have you done over your life to gain the freedom and finances to pursue as much travel as you have?

Beyond what I mentioned in terms of having an eye out for business opportunities in the early years, the main effort for me was not one of gaining finances so much as gaining freedom. I don't care about material things or comfort, and instead of a fancy hotel I would rather spend the night in a mud hut or a hostel, or couch surfing, before that was the name of a business. I've lived out of the same backpack for 24 years now, and I never had any camera or computer or phone, just a mosquito net, old clothes, and books. If it wasn't for all the photographers I keep meeting in remote areas, I wouldn't have such a nice collection of photos. This year, I'm writing about my life as a traveler, so I have a laptop, and I've been staying in each area for a month, to practice slowing down and make it easier to get chapters typed. This will be a new income source, I hope, to keep me going for years to come.

Was there ever a time you felt like abandoning this goal?

I've visited Russia a few times, but one was a very long trip, from the Baltics to the Pacific, over 9000km of travel, hopping on and off the Trans-Siberian and ending up in the Arctic to visit the Yakuti people. They taught me how to drive a reindeer sleigh, while drunk, as we were never without a bottle of vodka to stay warm. Hanging out with ethnic Russians was if anything harder on the liver. When I stopped in London after that trip it took me weeks to recover my health — the first week I scarcely left the couch I was crashed on.

What were your worst travel experiences (i.e. detainment, bribes, car accidents, sickness, etc.) and why?

Visa troubles are the bane of travelers. Only a dozen are truly nightmarish, however. Equatorial Guinea is such a place, for anyone except Americans. Over a three-year period I'd tried six times for this visa, mostly just wasting a day each time, but in Ethiopia I put in a ten day effort. My payoff was a hung-over ambassador scowling at my papers and demanding a $500 dollar bribe. I left to the sounds of the receptionist shouting, "Jesus loves you! Jesus loves you!" So I was off to Yaounde where I had tried and failed before, but my new plan was to check into the Ideal Hotel, a brothel right near the embassies (most mid-range hotels in Africa are brothels), were I sweated out a bout of falciparum malaria and worked all day, every day, for three weeks on this visa. I needed to manufacture four impossible documents. Example: a report from the Canadian police saying I'm an upstanding citizen. This is an impossible document since Canada isn't a police state, and they decline to get involved in sorting citizens into paragons or cases of moral turpitude. One of the documents was an invitation from a V.I.P. and was proving unobtainable even with the most brazen offers of bribery. I was worried that it might be a truly impossible document.

After trying ploy after ploy without success, I talked to a local who worked for the Canadian Embassy to find if he's ever heard tell of a Canadian obtaining this visa. He sympathized with my plight, and told me, "I'll arrange a document for you, saying that the Canadian government cannot help you in any way to obtain this visa." Thanks, I suppose, I said, but I don't see how that will help. He said, "They speak Spanish in Equatorial Guinea, and I'll write it in French, and cover it with as many official-looking stamps as I can fit. Also, slip my card under a paper clip — when they don't understand the French, they'll give me a call and I'll talk in circles." I thanked him, and spent a couple days winning access into the most holy of holies, where sat the scowling administrator. "Is this the document?" she said. I slid it over to her. A couple days later, the embassy guard gave me a high five. This was the first time someone had actually walked away with the visa; and mine said by special request of the Canadian government.

Of course, conditions for visas wax and wane in difficulty; if I'd tried a couple years earlier in Douala down by the seaside I could have had it in a few days. I've had maybe ten or so visas that were as hard as this one. For me, this kind of bureaucratic bullshit is the worst thing about travel; I've lost about six months of my life on these applications and the ensuing runaround, despite a well-stocked visa kit. You can never have too many passport photos.

What do you consider the most adventurous trip you have taken?

For years I'd been hearing the DRC (Democratic Republic of Congo) overland was difficult: the word among backpackers was you'd cross by volcanic Lake Kivu, and then police and bandits rob you blind, so you limp back to the Rwandan border practically naked and penniless. I got myself a deceptive U.N. card, and the right clothes: the area has a heavy armored U.N. presence in an effort to curtail all the mass rapes.

I was going to pass myself off as a security inspector who was checking road conditions pursuant to sending supplies. The head of U.S. Aid in Kigali was of the opinion that I wouldn't last a day, as the Rwenzori Mountains are full of genocidal hut rebels. I had to sneak around the U.N., as they were trying to force me to take a flight all the way to Kinshasa and over all the most exciting bits, but I managed to get out on the road and hitched a ride in an old truck. We passed through the mountains, and my card worked like a charm. Sometimes the truck was bristling with weapons and rockets, as bands of soldiers hopped on for a ride to the next village. But often we were alone, or passing mud huts and villagers with wooden bicycles, who were willing to sell me hot potatoes and handfuls of swamp minnows for a few coins.

Across the mountains were the primordial rainforest of the Congo basin; a Chinese-built dirt road for extracting minerals led west. I traveled a thousand kilometers by motorcycle deep into the forest and went to live with the Bambuti pygmy tribe, living in a leaf hut and hunting antelope with spear and net.

What were your most challenging countries to visit and why?

Usually the countries experiencing a hot war while I was trying to visit were the most challenging. I'd been in Iran pretending to be a professional photographer's husband so she could get photos of the underground party scene, and afterward I decided to tour Iraq, with a plan to bribe my way across the border, and hitchhike around dressed like a local and speaking as little as possible during the Operation Iron Grip phase of the Gulf War, watching the Americans battle the Iraqis.

On a couple occasions, the receptionist at my hotel wouldn't let me out onto the street. One time the guy was pushing against my chest until I sat down and waited. A few minutes later there was a burst of automatic rifle fire and explosions outside. The hotel guy must have known it was about to kick off, and decided to save their only tourist.

Tikrit was dodgy. The locals were from Saddam's tribe as this was his hometown, and were sore that he was captured and slated to be executed. I was eating in a large outdoor chicken and rice restaurant, and scores of locals were giving me the stink-eye, as I was talking in English with the guy who was giving me a lift north. I was worried that they would come over and chop off my head like what happened to the Japanese guy who tried to do Iraq the same way I did at the same time. Luckily I emerged unscathed. The only real trouble I had was in Mosul, where I was held at gunpoint by American Special Forces. They were trying to make an interrogation, but I managed to keep it light. The commander angrily said, "What are you doing in Iraq?"

"I'm on vacation... What? Are you guys working?" This produced some laughs. Anyhow, never a dull moment in Iraq.

What is the strangest thing you've seen/experienced while traveling?

So many odd memories, as to travel is to be a stranger in strange lands. Some that come to mind are riding out a typhoon in a top-heavy wooden junk in the sea north of Sumbawa, Indonesia, in the darkness watching the disco-blue phosphorescence of the giant waves thrashing us, while steel-hulled car ferries were sent to the bottom with all hands lost; a blonde-haired utterly dark-skinned girl on one of the Solomon Islands with her cheeks showing a geometry of delicate silver scars, scratched into her face by her mother when she was a baby using the sharpened wing-bone of a fruit bat, in homage to the shark god; suicide bombers in Kabul popping with a sound like opening bottles of Coke, after spraying the crowd on Chicken Street with machine pistols and then hurling themselves into the Ministry of Culture to explode; a deer staggering over to me walking on bone stumps, while the dragon that snapped off its legs lurches in for the kill; a factory for rendering the blubber of marine mammals on South Georgia in the Southern Ocean, it storage tanks now rusted and empty, R2 Whale-catchers forlorn and stranded, and the blubber saws and corroded machines colonized, ironically, by hundreds of frolicking black fur seal pups and enormous honking elephant seals, with a backdrop of herds of feral alien reindeer.

Which travel experiences stand out the most and why?

Comic situations stand out for me, such as when I was swarmed by killer bees and the local kids "helped" me by whipping them off with branches of a neem tree. For once, the little Islamic girls had an advantage from the hijabs they have to wear. When I'd run my hand over my back, it came away full of stingers. Turned out I was not allergic, and a beer or two in a roadside bar sorted me out. On another occasion I was hitchhiking around Central African Republic, and a nun who had given me a lift cautioned me against the road I was planning to follow on account of cannibals. I had a laugh, as I had thought I was born in the wrong century to hear that particular warning.

What are the most overrated and underrated countries you've been to in your travels and why?

French Polynesia is one of the most overrated. First off it's a part of France, and a playground for the super-rich, so everything is super-expensive. I'm not a fan of snobbery and excessive comfort anyhow, and while it is a lovely tropical paradise, I was turned off by the prices. Thinking to keep on budget and enjoy some authentic local food at the same time, I went to a parking lot where Tahitians were selling curry and rice on paper plates from the back of a truck, only to discover that it was 20 euros. Okay, it's a tropical paradise, but there are thousands of such tropical paradises, and many at a reasonable cost, such as Easter Island, a short flight away, with the famous stone heads and a nice hostel in town.

Yemen is the most underrated. Hardly anyone has heard of it, but it has amazing high-rise medieval architecture in Sana'a, and the Jabal Haraz mountains, each swirl of cliff and cornice topped with a tower or castle, lording it over the groves of narcotic shrubbery that suck up two-thirds of the scarce water in this parched and ancient land. Socotra Island has schools of dolphins, fairy forests of chest-high mini baobab trees, bulbous vase-like trunks with silver or bronze bark and branches like tentacles, each sporting a colorful flower, and flocks of beady-eyes Egyptian vultures hopping and hankering for fish bones and carrion. I scored an invitation to a wedding in the mountains, and was reminded of the times weddings were blasted by mistake with hellfire missiles. I discovered why: a Yemeni wedding consisted of men brandishing knives and scimitars, yelling and surging toward each other, while hurling bombs and firing assault rifles into the air. There is precious little difference as seen from the air to tell apart a wedding from a terrorist battle. Any lull in the general melee lasts only long enough for everyone to consume more of the stimulant drug, khat. I remember thinking, "Please, Mr. Obama, don't drone strike me…"

What are the best and worst meals you have ever had traveling and where were they?

Simple meals can be tasty if you are hungry enough. I used to carry tins of sardines for those days when I couldn't find any food at all. In the Sahel, sometimes all that is on offer is a greasy mix of goat guts and rice, unsifted and full of little rocks that chip your teeth. Sometimes in local bars along dirt tracks in the African jungle a guy will come through with wheelbarrows full of smoked monkeys. I don't fancy them: something about the little faces reminds me of concentration camp victims. Once, I was floating in a fiber-glass motor boat in the Cross River delta, laying atop sacks full of edible tree leaves (long story), and a passing police boat pulled alongside and said that a white man shouldn't be out here, on account of the kidnapping risk, and insisted that I pass the night on an island that housed the police headquarters. A huge friendly policeman offered his spot on the concrete floor, while he would sleep on the dock. He had a few slices of bread and some butter, and I had a tin of fish, which we shared, and in the morning, we picked some mangoes for breakfast, off a tree in the courtyard. I'm thankful for food, as I know what it feels like to starve and do without.

The most thankful diners are Buddhist monks. In Mandalay, I was trying to find a woman named Petra, who was staying in a monastery. She's told me to look her up if I was ever in Burma. The first monastery I checked at was the most austere and respected in the city. As a result they had the traditional right to beg from the poshest neighborhood. Housewives would compete to fill the monks bowls with the most amazing secret family recipes. Whereupon the monks would set them out on a table, and enjoy them in silent contemplation of the generosity of those who provided. I lucked out in that I came just before lunch and was invited to join them in this amazing meal.

What country made you feel most out of your comfort zone and why?

Generally speaking, I feel least comfortable when I arrive in a country to find myself arrested and detained, and under angry interrogation. In Nagorno-Karabakh, I was forced off the road by a trio of black SUVs and was taken to a military prison, where a guy was shouting in Russian that I would suffer worse than I'd ever suffered before. I pretended I could understand nothing, not even "Nyet" and "Da." They had to bring in a translator, and as luck would have it, it was a guy I'd had a friendly visit with the day before: he was the only one who could speak English in the area. The interrogator tries again, saying I would suffer blah, blah, blah. The translation came: they are angry that you have seen the ruined city of Agdan, where ethnic Armenians massacred Azeris; just sit tight. They'll run out of steam eventually and just deport you. With my translator, I could relay to them amusing stories about trying to pick up girls in bars, and I had six out of eight smiling and friendly after a day, and only two still scowling. The six mentioned waved me goodbye when they finally drove me to the border and kicked me out.

In the Puntland state of Somalia, I had a harsher reception than in Mogadishu. Local Somalis had told me that the government themselves were one and the same with the pirates that Puntland is infamous for, but I was relieved to find that this was not the case. When I arrived on a small propeller plane I was surrounded by shouting armed men, and put into detention, guarded by two guys with 9mm machine pistols. The Minister of the Interior came by to shout at me that things would go very badly for me if I was not a journalist. Okay, if you put it that way, I'm a journalist, he, he, he. Convinced that I was not a security threat, they decided that I should attend the Puntland poetry festival as a guest of the government and meet the President. I rode around in a convoy of technicals (Toyota trucks with box fed machine guns in the back) in the company of the minister for good governance and the minister of education. The best way to make the most of being detained or imprisoned is to try to connect on a human level, and try to entertain and joke around. Don't try to contact embassies or make threats or demands because if that's what your relationship with your captors deteriorates to, heaven help you.

Do you speak any foreign languages? If so, which have been the most useful for you besides English?

Languages come and go for me. If everyone is speaking Spanish, for instance, after a few months or a year, I find that somehow I'm getting by, but then some years pass before I hear it again, and it fades from my memory. At one time or other I was able to get by in French, Spanish, Bahasa, and Russian. All these languages are rusty now... More and more the language of travel is English. Anyhow, as I'm always on the move, especially off-the-beaten-path, often the local language changes more often than I'd change my shirt.

Looking back from when you started traveling to where you are now, in what ways, if any, have travel changed you?

Seeing as I've been traveling non-stop my entire adult life, it might be hard to tease out the effects of travel from simply getting older. I'm pretty sure I'm a good judge of character by now. People try to rip off or rob travelers all the time, but after a while you get an intuition for peoples' intentions. The trick is to hone and learn to trust this intuition. For example, if a guy at a market stall is trying to overcharge you, treat it as a lesson in intuition and try to attend to the tiniest flicker of expression across his face, or the tones and modulation of his voice — this is a precious opportunity to train yourself in human nature. The end goal is to be able to spend all your time in the company of good people, of which there are many in all nations, and avoid those who mean to rob or kill you. You can tap into that most essential network, which predates the Internet by millennia: the network of good and friendly people who can help you on your way.

Also, I've noticed over the years that everyone is equally human and much the same, even the most outlandish tribes and weird westerners. This fact is most easily apprehended when you are fair in your comparisons. Rural Mongolians are comparable to rednecks. Pygmies are much like hillbillies. New York bankers should be favorably compared to Lagos businessmen. It's remarkable how similar the various races of our species are under the skin.

And I've noticed that my memory is geo-tagged — certain cities or regions bring up certain thoughts and memories. Now I have an entire globe in my mind of such memories. I've always been fascinated by history and archeology and museums, and especially what I can learn from conversations with interesting people. Travel is a form of filter, straining out boring people for the most part — if you are wrestling your way through a jungle searching for the temple of the jaguar god, and you meet someone else doing the same, you can count on an interesting conversation around the campfire that night. All this experience means that, for me, the world doesn't seem so bewildering or complex. It makes sense, given our species' past and the forces at play.

What is the longest continuous trip you have ever taken? When was it and where did you travel?

It's all the same trip. My biggest break from travel was after 23 years, when I'd done Ireland, which I'd been saving for a while so that I wouldn't have done all the countries. But last year I couldn't resist any longer and popped over to backpack the Emerald Isle. There was quite a lot of media attention, more than when I'd done Mogadishu as a tourist during the height of the trench warfare between the A.U. and Al Shabab. I ended up doing six months of various interviews on television, radio, film, newspaper, Internet, etc., which was spread between Dublin, London, Ottawa, other Canadian cities, Hawaii, and L.A. That's not much travel for such a long stretch of time.

Up until then, I usually went to Canada or the U.K. to see family and friends, but this involved actually more travel than when I was traveling, as they are spread out into so many different towns and cities. It has been non-stop travel for me since I was in my early twenties.

What is your favorite "off-the-beaten-path" destination and why?

Tough one, but I'll say Lake Chad: the premier, in fact the only, tourist site in the nation of Chad. I arrived by riding in the back of a series of flatbed trucks, being careful to duck when thorny branches swept the deck. There were no hotels. But a purveyor of veterinary medicines helped me ask around until I secured a place to sleep: a concrete slab surrounded by corrugated metal sheets. I borrowed a couple plastic chairs and draped my mosquito net over them, to make a cozy, if somewhat hard, bed. Little village kids constantly peered through the cracks in the walls to spy the exotic foreigner. I was given a key to an outhouse full of smelly bats.

Activities for visitors included sitting at the lake shore amongst the bladders and stems of acrid devil plants, drawing animals in the sand with sticks, but to be careful to get back under cover before the sun sets, and the waves of malarial mosquitoes. Or you might watch a man disassembling a line of fat-horned cattle with a bloody battle-axe, and hanging the chunks in the thorny trees like an enormous shrike. The only restaurant was a goat carcass on a hook — simply point to what you want and a dude will chop it off, sear it over charcoals, and serve it to you on a scrap of brown paper torn from an empty cement bag. Places like this are my all-time favorite, for obvious reasons: never a dull moment.

What are the best and worst places you have ever spent a night?

There are so crazily many of each. Often I just sleep on the ground or in the ditch. Once I was trying to hitchhike from Cape Town to the Fish River Canyon in Namibia. A long-haul trucker was the last to drop me off near a dirt road going west from the main highway. He told me it was 80km to the canyon, and I might not get another ride, so he gifted me a surplus two liters of pop that he got for free with his last diesel fill-up. Good thing he did too, as the first day I walked 46 km, under the desert heat, under constant attack from biting flies, such that I had to swipe my hand non-stop over my face like a windshield wiper as I trudged along. Come nightfall, I put on all my clothes and lay down on my back in the sand, listening to the hyenas and the clicking and skittering of numerous prowling black hairy, wide-bodied scorpions. The next day was similar, but I saw the amazing canyon.

I've stayed at three cents a night hotels in war-ravaged Nicaragua, and you get what you pay for. Sometimes I've slept in piles of spare tires, or abandoned warehouses. Often I sleep in the ditch. Some hotels are amusingly seedy and terrible. One Christmas I spent in a brothel in Gau, Niger, the only accommodation left in town as everyone had fled because of an onslaught of Tuareg rebels. I'd come to talk to the Algerian consul, and chanced to see him in the market and say hi. But by the time I knocked on his door, I was told he'd been assassinated. The whores could speak English, but had assumed I must be an Arab, and unable to talk to them, so they left me alone. They gathered in the hall outside my door on Christmas morning to sing, "But for the love of Jesus I'd be a sinner."

My luckiest and best hotel is easy to name. I took a boat over to Koh Toa, a smaller island in the gulf of Thailand, popular with divers and backpackers. A tout working the crowd on deck told me of a hotel where I might snorkel and see sharks. The hotel stands all alone, amongst forest and mountainside, so if it turns out you are the only guest, it might be boring. I resolved to chance it, and rode in the back of a truck soaked in a tropical downpour. Having been dropped near the entrance and seeing the truck speed away back up the muddy mountain trail, I stepped into the lobby with some trepidation — would anyone be here to keep me company? Hmm... yes indeed. There happened to be two dozen western European girls, all in their early twenties (I was a young man myself back then) and all were volunteer English teachers in isolated rural Chinese villages, where they had taught for six months straight, and they had done such a good job that the organizer had rewarded them, flying all these ladies to Thailand, whereupon they had taken the ferry here, and had just opened their first beers. Before I finished two beers, the boldest girl stood up and announced, "I'm going to do something very unexpected." The lobby fell silent, as all of us wondered what she might do that would be so unexpected — until she strode over and grabbed me, and woman-handled me, if there is such a word, back to her hut. Do you think girls are afraid of giant spiders? There was one spread out the size of a baseball on the floor between us and her bed, which she promptly booted, sending it sailing over to strike the wall with a wet thump.

In your opinion, what country or place in the world feels the most authentic and untouched by tourism?

Pakistan. It used to be one of the highlights of the overland Asia trail, and now practically no-one goes there. But it's a fabulous country with friendly people, and so much to see. If you tire of the humidity and heat and yellow mangoes of Lahore, you can go up into the hills, or enjoy the walnuts, apricot orchards and ancient forts, and hikes through meadows and glaciers in the Karakorum Range, making your way to the Pamirs on one of the world's top overland experiences.

In your opinion, where is the most beautiful place on Earth?

When I first began to travel, I had an interest in beauty, and kept a growing horde of memories of beautiful places in my mind. Often they would shuffle and shift, or drop from the running, as my memory of a first encounter with a new sort of landscape, architectural or natural beauty would astound, but then I'd find better examples in the same category, and rate them like a connoisseur.

I'm not sure when it happened exactly, but at some point I stopped looking for beauty, and this was when I began to find it everywhere, even in slums and swamps. What was most real became most beautiful to me. For instance, I went to visit some

Bozo tribesmen. A family came over to shake my hand, except for one old man who shied away: a leper. He was the first leper I'd seen in years, as the disease is fading into history with modern medicine. He didn't have the contagious variant, and was surprised when I reached out and shook his hand. The expression on his face, there by his mud hut amid reeds and river, was beautiful.

What do you enjoy most when traveling (cities, nature, people, cultural spots, etc.) and why?

Mixing it up is best. For me ancient civilizations, high-tech mega cities, primitive tribes and astounding natural treasures are the most rewarding. Tourist traps and shopping don't do it for me, especially shopping. I don't buy anything unless I'm prepared to carry it on my back for the rest of my life.

What travel accomplishments are you most proud of?

Travel for me is just life. I suppose I'm most proud that I just managed to survive all this travel, without debilitating injury or disease. It's a minor miracle, but I must have done something right to satisfy the fates. I'm proud of it partly because it proves that I was right to think that there are friendly people to be found everywhere, and the Earth is not so scary a place, as modern media and their relentless negativity want to portray. Mostly I'm proud of it because of the favorable light it shines on human nature, and the hope it gives me for our collective future.

If you had just one personal travel story to share with someone, what would that be?

Afghanistan in 2008 makes for a compact travel tale, with a little bit of everything. At the time, I was seeing a Kazakh girl, who was sent to Kabul for a work-related meeting. She was scared, and wanted to tell her boss, "No." But I emailed her to say I'd fly over and meet her in Dushanbe, and we'd go together. Kabul and surroundings was interesting, and I have another story involving an illegal bar, the Minister for Preventing Corruption and a nargala full of Kandahar hashish. After a week, my girl had to leave, and I decided to explore the central mountains before exiting to the northwest through Herat to Turk-menistan.

Everyone agreed there were two possible routes to get to Bam-iyan, famed for its giant Buddha statues that the Taliban blasted to rubble. At the time, a lot of Taliban were active in the moun-tains, so it was not the best time to visit. The Taliban were stopping 80% of the vehicles on the southern road, and killing anyone they found who was not a Pashtu. But on the northern road, there was only a 30% chance of this outcome. But finding a public transport van required wandering around in Kabul at two in the morning, and hoping for the best. I found a four-wheel drive van heading that way, and I was getting settled with my Afghan fellow passengers, a young man said, "I can protect you."

"Are you a security guard, or a policeman?" I asked.

"I carve wooden spoons, like my father," he said. Okay...

It was a rough road, as bad as the road over Blue Mountain to see Lake Turkana in East Africa. We saw mud forts that would have been familiar to the great Khans, Afghan girls in colorful dresses climbing up trees to cut down leaves for goats, and nar-row canyons of golden stone. To either side was destroyed by Soviet armor and minefields. The road was so rough that it tore one of our wheels completely off and it went spinning free up the side of a mountain. As we skidded to a halt, I was thinking, "Who will have to go fetch that wheel through the minefield?" But in a minor miracle, it wobbled and then turned, and rolled all the way back down the mountain, to stop exactly near to the hands waiting to cram it back onto the axle.

The helpful young man suggested that I might sleep in his un-cle's restaurant. This was atop a platform near the center of town, and he showed me a ladder in case I had to climb down and piss in the alley, and a carpet in the corner to lay my pack and sleep. Supper was a camel knee served on a dented metal platter. Bamiyan was grand, but there came a time when I was ready to get a move on. As I was climbing into a van in the market, that same young man rushed up to me and said, "Not that one." I got out, and he said, "That one is heading down the 80% chance of death road".

"Thanks," I said, and started climbing into the adjacent van.

He said, "No, not that van, it's worse."

"What is it," I asked, "The 100% chance of death road?"

"I know this van from around town. It has no shocks."

"Thanks, you just saved my life," I replied.

Besides your home country, where do you find yourself returning to over and over and why?

It's helpful to have a city you know as a gateway for getting into a continent, that way you can get off these long intercontinental flights and quickly orient yourself, check into your usual hostel or hotel, and to hit the ground running in terms of foraging for visas, so much easier when you already have a good idea where the embassies are concentrated. Buenos Aires and Lima are good for South America, London and Amsterdam for Europe, Cairo, Addis Ababa, Pretoria, Dakar, and Yaounde for Africa; Bangkok, Bali, Kathmandu, and Hong Kong for Asia. Almaty is a good way to get into Central Asia to start the torturous process for those lands to the east of the Tien Shan Mountains. London was a special favorite for me, as I'd always take the time for a squat party or massive rave with the many U.K. based friends I've met in far away places.

What is the ideal amount of time you prefer to travel each trip before you are ready for home and a break?

A year to two years is the perfect span between visits to family and friends. This is about how long it takes to fill a 48-page passport, so I would get a flight to Ottawa, get a new one at the central office in just a matter of days, and then hop across some cities and towns in Canada, visiting friends and family for a few days or a week each, and end up on the Pacific coast in Vancouver, where it's easy to get on a cheap flight to Asia or South America, or whatever continent most captivated me at the time.

If you had an unlimited budget and space and time was no object, what would your perfect travel day look like? (for example: start your morning in Bora Bora; afternoon on a safari in Kenya; night in Australia, etc.)

When I can follow natural features, and the human geography these features sculpt from our cultures, I feel it's more meaningful and I learn things that I'd miss if I was engaging in a disjointed sort of travel, where I'd flit from wonderful place to wonderful place, in a quest for some sort of abstract notion of beauty or perfection. I'm fascinated, rather, by what is real, and long uninterrupted journeys through various ecosystems and cultures makes the strongest impression.

For example, the long winding road from the Tibetan plateau to the valleys of Nepal passes through the most amazing scenery and towns, and even a city perching like a falcon in its misty aerie on a switch-backed cliff-side. There is no better way to appreciate the lofty heights and immense fractal roots of the Himalayan peaks. River journeys can be just as powerful, such as floating down the Amazon, from the Andes to the Atlantic, or slowly hitchhiking up the Nile from Egypt across Lake Nasser and through the Sudan, taking a left at the Blue Nile and following it to its headwaters at Lake Tana and on past the ancient fortress city of Gondar into the Simian range.

For those looking to travel to every country, what is the best piece of advice you could offer them?

My advice is this: simply travel. If you should happen to visit every country, so be it. Whatever you do, don't try to travel to every country. This is a gimmick and epic fail as a traveler. I've met thousands of backpackers, and if I were to make a graph of who has the most interesting tales of adventure, the slope of that graph would be up until it peaks around 65 countries, and then all the way back down. I've sat at a table where there were travelers besides myself with over 100 countries (I think I had seen all but a few at the time). Also, there were a couple just out of their teenage years who had seen only a handful of countries. The youngsters were thrilled to be sitting with so many extreme travelers and wanted to hear tales of adventure. I could oblige, but the others had only a few stories of hotels, taxis, and plane trips. It turned out the youngsters had a travel tale of a jeep trip in Asia, and the 100 plus country folks had nothing.

Try only to travel and have fun. If you think you will have sixteen solid years to devote to travel, because that's how long it takes to get a feel for every country, then try to see all the countries in whatever zone you find yourself in, to cut down on expensive flights. But otherwise, travel for knowledge and experience and for sheer joy. Travel is not transportation. It is much more, and those who diminish their experience of cultures and continents chasing some record are making a gimmick of what could have been a noble pursuit. The use of the metric of the number of countries visited only works when all else is equal, and breaks down if some people game the system by making short visits or sticking their feet over borders as if they were stamp collecting. An ancient philosopher said it best, "For suppose you should think that a man had had a long voyage who had been caught in a raging storm as he left harbor, and carried hither and thither and driven round and round in a circle by the rage of opposing winds? He did not have a long voyage, just a long tossing about."

Which is to say, in the immortal words of Seneca: don't be a "tosser."

For someone that has been almost everywhere, what still gets you excited about packing your bags again?

Visiting friends all over the place. I've been blessed to have met so many fascinating people, and I love to stop in and see how they are getting on, and catch up on old times. Recently I stopped in at Saint Petersburg for a visit, and went down through the Balkans, which I hadn't seen since the war, and to Turkey with a guy who was seeing it for the first time. It was my fourth time in both Russia and Turkey, so I didn't see much that was new, but travel in good company is worthwhile in and of itself.

Do you feel you have missed out on certain aspects of life being away from home so much?

Wife and family come to mind. However, only the shadow knows what the future holds. Maybe I'll settle down as a husband and father — stranger things have happened and I still feel full of life and energy.

To quote Francis Bacon, his essay "Of Marriage" begins with: "He that hath wife and children hath given hostages to fortune; for they are impediments to great enterprises, either of virtue or mischief."

Looking ahead, what travel plans and goals are you still pursuing, and what is on your "Bucket List"?

I don't have a bucket list anymore: I was pretty thorough in seeing everything that interested me in every country. Freestyle travel used to be my all-time favorite, where you come in with a modicum of research, but then discard any plan and your guidebook, since it's most fun to just go with the flow for max-imum flexibility and fun. Besides, no travel plan survives con-tact with friendly forces. Lately I'm working on a book, so I'm dropping in on places where I can spend a peaceful month, such as Olympus in Turkey or Chernivtsi in Ukraine, and get some chapters written. In the future, I'm thinking to concen-trate more on expedition-style travel, to see places in the deep wilderness that are tougher to get to under a more casual ap-proach.

Wojciech Dabrowski, Poland

(Wojciech Dabrowski)

Where did you grow up and what was your early life like?

I was born in Gdansk, Poland, where my parents settled after WWII. It was just 100 meters from our flat to the canal of Gdansk commercial port, so as a boy I saw many foreign ships passing by. Every day I saw sailors from different countries, speaking strange languages. They were from another world.

Once I was in school I started to eagerly read books about the world and to dream about distant mountains, islands, and waterfalls. At that time, the Iron Curtain isolated us from the rest of the world.

When did you go from casually traveling to making this a full-time goal, and what motivated you to travel to every country?

For the first time I was allowed to cross the border (to socialist Czechoslovakia) when I was 14. Ten years later they allowed me to see Spain — my first western country. Only starting in

1988 did authorities allow me to freely travel the world. Traveling to every country was not my goal. The goal was to see all fascinating places around the world I was reading about. All the unknown countries were also on this list because every unknown country was like a fascinating enigma until I entered it for the first time.

Do you remember the point where you said to yourself, "I can really accomplish this"?

No. As a rule I travel alone and I organize my voyages by myself. In traveling I use common sense: I do not go to dangerous areas, and I do not want to be a hero, even for myself. But many people use the number of visited countries to assess the achievements of a traveler. I was asked so often, "How many countries did you visit?" that I finally decided to publish a "common sense list of the countries" on my website — so everybody can see it and can check. I am not on the MTP (Most Traveled People) list because I do not travel for points or for the better position on the list.

What have you done over your life to gain the freedom and finances to pursue as much travel as you have?

I was worked for 31 years as a telecoms engineer. To save extra money for travel, I started to write articles for the press about visited countries. I was giving thousands of paid lectures and slide-shows about the world in public libraries, clubs, and schools. Finally I published a book, *To the Seven Continents*. I travel on a budget level, and my travelers knowledge and experience allows me to reduce the cost of my solo expeditions.

Was there ever a time you felt like abandoning this goal?

No, never. I still have a long list of places I want to visit. Some of them are postponed because the authorities do not allow you to visit specific areas, or it seems to be too dangerous. For example, I would like to travel along the whole Himalayan Range on the Tibetan side all the way over from Yunnan to Kashgar. I believe it will be possible in the future.

What have been your worst travel experiences (such as detainment, bribes, car accidents, sicknesses, etc.) and why?

I once escaped a train that was on fire. It was in the Nubian Desert. The train was going from Khartoum to Wadi Halfa. The fire started in one end of my car and I ended up jumping off the train into the sand.

What do you consider one of the most adventurous trips you have taken?

That would be my trans-African voyage from Ceuta to the Cape of Good Hope with only one air segment over the DRC (Democratic Republic of Congo). I spent four months using just local transport.

What were your most challenging countries to visit and why?

Saudi Arabia. It took me a few years of attempts until I finally received a visa (for 72 hours). I rented a car in the Jeddah airport and drove through the desert to see my dream — Madain Saleh.

What's the strangest thing you've seen/experienced while traveling?

The noise made by the melting glaciers at sunrise on the summit of Mt Kilimanjaro.

Which travel experiences stand out the most and why?

There are two: my trans-African solo voyage mentioned above and my Everest trek from Jiri to Kala Pattar. Both required a lot of determination, effort, and experience.

What are the most overrated and underrated countries you've been to in your travels and why?

It depends a lot on what is most important to you during your voyage: people, monuments, nature?

Overrated: Nigeria; it was unfriendly, corrupted, and polluted.

Underrated: The little insular countries of the South Pacific like Tuvalu or Kiribati — they are little-known because few travelers go there. These are friendly, quiet and picturesque.

What are the best and worst meals you have ever had traveling and where were they?

Worst: Tsampa in Tibet: Tasteless, sticky, and hard to accept by Westerners.

Best: Polish dumplings filled with white cottage cheese — delicious!

What country made you feel most out of your comfort zone and why?

In Libya twenty years ago the officials treated me like a servant. I had a feeling that they considered themselves as a chosen nation.

Do you speak any foreign languages? If so, which has been the most useful for you besides English?

Spanish in Latin America, French in West Africa and the former French colonies like French Polynesia, and Russian in the former Soviet Union republics and Mongolia.

Looking back from when you started traveling to where you are now, in what ways, if any, has travel changed you?

I am more open to the people. I learned a lot. Let's just say that now I can give a lecture about every single country of the world. Travel broadened my horizons.

What was the longest continuous trip you have ever taken, when was it, where did you travel?

My 8th around the world voyage in 2009 to Africa, South and North America, the Pacific, and Asia.

What is your favorite "off-the-beaten-path" destination and why?

Christmas Island in the Pacific — unspoiled and isolated with friendly people and beautiful landscapes.

What are the best and worst place you have spent a night?

Best: a fale on the beach of the Savai Island in Samoa.

Worst: a primitive hut in the Ethiopian village on the road from Gondar to Metema.

In your opinion, what country or place in the world feels the most authentic and untouched by tourism?

For me, it is the Republic of Tuvalu in the South Pacific. Also the atolls of Tokelau. They have preserved their native culture and lifestyle.

In your opinion, where is the most beautiful place on Earth?

To be precise I must give two answers:

In my opinion the most beautiful place to be for a short time and to enjoy the beauty and the majesty of nature is the summit of Kala Pattar in the Himalayas — at the end of the Everest trek. It gives a 360 degree, breathtaking panorama of the highest mountains on the Earth. Everest, Nuptse, Pumori, and other peaks are in front of you. I suffered a cold and headache there due to the altitude — 5643 meters — but for me, it is still the place of the highest enchantment.

But if I think about the most beautiful places to stay longer than a few hours, to enjoy not only the landscape but also the friendliness of the local people, I must say: the small islands of the South Pacific. There are many islands I enjoyed. Coming to a choice of the most beautiful is very difficult. But in my opinion it could be Aitutaki on Cook Islands or Kiritimati/Christmas Island of Kiribati.

What do you enjoy most when traveling (cities, nature, people, cultural spots, etc.) and why?

Nature and people. Nature can surprise you by its beauty — you see much nicer landscapes than you can imagine. The meetings with friendly people are also unforgettable — but, sorry to say, there are also unfriendly people around the world.

What travel accomplishments are you most proud of?

My trans-African voyage from Ceuta to Cape, my Everest trek, and my 11 Around the World expeditions — all solo and organized by myself.

If you had just one personal travel story to share with someone, what would it be?

That would be the story about my Christmas on Christmas Island. It was the only time in my life I was forced to spend Christmas far from home. I spent it with the friendly and hospitable people of Kiritimati — and I was invited to celebrate during the three days this big event was held in the middle of the Pacific Ocean, close to the equator.

Besides your home country, where do you find yourself returning to over and over and why?

I do not think I have such a place. I always like to discover new places, and I still have my own list with enough new destinations I want to go to.

What is the ideal amount of time you prefer to travel on each trip before you are ready for home and a break?

From my experience, I know that after three months on the trail I begin to strongly feel homesick. This is the signal that it is time to come back.

If you had an unlimited budget and space and time was no object, what would your perfect travel day look like? (for example: start your morning in Bora Bora; afternoon on a safari in Kenya; night in Australia, etc.)

Spend a morning at Ayers Rock, an afternoon in the Himalayas, and an evening on Fatu Hiva (the southernmost island of the Marquesas Islands).

For those looking to travel to every country, what is the best piece of advice you could offer them?

Do not rush! Give yourself time to understand every country you visited. You are not going there just to check off countries on the list, are you? Do not treat your traveling as a sport — do not go out to beat any records.

For someone that has been almost everywhere, what still gets you excited about packing your bags again?

Knowing that a new adventure awaits me beyond my front door; I still have new places to discover, new interesting people to meet, new landscapes to enjoy. What is life worth without dreams?

Do you ever feel you have missed out on certain aspects of life being away from home so much?

Yes I do, but it is my choice. And that is the price I'm willing to pay.

Looking ahead, what travel plans and goals are you still pursuing, and what is on your "Bucket List"?

A great journey from east to west Tibet at the bottom of the Himalayas; Emperor penguins in the Antarctic; Chilean Fjords; Western Siberia… and much more!

Charles Veley, U.S.A.

(Red is the color of the day, at the sunburn capital of the world, Howland Island)

Where did you grow up and what was your early life like?

I grew up with my father in and around New York City, and spent summers with my mother on a farm in rural West Virginia. My three half-siblings didn't start appearing until I was ten, so as an only child adapting to two very different environments, I probably developed some basic traveler skills. From the start, I was known as a wanderer with an unnatural fascination with geography. Once, as a toddler, I escaped my parents' notice out the back door, and was recovered several blocks away by a concerned neighbor. In first grade, I began riding the subway to school alone, and hand-drew complete street maps of every borough in New York City by taping together dozens of pieces of 8.5x11" paper; this took up much of the floor area of our townhouse. When we moved to the suburbs, long before the days of Google Maps, I began expanding my boundaries by bicycle, venturing for hours in a different direction each day, with the goal of developing a complete understanding of my geographical surroundings. One day, my bicycle and I turned up at my aunt's house in another state, and my father was none too amused at learning he would have to drive an hour to come pick me up. My parents didn't have much money, nor interest in adventure travel, so my first and only overseas trip prior to university was to Spain in 1977 — a work-related trip for my father. Neither my father nor stepmother spoke Spanish, and at age 13, with a full three years of grade school Spanish under my belt, I wound up leading them and my baby sister around Andalucia by car. That was my first lesson in the power of local language. Four years later, I matriculated at Harvard on an Air Force scholarship, and, at 19, faced with a service commitment of ten years, I convinced the somewhat introverted Administrative Board that my computer science curriculum was lacking in "Australian Studies," and that I needed a semester abroad in Australia. A helpful travel agent found me a Circle Fare ticket, unlocking such unspeakably exotic (to me at the time) destinations as Tahiti, Fiji, New Zealand, and Hawaii. This was my first introduction into complex tickets — a topic that would later become an obsession. After graduation and the better part of a year spent burning jet fuel in the military airspace above Arizona, I was obliged to return to civilian life, since a routine flight medical exam revealed deterioration in my right retina. In response, I purchased a three-month Eurail pass, and — just as I had always dreamed of doing on the New York Subway — rode every line I could to its outer limits, from the bottom of Sicily to the top of Norway, and everywhere in between. This was Europe before Schengen and the euro, where every border crossing meant a hard change in language, food, currency, and sometimes even the train car itself! I loved it all, and have been hooked on travel ever since.

When did you go from casually traveling to making this a full-time goal, and what motivated you to travel to every country?

For a brief period of time in 1999 and early 2000, I was wealthy following the IPO of my employer, and so I decided to stop working and take a year abroad to study languages, and to introduce my then-newlywed wife to some places already familiar to me. I purchased my first ever 'round-the-world (RTW) tickets for that journey and rented apartments in Paris and Munich for three months each, while attending language school. At the close of 2000, my travel awareness consisted of Europe, the U.S., Australia/NZ, and a few Asian cities. Additionally, the high-flying stock which had enabled my decision to travel for a year had crashed hard, forcing me to consider going back to work. But then two things happened: A three-week trip to Southern Africa completely expanded my horizons, enabling me to consider previously ignored destinations such as Botswana, Zambia, Malawi, and Mozambique. I realized that there were many more regions and places I wished to visit, and that the 'round-the-world tickets were a reasonable vehicle for doing so. Simultaneously, the disappointing result of the U.S. presidential election caused me not to want to return to the U.S. If not now, when was I going to have the opportunity to visit China, South America, and other locations? I elected to extend the time abroad for a second year. More and more people began asking how many countries I had been to, and when I tried to tally them up, I realized that this is not a straightforward question. For example, I had been to Tahiti, which was (and is) technically part of France. However, it is on the opposite side of the world. Surely it should "count" separately! Similarly, I had been to Puerto Rico, the U.S. Virgin Islands, and other possessions which were not technically "countries," but which seemed as though they should count in a person's travel tally. I said to myself: "Someone should make a list of all the 'Travel Countries' in the world!" Sometime in early 2001, I stumbled across a blurb about the Travelers' Century Club in an in-flight magazine, and thought "These people have created 'The List!' " At that point, I realized that at 75 or so TCC countries, I didn't even qualify to join the TCC, and resolved to get to 100. Soon thereafter, I recall adjusting an itinerary within my RTW ticket. Instead of flying from Seoul to Hong Kong non-stop, I chose to spend a day in Taipei. Upon making that change, I realized that list-driven country maximization behavior might become something of an obsession. 100 soon became 200, two years became three, then four, then five. The rise of airline alliances and concurrent universe of RTW ticket possibilities supported my daily habit of travel planning.

Do you remember the point where you said to yourself, "I can really accomplish this"?

In the early 2000s, the only legitimate authority on counting travel destinations was the TCC, so I was following their list, which were 314 countries at the time. I was completely focused on building beautiful itineraries, and creatively planning around locations which had been described as difficult. For example, many top travelers had described to me their frustration at being unable to visit the British Indian Ocean Territory (BIOT), due to the highly secure and inaccessible American naval base there at Diego Garcia. While staying in the Maldives, I had a long conversation with my resort's Danish general manager, and we both realized that the southernmost Maldivian island of Gan was a seaplane's ride away from the northernmost atoll in BIOT. I audaciously reached out by email to the naval commander of Diego Garcia. Surprisingly, he responded, and referred me to the British Governor of the territory, who was receptive to my overtures. He told me that any seaplane access attempt would be (literally) shot down, but that I was welcome to arrive in the non-restricted northern atolls by boat. My new Danish friend used his Maldivian connections to suggest a boat, and I quickly rounded up three other top travelers to share costs. The voyage went off without a hitch, and the governor even sent out a special patrol boat overnight from Diego Garcia to give us passport stamps up on our arrival. This success gave me confidence that with the right gumption, creativity, respect, and hard work, any destination in the world could be reached.

What have you done over your life to gain the freedom and finances to pursue as much travel as you have?

I was an early employee at a software company, which went public in 1998 during the first Internet bubble. In 1999 and early 2000, the company had an astronomical valuation, which led me to stop working and decide to travel for a year. I sold a small portion of my stock, and begun the journey. In March of 2000, shortly after I began traveling, the stock crashed heavily, and continued a downward trend until stabilizing in 2002. At that point, I had to seriously consider going back to work. However, the stock rose slowly again until 2008, leaving me comfortable enough to continue traveling, albeit with a stricter budget. In 2008, the stock crashed again, and, with three children now in the world, I could not afford the luxury to travel extensively any more. I returned to work in 2010, and now try to make one or two journeys a year to new places.

Was there ever a time you felt like abandoning this goal?

The goal to "go everywhere" is a lifetime aspiration, so death would be the only true abandonment of that goal. I have faced major setbacks over the last 5 years which caused me to cancel or postpone indefinitely many trips and plans, but those would never cause me to totally abandon the goal to visit as many new places as possible. Having experienced many twists and turns in the road of life over the years, I realize that I may not be able to see the road ahead, but I am optimistic that it will turn back in my favor at some point, and when it does, my bags will be packed and ready to go to new destinations.

What were your worst travel experiences (i.e. detainment, bribes, car accidents, sickness, etc.) and why?

I generally find the silver lining in most travel experiences, but there was little to recommend the M/V *Bounty Bay* and its company Pacific Expeditions, run by the criminal Graham Wragg. I am probably one of the few repeat customers ever to sail on the "Bouncy Bay," and wish I hadn't either time. Although it did bring us to land on Howland and Baker Islands, as well as three of the Phoenix Islands, the unpleasantness of the boat forever tarnished the memories. A small steel catamaran, with sardine-can bunks in the unventilated pontoons, the *Bounty Bay* could barely make five knots under most conditions. It was dripping with cockroaches and reeked of diesel, and rode every Pacific wave it could find through full peak and trough. There was never sufficient water, the electrical system was overloaded and jury-rigged, and the crew was perpetually angry, since they inevitably hadn't been paid and were going to quit. Suffice it to say, the voyages never elapsed as advertised. On my first voyage, we spent nearly four weeks at sea, from Apia to Swains, Tokelau, Phoenix Islands, Baker, Howland, and then a seven-day run back to Funafuti, Tuvalu. Although we wished to kiss the ground in Funafuti, we were detained for several hours from doing so, since Graham hadn't registered the boat, or paid customs, and of course the captain was reticent to part with his personal funds to the Tuvalu authorities. I remember one low point from that voyage, where I was SCUBA diving with U.S. Fish and Wildlife people who were collecting fish and coral samples. The blood from the fish-spearing was attracting sharks, and at least six of them were circling my legs as we called the dive short and surfaced prematurely. Somehow, the crew had lost a visual fix on our dive spot, and allowed the vessel to drift off at least a mile away, and now could not find us in the setting sun. We treaded water in strong chop for at least 45 minutes while fending off the circling sharks. At one point a booby landed in the hair of one of the female Fish and Wildlife officers, and tried to sit down and nest on her head! I will never forget the surprise on her face! I personally realized how far away from help we were at that moment, and, were anything to happen, we would almost certainly die. Two years later, and against my better judgment, I signed up again to ride on the "Bouncy Bay" in hopes of finally visiting all four Pitcairn Islands over the course of two weeks. Again, problems were evident from the start as the sailing was delayed in Mangareva, and the irate, unpaid captain told us his detailed opinions about Graham the owner. On the first night, one of the engines failed, and we hobbled into Pitcairn on a detour from the original route. For two days, a junior mechanic and ship's mate took apart the faulty engine and tried and failed to put it back together again, at which point the remainder of the trip was abandoned. We limped back to Mangareva on one engine a week early, without accomplishing any of our itinerary — and none of us ever saw a refund.

What do you consider the most adventurous trip you have taken?

I was 72 days at sea on the *S.A. Agulhas* from Cape Town, landing on Bouvet by helicopter, visiting SANAE at the Ross Sea Ice Shelf, stuck in ice for two straight weeks, and celebrating Christmas and New Year's onboard with the crew. We also crossed the Southern Atlantic, dropping weather buoys regularly, before landing on South Thule Island, the southernmost of the South Sandwich Islands, and a little-known key point in the Falklands War. Upon my return to Cape Town, I marveled at and was overwhelmed by the bustle of the city, not to mention modern-day conveniences such as ATM's. I felt like a caveman caught in a time warp. After so much time at sea, adjusting to civilization and mild temperatures took several days.

What were your most challenging countries to visit and why?

Of the UN countries, Saudi Arabia was always one of the most difficult places to obtain a visa. Saudis have little interest in welcoming those who are not Muslim, and who have no business interests there. Over the years, I must have stopped by 12 different Saudi embassies inquiring about a visa, but was always rebuffed. Eventually, as a temporary solution, I was able to purchase flights into and out of Jeddah, and was approved for a 24-hour transfer visa. I spent a day and night in Jeddah during the Hajj season, and thought that might be the last of it. However, through my return to work in 2010, I met a few Saudi princes, one of whom was interested in exploring a joint venture. One day in New York, he asked for my passport, along with the passports of four of my colleagues. Within one hour, we all received five-year, multiple entry TOURIST visas for Saudi Arabia. Since then, I have been to Riyadh twice with much better hospitality than my initial experience — proof that you should never stop trying, even when progress seems impossible. For example, to visit Peter I Island off the coast of Antarctica took five years, with many false starts. In 2005, the whole Peter I Island team flew to Ushuaia, after three years of fundraising, only to have the chartered boat be a no-show due to mechanical failure. Those hardships only make the eventual arrival to a place more satisfying. I am still awaiting that satisfaction for both Nicobar Islands and Paracel Islands, after ten years of frustrated attempts. I suppose that the most challenging "countries" to visit will always be, by definition, the ones not yet visited.

What is the strangest thing you've seen/experienced while traveling?

I recall a scene in the Mogadishu Airport in Somalia — the one about 50km out of town, which was the only one in commercial use in 2003 — where two men loaded a passenger aircraft through the nosecone with raw camel meat. Now, this was not processed meat; these were primitively butchered parts like full legs and carcasses. And two guys in flowing dishdashes were making runs from their pickup truck to the nosecone storage compartment of the aircraft. Together, they would deadlift, clean, and jerk the giant camel part from the ground, approach the aircraft with the odd, bleeding cargo at arm's length overhead, then jump up and slam the meat into the storage area, with a minimum of both decorum and sanitary consideration. They seemed to make light of this bloody work, prosecuting the camel alley-oop with a jaunty air. When I asked them who wanted this grisly product, and why they were pursuing such a gory profession, they replied: "Saudis like it."

Which travel experiences stand out the most and why?

I recall an unlikely revelation while standing on the most unimpressive rocks of Kingman Reef, 33 miles off of Palmyra Atoll in the South Pacific. This reef barely surfaces, so only just qualifies as a "land area" according to the DXCC, the official body regulating Ham Radio geography. A land area is required to exist consistently above sea level for 100 meters in a straight line at high tide, and Kingman Reef only just qualified. We had sailed to Kingman from the relatively lush and verdant Palmyra that morning, and landed by rowboat, only to find no more than a pile of rocks and coral, smoothed by wave action over the aeons, to form somewhat of a rocky mound no more than ten feet across, and four to six feet above the water, extending for maybe 200 yards at most. It was a lifeless pile of small rocks and sand. Or was it? As I turned away to go, disappointed, I noticed that there was a stray coconut, or two, or three, perched there on the mound. What were coconuts doing there? There were no trees for at least 33 miles… And then it stuck me. Those coconuts had floated across the sea. They had randomly arrived on Kingman, and been propelled into a stable place on the rocks by tidal and wave action. And they hadn't just arrived. They were sprouting! They were attempting to lay down roots in this desolate and unpromising place! Of the hundreds of thousands of coconuts which must have fallen on Palmyra in the past year, these three were the ones who had made it on this particular 33 mile journey, and had climbed on-to the reef. It then struck me — stunningly — how perfectly these little vessels of life had been constructed for the journey. Round, hollow, with durable sides, and energy-filled interiors, they had sailed and rolled through the harshest of environments, and now had stationed themselves on the reef. Not only that, but they were now transforming themselves and consuming their own flesh in support of their sprouting stalks and roots in an attempt to settle here in these rocks. I could see now that this attempt was futile — that these coconuts would consume themselves and die, but the sheer AUDACITY that they would even attempt such a feat fully impressed me with the magnificence and power of nature, and of natural selection, and the life force always at work on Earth. Sometimes it takes the most extreme and austere conditions to make plain the simplest and most beautiful of principles.

What are the most overrated and underrated countries you've been to in your travels and why?

For some reason, I have found diving in the Great Barrier Reef to be a huge disappointment. I have tried diving there on five separate trips and every time seems to be following a storm, leaving close to zero visibility. While I love all parts of Australia in general, this supposed natural treasure has kept its charms elusive from me. Meanwhile, Slovenia stands out as an under-rated place. You never hear much about Slovenia, but I have driven through all 230 provinces in the country, and every twist and turn of road feels like a postcard. There are few more picturesque places on Earth. The country has good food, wine, friendly people, a stable economy, beaches, mountains, and river valleys, and all in a compact, first-world location, with reasonable prices. What's not to like?

What are the best and worst meals you have ever had traveling and where were they?

While living in Paris for three months, I realized I only had a month to go before moving away, and so began booking three-star Michelin restaurants one after the other. Soon I began experiencing debilitating pains in my side, and my complexion turned gray. I visited a local doctor. He informed me that I might want to cut back on the Michelin stars; that the human body wasn't built for that sort of thing, and that my tiny, inadequate gall bladder was backed up and overflowing with caloric richness. While those meals were all good, and I have enjoyed hundreds of similar gourmet meals, there is something to be said for a gigantic fresh lobster at Robinson Crusoe Island or Tristan da Cunha, or sashimi on the spot, from a fish just caught at sea. To me, the worst food is always a standard bag of junk food or tasteless sandwich or pizza in a gas station or airport snack shop, just because it has no sense of place, and signifies a lack of choice. I remember once waiting all day in airport queues in St Thomas to fight my way onto a flight to escape an impending hurricane. At that point, I had been on the road for six months or so, and was tired. And few places evoke less sense of place than the airport in Saint Thomas. Once through security, I found a single, horrible snack shack at which, hungry from the hours of fighting the crowds, I selected a single, horrible snack for the airport-inflated price of $5. Having only euros on-hand, I gave five euros, but received no change. When I inquired, the single, horrible snack shop lady said, "Exchange rate is 1-1." When I protested that wasn't generally the case around the world, she dismissed me haughtily with: "You need to travel more." I can't remember a meal less satisfying than that unmemorable, depressing snack.

What country made you feel most out of your comfort zone and why?

Clipperton Island is a horrible and spooky place, with a gloomy history of death, madness, and destruction to all who have attempted to settle there. Go read the stories of the reign of terror of Álvarez the Giant, the "Tyrant of Clipperton," who was eventually murdered by the very women he enslaved there. I visited Clipperton aboard a sportfishing vessel, since the tuna fishery surrounding Clipperton is world-class. Our group fed many friends and relatives that year with the tuna we caught. Franklin Roosevelt himself came here as President of the U.S. for sport fishing, and tasked U.S. Marines standing alongside him to shoot the inevitable shark or three which went after any tuna ensnared on his line. The surrounding sea is indeed rich with life. But the morbid ring of sand called Clipperton which circumscribes a brackish green lagoon is another story. First off, landing on the island was challenging, and I had to swim to shore through treacherous reefs and hundreds of sharks. Once on the beach, I was deafened by the horrible screams of thousands of nesting boobies, and tormented by the millions of beady, red-eyed crabs who comb every square inch of sand, ready to devour any organic material in their path. There was no other life to speak of — only the ruins of American WWII gear left by the U.S. Navy, who lost six ships attempting to build a proper landing on the island, with the idea of establishing an alternate wartime airfield towards the South Pacific. As I climbed the solitary guano-encrusted rock formation which forms the stone to Clipperton's gruesome ring, I could almost feel the ghost of Álvarez the Giant — the former Tyrant of Clipperton — haunting the spot. Soon I ran senselessly in fear — I ran around the entirety of the island, to escape the haunting screeches of the boobies and the relentless crabs. After ringing the island and finding it all eerie, frightening and worthless, I plunged back into the surf and risked the sharks to escape that horrible place. Simply put, I have no desire to return to Clipperton.

Do you speak any foreign languages? If so, which has been the most useful for you besides English?

I speak Spanish and French pretty well, and those both have been very useful in Latin America and the Francophone world respectively. It is easier to find English-speakers nowadays than ten years ago when I was traveling more extensively, but an effort in the local language nearly always brings advantage. I also speak Italian and German passably, but would trade those in an instant for Russian and Arabic — both languages which make an enormous difference in the quality of one's experience where they are spoken extensively. I can also order beer and come up with some basic words and phrases in a dozen or so other languages.

Looking back from when you started traveling to where you are now, in what ways, if any, have travel changed you?

I now have a much more complete worldview than in the year 2000. Even though I had been to roughly 50 TCC countries at that time, my understanding of the world was restricted by the Euro-American filter which I had experienced before then. Now, I can read through *The Economist* or *The New York Times* with a complete picture of what people are feeling in those areas, how they relate to their neighbors and their historical trade or colonial partners. A worldview is like a jigsaw puzzle, and mine had only a few connected pieces in place. I didn't even realize how many pieces there were at the time! Now, my puzzle is nearly complete, but still blurry in parts, and changing over time. I can only hope that it will continue to clarify and resolve to completion as the opportunity to travel further unfolds.

What is the longest continuous trip you have ever taken? When was it and where did you travel?

During the nearly four-year period from January 2000 to October 2003, when my first child was born, I was traveling full-time, with a stop at my apartment in San Francisco only for a day or two once every three-six months for special events or to run errands. That apartment felt like no more than another hotel during that stretch. The longest absolute time away from San Francisco was the first nine months of 2000, during which I traveled to Fiji, New Zealand, Australia, Bali, Hong Kong, Thailand, Nepal, Bhutan, India, Germany, France, Switzerland, Netherlands, Italy, Greece, and Pennsylvania (for my sister's wedding). I lived in Paris and Munich for three months each during this time, and returned to San Francisco only to attend a pair of social events.

What is your favorite "off-the-beaten-path" destination and why?

Lord Howe Island has been one of my "favorite places that no one knows about" since I first stopped there in 2001. This gorgeous island territory of Australia in the Coral Sea is a volcanic semi-crater a la Santorini, but much more fertile and lush than Santorini. Lord Howe is both a World Heritage Site, and an Australian national park. It is a tropical island, but not "too tropical," in that it is situated at 31 degrees south latitude — enough to have both palm trees and Cook pine trees. It has beautiful, desolate white-sand beaches for swimming or surfing, and offers fishing, bicycling, mountain-climbing, and hiking. Besides that, it has a small, picturesque village with friendly Australians offering good food and wine, none of the poverty or garbage associated with most tropical islands, and has a legal limit of 400 guest beds, which means it will never be overbuilt.

What are the best and worst places you have ever spent a night?

I've spent many nights in bad places, but perhaps the worst place was on Peter I Island, 400 miles off the coast of Antarctica, trapped overnight in freezing temperatures with three Chilean sailors, and without supplies. The four of us served as helicopter crew, and were offloading people and gear from the island to our ship following a two-week Ham Radio expedition (which won Expedition of the Year for 2007). In Antarctica, one must remove everything one introduces, and we had just finished evacuating our entire team and most of the small village which the team had constructed. All that was remaining were a few wooden pallets which had served as flooring, and a few odds and ends such as burlap sacks. With about five helicopter slingloads to go, the weather closed in, and the helicopter pilot bugged out, too scared to approach the surface of the island for fear of crashing in the snowblind. We were stranded. We fashioned a makeshift lean-to with the pallets as shelter, and lay together inside of the burlap sacks to conserve warmth. The Chileans' radios failed, and it was left to me to serve as communications manager and translator. When we signed off that night to conserve battery power, the feeling in my stomach was lost and forlorn. This was one of the most remote places on Earth. No other vessel of any kind — let alone one which could support helicopter operations — was within five days sailing; we were on our own. And it was difficult to sleep. One of the sailors snored so loudly in general that he was not allowed to share a cabin while on the ship; he slept in the "hospital" room on his own. The other three of us joked that the sound of his snores was the helicopter arriving to rescue us. Fortunately, about 21 hours later, a window in the clouds opened up, and the helicopter indeed came through. Two days later, the four of us returned to the island to finish evacuating the last five sling loads. I boarded the helicopter last, carrying the final item, an American flag which we had placed in the snow to mark the camp.

As for the best place to spend the night, there have been many, many castles and hotel suites and mansions and beach bungalows, but there is nothing better than waking up in the arms of your one true love, no matter where she may be.

In your opinion, what country or place in the world feels the most authentic and untouched by tourism?

Among UN countries, Bhutan used to feel a world apart, but was already rapidly changing last I visited in 2007. Vast portions of Russia are almost completely un-touristy, which is not to say that they are comfortable for travelers! The world has thousands of wilderness islands such as Peter I Island which have barely been touched by humans, and where humans must take extreme precautions to survive, but which are bursting with animal activity both above and below the water. To spend extended time among penguins and seals in their extended native colonies is to truly appreciate nature, and the beauty of life.

In your opinion, where is the most beautiful place on Earth?

It is so difficult to select a single spot as the most beautiful place on Earth, since perspectives and weather change from day to day and hour to hour. So many of the places considered "beautiful" on a clear day are picturesque because they are verdant, which means they are rainy much of the year. Many "beautiful" tropical islands lose their charm somewhat during cyclone season, and many beautiful mountain vistas are less appealing when swathed in fog. Over the years, I've noticed a phenomenon I'll call "West 45", which means that the west coasts of places around 45 or so north or south latitude all seem to be pretty gorgeous. This includes the west coast of the South Island of New Zealand, the west coast of Tasmania, the Chiloe Island area of Chile, the west coast of Vancouver Island, and (higher up due to the Gulf Stream), the west coasts of Ireland, Scotland, and the Fjordlands of Norway. Of course, the weather in these places is hit or miss, so you might get the most beautiful day of your life, or you might be miserable and wet. If I had to pick a few places which stun me every time I visit, they would be:

1. The Grindelwald and Lauterbrunnen Valleys in the Berner Oberland, Switzerland

2. The north shore of Kauai (including the Na Pali coast)

3. A stretch of road north of Punakaiki, South Island, New Zealand, where the black sand beaches lead to oversized primordial ferns at the base of the majestic snow-capped Southern Alps.

What do you enjoy most when traveling (cities, nature, people, cultural spots, etc.) and why?

I enjoy crossroad places where people congregate and interact, such as markets, transport hubs, and bars and restaurants. It is easy to strike up conversations, to find out what people value, and learn where they aspire to go. These are also likely spots to find fellow travelers, and apt to be crowded and lively. Few things bore me more than a dusty old museum!

What travel accomplishments are you most proud of?

I'm proud to have created the Most Traveled People community of travelers, which was conceived as a way to share information, and to help fellow travelers avoid many of the pitfalls which I had encountered. It was also the first open system of record about who had actually gone where, as well as the first democratic voting system among travelers about what constitutes "everywhere."

If you had just one personal travel story to share with someone, what would that be?

When I was 22, and a young professional in Boston, I flew to Las Vegas to hike the Grand Canyon with an Australian friend. We drove through the night and started down the Bright Angel Trail at daybreak. It was the height of summer, and temperatures at the bottom of the canyon were well over 110 degrees. My friend wasn't drinking enough water, and she began experiencing circulatory problems towards the bottom, then passed out. This was long before the days of cell phones or other emergency trackers. I carried her to shade, then left her in the care of two campers who were trying to purify water from the Colorado River, and ran two miles in the heat to the ranger station to get help, then ran two miles back to her while the ranger walked quickly behind. He told me to force her to drink water, which he handed to me. When it became evident that we would need more water for her, the ranger asked me to run back again to the ranger station to collect more water, so I ran another four miles to and fro in the blazing summer sun. Fortunately, all of the attention prevented her from heatstroke or worse, and she fully recovered, remaining in the shade until the direct sun had passed. As dusk approached, she leaned on me while we walked on to Phantom Ranch. Their chili dinner was even more delicious than usual that night, and I slept very soundly before hiking up again the next day. As for her, she elected to ride up on a donkey, and I had no qualms about handing over that burden!

Besides your home country, where do you find yourself returning to over and over and why?

Some of my favorite spots in the world, which I always go out of my way to visit, and in no particular order, are: London; Paris; Sydney; Hong Kong; Lauterbrunnen/Berner Oberland, Switzerland; North Shore of Kauai; Tofino, BC, Canada; Lord Howe Island; and Cape Town. The common theme here is natural beauty, good food, and interesting culture.

What is the ideal amount of time you prefer to travel each trip before you are ready for home and a break?

I truly don't know the answer to this question. It might be that when I am traveling, I feel most at home. During 2000-2003, when I had the time and the resources, I only returned home out of necessity for a day or two, for notable social events such as weddings, or to catch up on things which required my personal presence. Aside from that time, I have always had time restrictions due to work and children. Whenever I am traveling, I want to continue — to spend another day, to move to the next place, to eat at the next restaurant, to turn down the next unexplored side alley. So it may be that I prefer never to return home.

If you had an unlimited budget and space and time was no object, what would your perfect travel day look like? (for example: start your morning in Bora Bora; afternoon on a safari in Kenya; night in Australia, etc.)

I would follow the sun and travel westward, stretching one day into two, and all locations would be new ones. My day would by start watching the sunrise from Minami Torishima in the Pacific, whereupon I would zip through Oecussi for breakfast, go for a morning walk in the mountains of Mustang, and cool off with a dip in the Indian Ocean waters off of the Nicobar Islands. All terrorism and unrest would magically cease in Pakistan, as I set out with my picnic lunch on a drive through my remaining three provinces, after which I would track nesting giant tortoises in the Aldabra's. After tanning for 30 minutes in Darfur, I would leap north to Jan Mayen and Bjornoya to commune with polar bears, prior to heating up again in Trindade and diving at Saint Peter & Saint Paul Rocks. I would then dine on fresh lobster on Saint Felix Island, prior to enjoying the sunset sequentially through Ducie, Henderson, and Oeno. For dessert, something cold at South Orkney Island, after which I would humbly request the U.S. Navy let me spend the night at Guantanamo Bay, Cuba.

For those looking to travel to every country, what is the best piece of advice you could offer them?

Plan as if every minute will be accounted for, but then be prepared to throw away the plan. The advance planning about things like driving distances, flight schedules, visa requirements, and opening hours, will help you make good decisions when the inevitable complications arise. Weather, labor strikes, insurrections, mechanical failures, high seas, and other annoyances large and small, have a way of cropping up just as you arrive in a location, and especially in remote areas. Armed with knowledge and flexibility (and the required three travel virtues: patience, persistence, and politeness), you can normally turn hostile situations into unexpected opportunities for unforgettable memories. And when all else fails, be prepared to walk away and revisit a target destination months, years, or even decades later. Time and time again, I have begrudgingly abandoned carefully laid plans of arriving in places, due to circumstances beyond my control, thinking that I would never again be in such proximity, only to find myself arriving years later via a better way.

For someone that has been almost everywhere, what still gets you excited about packing your bags again?

"The more you know, the more you know that you don't know." I think this truism applies to the Most Traveled People. They, more than anyone, realize that it is impossible to "go everywhere" in one lifetime, and so get more and more motivated for each new journey. Every takeoff on a flight, every embarkation, every train and car departure is a new opportunity for adventure. Even familiar places change over time, and so revisiting old haunts can be just as informative as new ones. The road always beckons.

Do you feel you have missed out on certain aspects of life being away from home so much?

No. I had the good fortune to be able to travel full-time for many years, and never say to myself "I wish I hadn't."

Looking ahead, what travel plans and goals are you still pursuing, and what is on your "Bucket List"?

I will always maintain the goal "to go everywhere," as long as I live. At present, my main geographic goals — in no particular order — are to visit the remaining three Pitcairn Islands (Henderson, Oeno, Ducie); to visit my three remaining Pakistani provinces, to hike to the Himalayan Kingdom of Mustang, and to bring my girlfriend on her first 'round-the-world itinerary for our honeymoon.

Michael Novins, U.S.A.

(Michael Novins in front of the Church of Saint George, Lalibela, Ethiopia, January 2013)

Where did you grow up and what was your early life like?

I was born in Brooklyn, NY in 1964 and my family moved to central New Jersey, an hour outside of New York City, in the late 1960s. We traveled frequently during my childhood, mostly during summer vacations, but our family trips were typically road trips along the I-95 corridor to Florida. I didn't travel outside the Eastern Time Zone until 1986, when I left to attend law school at the University of Chicago, or overseas until 1992, when I made my first trip to Europe (two weeks split between London and Paris).

When did you go from casually traveling to making this a full-time goal, and what motivated you to travel to every country?

During much of the 1990s, I was a corporate attorney at one of the world's largest law firms. Before I joined the firm in 1994, I had made a few overseas trips to Europe, but hadn't really traveled widely. A little more than a year after joining the firm, an opportunity arose for me to spend a few weeks practicing out of the firm's office in Hong Kong, so, in November 1995, I boarded Cathay Pacific for the flight from JFK to Kai Tak Airport (with a pit stop in Vancouver — at that time, flights couldn't make it from New York to Asia without a refueling stop). Over the next several years, I worked on projects around the world, mostly out of the firm's offices in London, Madrid, Moscow and Warsaw in Europe and Hong Kong and Jakarta in Asia, but I also spent time working in destinations in Africa (Cairo), the Indian subcontinent (Mumbai), South America (Caracas and Rio de Janeiro) and Australia (Brisbane). I quickly realized that if I had a meeting scheduled for a Monday or Tuesday, I could leave New York on the preceding Friday and spend the weekend either in my destination or somewhere along the way and could do the same on the return. So, by way of actual examples, I might stop in Dublin on the way to London and Reykjavik on the return, or in Honolulu on the way to Jakarta and Sydney on the return. So long as the airfare was less than or equal to what I otherwise would have paid for a more direct routing, the firm was indifferent (and if the fare was more, I would pay the excess). Even though I was limited to four weeks of vacation each year, I mixed in trips to new countries between my business trips, and by the time I left the law firm I had visited dozens of countries on six continents.

Do you remember the point where you said to yourself, "I can really accomplish this"?

I'm not sure I ever thought that it would be difficult to visit all of the countries. Rather, I think that it will be much more difficult to visit all of them well — by that I mean, to visit all of the most interesting museums (art, archeology and natural history are my primary interests); World Heritage Sites; birthplaces, residences and graves of the famous and infamous; zoos and aquariums; historic hotels, restaurants and bars; the best wildlife experiences; and natural wonders. While I would like to visit all of the countries in the world, it is much more appealing to me to try to visit all of their first level administrative divisions *(e.g.,* states, provinces or oblasts), at least for the larger countries, which will provide a much broader survey of each country, and to make a significant dent on the list of World Heritage Sites. Since my interests are much broader than just visiting all of the countries, I find myself returning to countries rich in World Heritage Sites, like Spain, where I recently (November 2014) undertook a 1,500-mile driving tour to visit 11 World Heritage Sites and my final four autonomous communities (it was my fourth vacation to peninsular Spain, not counting several business trips to Madrid or trips to the Balearic and Canary Islands). I made a similar trip last summer (August 2013) to South Africa to visit my final four provinces, two World Heritage Sites and three major national parks: Addo Elephant National Park in Eastern Cape, Kruger National Park (my second visit, this time to the northern portion in Limpopo) and Pilanesberg Game Reserve in North West (it was my fourth trip to South Africa).

What have you done over your life to gain the freedom and finances to pursue as much travel as you have?

Since I travel frequently for work and take advantage of mileage-earning credit cards, I am often able to redeem frequent flyer miles to purchase international tickets. With a little research and a long lead time (sometimes 11 months in advance), I have been able to use frequent flyer miles to get plane tickets for many of my international trips. For example, later this month (December 2014), I'll be flying to Darwin, Australia and back from Bangkok, with a stopover in Seoul, with a ticket that I obtained using Delta SkyMiles. I also recently redeemed Delta SkyMiles for a round trip ticket from Los Angeles to Port Moresby in August 2015, with a stopover in Brisbane on the return, when I'll fly on Qantas to Lord Howe Island, which I obtained with my Alaska Airlines miles. In recent years I have also been able to redeem miles for trips, by way of examples, to

Madagascar, Kazakhstan (with a return from Turkmenistan), Easter Island, Palau, Cape Verde, Ethiopia, Angola and Mongolia, all of which would have been expensive to purchase. For me, I am far more limited by time than resources, since I only have four weeks of annual vacation. So, I try to maximize my vacation time by departing on Fridays and returning on the next succeeding Sunday (to stretch a one-week vacation to nine days) and traveling over every holiday weekend. Over the several three-day holiday weekends each year, I try to visit a nearby destination in the United States, Canada, Mexico or the Caribbean, and then make longer trips during my week-long vacations.

Was there ever a time you felt like abandoning this goal?

One of the nice things about trying to visit most of the World Heritage Sites is that new sites are added to the list each June. So, chasing the list of World Heritage Sites encourages repeat visits to countries that I may have already visited several times. For example, during my second trip to Israel and Palestine in March 2014, I visited all of their World Heritage Sites then on the list, but new sites were added in both places in June 2014, so I'll need to plan a return.

What were your worst travel experiences (i.e. detainment, bribes, car accidents, sickness, etc.) and why?

Fortunately, I have largely avoided major mishaps, so aside from the expected border shakedowns, I haven't had any major incidents, except maybe for a motorbike accident on Easter Island. Easter Island is not a place where you want to get a third-degree muffler burn on your leg, which is what happened to me when driving too quickly on rain-soaked dirt roads in the island's interior. I crashed my motorbike the day before departure and flew to Rangiroa with my calf wrapped in toilet paper. The wound got progressively worse and the owner of the inn in Rangiroa kindly arranged for me to visit a local physician, who had me bite down on a dowel while he scraped off layers of burnt flesh and cleansed the wound. Even though the doctor advised me not to get the wound wet, nothing was going to stop me from drift-snorkeling with sharks and large schools of fish through the Tiputa Pass in Rangiroa. Notwithstanding that

I ignored the doctor's instructions, the wound healed and disappeared.

What do you consider the most adventurous trip you have taken?

I spent November 1997 in Jakarta on business and decided that I was going to celebrate the Thanksgiving holiday with a short visit to Komodo Island. There was at the time very little information available on the Internet about visiting Komodo, so the best I could do was to fly to Labuan Bajo's airport (since renamed Komodo Airport), the closest airport to Komodo Island, and hope that I'd be able to make arrangements after arrival. There were a few fishermen outside the airport willing to take me (along with a couple that I met at the airport) to Komodo Island. I stayed at the ranger station at Loh Liang, which had very basic bungalows and a restaurant, and the rangers organized a hike to the Banugulung viewing area, an hour from Loh Liang. There were several Komodo dragons at the Banugulung viewing area, but it was also easy to see them while walking around the grounds at Loh Liang. I grew up watching *Wild Kingdom* and *National Geographic* documentaries and I thought the places that they featured were for the very few who were able to mount an expensive expedition, like David Attenborough in *Zoo Quest for a Dragon*. Getting to and wandering around Komodo Island showed me that it wasn't that difficult to visit interesting wildlife destinations and that trip has spurred many others.

What were your most challenging countries to visit and why?

By 2001, I had earned enough frequent flyer miles to visit Saudi Arabia — the only obstacle was obtaining one of the world's most notoriously difficult visas. At that time, my law firm had an office in Riyadh and they helped me obtain a business visa. Aside from jumping through the bureaucratic hoops to obtain the visa, travel inside Saudi Arabia was surprisingly easy, and I spent a week split between Riyadh and Jeddah (where I visited a site in each city that would much later be added to the list of World Heritage Sites). Some other countries, notably Belarus, Angola and Libya, make it difficult to get a tourist visa, but with persistence, creativity and a good local contact, I was able to get visas to visit all three of those countries.

What is the strangest thing you've seen/experienced while traveling?

I very often try to experience a country through its cuisine, where some of the dishes are unusual, such as green turtle, which I ate many years ago in the Bahamas (on a separate trip, I managed to access the turtle farms in Grand Cayman). On other trips I dined on scorpions in Beijing, llama in Bolivia, musk ox in Greenland, hákarl (or putrid basking shark) in Iceland, minke whale at Tokuya (one of the world's most famous whale restaurants) in Osaka, dog-meat soup in North Korea, camel in Libya and Syria, tenrec in Mauritius, moose in Newfoundland, cuy (guinea pig) in Peru, and flying fox (or fruit bat) in Vanuatu, only some of which were delicious. Equally strange are some of the markets that sell these items and the strangest markets that I have visited are Qingping Market in Guangzhou, a veritable edible zoo (with cages and buckets full of snakes, cats, raccoons, turtles, monkeys, etc.); Marché Mont-Bouët, the largest market in Libreville, Gabon, which has a bush meat section located deep in its center (which during my visit was selling enormous pythons and their eggs, bush pigs and assorted primates); and Akodessewa fetish market in Lome, Togo, reputedly the world's largest, with an array of animal skulls, skins, teeth and feathers.

Which travel experiences stand out the most and why?

I have visited many of the world's best wildlife destinations, many of which rank among my most memorable travel experiences. My most incredible wildlife trips include seeing grizzly bears pluck salmon out of the air at Brooks Falls in Katmai National Park, Alaska; closely approaching Pacific grey whales in Laguna San Ignacio on the Baja peninsula, Mexico; feeding hyenas by hand in Harar, Ethiopia; seeing giant tortoises (including Lonesome George, the last known Pinta Island tortoise, since deceased) on the Galapagos Islands; boating with humpback whales in Greenland and sperm whales near Kaikoura, New Zealand; seeing the great wildebeest migration in the Masai Mara Game Reserve, Kenya; getting within a few feet of

Komodo dragons on Komodo Island, Indonesia; seeing and hearing the Indri, the world's largest lemur (with a booming call) after a long, muddy hike in Andasibe-Mantadia National Park, Madagascar; taking the Tundra Buggy to see polar bears near Churchill, Manitoba; seeing one of the world's few remaining pink pigeons on Ile aux Aigrettes, an island nature reserve in Mauritius; swimming in a virtual lava lamp among thousands of jellyfish in Jellyfish Lake, Palau; making a one-hour climb by horseback to Cerro Pelon to see enormous gatherings of monarch butterflies in their overwintering grounds; driving alongside wild dogs while on the hunt for impalas in the Okavango Delta, Botswana; riding an elephant to penetrate the thick grass to see Indian rhinoceroses in Chitwan National Park, Nepal; taking a boat to see entire trees flashing with fireflies in Kuala Selangor, Malaysia; trekking to see mountain gorillas in Parc National des Volcans, Rwanda and Bwindi Impenetrable National Park, Uganda; seeing all sorts of marsupials, like koalas, kangaroos, wallabies and echidnas on Kangaroo Island, Australia; snorkeling with whale sharks in the Maldives; and cage-diving with great white sharks in "shark alley" near the fishing village of Gansbaai, South Africa.

What are the most overrated and underrated countries you've been to in your travels and why?

While I haven't been to any country that I would classify as overrated, I have been to popular parts of some countries that weren't particularly interesting, at least not to me. For me, international travel is about seeing that which is unique in each country, so my first category of overrated destinations are those that seem manufactured, where most of the history has been erased and which are inauthentic. In this category, I would lump Dubai, Las Vegas and Orlando, probably three of the least interesting places that I have visited, but all of which seem to attract an enormous number of visitors. My second category is beach destinations. While there are very interesting sites in most of the Caribbean countries, it seems odd to me to travel so far to spend the day reclining on a beach, experiencing nothing that makes a place different from its neighbors. I have many more countries in my underrated category, which I would top with Mexico. Since Mexico is an easy trip from New York, I have made more than two dozen trips to visit all of its 31 states. Mexico offers 32 World Heritage Sites (of which I have visited 28) scattered around the country, most of which are easy to reach by bus (and Mexico has one of the world's best and most comprehensive bus systems). Second on my list is Nigeria. Before visiting, I had read mostly negative reviews of Nigeria; however, having visited, I regret only spending a couple of days in Lagos and not seeing more of the country. Lagos is one of Africa's most vibrant cities and is a great place to see live music, particularly at New Africa Shrine, a club established by Femi Kuti (Fela's son), or the Nimbus Art Centre, located next door to Bogobiri House, an excellent boutique hotel, where I stayed. Third on my list is Sri Lanka. The island nation is small and easy to cover during a week-long vacation, with several World Heritage Sites, colonial buildings and national parks with a wide variety of wildlife. Sri Lanka is very easy to get around by inexpensive hired car (with driver) or train. Fourth on my list is Syria (or at least it was during my visit in 2009), which likewise has several World Heritage Sites, great cuisine, one of the world's best bus systems and historic hotels (I stayed in room 203 of the Baron Hotel, Aleppo, the oldest hotel in Syria, the same room where Agatha Christie wrote the first part of *Murder on the Orient Express*).

What are the best and worst meals you have ever had traveling and where were they?

For me, a great meal is not only about the quality of the food, but also the atmosphere and authenticity (which is why I generally avoid restaurants established by celebrity chefs who have restaurants around the world but who are rarely in the kitchen). I have eaten at some great Michelin three-star restaurants, my two favorites being Taillevant in Paris and Arzak in San Sebastian, but I've had equally great meals at less well-known restaurants, like Taverna Dajkua Paidhaqe in Tirana, which served the best grilled lamb chops I've ever had (I went twice during my time in Tirana and I rarely revisit a restaurant during a short visit); Brasserie des Facultés in Algiers, Algeria (because the restaurant-bombing scene in *The Battle of Algiers* was filmed at the restaurant); El Obrero in Buenos Aires, probably the best steakhouse I've eaten at; Ristorante Castelli in Addis Ababa, one of the best Italian restaurants outside Italy; and Schwartz's in Montreal, which serves the world's best smoked meat sandwiches (which — speaking as a New Yorker — is difficult to concede).

What country made you feel most out of your comfort zone and why?

I visited Libya in May 2013, during a relatively safe period for travel, where I was the only guest at my hotel, one of very few at the restaurants and the only overseas tourist at Leptis Magna and Sabratha. I also spent time wandering around the ruins of Bab al-Azizia, the partially demolished military barracks and compound that served as the main base for Muammar Gaddafi until its capture by anti-Gaddafi forces in August 2011. Throughout my trip, an armed guide accompanied me, but he wasn't with me while I was wandering around Tripoli listening to sporadic, nearby gunfire.

Do you speak any foreign languages? If so, which has been the most useful for you besides English?

I only speak English (along with traveler's Spanish). While English may only be the world's third most spoken language, it must be the world's most widely spoken second language and is the most useful language for travelers.

Looking back from when you started traveling to where you are now, in what ways, if any, have travel changed you?

As hackneyed as it may sound, international travel has made me better informed and has also allowed me to challenge stereotypes and myths propagated by various governments (including my own).

What is the longest continuous trip you have ever taken? When was it and where did you travel?

I spent November 1996 traveling around India and Nepal, but since I have worked full-time since graduating from law school in 1989, my longest trips otherwise have been two-week trips between jobs or over the December holidays.

What is your favorite "off-the-beaten-path" destination and why?

Nowadays, most of the world is "on the beaten path", but my favorite regions that perhaps see fewer visitors than other more popular regions are Central Asia (specifically Uzbekistan) and the Maghreb (from Algeria through Libya to Tunisia).

What are the best and worst places you have ever spent a night?

The best place that I have stayed is a villa at the Conrad Maldives, where I ate at the world's first underwater restaurant. The resort offers amazing activities, like snorkeling with whale sharks and watching manta rays feed from the bridge that connects its two main islands. I would also include on my list of "best hotels" the American Colony Hotel in Jerusalem, Hotel El-Djazair in Algiers, Hotel Arctic in Ilulissat, western Greenland (for its view), and the Lake Palace Hotel, set on an island in the middle of Lake Pichola in Udaipur, India.

I haven't stayed at too many bad places, but one that comes to mind was the hotel in Almetyevsk, Tatarstan, Russia, where the cleaning staff left my room's windows open during the day, so by nighttime the room was abuzz with hundreds of mosquitoes. Fortunately, the bathroom door had remained closed so that room was mosquito-free. I spent the night sleeping on bedding dragged onto the bathroom floor.

In your opinion, what country or place in the world feels the most authentic and untouched by tourism?

As odd as it may sound, because the country welcomes more than six million visitors each year, India is one of the world's most authentic travel destinations. The six million visitors represent less than 1% of India's population, so the impact of tourism is highly diluted, especially away from the most popular sites. India is the world's most overwhelming and exasperating country to visit, but also one of the most interesting. While many other places around the world have become homogenized, much of India seems as if it hasn't changed in hundreds of years.

In your opinion, where is the most beautiful place on Earth?

Since all of my lengthier trips are to overseas destinations, I spend less time traveling around the United States and sometimes forget the great beauty of my home country, especially in the western national parks. In 2008, I visited Bryce Canyon National Park and the view of Bryce Canyon Amphitheater from Sunrise Point may be the most incredible landscape I have seen. I have been similarly awestruck during visits to other western national parks like Yellowstone National Park, with its geysers and other geothermal features, the eroded buttes of Badlands and Theodore Roosevelt National Parks, and the rock formations in Yosemite National Park.

What do you enjoy most when traveling (cities, nature, people, cultural spots, etc.) and why?

I have broad interests and am trying to visit all of the World Heritage Sites (but realize that while I may be able to dent the list, I won't finish it since some of the sites are very difficult to visit and new sites are added to the list each June). My favorite destinations are cities, where I try to visit all of the interesting museums (especially art, archeology and natural history), zoos and aquariums, markets, major historic sites and places associated with the famous and infamous (like birthplaces, residences and graves), and where I try to eat and drink at historic restaurants and bars and stay at historic hotels.

What travel accomplishments are you most proud of?

While I haven't been to as many places as some of the people interviewed for this book, I have been able to eat at or stay in a significant portion of the world's historic restaurants and hotels, visit more than a third of the World Heritage Sites and visit many of the best wildlife destinations. I also don't consider a country or region to have been visited if I merely fly through its airport, pass through by bus or train, or otherwise don't reasonably familiarize myself with an interesting city or site, at a minimum. My goal is to more slowly see more of less, rather than rushing to complete any list.

If you had just one personal travel story to share with someone, what would that be?

In August 2003, I went trekking to see mountain gorillas in Parc National des Volcans in northwestern Rwanda (earlier on the same trip I did the same in Bwindi Impenetrable National Park in Uganda). During the pre-trek briefing, we were instructed to maintain a safe distance from the gorillas, 20 feet or so as I recall, because they are unpredictable and highly susceptible to catching human respiratory infections. No one apparently told the gorillas, because while I was standing still and taking photos of the large silverback, a much smaller gorilla blindsided me and grabbed my leg. I probably should have retreated, but I had been surprised and was completely surrounded by other gorillas so it seemed more prudent to freeze and wait for them to pass. After what I'm sure was very brief contact, but which seemed much longer, the gorillas continued down the path. Wildlife encounters don't get much closer than that.

Besides your home country, where do you find yourself returning to over and over and why?

I have visited Mexico more than two dozen times, in part due to its proximity, so it's an easy destination from New York over a long weekend, but also because it offers a lot to see, like its wildlife destinations (such as the monarch butterfly migration in Michoacan and the Pacific grey whale nurseries in Baja California Sur), historic cities (like Guanajuato, Zacatecas and Morelia), archaeological ruins (like Uxmal, Palenque and Monte Alban), the most interesting city in North America (Mexico City) and one of the world's best cuisines, combined with affordability and an easy-to-use public transportation system.

What is the ideal amount of time you prefer to travel each trip before you are ready for home and a break?

Since I work full-time, I am restricted in the amount of time that I can travel, so I haven't given any thought to how long an ideal trip would be, but rather what is realistic given my responsibilities. So for me, most of my trips extend over one week, and I am usually able to travel for a two-week period over the December holiday period.

If you had an unlimited budget and space and time was no object, what would your perfect travel day look like? (for example: start your morning in Bora Bora; afternoon on a safari in Kenya; night in Australia, etc.)

I have had a lot of perfect travel days, so instead of fantasizing about an impossible travel day, if I had an unlimited budget I may revisit some of my favorite days (not already mentioned above), like running with the bulls in Pamplona, Spain; hiking the so-called wild sections of the Great Wall of China without anyone else in sight; taking a catamaran to Devil's Island in French Guiana; sightseeing in the Potemkin village that is Pyongyang, North Korea; spending the day hiking around Bayanzag (also known as the Flaming Cliffs) in the Gobi Desert, Mongolia; climbing the world's highest sand dunes in Sossusvlei, Namibia; watching Valery Gergiev conduct Tchaikovsky's *Swan Lake* at the Mariinsky Theatre in Saint Petersburg, Russia; more safely traveling around Easter Island by motorbike to see the various Moai sites; or spending the day wandering around Venice or Jerusalem.

For those looking to travel to every country, what is the best piece of advice you could offer them?

Read widely, especially a newspaper with a large international section, like *The New York Times* — you'll soon follow story lines and may decide you'd like to see the locations where the events unfold. I would also suggest getting a credit card that allows its user to earn miles in one of the major frequent flyer programs (so long as you pay in full the credit card balance each month).

For someone that has been almost everywhere, what still gets you excited about packing your bags again?

I have only visited a little more than one third of the World Heritage Sites, so I have a lot more to see, and am glad that UNESCO adds new sites to the list every June, so the list will continue to expand.

Do you feel you have missed out on certain aspects of life being away from home so much?

Since I have worked full-time since I began traveling, I have taken advantage of long holiday weekends for many of my trips, so I have missed most family holiday gatherings over the last several years and expect that pattern to continue.

Looking ahead, what travel plans and goals are you still pursuing, and what is on your "Bucket List"?

My next trip will be in May 2015, when I am scheduled to visit Georgia and its Adjara autonomous republic. Later in the year, I have international trips planned in August to Papua New Guinea (including New Britain and New Ireland) and Lord Howe Island; in November to Fiji and Kiribati; and in December to Micronesia (Marshall Islands, Pohnpei and Chuuk) and Japan (Okinawa plus a few World Heritage Sites). In between those overseas trips, I have North American trips booked in April to Louisiana (to visit the Monumental Earthworks of Poverty Point, the United States' most recent addition to the list of World Heritage Sites); in July to Calgary (to visit its two nearby World Heritage Sites, Dinosaur Provincial Park and Banff National Park, part of the Canadian Rocky Mountain Parks World Heritage Site); and in October to Los Cabos, Mexico to visit some of the locations in the Islands and Protected Areas of the Gulf of California World Heritage Site.

I would like to visit many more World Heritage Sites and the remaining countries that I haven't seen, as well as to revisit those countries that I didn't properly explore on my first trip, like Nigeria (where I only spent time in Lagos), Venezuela (where I only spent two days on business in Caracas) and Tajikistan (where I only made a day trip to Penjikent).

Terry Last, England

(Terry Last in Mogadishu, Somalia, January 2015)

Where did you grow up and what was your early life like?

I grew up in Bethnal Green, East London, UK. It was a poor part of London which experienced plenty of crime and social problems. At the same time, it was a united community. People rarely went on foreign holidays but the seaside was great fun as kids. School was a hit and miss affair which included skipping lessons to play pool in the pub at 14. In the summer during the school holidays we (the estate kids) would usually play football (soccer), cricket, or go swimming over at Victoria Park Lido. I remember in the summer of 1972, Bob the bus conductor, went to Spain for his holidays and us kids spent the whole six weeks holiday discussing his holiday. He was like a God to us.

When did you go from casually traveling to making this a full-time goal, and what motivated you to travel to every country?

From about the age of 13, a family friend, Harry, used to visit and tell us his traveling stories. At that point, he had visited 33 countries and he and a German friend used to go backpacking together. My brother John and I loved hearing these stories and in effect got the travel bug before we had even left England. I would imagine it were all these far-flung places which really gave me a travel appetite. I first went abroad to Italy in 1980 to watch a football tournament and from then on continued following football (later other sports) as an excuse to travel. In 1983, when I had no football to watch that summer, I went to Egypt with John on my first foreign trip not involving football. After this trip, I mentally decided, should finances and time permit, I would like to visit all of the countries. The following year, I made many foreign trips and from then on began visiting new places.

Do you remember the point where you said to yourself, "I can really accomplish this"?

I was in Svalbard in 1993 and on the ship met a traveler who gave me a copy of the Travelers' Century Club (TCC) list. I looked at it and found some places listed were surprising, but I felt visiting all these places would be great fun and enjoyable, and being 30 years old at the time, I felt it was possible. Of course, I was ignorant at the time of some places needing a hard-to-obtain permit or that there would not always be ships going to the more remote islands. I did some research on my return and found various lists: UN members and territories (the main list for all); TCC (viewed more for Americans it seemed); the Guinness list (was for Britain and her former colonies); and CIGV (mainly for French speakers). I wanted to visit them all. Since 1993 I have averaged around two trips a month.

What have you done over your life to gain the freedom and finances to pursue as much travel as you have?

In 1993 I took a career break from work so I could travel — a big decision for me at the time. I then spent many months per year traveling. Then, after five years, my former employer said it was time to decide if I was to go back to work or not. I chose the latter. Due to some solid investments, I had the finances to travel frequently without working and still travel many months a year. I now have my own personal list of places I would like to visit, so "touch wood" that my finances will hold out.

Was there ever a time you felt like abandoning this goal?

I don't feel I have ever felt like abandoning my travel goals. I have in the past become jaded with travel, which has been mainly due to doing many similar trips on the bounce. I now try to mix trips so if I am in a cold climate on one trip the next trip may be historical, then a beach and so on.

I found an open conversation on the Wake Island trip in 2009 disturbing and slightly off-putting for travelers. The topic was sea territories, and if you are in a specific sea territory you can count the places nearby as a destination visited! I was truly amazed with the whole debate and half the people (a total of about ten) agreed with this. I guess we all have our own values on things, which is what makes life interesting.

What have been your worst travel experiences (such as detainment, bribes, car accidents, sicknesses, etc.) and why?

Several times in Africa the police have stopped me requesting a bribe, which is not very pleasant. In the Ivory Coast, I was held standing up against a wall for several hours in the sun, which was not fun. I was leaving that day and had all my valuables at the hotel, so I had no cash on me to give them as bribes. Eventually they gave up and left. In Togo, I was in a fetish market and failed to give a witchdoctor-type woman any money for apparently blessing me. Next thing I know I am surrounded by the screaming women and then men all shouting and shoving me. Luckily a local spoke English and sorted it all out. I guess I have been quite lucky traveling and most of my bad experiences have come in the U.S. because I do not drive and have to rely on public transport, which has often been not a great experience. For example, a couple of years ago in Raleigh, North Carolina at 5 a.m., I was waiting for a Greyhound bus to go to

New Bern when a group of black youths arrived on a bus and already at the station were another group of black youths. In no time at all a fight broke out with plenty of blood. I was the only white person present and had nowhere to go. Several black women moved to stand near me. The police finally arrived and dealt with the issue. Later on my bus some of the black women were on board and I asked why they stood near me and I was informed the police do not make arrests unless a white person gets caught up in the trouble and the gangs know this as well so they stood near to me guessing (correctly) that the fighting youths wouldn't come near me. They were also correct in that no one got arrested.

What do you consider one of the most adventurous trips you have taken?

Visiting the South Pole I would say, although just flying to places might not be considered an adventure. Seven of us ended up getting stuck for ten days at the camp, which really added to the feeling of remoteness. Traveling overland in Africa and even Asia can also be very adventurous with the added dangers it can bring.

What were your most challenging countries to visit and why?

Any country that requires a visa can be difficult and some countries make obtaining visas very difficult. I have been refused visas by several countries. Then, on the other hand, countries that are dangerous are also challenging. I just completed a three-day city tour of Mogadishu, Somalia, which is arguably the most fear-generating country to visit. The majority of people who I have met who tell me they have been there just visited the airport; under my personal criteria I do not count airports as a visit.

What's the strangest thing you've seen/experienced while traveling?

On the Banana Islands in Sierra Leone, I had given a family group a ride on a small boat taxi I had hired to get to the islands. For giving them a ride I was invited to attend a funeral. Their six year old boy had been alive at 5 p.m. the day before and at ten p.m. the same night he was found dead. A local island man checked him over and found no bites or cause of death. So he just waited for the rest of the family to arrive (I had given a lift on the boat to the father) and then they just buried the boy. No police, no government officials, etc. — just buried and that was it.

A private one week tour to North Korea brought about many conversations with the guides at the various tourist sights. They would ask many questions, and then once I had answered them they would tell me I was lying, or I was just repeating what the lying western media said, while at the time they would tell me stories such as how the Americans had murdered the Romanian leader Ceausescu in New York and I would then inform them their media had lied to them... so we had to agree to differ.

Which travel experiences stand out the most and why?

Since I was a boy, I had always wanted to visit Pitcairn Island. The book/film *Mutiny on the Bounty* was of major interest to a young boy in England at the time and conjured up many images. So I finally made it there and spent four nights on the island. Each place on the island had a unique name, such as Down Rope, Bitey-Bitey, Where Dan Fell, Nancy's Stone, etc. These names all added to the island's intrigue. The people there speak a great pidgin English. They are very friendly and make you feel really welcome.

In the mid 1990's, I spent a week on Kiritimati Island (also known as Christmas Island). In those days it only had a fisherman's charter flight once a week from Hawaii. On my second day there I was in the main village, London, and a huge Russian yacht arrives with two very pretty Russian women who get dropped off by the yacht's small boat with just their clothes they are wearing, and then the yacht sails off. By the time I had left the women were still there and I was told it was without a passport, so they would not be allowed to board the flight to Hawaii but would have to wait until the quarterly supply vessel from Tarawa arrived to take them off to the mainland.

In Guyana I stood atop of Kaieteur Falls drinking the water direct from the waterfall, and that left me with a wonderful feeling hard to beat.

What are the most overrated and underrated countries you've been to in your travels and why?

I guess I am most disappointed when I have put a country on a pedestal which then does not live up to my perceived expectations. It does not mean there is anything wrong with the country, but more that my own expectation was unrealistic. Egypt would fall into this category. In terms of underrated, Guyana and Ghana stand out for me. Guyana may have lots of crime in the capital but outside it has fabulous wildlife which feels untouched, whereas Ghana has plenty of sites to see, friendly people, and the coastal route has numerous places to relax and enjoy life.

What are the best and worst meals you have ever had traveling and where were they?

My best meal was in Padstow, UK. I visited Rick Stein's Fish Restaurant, which was fantastic. In Russia I have had many poor meals and am usually disappointed as the food regularly seems stale, can be cold, and has little flavor. When I travel I usually make a big effort to try local and unusual foods. In French Guiana I had a very life-like bat in red wine sauce with steamed rice. In China the roasted rat was very nice and I went back for seconds. In the jungle in Ecuador the lemon ants tasted just like lemon sherbet and were good. In Thailand the fried bugs taste a little like crisps (chips). I did not really enjoy boiled sheep brain in Turkey, though. I suppose our tastes are products of where we are brought up.

What country made you feel most out of your comfort zone and why?

Wallis Island. I got stuck there for ten days back in the 90's due to an airplane strike and I never found anyone who spoke English, which made life very difficult. Finding information out proved very hard. So I had to return to the airport every day just to find out what was happening. I did, however, meet Tony

Wheeler (he started the Lonely Planet guides) on my return flight, as he had got stranded on Futuna Island.

Do you speak any foreign languages? If so, which has been the most useful for you besides English?

I only speak English, and other than a visit to Wallis Island in the mid-1990's, I have never needed another language. Although, I do believe speaking the local language is likely to open a few doors that would otherwise be closed.

Looking back from when you started traveling to where you are now, in what ways, if any, has travel changed you?

When I first started to travel, my information on my destination usually came from school and the British media. By traveling I have learned that much of what I learned and thought I knew was wrong, such as why some people from other countries hold the views that they do, and also being more understanding of other cultures. Some years ago an incident occurred in the Middle East and within a few days I was in USA, Australia, France, and the UK. Each country's media took a different view on the events occurring, mainly for political reasons. In this instance, the Aussie media was clearly the better, probably because they had no real interest in what was happening, while if it was happening in the Pacific they too would probably have had biased reporting.

What was the longest continuous trip you have ever taken, when was it, where did you travel?

I had a three month trip to Asia and Australia back in 2004. My then-girlfriend (now wife), Natalie, came with me and we had our best-ever holiday together going all over Australia. I picked Australia because you cannot fail to enjoy it. In my backpacking days, groups of all nationalities would always gather together and have drinks and then the usual question, "Where is the best place to visit?" would come up. Only two countries really featured in the answers — Australia and New Zealand. With so many nationalities and age groups holding the same views, those countries must have something special.

What is your favorite "off-the-beaten-path" destination and why?

The Faroe Islands. It is not a scary or hard to get to place, but it's not well visited either. Very green (often wet), very clean, good people, and an incredible public transport system. It has great walking, which I really enjoy without people, and the islands have bundles of routes to take. Easy place to relax in and very scenic.

Another great country not visited a lot is Guinea-Bissau, and the Bijagos Archipelago there are particularly nice. Great, friendly people, superb food, very safe and plenty to see and do.

What are the best and worst places you have spent a night?

In Bangkok, Natalie treated me for my birthday to a couple of nights at the Oriental Hotel, which is one of the original colonial gem hotels dotted about the planet. Superb service (including a butler) with history thrown in.

My worst was spending several nights up on a mountain in the giant panda reserve near Wolong, China in 1994. Eight of us had a hose pipe for all our ablutions and we had sleeping bags on a platform. Each night the rats would jump on our legs, sniff around our face and generally stop any possible sleep. To top it all, we never saw any giant pandas in the wild!

In your opinion, what country or place in the world feels the most authentic and untouched by tourism?

Maybe North Korea, although now it is running alive with Chinese visitors who can even go on one night trips there if they want. The more usual untouched places I find are affected by media. Finding a group of people without mobile phones is an example. While the North Koreans, it would seem, have less access to our media and therefore less affected by the outside world.

In your opinion, what is the most beautiful place on Earth?

Of course, like all my answers, many of them are probably mood-dependent, and on a different day it could be a different answer, but I would say South Georgia Island. It is just a really stunning place. I have been there five times.

Closer to home it is difficult to do better than the Shetland Islands. The scenery is fantastic, the walking great, the food is fresh and it is easy to find yourself all alone with just the incredible scenery and wildlife to keep you company.

What do you enjoy most when traveling (cities, nature, people, cultural spots, etc.) and why?

I enjoy nature the most. Seeing wildlife in its own environment is always an experience. Sometimes if you are lucky you might get an encounter. I enjoy just walking out in the countryside with no people. When I read the growth rate of the human population, it leaves me wondering if there will be space for wildlife in the future or will the planet be filled up with buildings and farms? What is going on in China, India, and Brazil is really worrying.

What travel accomplishments are you most proud of?

I am not really sure. Maybe finding out how to get to a place at a reasonable cost rather than joining a charter group at a much higher cost, which is easier if you have the cash. Recently I went to Market Reef in Finland and I was ready to charter the helicopter like I was advised to do by other travelers who had been there, but a chance meeting with a Finnish man lead me to learn about a regular boat and I went for only 80 euros after having been prepared to pay the 1200 euros helicopter fee. Knowledge is king, but acquiring it regarding travel is not as easy as some people might suspect, like tapping it into a search engine on the web.

If you had just one personal travel story to share with someone, what would it be?

When you meet people who tell you something that you think you know about, don't just dismiss the new information. On one of my expedition cruises, I met an American man who told me he had visited the sewers beneath London on an organized trip. Being born in London and having tried to do this but told it was simply not allowed, I felt I was being fed a pack of lies. However, he promised to email me some information. I later got the information and two years later I did the London sewer tour. They allow 64 people a year over two days, with priority given to former employees and their families. So before you dismiss something you hear, you should look into it.

I stayed at an hotel in American Samoa once that was run by a few Polynesian women who were very flirty and suggestive all the time. I remember the toilet and bathroom had many holes and while I filled them with toilet paper each time I used them the very next time the holes were unplugged. A rather nondescript British man with a limp, who was also staying there, seemed to have fallen in love with the place!

Besides your home country, where do you find yourself returning to over and over and why?

Certain places I return to a fair amount because I need to go there to pick up a boat or something. I have been to Ushuaia, Argentina at least ten times to pick up a boat to Antarctica. Mauritius and Fiji so I can again pick up boats or fly from there to other places more conveniently. For other reasons, I am often in the USA, Spain, Italy, France, etc., watching sporting events, which is mainly football.

What is the ideal amount of time you prefer to travel on each trip before you are ready for home and a break?

I feel three weeks is a nice amount of time. It allows enough time in a place to get some sort of feel for it while not leaving you feeling that you have exhausted all the things you may want to see there. I prefer to leave a place wanting to go back if possible. So having a few sights left to see is good for me. I would not really want to spend several months in one place as you only have so much time, and I want to see as much diversity as possible.

If you had an unlimited budget and space and time was no object, what would your perfect travel day look like? (for example: start your morning in Bora Bora; afternoon on a safari in Kenya; night in Australia, etc.)

Wake up in the Maldives; breakfast at the Oriental Bangkok; early morning sightseeing around South Georgia Island; elevenses at the Savoy London; late morning sightseeing at Victoria Falls; lunch at the Peninsular Hong Kong; early afternoon sightseeing at Ha Long Bay, Vietnam; afternoon tea at Belmont Reid's in Madeira; late afternoon sightseeing in Petra, Jordan; pre-dinner cocktails at The Taj Mahal Palace in Mumbai; dinner at the Raffles Singapore; evening sightseeing in Sydney; drinks at The Strand Hotel in Yangon; midnight sightseeing at the North Pole; bed at the Claridge's London.

For those looking to travel to every country, what is the best piece of advice you could offer them?

Try to get visas from difficult countries as early as possible and visit them now so you are not left with all the hard places to go. If you have time and money, do not rush to visit every country as quickly as possible and try to enjoy each one. For more expensive and time-consuming trips, combine countries on each trip. Research destinations which are hubs for visiting other countries and then do not visit the hub unless you are going elsewhere as well.

For someone that has been almost everywhere, what still gets you excited about packing your bags again?

I just love visiting somewhere new. The sense of anticipation and not really knowing what to expect adds to a new destination. Finding a nice place not mentioned in the guide books gives me a buzz. Packing my bag is enjoyable as I question what I need and why, which brings with it an image which may be way off but still nice to have.

Do you ever feel you have missed out on certain aspects of life being away from home so much?

I am currently 52 years old. I am married with no children. Had I not been traveling so much it is quite likely children would have been on the scene. When I see my mother and other grandparents and the pleasure they get out of seeing their grandkids, I do sometimes wonder how much I will regret this. Being away so much you do not have the friends you would have with a more regular life. People I know who spend their lives working spend much of their social time with their colleagues.

Looking ahead, what travel plans and goals are you still pursuing, and what is on your "Bucket List"?

I would hope to visit all the UN countries (seven remaining). I will not rush this, though, as every new country (as opposed to a region or territory) I visit is special. While I only have a handful left, one new UN country a year is good for me, and I visit them slowly on purpose. My personal list of places to visit is quite large, but part of it is the Guinness list, which I would love to complete. I met a Swedish man, Jarl, who completed the list on our 2006 Bouvet Island trip, and he may be the only person ever to do it. I love going to different islands and the Nicobar Islands would be great, as would the Paracel Islands.

Steve Warner, U.S.A.

(Steve Warner)

Where did you grow up and what was your early life like?

My father was a U.S. Army Officer. Besides living in Hawaii and CONUS (Continental U.S.), my family resided in Germany and England. During our two years in Germany, my father studied the Russian language at the Defense Department Russian Language Institute in Regensburg. During each summer he would serve as a diplomatic courier traveling behind the Iron Curtain. When he returned from these trips, he would show my brother, sister, and me, pictures he had taken in Eastern Europe. He would also bring us little toys and presents from the Iron Curtain countries. We siblings were mesmerized. During his leave, he would take our family all around Germany, France,

Italy (Rome & Vatican City). When he was assigned to England, the family moved to London. While there for two years, we traveled extensively around England and Scotland. I was active in the Scouting Movement. Our Air Explorer Squadron traveled to Germany; Italy (Rome); and to a survival school in Scotland. Living overseas introduced me to travel. I fell in love with traveling.

When did you go from casually traveling to making this a full-time goal, and what motivated you to travel to every country?

While in college at the United States Military Academy at West Point, I found myself traveling during the summer months, both in CONUS and overseas. During my Army career, I was stationed in Vietnam and Saudi Arabia. Following my Army career, I had a second career in the Army as a civilian. I had assignments in Saudi Arabia (for a second time) and in Germany, where I spent 15 years. Throughout my careers, I continued my travels. By the time I worked in Civil Service, I had been introduced to the Travelers' Century Club (TCC). The TCC's travel destination list became my standard and my inspiration. This list also motivated me to visit every country.

Do you remember the point where you said to yourself, "I can really accomplish this"?

When I reached number 300 on the TCC's list. Country #300 was North Korea. I never dreamed of being able to visit North Korea. I came across a company called Koryo Tours. This company had (at the time) exclusive rights to bring tourists to North Korea. Koryo Tours was well-organized and had many local contacts in and around Pyongyang to make the visit both comfortable and extremely interesting. I was in North Korea about ten days. I found the capital, Pyongyang, to be very modern and cosmopolitan. The people were very friendly and approachable. The streets were wide and clean. The buildings modern. There were many monuments to the Communist leaders. I saw no signs that were indicative of any hatred toward their supposed enemy, South Korea, or even anything derogatory about the 'great Satan', the United States. I also did not observe any large military presence in Pyongyang. Also group made a day long trip to the DMZ. En route I saw a lot of poverty; poor housing; and pallor. The DMZ (from the North) was well-guarded and robustly fortified. I had been to the South Korean side of the DMZ before, so I had an eerie feeling looking south from the North Korean side of the DMZ originally, but I found the North Korean officers and soldiers to be very friendly, and a number of them who spoke English. I engaged one North Korean officer, telling him I was a retired U.S. Army LTC. I gave him a United States Army coin, a habit I have had when I travel and meet interesting people. I would say visiting the DMZ from the North was one of the highlights of my visit to North Korea.

What have you done over your life to gain the freedom and finances to pursue as much travel as you have?

Probably five reasons:

1) Life as an Army Brat.

2) Army and Civil Service Careers.

3) Having indexed retirement incomes.

4) Being single most of my adult life.

5) No children to raise.

Was there ever a time you felt like abandoning this goal?

Never.

What were your worst travel experiences (i.e. detainment, bribes, car accidents, sickness, etc.) and why?

My inability to get into Libya without a visa, despite my pleading with the Chief of Border Customs; I was able to visit Libya on a later trip.

There was a second "worst travel experience" — While traveling from Greece through Macedonia and Kosovo to reach Serbia (in order to travel west to reach Srpska), we were refused entry into Serbia for a political reason. Bill Clinton authorized the bombing of Serbia in the 90's, to protect the Kosovo Muslims from the Serbs. We had to backtrack 500 miles through Macedonia to reach Serbia.

What do you consider the most adventurous trip you have taken?

A month-long trip to Papua New Guinea and Indonesia (Irian Jaya and the Komodo Islands) where we visited primitive tribes; whitewater rafted; and saw the Komodo dragons.

What were your most challenging countries to visit and why?

Angola: I had difficulties in obtaining a visa.

Iraq: I could not get in due to the ongoing war.

North Korea: I had difficulties in obtaining a visa.

What is the strangest thing you've seen/experienced while traveling?

Seeing penises on Tonga currency and in other locations on the island of Tonga.

Which travel experiences stand out the most and why?

1) A three-month cruise on Windjammer's *Yankee Trader* (which circumnavigated the world in 1977). It opened the world to me.

2) A month-long Malaysian Air Pass trip which opened the doors to locations in Malaysia and Indonesia, in 2005.

3) Spending two tours in Saudi Arabia (1972 and 1980) which allowed me to visit throughout the Kingdom, to include the Empty Quarter; the Asir; Riyadh; Jiddah; Mecca and Daharan.

4) Making an around the world trip in 2009 that took me from the U.S. to Vietnam and Laos and on to Europe for a cruise down the Danube from Budapest to the Black Sea; and then home to the U.S.

What are the most overrated and underrated countries you've been to in your travels and why?

Most overrated: England and France. (No comment.)

Most underrated: Uzbekistan; Mongolia; and North Korea.

What are the best and worst meals you have ever had traveling and where were they?

Best: Eating garlic laced food in Portugal.

Worst: Drinking a yak butter beverage in Kathmandu, Nepal.

What country made you feel most out of your comfort zone and why?

I found the islands of Cape Verde to be a little outside of my comfort zone. There wasn't hardly anything to see. It was terribly hot. Their beaches were nothing to speak of. I found myself bored with nothing to do. I really have no lasting memories of these islands.

Do you speak any foreign languages? If so, which has been the most useful for you besides English?

While I have been exposed to the following foreign languages — French; Latin; Russian; Vietnamese; Arabic — I have retained next to nothing.

Looking back from when you started traveling to where you are now, in what ways, if any, have travel changed you?

Travel has given me a deeper appreciation of my beloved home country, The United States of America.

What is the longest continuous trip you have ever taken? When was it and where did you travel?

In 1977, I made a ten-month trip aboard Windjammer's *Yankee Trader* around the world. While I got off the Trader after three months, my wife and I continued westward around the world, returning to the U.S. ten months later. It cost us, for two people: $16,000. (That was 37 years ago.)

What is your favorite "off-the-beaten-path" destination and why?

Pitcairn Island. Meeting the 48 inhabitants of the island, including Fletcher Christian's great, great, great, grandson.

What are the best and worst places you have ever spent a night?

Best place: Bali, Indonesia.

Worst place: Cape Verde — Little vegetation; little water; nothing to see.

In your opinion, what country or place in the world feels the most authentic and untouched by tourism?

Reykjavik, Iceland. I found the city of Reykjavik to be filled with architecture that is distinctly Icelandic. Iceland is a very conservative country. The people are warm and friendly. I wish I'd had an opportunity to venture out into the countryside.

In your opinion, where is the most beautiful place on Earth?

Bora Bora, French Polynesia.

What do you enjoy most when traveling (cities, nature, people, cultural spots, etc.) and why?

1) Visiting the cultural highlights of a city/country in order to see what made that city/country famous/memorable.

2) Meeting and interacting with locals to try and understand some of their core values; what made their city/country what it is today.

3) Obtaining a soil sample. I have a dirt collection of over 650 small, labeled, jelly jars containing soil from places around the world I have visited. My most prized are two jars of dirt and sand from Mecca/Medina, Kingdom of Saudi Arabia, which a friend gave me.

What travel accomplishments are you most proud of?

Visiting the remote islands of Pitcairn; Tristan da Cunha; and St Helena.

If you had just one personal travel story to share with someone, what would that be?

In 1977, while on a trip around the world aboard the Wind-jammer *Yankee Trader*, we were out in the middle of the South

Pacific. I struck up a conversation with the ship's doctor, "Doc Purdy." He was a U.S. Army OBGYN doctor, stationed at Ft. Sill, Oklahoma, just after WWII in 1946. My sister Randy was born at Ft. Sill in 1946. When I returned home, I dug up a picture frame my father had given me. The picture frame contained three military "orders" my father made announcing the births of myself; my brother; and my sister, Randy. At the bottom of each order were my Dad's signature and the name of the physician who delivered us. Sure enough, you guessed it; on my sister's order was "Doc Purdy." He had delivered my sister, Randy.

Besides your home country, where do you find yourself returning to over and over and why?

The Czech Republic, specifically Prague. While stationed in Grafenwoer, Germany, I often traveled to Prague, where I met many wonderful friends, friends whom I have maintained contact with for many, many years.

What is the ideal amount of time you prefer to travel each trip before you are ready for home and a break?

Three to four weeks.

If you had an unlimited budget and space and time was no object, what would your perfect travel day look like? (for example: start your morning in Bora Bora; afternoon on a safari in Kenya; night in Australia, etc.)

Spend a morning and afternoon on St Helena; and evening on Pitcairn Island. I love visiting islands all over the world.

For those looking to travel to every country, what is the best piece of advice you could offer them?

Persevere; do NOT give up; have patience; have adequate resources; research your destinations as much as possible.

For someone that has been almost everywhere, what still gets you excited about packing your bags again?

The thrill of reaching a destination you have never been to.

Do you feel you have missed out on certain aspects of life being away from home so much?

Perhaps not raising a family would be one such aspect.

Looking ahead, what travel plans and goals are you still pursuing, and what is on your "Bucket List"?

The current TCC List contains 324 destinations. I have visited 321 TCC destinations.

My "Bucket List'" is therefore:

Norwegian Antarctic Territory

French Antarctic Territory

Galapagos Islands

Tan Wee Cheng, Singapore

(Tan Wee Cheng on an old battlefield near Hargeisa, capital of Somaliland, 2008)

Where did you grow up, and what was your early life like?

I was born and raised in Singapore, in a middle class family. Tiny Singapore is a nation that has transformed within 50 years from a poor Southeast Asian backwater to one of the world's wealthiest countries and an international financial center. Singapore of the 1970s and 1980s that I grew up in was one where most families were careful with money and saved what they could for their children's future education. I always recall Mum saying that she used to buy oranges only for my sister and me, as they were too expensive for her and Dad to eat.

Travel was considered a luxury that only the rich could afford. Even today, some Singaporeans above 60 years old consider extended travel as a hedonistic pursuit associated with irresponsible youth and plain idle hippism. Contrast that with today's Singapore where some schools send their teenage students on enrichment holidays in Europe, China, Japan, and even Mauritius.

I have always been fascinated with faraway places and exotic lands. Mum worked in a firm that had international clients, and she would pass along to me stamps stuck on letters and parcels sent from around the world. I was intrigued by these tiny souvenirs from countries whose names I could not even pronounce, and even more so in the stories behind the colorful images.

When I was in secondary school, I realized that embassies and tourist offices were giving out free books, tourist brochures, and maps as well as all sorts of political propaganda publications. I learned a great deal about countries and their history and politics from these publications. I became obsessed with visiting and writing to all the foreign missions in Singapore to ask for their publications. There were some embassies where I would write twice a year just to check if they had new publications that I did not collect previously.

The Soviet Embassy was one of those that I enjoyed collecting stuff from. They always had beautiful propaganda books and leaflets about their "workers' paradise." I had collected so much from them that they could tell me what was new from my last visit. That was still in the Cold War-era and Singapore was anti-Communist, so not all their publications were authorized for public distribution in Singapore. There was one occasion when I visited the Soviet Embassy's press office, and they decided to bring me into a storeroom with books and brochures laid out on the shelves. The press officer scanned through what he had, telling me which I could take and which I could not because the Singapore government would not approve. I had so much amazing Soviet propaganda that some classmates nicknamed me "KGB."

When I was 18 years old, I had to serve two years of compulsory military service that all guys in Singapore were legally obliged to. I had quite a bit of spare time then. On boring humid nights when I had to perform guard duty at military installations, I found myself running through a mental map of the world, naming all the countries and their capitals, and even states and provinces of major nations. I even challenged myself to find a line or two to say about these places. During free weekends, my fellow conscript soldiers went for movies with girlfriends whilst I hunted for books about exotic places in libraries and book stores.

When did you go from casually traveling to making this a full-time goal, and what motivated you to travel to every country?

My first holidays were with my parents and sister, on package tours to Malaysia and China. I enjoyed myself and thought that I could try to be more adventurous by doing a bit of backpacking later on, just like the many young European and American backpackers that passed through Singapore on their way to other parts of Southeast Asia did. By the early 1990s, Singaporeans had some spare cash to travel but most people were intimidated by the notion of traveling on their own in foreign lands. Joining package tours was the norm.

When I completed university, I wanted to do Western Europe before starting to work. My parents offered me to pay for the trip as a reward for completing my education. The idea of me backpacking, however, horrified them, and one of Dad's closest friends told him it would be a terribly dangerous and reckless thing to allow his son to backpack. I had to try very hard to assure them that I would be careful and nothing would go wrong. My best friend was supposed to travel with me and I spent an hour on the phone with his parents persuading them that their son would survive this journey safe and sound.

We survived the trip and I came home deeply bitten by the travel bug. In the years that followed, I used all my annual leave entitlement to travel — Eastern Europe, then Turkey, the Middle East, and Indonesia. Even then, I thought I would only go to the more touristy destinations. There were more than enough of such places to do in my lifetime, I reckoned then. No, I wouldn't risk my life or discomfort, or spend reckless sums of money to do off-the-beaten-track places that only crazy Westerners would do.

In 1997, I went to graduate school in London and stayed on to work for an investment bank in the city. With constantly concerned family now far away, the floodgates of frequent travel were opened. Before long, I found myself in the Baltic States, Patagonia, Central America, Central Asia, and the Caucasus. Every new trip lifted my threshold for discomfort, uncertainty, and even danger. It was in a Vilnius hotel lobby when I bumped into an elderly Spanish man who exclaimed that he had just done his 100th country. At that point, I was 30-odd countries away, and I thought — why couldn't I do the same? Perhaps I could even aim to complete all the countries in the world.

By 2002, when I was to head home for good, I decided to spend a year on the road. That was something I used to think only mad Englishmen would do. I spent half a year in Latin America, and the other half year overland from London to Singapore — after all, I have told friends I would go home by land one day. Even though I had to fly back to Singapore from Moscow to attend an uncle's funeral midway through the trip, I returned to Russia one week later to resume my overland journey. I still recall how shocked Mum was when she realized that my return during the funeral was only temporary.

Do you remember the point where you said to yourself, "I can really accomplish this"?

We live in an era where most places are physically reachable so long as you are willing to spend the money getting there. The biggest constraint, apart from money, in my view, is border bureaucracy.

When I first began traveling over 20 years ago, when Singapore was still a Third World country, Singaporeans required visas to visit many countries, and it was a painful process applying for them. As Singapore became steadily wealthier, more and more countries waived visa requirements for Singapore passports.

The Singapore passport is now ranked the 5th best passport to have in terms of number of visa-free countries one can visit.

Even then, as there are only three million Singapore citizens, many border posts have never encountered any Singaporeans, and have little idea what we looked like. Often, even if we are not required to have a visa, Singaporeans are asked to stand aside while border officials ring their headquarters to find out what to do with us. That's not fun if you were on a remote Moldovan border post in the freezing night or in a flooded Ecuadorian-Peruvian border post when overflowing river waters were threatening to wash away anything and everyone in their pathway.

There remain some stubborn countries where Singaporeans need visas and yet they have no embassies nearby. I had to make extraordinary efforts to get such visas. Guyana was one such country. Their nearest embassy was in New Delhi. Fortunately, I was planning to visit India two months before the Caribbean trip, and so I was able to visit the Guyana Embassy to get the visa. The extensive correspondence with the Guyana Embassy before the New Delhi visit, and ultimately getting the visa convinced me that I can go anywhere I want, provided that I try hard enough, or can wait for the right opportunity.

In 2002, I was denied a Bolivian visa — as were many Singaporean travelers in that year. I never knew the reason, but eventually, they allowed Singaporeans to get visas on arrival, and I visited that beautiful country in 2014. The Marshall Islands currently require Singaporean visitors to get visas in advance, by sending all the way to the Director of Immigration in Majuro, their passport, a police certificate proving one's clean criminal record and a medical certificate with results from their HIV test. Would you want to post your passport to the Marshall Islands? The Democratic Republic of the Congo (DRC) requires all foreigners to apply for the visa in their country of residence. But there is no DRC embassy in Singapore. Nevermind. I can wait. Some day in the future, it might become easier for Singaporeans to visit the Marshall Islands and the DRC.

I consider myself a moderate traveler-next-door, not an adventurer. I do not undertake expeditions to the North Pole. Nor walk across the Sahara. I do suffer minor discomfort from time to time, but nowadays generally try to ensure that I have a clean, nice, air-conditioned room with attached bathrooms. I do go to places perceived as dangerous, but do so only after careful consideration and taking steps to ensure my safety (e.g., getting a local fixer or booking a taxi for the entire day in rough places, as the taxi driver can become an informal bodyguard).

There is also no rushing to get to places with an ongoing conflict. When I was in Croatia in May 1995, I contemplated visiting Bosnia during a ceasefire. That would have been silly, for no one knew when the fighting would resume — and it did resume shortly after. By the end of the year, the war ended with the Dayton Agreement, and I visited the country in 2002. So, I tell myself sometimes, no hurry — there is no race to complete all the countries. There will be a time when a place is safe to visit, and it is good to do so at that time.

What have you done over your life to gain the freedom and finances to pursue as much travel as you have?

I have done well in my career to gain financial freedom to pursue my travel dreams. I am not rich but am doing okay. I began my career as an auditor, then a banker, a regulator and then chief financial officer of a small listed company. There are those who say that life as an accountant and banker is stressful, and it would be impossible to achieve a work-life balance. I disagree. I believe that, if one works hard and adds value to organizations, one is able to negotiate for time for extended holidays or anything one deems important. As one rises through the ranks, it also becomes easier to plan one's schedules. Of course, one sometimes may have to abort an occasional vacation due to urgent work matters — as I had done on a few occasions, even giving up non-refundable air tickets.

When I finally left my last corporate job, I had a minor windfall from the stock market. I decided to switch to an adjunct academic job that pays me enough for my travels and running costs (notwithstanding a major pay cut) and yet allows me practically three months of travel every year.

As I have told many students who are travel enthusiasts, it is important to plan one's career and do well in work. You can, of course, travel as a backpacker and spend very little. With time, however, you may need to spend a lot more when you run out of cheap places to visit. For instance, you need to spend much more for customized transportation arrangements in remoter parts of the world. As I age, comfort becomes important, and I enjoy good food. No more hostels and dollar pancakes for me! You need a good career advancement and financial independence to be able to afford the good things while traveling.

Was there ever a time you felt like abandoning this goal?

Not at all. I cannot imagine how this could ever be the case. There are endless places to visit; there are many unvisited regions in countries I have visited. Besides, countries also change with time; hence there are many countries that I would love to revisit again.

What were your worst travel experiences (i.e. detainment, bribes, car accidents, sickness, etc.) and why?

I have been relatively lucky in that I had not suffered in any major way during my travels (knock on wood). I have had my fair share of minor detainment or experienced bribery attempts by corrupt or overzealous officials in Uzbekistan, Ukraine, Russia, Bulgaria, Transnistria, Guatemala, Guinea, Cameroon, Togo, and Mali; I met with an accident in Albania, got pickpocketed in Jerusalem and Saint Petersburg, and almost becoming a victim of crime in Peru, Brazil, and Lesotho. On other occasions, my taxi drove into a riot in Ouagadougou, Burkina Faso and another in Hyderabad, India; on both occasions, the drivers retreated and drove to safety via small lanes and side streets.

My most frightening experience occurred in Liberia. When I flew into Monrovia Airport one late evening, I was dehydrated and suffocated after a long wait in a humid airport hangar for the baggage to be manually offloaded from the plane, laid out on the ground, and then collected. Then we were suddenly pushed out of the airport compound. Most of my fellow passengers were diplomats or NGO's, who had people to pick them up. I had no one, and was suddenly mobbed by aggressive touts and former child soldiers who tried to lead me into their ramshackle cars. Terrible dilemma, as the city center was 56km away and it was almost 11 p.m. by then. If I did not get into one of the cars, I might get stuck in the middle of nowhere.

I was pushed into a car already partly occupied by a few dodgy characters. The touts were shouting away with their palms outstretched screaming for tips for "finding the taxi." Yet, just as the vehicle was about to move, a lady official waved her badge around and appeared at the door of the taxi, "You need help? Are you sure you want to go with these people?" She was the angel who appeared at my hour of need. She shouted at the people inside and outside the vehicle, warning them about her official status. She got me out of the car and gave me a lift to town. Who knows what could have happened if she had not appeared?

Another incident was on the crowded main street of Maseru, Lesotho, when a gang of robbers tried to rob me and my friend, but failed and ran away. I was pushed onto the ground and fell on a stall selling cooking utensils. The fall caused enormous pain and I stood up with great difficulty. Yet, no one helped me. The locals simply pointed at us — some shouted "Chinese!" and many laughed loudly as though to say, "You deserve it." I was shocked by not just by their apathy but what could be a kind of hostility towards Asians.

In an era when businessmen and tourists from China have appeared everywhere, all East Asian people are often mistaken as "Chinese" and any hostility (and sometimes, though rarely, affection) towards the Chinese are also hurled towards these Asians. Anecdotal evidence as well as my own experiences seems to suggest that many corrupt officials see Chinese businessmen and travelers as walking cash machines, as the Chinese are often too quick to offer huge sums of bribes whenever overseas. As many people in such places cannot distinguish between Chinese and other Asian nationalities, Singaporeans, Japanese, Korean, or Malaysian travelers are often adversely affected as a result.

What do you consider one of the most adventurous trips you have taken?

I do not think any of my trips are truly adventurous. Not sure if you would count these: I have taken some long West African bus or mini-van journeys across very bad roads from the capital city to the border, crossed the border by foot, and then hopped into another vehicle to the nearest big town. And of course, along the way, either the vehicle broke down several times, or the driver allegedly ran out of cash for fuel in the middle of nowhere and demanded additional sums from the passengers. As usual, they always tried to get more money from the perceived rich foreigners. Sometimes, we had to drive across running rivers and muddy potholes. By the time we reached our destination, we would be completely covered by a thick layer of bush dust and dried mud. Countries such as Liberia, Sierra Leone, Guinea, Guinea-Bissau, and Cameroon would be stuck in my mind for a long time for these reasons.

I also recall occasions where I was the sole passenger on barges upriver in remote parts of Myanmar such as the Rakhine and Chin States, traveling on rivers and canals through tall grass and mangroves. I asked myself, "Why did I allow myself in such a position whereby the barge captain could kill me and nobody would ever know that I was ever there?"

What were your most challenging countries to visit and why?

Sub-Saharan African nations — though not South Africa and Namibia: bad or non-existent roads, open sewerage, law and order issues, tedious visa regimes and high cost of decent tourist class travel make most of Africa the most challenging region to travel around. Worst of all were the corrupt police who demand bribes on the streets, road checkpoints, and airports. I hate these beggars with guns.

What is the strangest thing you've seen/experienced while traveling?

I will give you three since I am not sure which is the strangest:

First was driving around a desert reserve outside Niamey, Niger, in a well-beyond-scrap-date taxi searching for the elusive Sahara giraffes. Before we realized it, we were chasing them in the reserve, as the driver was more excited than us.

Another incident happened in Pyongyang, North Korea. We were strolling in a park and then were asked by a group of picnicking locals to dance with them. That evening, we found ourselves on Pyongyang TV, which said that we were foreigners in Pyongyang to celebrate the birth anniversary of the late President Kim Il Sung and were dancing in his honor.

Third was watching dozens of Peruvians dancing wildly to loud band music in a cemetery, at the remote highland town of Paucartambo, during the Fiesta de la Virgen del Carmen. For an East Asian, dancing in cemeteries is an absolute taboo.

Which travel experiences stand out the most and why?

Watching Inuit seal hunters at work in Greenland. I was instantly awed by the sheer whiteness and grandeur of the environment, of both the perpetually snow-capped mountains and the massive icebergs. The Inuits, in a land where neither farming nor industry was viable, had to hunt for subsistence. The seals may seem cute and cuddly to us, but the Inuits have no other viable livelihood choices. The only main alternative was to receive welfare handouts from the Danish Government and risk destroying their dignity in the process. I was impressed by the hardy Inuits operating in such a harsh environment, as well as the care taken by the hunters to minimize the seals' suffering during the process. No, the Inuits that I saw did not club the seals en masse. The Inuits only shot or harpooned what they needed.

What are the most overrated and underrated countries you've been to in your travels and why?

Every country is different in its own ways, and I can hardly say any nation is overrated. Iran is the one that is super-underrated. Dogged by U.S. political attacks, the country has a terrible international image as a dangerous and extremist terrorist state. Yet, this is a most diverse nation with much to see and do; and its greatest asset is its hospitable people. Every other day, I received invitations by strangers to stay at their homes. On long distance bus journeys, people fought to buy me tea and snacks. In restaurants, I sometimes had to insist on paying the bills. In the parks where families picnicked after work hours, I was invited to join them and indulged in an endless flows of tea and cakes.

What are the best and worst meals you have ever had traveling and where were they?

I have had many bad meals around the world that I hardly knew which the worst was. It is certainly much easier to find bad meals than to find very good meals in places one isn't familiar with.

It is difficult to rank the good meals too, but I have had many good meals — some of which were simple street food — in Bangkok, Melaka, and Penang. And I would return to the same nice restaurants and food stalls again and again, on numerous repeat visits to these cities. Bangkok, in particular, is the food capital of the world. And I cannot have enough of it.

What country made you feel most out of your comfort zone and why?

I feel I stand out like a sore thumb in cities of Sub-Saharan African countries. The risk of getting mugged by criminals and getting extorted by corrupt officials, as well as the fairly frequent and hostile taunting by young people (either "China!" or "Ching Chong!") keep me on the guard all the time in these places. Unfortunately, this also takes away much of the fun of travel.

Do you speak any foreign languages? If so, which has been the most useful for you besides English?

I have never been good at languages. I am fluent in English and Chinese/Mandarin. I try to learn ten foreign words or so in the countries I visited but could hardly string complete sentences. And what I knew quickly gets overwritten by a new language once I cross international borders.

Interestingly, over the last decade, I found myself speaking Chinese to the many new Chinese migrants that have appeared everywhere in the world (in places as diverse as Chad, Samoa, and Paraguay), mostly running businesses. Whilst many of these Chinese business people have little knowledge or interest in places to visit, they often provide good tips on where to find Asian comfort cuisine and dangers to be alert to. I have even been offered consular protection by Chinese diplomats in case I get into trouble. The offers were given notwithstanding I wasn't a Chinese citizen. but simply because I spoke the Chinese language and was of Chinese descent.

Looking back from when you started traveling to where you are now, in what ways, if any, has travel changed you?

Travel has taught me to appreciate different viewpoints and perspectives. The media that we are exposed often present events in a manner that is influenced by the predominant perspective of where we live. It is when one travels that one opens the mind towards alternative ways of looking at things, and realizes that the world is more diverse and varied than what one believes.

What is the longest continuous trip you have ever taken? When was it and where did you travel?

That was during my first career break when I took one year off. During that year, I went to Brazil, Paraguay, Chile & Easter Island, Peru, Ecuador, Colombia, Costa Rica, Nicaragua, Honduras, El Salvador, Belize, Mexico, Florida, Bahamas, UK, Faroe Islands, Greece, Macedonia, Serbia, Croatia, Bosnia and Herzegovina, Montenegro, Kosovo, Albania, Switzerland, Liechtenstein, Turkmenistan, Azerbaijan, Russia/Kaliningrad/Murmansk/Siberia, Mongolia, China, Laos, Vietnam, Cambodia, Thailand, and Malaysia.

What is your favorite "off-the-beaten-path" destination and why?

The French overseas territory of Wallis and Futuna is not your average South Pacific tropical isle, but an often forgotten protectorate of three feudal kingdoms whose kings still wield significant power. I was fortunate to attend a traditional ceremony graced by one of the kings and the French administrator, and enjoyed much of the local color and festivities.

What are the best and worst places you have ever spent a night?

The best city hotel I have stayed is probably The Sukhothai Bangkok. An oasis of calm and luxury located downtown. I have also stayed in some nice safari lodges in Africa. One that I always remember is Camp Kipwe in Damaraland, Namibia. Each bungalow has a fantastic view of the many unusual granite domes scattered across the timeless Damara plains. I will forever remember the beautiful sunset.

Worst places? A ramshackle hut in Ouagadougou on a hot, humid night. We arrived in the city late and had to make do with it.

In your opinion, what country or place in the world feels the most authentic and untouched by tourism?

Bhutan — I loved the country from the moment the plane began to descend into Paro Airport, the navigation into the narrow Paro Valley surrounded by green mountains, followed by the magnificent fortresses that we saw even while the plane was landing. There are people walking everywhere in traditional costume. It's like a journey back in time.

Another country was Yemen. Yemeni men walked around with jambiya, their ceremonial short daggers, and often, together with firearms. This, together with the amazing ancient skyscrapers, felt like a movie set in a *Thousand and One Nights*. However, unlike Bhutan, which seems to be successfully moving into the modern world with the Internet and mass education, Yemen looked authentic only because it was socially, economically, and politically backward.

I often hear Western travelers complaining about how places are no longer "authentic" or "untouched" when they noticed economic development, shopping malls, and modern infrastructure. As an Asian, I find it hard to approve of such sentiments even though I do love taking photos of people in traditional costume and quaint old architecture. At the end of the day, people do want to live in modern housing with plumbing and electricity. They also want an increase in income and the opportunity to buy the best they can afford in life. They want their children to go to schools and they want to get to places fast and safe. The people of countries such as Singapore, Taiwan, Korea, and Japan have now achieved this, and I hope to see more Asian countries achieve the same as well.

In your opinion, where is the most beautiful place on Earth?

Difficult question. Depends on the time and day of the year, and one's mood as well. I would say it is perhaps the Canadian Rockies in Alberta.

What do you enjoy most when traveling (cities, nature, people, cultural spots, etc.) and why?

I love cities — in a world where more than half the population is urbanized, cities are the real heartbeat of nations. The historical monuments and museums in cities were the focal points of historical development and repositories of a glorious past; whilst the shops, public buildings and infrastructure are hints of where the future lies. As a business professor and former banker, I love visiting the traditional bazaars and modern supermarkets to find out prices of products, the range of what's on offer, and the latest retail trends — not to mention photographic opportunities at traditional markets. I love restaurants, eateries, and street stalls that serve local cuisine, which to me is one of the finest manifestations of national and regional cultures. I love to sit in cafes and drop by book stores, to see how people interact and what they are interested in.

What travel accomplishments are you most proud of?

As mentioned earlier, I see myself as a traveler-next-door. I do not have any extraordinary travel accomplishment; with patience, perseverance, life-scheduling and careful career planning, everyone can achieve what I have done. I enjoy visiting new places all the time, and revisit old places to see what is new. I am a history aficionado and always add places I read about to my wish list. I have done slightly less than half of all the UNESCO World Heritage Sites and would endeavor to visit as many as I can if practicable. I am not competing with anyone and they aren't accomplishments per se; but there is always an enormous pleasure as I cover more places.

If you had just one personal travel story to share with someone, what would that be?

When I was in the historic old town of Massawa, Eritrea, I came across an elderly, one-legged Japanese-American. And he amazed me with his life story — how his entire family was deprived of their American citizenship and exiled to a concentration camp in the Californian desert during WWII, forced deportation to Japan after the war, his realization that Japan was entirely foreign to him despite ancestral roots and then his return to the U.S. He also spoke about how he came to Eritrea to help develop agriculture and fell in love with this land, and eventually spent large parts of the year meeting old friends here. I was mesmerized by his stories and by how I got to know him in this unexpected setting.

Besides your home country, where do you find yourself returning to over and over and why?

I have become very much a foodie and I tend to return to my favorite food cities in Asia again and again.

Bangkok: for the great food and shopping. I can never run out of great places to eat in this fabulous city. I go to Bangkok at least once a year, sometimes several times a year.

Melaka: a small historical city in Malaysia with amazing street food at affordable prices.

Taipei: the wonderful and hospitable capital of Taiwan. Again for food and jolly good times to catch up with my friends in this city.

What is the ideal amount of time you prefer to travel each trip before you are ready for home and a break?

At least two weeks, if not one month. I also go on frequent weekend trips to nearby destinations.

If you had an unlimited budget and space and time was no object, what would your perfect travel day look like? (for example: start your morning in Bora Bora; afternoon on a safari in Kenya; night in Australia, etc.)

I would be provided endless capacity to eat: Getting up to the sounds and smell of the Iguazu Falls at Belmond Hotel das Cataratas. On to Michelin-rated Tim Ho Wan at Hong Kong's Sham Shui Po area for dim sum breakfast, followed by a casual stroll and a reading of excerpts from *Grænlendinga* (the Icelandic epic about the voyages of Erik the Red in Greenland) in the serene meadows of Þingvellir (Thingvellir). Lunch will be a gorgeous spread of Indonesian cuisine, nasi padang or rijsttafel style, in a nice restaurant in Jogjakarta. After that, I will marvel at the wonderful reliefs of the Assyrian lion hunt at the British Museum, before a short hop to Piccadilly for champagne high tea at The Ritz. Fully recharged, I would be ready for a late afternoon rhino safari in the plains of Kaziranga National Park in Assam, maybe even having good luck to spy on a Royal Bengal tiger by the Brahmaputra; and then on to Bloubergstrand to admire the gorgeous sunset over Cape Town's Table Mountain. Dinner has been reserved at Astrid y Gaston in Lima, followed by a nice evening of Beethoven's Fidelio at Teatro alla Scala in Milan. End the day with a good night sleep at the romantic Taj Lake Palace Hotel in Udaipur, Rajasthan.

For those looking to travel to every country, what is the best piece of advice you could offer them?

We live in a beautiful world of wondrous diversity. Don't rush to tick off the boxes. Do pause and spend a decent amount of time in each country. I have heard of way too many people who considered countries done when they transit airports, or visit places like Kazungula, where Zambia, Zimbabwe, Botswana, and Namibia meet.

For someone that has been almost everywhere, what still gets you excited about packing your bags again?

There are still many places I haven't been to within countries I have visited. And I do enjoy revisiting countries years after a previous visit, to see what has changed. I still get excited about travel and believe that will never change.

Do you feel you have missed out on certain aspects of life being away from home so much?

I do miss family and friends during my travels, increasingly so. That being said, the advent of technology has allowed me to keep in touch with people via Facebook and whatsapp. When those means of communications break down, however, I often feel a sense of loss and worry.

When I first began my travels over two decades ago, it was difficult and expensive to keep in touch. Every few weeks on my extended travels, I had to go to the local PTT offices at weird hours to try and ring home to tell them I was still alive. It was an expensive hassle and I sometimes could not care less in my younger, perhaps more reckless days. Nowadays, it is so easy to chat on the road by getting a local 3G SIM card. On a recent trip to Ladakh, I realized that the Internet was down due to catastrophic flooding in neighboring Kashmir. As a result, I could not chat with my elderly parents and was very worried about their well-being. (The lack of Internet also meant I could not deal with certain urgent work matters as well as to check air tickets and other logistical details.) That was a little upsetting, but it also reflected my changing priorities and concerns in family life and how those impacted my travels.

Looking ahead, what travel plans and goals are you still pursuing, and what is on your "Bucket List"?

There are still a few countries and political entities I have yet to visit, and a few significant places I haven't done. Among them include the DRC, Angola, Saudi Arabia, Algeria, Iraq, Tibet, Xinjiang, Alaska, Falkland Islands, and West Papua. In fact, I would also like to cover all the political subdivisions of China, India, Indonesia, Myanmar, Pakistan, Australia, Spain, Italy, France, Germany, and the USA, as well as the ethnic republics and regions within the Russian Federation.

I need to redo most of Europe again, and do them in a more thorough fashion, with greater focus on museums and gastronomy. I am very keen to visit all the World Heritage Sites (WHS) worldwide and all major archaeological sites which are not WHS. I would like to do a couple of road trips, along the Trans-Sumatran Highway, the Volga and the Lena, and across the U.S. The list is so long, and you give me another day, I could easily list another few pages of to-do places.

Phillips Connor, Singapore

(www.MadExpat.com)

Where did you grow up and what was your early life like?

I was born in Washington D.C., but grew up in suburban Chicago. My parents were lawyers and heavily involved in local politics, which my sister and I were often roped into as "letter-box-stuffers" — so I suppose that the constant canvassing up and down every block of the neighborhood were my first "travel" experiences. We were always discovering new and peculiar things in the neighborhood!

I had a comfortable and predictable "All-American" childhood. Relative to this discussion however, I suppose is the fact that my parents held strong views about international travel. Though we did many road trips throughout the U.S. as a family in the 60s, they held to strong beliefs that travel overseas would be wasted on children. As such, I was not allowed to travel beyond domestic borders until I was sixteen. The upside of this, is that once having reached this age, and having watched my parents travel the globe in the interim, (much to my jealousy in these early years), at age sixteen I was finally allowed to "choose" where I wanted to travel to.

Of course, I picked the most exotic destination that I could think of at the time: Egypt. It turned out to be the biggest mistake of my life however; because almost no other experience of antiquity has lived up to that trip.

When did you go from casually traveling to making this a full-time goal, and what motivated you to travel to every country?

In university I never had the means or the time to even consider much travel. In fact, though I spent a semester abroad studying in Copenhagen and living with a local family there, I was truly convinced by the end of that semester that I would never be able to return. When I think back to that time, it almost seems laughable!

It was only after I started working professionally that I realized I could make the money and the time to do what I wanted. I started as an armchair traveler, but heavily interested in logistics, devouring all the *Lonely Planet* guides to any and all destinations, scrutinizing and marking up maps, memorizing ways to get around the country, bus timings, etc. — plotting out detailed and complex itineraries for trips that I might make one day.

As my career blossomed and I found success, I also found the power to be able to tell people that I worked for/with that I would take significant time off and start realizing some of these trips.

Accepting a job offer out of the blue in Singapore, at which point I'd never even been to Asia, sealed the deal. The new found seniority, proximity of exotic destinations and disposable income fueled my rapid exploration of the region. It has been my obsession ever since.

Do you remember the point where you said to yourself, "I can really accomplish this"?

In my mid-thirties, I suppose, when finances were no longer so much of a survival issue and my business and career were already well-established. At that point, it was really just a matter of finding those pockets of time and investing the time into logistics to make things work out, by a self-imposed "50 years old" deadline, that I was able to complete my goal.

What have you done over your life to gain the freedom and finances to pursue as much travel as you have?

1) I've always worked incredibly hard and have been lucky enough to be recognized as a leader in my industry.

2) Not shying away from opportunities, even if risk was involved, and making the most of every moment.

3) I've always pushed the limits of tolerance of my clients, co-workers, and family — to take "that extra time" to travel before and/or after every business trip and take liberal leave throughout the year, defying the "accepted norm" regardless of my position. Lucky to be talented enough to be considered too valuable to piss off, so rarely denied any of the time off I asked for. And, of course, running my own company for many years has helped to reduce the barriers as well.

Was there ever a time you felt like abandoning this goal?

No, I just had to re-regulate time expectations over and along the way.

When I first arrived in Singapore at 25, I thought I could try to finish them all by the time I was 30; but I still just had to work too hard.

I set a new deadline of 40, but getting married and having a child kind of got in the way of *that* deadline.

Slogging away at this goal through my mid-forties brought me close enough to realistically set a deadline of "by the time I am 50"; for which I still needed to take off the last few months to travel through some difficult sectors of central and West Africa.

What were your worst travel experiences (i.e. detainment, bribes, car accidents, sickness, etc.) and why?

Kiribati — Threatened to be imprisoned in a corrugated iron shed in the hot sun, due to a change in visa regulations (U.S. Congress repealed all foreign aid to the country the day before I arrived).

Gabon — Detained by the presidential guard for a day after local police tried to extort bribe money from me and contingent parties; (I was foolishly taking photos of the venue where a world African congress was to be held and an over-officious gendarme snagged me). I was finally able to talk my way out of it, as the commando that was holding me was a Polish mercenary. So naturally we bonded, even with my broken French, after I told him that I was from Chicago, where there are more Polish people than anywhere else outside of Warsaw! A curious full-circle twist to this is that years later, when visiting Gabon again for the total solar eclipse in a remote village, I got to meet and have a photo with the President himself!

Otherwise I've been incredibly lucky — no real serious incidents, even the illness episodes have been more funny that terrible usually; but then I've always planned very carefully.

What do you consider the most adventurous trip you have taken?

A four-week 4x4 expedition through the deserts and mountains of southern Algeria and Niger. In 2006 I joined a small group on this trip, the primary objective of which was to view the total solar eclipse in the Tenere desert near Bilma, Niger.

Camping every night for several weeks and the harsh desert driving and mountainous conditions made for a truly memorable experience; we got lost, encountered many obstacles and a few hardships. But the Algerian team managed to overcome most issues.

Certainly we were lucky enough to not have to experience any of the more serious issues that regional peoples in these areas have to contend with these days. Exploitation, starvation, and abandonment are now common along this same route, as it is now one of the primary conduits for transmigration across the desert from Sub-Sahara Africa to Europe. Who would've known in those days…?

What were your most challenging countries to visit and why?

My challenge has always been time. Keeping at the forefront of my career, combined with obligations to family and friends have always rather limited the duration of my trips. The most challenging countries to visit thus have been because of basic logistics issues. Infrequent flights or land connections have made it most difficult to visit a few of the less traveled West African countries in a "reasonable" amount of time. Countries such Sierra Leone, Liberia, Guinea Bissau, and Mauritania were the very last few stops in my quest to travel the world before I turned 50.

Other than this, I've found virtually every place is pretty easily "accessible" these days. With the right amount of due diligence, I've always found it possible to make the most out of my visit, no matter how short or long it may be.

What is the strangest thing you've seen/experienced while traveling?

One of the funniest things I've ever seen is such careful atten-tion to detail in Perge, Turkey, along the Lycian Way, where the telephone pole was so perfectly coordinated with the ruins of ancient columns!

Strangest, however, would have to be an experience I had in Afghanistan. Driving up into the mountain ridges surrounding Kabul one afternoon, I stopped at a picturesque mosque, perched along a crest about halfway up, overlooking the city spread across the valley below. Miraculously, a thin and sinuous "dust devil" descended from the sky, touched the ground, and spun around for a few seconds, then retracted back up into the clouds. It was so perfectly formed, spontaneous and unusual,

I've never forgotten it and was lucky enough to have caught this fleeting apparition on film.

Which travel experiences stand out the most and why?

Too many to count…

I always take something memorable from *every* experience; that's why travel is so rewarding for me. I always insist on looking at the world as a "glass half full" not empty, and am rarely disappointed.

Certainly my first overseas trip, to Egypt in 1975, stands out. Unbelievably atmospheric and immersive travel, those experiences have literally "haunted" me ever since. Almost nothing else has been able to compare to the rich cultural experiences from that first significant overseas trip.

Multi-week trips through West Africa, for rich cultural heritage, mask dance traditions, and the people. One particular hike along narrow cliffs high in the escarpment of the Dogon in Mali stands out for the way our guide described it, "Easy but deadly!" That is, not particularly difficult to hike or climb, but one misstep and it's all over!

Antarctica also comes to mind due to the sheer majesty of the icebergs and their inhabitants

What are the most overrated and underrated countries you've been to in your travels and why?

Overrated — Botswana

Wildlife too sparse, expectations too high, accommodations and arrangements too expensive — compared with other African game destinations — "boring…"

Underrated — Burkina Faso.

It is so much better than anywhere for its festivals and rich cultural traditions — even better than it's somewhat overrated neighbor, Mali. "Stupendous!"

What are the best and worst meals you have ever had traveling and where were they?

I'm not food-centric at all, so nothing particularly fazes me one way or the other.

The most shocking meals that I've had would be the pigs' blood concoctions in Tana Toraja, Sulawesi, Indonesia, as well as all the other homemade fare for the various funerals, housewarmings, and harvest festival celebrations that I was lucky enough to attend in one trip.

Particularly memorable were the many bloody heads of cattle randomly strewn amongst the "picnickers" in the field comprising the front lawn of the house warming; interspersed with frequent villagers briskly walking along with both live squealing and seriously charred BBQ pigs lashed upside down on poles stretched between two carriers.

If you do not understand enough French in Reunion to realize that when ordering kidneys in a white cream sauce, you might respond "rare" when asked how you'd like them "done." What a bloody mess!

But for sheer comfort food, I always come back to my favorite of all favorites, "Hot Dog Stick" on the beach in Santa Monica; fabulous corn dogs, cheese dogs, and the best fresh lemonade anywhere!

What country made you feel most out of your comfort zone and why?

Central African Republic — very bad vibe in the air, unhelpful people, downtrodden society. Everything was difficult; I couldn't wait to leave.

That said, I do seem to have a bit of a bad, (or some would say lucky), track record. I've visited Yugoslavia, Libya, Syria, and Egypt, all within months preceding their various uprisings. In retrospect — the "bad vibe in the air" was palpable in each of these places as well.

Egypt — working on a new building construction project in a small town outside of Cairo for a month in 1983. Having worked late at the site one evening, I walked out about 3AM, and had to walk a few miles to the main road to pick up a taxi. Unfortunately, for most of this way I was stalked by various packs of menacing, growling, and rabid-looking dogs, each protecting their own distinct patch of territory. I managed to keep my cool, and pass from group to group without being attacked, but it was one of the most unnerving and helpless times that I have ever experienced.

Do you speak any foreign languages? If so, which has been the most useful for you besides English?

Not with any reliability unfortunately; I'm a victim of the American education system.

I've had years and years of French, so I have a massive vocabulary, but very little grammar with which to string sentences together!

These days, through my design project work in various countries throughout Asia, I "collect" key words that I hear a lot in project meetings. For example: "Mei Oh" in Chinese — "Don't have, No, Nothing, Don't want, Won't," etc! (*very* useful in almost *any* situation!); and "Bilum" in Bahasa Indonesia — "Not Yet" — kind of like a "menana" for this part of the world to cover over lazy behavior, lack of performance.

Looking back from when you started traveling to where you are now, in what ways, if any, have travel changed you?

I've become:

More geographically knowledgeable

More culturally sensitive

More attuned to body language

Even more inquisitive

Yet I suppose also more "demanding" — in that I know how short time is and always want to achieve the maximum experience(s) from any situation or locale. (When traveling I'm always out and about, rarely pausing to rest, for any reason, if at all possible.)

Overall, I hope I'm a more interesting person.

What is the longest continuous trip you have ever taken? When was it and where did you travel?

Six weeks through South Africa, Ghana, Togo, Benin, Burkina Faso, Mali, Senegal, The Gambia, Guinea, and Cote D'Ivoire. This was a trip centered around the cultural traditions of Benin, Burkina Faso and Mali, primarily, but ended up taking me even further afield in the region.

It was an exceptionally immersive trip that I will remember the rest of my life for the expedition nature of it, the untouched traditions we witnessed with our very small group and the impact of the people.

What is your favorite "off-the-beaten-path" destination and why?

Papua New Guinea for the sheer isolation and pureness of the cultural traditions and genuine warmth and curiosity of the people.

Kerala for its serene natural beauty.

Greenland for the majesty of scenery and environment.

The Vesteralen Islands along the northern Norwegian coast for picture perfect landscape settings that seem world's away from their ready accessibility.

And, of course, always Antarctica.

What are the best and worst places you have ever spent a night?

For the worst, it would have to be a three-way tie.

1) An open air shack in Moroni, the capital of the Comoros — A dishearteningly poor and destitute place. Very, very sad. Even the goats roaming this capital city appear inconsolably malnourished.

2) The dining car on a 33-hour Chinese hard class train journey. In the early '80's, before much tourism had developed, despite it being a dining car, we had no access to food except for a very limited time period once a day. Maddening in such a horrible tortuous way!

3) The Cosmopolitan Hotel in Cairo, Egypt in 1975. The combination of eerie night-long clanking sounds of a 19th century iron cage lift, echoing amongst vast cavernous areas on the upper floors of an aged tiled building (think *The Shining*), 45 degree heat, "herds" of cockroaches scurrying on the floor, all conspired to inspire terror and sleeplessness during my first ever stay at an overseas "hotel."

For the best, I guess I'm still looking. As a designer, my expectations are very, very high... Though I do always enjoy a bit of a camping experience and am particularly fond of the "Teletubbies Chalets" at Haus Poroman in the highlands of Papua New Guinea.

In your opinion, what country or place in the world feels the most authentic and untouched by tourism?

The remotest areas of Papua New Guinea, where modern society has not numbed the age old cultural traditions, yet one can appreciate and discuss the nuances of this with the locals, as many speak perfect English!

I found it to be an unbelievable, untouched society. It took me several days to realize travelling there "felt" so different from Malaysia or Indonesia, which the environment and cultures resemble. It finally struck me that the difference was that there was no PLASTIC. Sure: no power, no roads, etc. — but the fact that all everyday articles were fabricated from natural materials was truly amazing. Not even the ubiquitous pink plastic bag blowing and tumbling along in the wind that every traveler through Asia has seen time and time again.

In your opinion, where is the most beautiful place on Earth?

There are *so* many, and so often their "beauty" is determined by the serendipitous convergence of circumstances. *Every* place looks better in the context of local celebrations or festivities, and often the people from there, (or with you), add so much to the "experience," which is the "real beauty" in any place to me.

For sheer physical/natural beauty, I would have to say that the crater rim edge of Rano Kau on Easter Island is definitely one of my favorites. Not particularly well known, or heralded as a signature "wonder of the world" site (like any of the ancient antiquities sites of Egypt, Greece, Machu Picchu, etc.), this tiny ridge, and the views from it, really gives one a sense of awe and wonder.

Runner up is definitely the vistas in Mongolia; always serene and inspiring.

What do you enjoy most when traveling (cities, nature, people, cultural spots, etc.) and why?

Tribal festivals — rich, diverse, unique, authentic, and "immersive!"

And in a more urban context: any fantastic examples of environmental design, like in the BMW Museum in Munich, Germany.

What travel accomplishments are you most proud of?

Organizing travels for others and creating the most memorable experiences for all.

A good example would be an "expedition" I put together with 16 friends to scale the summit of Anak Krakatau in 1991. Twelve of us made it to the top caldera, after several hours of ups and downs on the scrabbly rock and cinder cones. The four-hour boat journey from the west coast of Java was particularly arduous on the nighttime return, through rough seas and foul weather. A few months later, a couple of people on another expedition died from unpredictable gas fumes which periodically vented out of the slope.

Another aspect that continues to fascinate me is the serendipitous nature of travel. Literally "stumbling upon" "the Flaming Crater" in remote northern Turkmenistan, yielded a one of a kind experience and video footage that continues to lead in YouTube ratings to this day.

If you had just one personal travel story to share with someone, what would that be?

My most frightening wildlife experience was in Stromness Harbor, South Georgia, British Sub-Antarctic Territory, in 2011.

The day starts early and I set off with a small group on a long hike to the waterfall at the back of a long valley. It seemed an idyllic setting: a long flat valley with a serpentine stream-bed passing down through it to the beach, and periodic hillocks with picturesquely positioned herds of reindeer atop them. Pausing for many photos of this lovely setting, the group soon gets stretched out, with most of the others far ahead of all but three of us stragglers.

Soon we come across an extremely aggressive fur seal: large, sharp toothed, and bloody mouthed. It refused to be dissuaded from his/her mission to attack us. Going after each of us successively, neither sticks, nor shouting, nor clanging rocks in front of its nose would do any good. We ended up spending the next 20 minutes trying to fend it off, with our calls for help to the rest of our hiking party far ahead going totally unheeded.

I was the last to have to deal with this beast individually. It chased me across a shallow riverbed twice, came to within six inches of me and constantly lunged forward so many times that I thought surely that I would be bitten. Holding hands above my head, clanging rocks together, shouting… nothing would stop it. I even got blisters on my hands from so much rock banging. Every step backward was met with a further lunge forward from it to match me. It was the most frightening moment in my life.

It continued for so long that I was consciously thinking, "Well, I'm going to be bitten, but what do I do then? Continue to let it bite me? Run? Fight back? What?" (We'd been told previously that seals can "run" up to 35 miles an hour!) Until then, I couldn't imagine being in such a hopeless situation. I was extremely lucky this time. Eventually it seemed to be a bit distracted by the others and I was able to inch backwards bit by bit.

I spent the rest of the hike to the waterfall at the end of the valley in a state of shock over such a narrow escape. There was something seriously wrong with this seal. We learned later that the same seal had attacked another group and cornered them with two other "seal accomplices" for 15 minutes. One person fell down and had their jacket's hood torn off by the seal; again with none of the usual abatement treatments working. It was from this point that the seals ceased to become "cute" and I became extremely wary of all future encounters. I can only imagine how bad it would be a few weeks later, when the next trip comes through this locale, and these same seals are so much bigger, and even more aggressive.

It made me realize how tenuous and fragile our relationship with nature, wildlife, and the environment can be and how much we should cherish every moment that we have…

Besides your home country, where do you find yourself returning to over and over and why?

England for family connections; California for the buzz and friends; but anywhere in Africa for the irresistible "pull"!

And of course, anywhere NEW!

What is the ideal amount of time you prefer to travel each trip before you are ready for home and a break?

I prefer trips of two to three weeks if at all possible, but with distance and logistics, longer durations are often required to achieve anything substantial. It's good to get back and re-sort through things in between more shorter length trips, so as to maintain a good understanding of what you've seen and why.

I find that with trips of a month or more, you can often lose sight of what the beginning of the trip was about, and of course have a mountain to catch up on when you return. Maintaining a family and a full-time job, it is also necessary to be "available" with some continuity!

If you had an unlimited budget and space and time was no object, what would your perfect travel day look like? (for example: start your morning in Bora Bora; afternoon on a safari in Kenya; night in Australia, etc.)

A single day only? Then ideally it involves no travel at all, but kicking back and appreciating where I am. Ideally in an unspoilt natural landscape anywhere, with a mixture of good friends and people I've never met, but all participating in a festival or celebration of some sort.

For those looking to travel to every country, what is the best piece of advice you could offer them?

Be organized and interested in the logistical planning. Do it yourself; don't leave it to others. Don't waste time traveling "backpacker style." Life is too short to wait a few days or a week for a bus or other transport connection when you could have planned a more synchronistic schedule/route and seen more.

Pick your "sacrifices" carefully! I've been lucky not to have had to sacrifice much in my life to achieve my travel goals. Cumulatively I'm sure it would be considered an expensive goal, but the in-depth cross cultural understanding and knowledge of the world gained from it to me, is priceless. Definitely to be considered an investment, not a sacrifice.

For someone that has been almost everywhere, what still gets you excited about packing your bags again?

Almost every place I can and do travel to always feels "new" to me. Different experiences, people, encounters, and weather add depth and nuance to even those destinations I've been many times. It is this continual "newness" that excites me. The endless opportunity for discovery is really exhilarating.

A good example is a business trip I took to Paris many years ago. Though I had been there a few times before, on this occasion it surprisingly coincided with Christo's "wrapping" of the Pont Neuf bridge; a once in a lifetime event. I had no idea it was happening and just "happened" to see a glimpse of it out a taxi's window as we sped along. I certainly felt lucky that day: proving the "right place, right time" adage without a doubt.

Do you feel you have missed out on certain aspects of life being away from home so much?

No, it adds value and depth to your relationships with those at home and in business as well.

Looking ahead, what travel plans and goals are you still pursuing, and what is on your "Bucket List"?

When I can, I'm gradually working my way through the "Extended List" of specific geo/ethno/socio distinct regions/states/provinces around the world as evidenced on MTP's and TBT's master lists. Of course, attention to the UNESCO World Heritage list is also important to me.

More than anything else however, I try wherever possible these days to travel for events or celebrations. I've found that these cultural highlights add additional value to the destination, and seeing everyone in a special festive mood, best decorative outfits, etc. is that much more special.

Some of my favorites include the Day of the Dead in Oaxaca, Mexico; Inti Raymi in Sacsayhuanman, Peru; the various Teschu festivals in Bhutan; Songkran in northern Thailand; the Mass Games in Pyongyang; Yadnya Kasada at Mount Bromo; the nightly Wagah Border closure in Amritsar; and of course the many, many African festivals, etc.

Thomas Flannigan, U.S.A.

(Thomas Flannigan in Detroit, Michigan)

Where did you grow up and what was your early life like?

I grew up on Chicago's South Side. My father was a postal worker, my mother a housewife. My mother hated travel but my father loved it, and we did some road trips to Canada and New York. Nobody we knew traveled abroad but the public library was full of books that fed my wanderlust. Alaska was the first place that I fell in love with and other places followed quickly.

When did you go from casually traveling to making this a full-time goal, and what motivated you to travel to every country?

My first trip abroad was in 1975, which was a six-week Euro-Rail pass trip in Europe. My first journey around the world, through all 24 time zones, was in 1978. I figured that would get it out of my system. Around this time, I realized that I wanted to keep planning more trips and the wanderlust was not going away.

Do you remember the point where you said to yourself, "I can really accomplish this"?

At some point, when I was around 22, I had read enough travel books to realize that the writers were not exceptional people. They were usually not rich or connected. I figured if they could do it, I could do it!

What have you done over your life to gain the freedom and finances to pursue as much travel as you have?

I am a lawyer, not the easiest job to combine with long trips away from the office. I planned journeys years in advance. I planned four to six month journeys before and after grad school, before and after law school, after a judicial clerkship, and so on. After I got married, I talked my wife into quitting our jobs and working in Tokyo law firms. Of course, we took at least three months to get there and five months to get back.

Was there ever a time you felt like abandoning this goal?

I briefly thought about it when I started working for a big law firm, but it did not take long for the dreams to return.

What were your worst travel experiences (i.e. detainment, bribes, car accidents, sickness, etc.) and why?

I was mugged at knife point near the Nairobi Youth Hostel in 1980. Only a British Airways van, taking the crew from the airport along Kenyatta Avenue, saved my life. I still went back to Kenya for my honeymoon eight years later.

In 1983, I took a small plane on Air Zanzibar from Zanzibar to Dar es Salaam. A truck blocked the runway and the pilot pulled out at the last minute. He was as terrified, as we all were, all six of us. He tried two more times to land but had lost his nerve. He was almost out of fuel and had one more shot at it and made it.

What do you consider the most adventurous trip you have taken?

I have taken 14 journeys around the world and the second one, in 1980, was the longest and most exotic. I was gone for seven months and not only traveled through the 24 time zones but went from Invercargill, New Zealand, the southernmost city in the world according to some measures, to Kiruna, Sweden, which claims to be the northernmost city in the world. It cost $6250 total, but I hitchhiked everywhere that I could.

What were your most challenging countries to visit and why?

Iran — because I tried to get a visa for years and finally got a short transit visa in November, 1997. My wife and I were the first independent travelers from the U.S. to visit Iran in 18 years. The visa was the hard part. Once we got to Iran, it was easy to travel on your own. We were also the first independent Americans to visit Libya in many years when we finally got a visa in 2003. Our youngest daughter took her first steps in Ghadames, in the Sahara Desert.

What is the strangest thing you've seen/experienced while traveling?

That was probably on February 28, 2001, in a small soccer stadium in Columbus, Ohio. My wife and I went to the U.S.-Mexico World Cup Qualifier in freezing temperatures. The U.S. had never beaten Mexico in a qualifier and was given no chance to win, but fanatical fans, wrapped in American flags, created the most incredible atmosphere I have ever seen, and would not accept defeat. The inspired team pulled off a win at the end. A transcendent experience.

Which travel experiences stand out the most and why?

The first time I traveled abroad in 1975. It was all new. The more you travel, the harder it is to find a new thrill. In a way, it is a personal search to duplicate the earlier, unique experiences.

What are the most overrated and underrated countries you've been to in your travels and why?

I think Mexico is underrated because you hear so much about crime and so many travelers head to the beaches but never see the amazing cities, and that includes Mexico City. I love New Zealand but think it is overrated because Australia is next door and the Australians are more extroverted and zany than the New Zealanders.

What are the best and worst meals you have ever had traveling and where were they?

Best: A vegetarian dinner for Hindu pilgrims in Madurai, India, was one of the best meals I have ever had, $1.90 US for two people, during my fourth visit to India in 1998.

Worst: A Chinese buffet, run a by a Korean guy in Prince George, Canada, which we visited when we drove our old Saturn automobile to Alaska and back in 2009, with the kids in the back seat, was awful. Who ever heard of a bad Chinese restaurant? For that matter, who ever heard of a bad Korean restaurant?

What country made you feel most out of your comfort zone and why?

China in 1983. I have never been stared at like that. Thousands of people on the streets in Beijing would stop to look at me. When I returned in 1984, very few people stared. In 1987, nobody did.

Do you speak any foreign languages? If so, which has been the most useful for you besides English?

I speak Japanese fluently, having studied it, mainly at Buddhist temples, for 34 years. I am not a Buddhist, but a devout Catholic. I also speak some French, Spanish, Hungarian, Estonian, Russian, and Korean. I also speak a few words of about 50 other languages but only a few words. I am a bad linguist, but I have found learning even some words of a nation's language opens the doors of perception for the traveler. You also get treated much better. French has been the most useful language for me, followed by Spanish, Russian, Mandarin Chinese, and German.

Looking back from when you started traveling to where you are now, in what ways, if any, have travel changed you?

I realized early on that I was lucky to be born in a rich country like the U.S. I have met many smart, hard-working people in poor countries who did not have that luck. I also learned to always try to see how other countries deal with a problem and take that into account when dealing with a similar problem in the U.S. I have also learned that you cannot judge a stranger by how they look or how they are dressed. As soon as I start thinking that way I am brought back to earth.

What is the longest continuous trip you have ever taken? When was it and where did you travel?

In 1980, I was gone seven months and visited Los Angeles, Tahiti, Fiji, New Zealand, hitchhiked across Australia, Indonesia, Southeast Asia, Nepal (including the Mount Everest Base Camp trek) India, Sri Lanka, Kenya, Sudan, Ethiopia, Egypt, Israel, and then took three months hitch-hiking from Athens to London and flew back to Chicago in time to start law school.

What is your favorite "off-the-beaten-path" destination and why?

Siberia. It is the size of Australia but has almost no foreign tourists. In general, more tourists in a place mean you will be treated worse. Paris is a fantastic place but don't expect special treatment at the tourist office on a hot August afternoon. In Siberia, you may be the first foreigner that the Siberian has ever met, or ever will meet.

What are the best and worst places you have ever spent a night?

The worst place was in the back of a flatbed truck in northern Peru, when hitchhiking to Lima in 1983. Floods had wiped out many roads, and the locals turned hostile in the middle of night. I was lucky to survive.

The best place was a tea house in Thyangboche, Nepal, at 4,700 meters, on the Everest trek in 1980. The scenery was incredible, the food good and company outstanding. A lawyer from Austin, Texas had carried the complete works of Shakespeare in his backpack, and a young English hiker and he performed parts of a few Shakespeare plays surrounded by candles and sleeping yaks.

In your opinion, what country or place in the world feels the most authentic and untouched by tourism?

Myanmar. It had not changed a bit between 1980 and 1995, but I think I would be a bit shocked if I went back there now.

In your opinion, where is the most beautiful place on Earth?

Naggar Castle, Kulu Valley, India. Naggar Castle is located about 20 kilometers south of Manali in the state of Himachal Pradash. The Kulu Valley is a narrow, lush valley surrounded by towering peaks on both sides. Naggar Castle is also home to one of the Nicholas Roerich Museums. Roerich, a Russian Asiaphile who talked Stravinsky into dropping out of law school and designed the sets for *Rite of Spring*, died here in 1947, after almost 15 years of overland expeditions through Asia. He painted thousands of canvases and may well have picked the most beautiful spot to settle in for his final years.

Naggar narrowly beat out Karimabad, Hunza, Pakistan; Milford Sound, New Zealand; Tyangboche, Nepal; Peyto Lake, Canada, and the Glenn Highway, Alaska.

What do you enjoy most when traveling (cities, nature, people, cultural spots, etc.) and why?

The people are the best part. I have missed lots of famous temples and churches around the world but have stayed in about 1,200 youth hostels, and learned so much from the travelers I met in hostels. I am a city boy and like cities, especially old and charming towns, but outdoor adventures like the Milford Track in New Zealand and the Kungsleden in Swedish Lapland really made an impression as well.

What travel accomplishments are you most proud of?

Pulling off the first trip around the world in 1978; after that, it got a lot easier.

If you had just one personal travel story to share with someone, what would that be?

In 2002, my wife and I were cheering on the U.S. National Team at the World Cup, and taking the hydrofoil from Busan, South Korea to Shimonoseki, Japan. Our oldest daughter was five weeks old at the time. A Korean woman came up to us, grabbed the baby, and looked her straight in the eyes, then walked over to the other side of the ship and sat down. We were surprised but not afraid, and walked over to her. She spoke no English but was with a Korean man who did, and he said she loved children, could she play with our child for a short time? We said sure and went back to our seat. Our baby was in good hands. They were having a great time. After an hour, we went back and the man said, "Can you given her a few more minutes? It would mean a lot to her." Finally, we were docking in Japan and there was no time left. We went to her seat and she cuddled the baby, handed her over, and burst into tears.

Besides your home country, where do you find yourself returning to over and over and why?

Russia, especially Siberia. Tourists can now go to all kinds of places that was once off limits to foreigners. Novosibirsk is my favorite city in the world besides my hometown of Chicago.

What is the ideal amount of time you prefer to travel each trip before you are ready for home and a break?

I think two or three months make the most sense. You are not gone so long that you lose touch with your own life at home, but you do have the time to do some strange things that you cannot do on a two or three week trip.

If you had an unlimited budget and space and time was no object, what would your perfect travel day look like? (for example: start your morning in Bora Bora; afternoon on a safari in Kenya; night in Australia, etc.)

Morning in India, when it is still cool and quiet, afternoon in Alaska or Siberia, late afternoon in Buenos Aires and night in Tokyo, a city that really comes alive when the sun sets.

For those looking to travel to every country, what is the best piece of advice you could offer them?

I would not try to go to every country, because it is so expensive and there is real danger, mainly from disease in many places. I would follow your dreams and try to visit a different place on every trip, challenge yourself and take a chance here and there. But don't go to a place just to say you have been there!

For someone that has been almost everywhere, what still gets you excited about packing your bags again?

Going to some new place, or a place that I visited a long time ago; I like the thrill of the unknown.

Do you feel you have missed out on certain aspects of life being away from home so much?

Of course, you miss a lot when you are gone for long periods of time. You also pay a career penalty by being gone for so long. The hard part is striking a balance between love of travel and something of a conventional life at home.

Looking ahead, what travel plans and goals are you still pursuing, and what is on your "Bucket List"?

I am planning three more trips around the world, number 15, 16 and 17, in the next three years. My bucket list keeps growing: Kamchatka, Tobolsk, St. Helena, the Savitsky Collection at the State Art Museum of Kara-Kapakistan, touching the Musikverein and attending a concert of the Vienna Philharmonic in the Musikverein, the Ogasawara Islands in Japan, finally seeing the Aurora Borealis after six or seven close misses, the churches at Lalibela, Ethiopia, seeing a performance of Rabindranath Tagore's opera, Valmiki Pratibha. The list goes on…

Tony Childs, U.S.A.

(Tony Childs in the 1980s in Africa)

Where did you grow up and what was your early life like?

I grew up in Los Angeles. Even though we were in the city, we lived next to the Santa Monica Mountains so we had lots of open space in which to roam. We had considerable freedom and I started hitching to the beach early in Junior High School. I grew up with an older brother and loved to read, starting with stacks of comic books and soon moved on to the *Landmark History* series. Those books and the *National Geographic,* plus a father, who had traveled extensively, expanded my radius of what was available to see in the world. I loved books on archeology, and for a period wanted to be one. My mom told me that when I was two I climbed over the back fence and went off exploring — at least as far as a two year old can scramble. I have never yet seen a horizon I didn't want to explore. And movement is important. Lakes are not so hot but oceans and rivers fascinate me — the constant change. This is a part of most true travelers which is poorly understood; the need for movement. The journey is as important as what you see. Often a tourist will go to see specific things. A traveler is content to throw themselves into new situations and experience whatever happens. I guess I am easily bored. I love new stuff — new places, new faces, new unfamiliar customs and events. I am planning another trip to India with my wife (our fifth) and I just wrote to the woman in India that we were not too excited about seeing old temples *unless they had current use*. When you have traveled as much as we have there gets to be a point where you start to ignore the obvious major tourist points and look for the unusual around them. So if we walk by the Eiffel Tower, the people visiting it are now more interesting to us than the structure.

Between his first and last marriages, my father was a real estate broker in Beverly Hills in the 1930's. He sold an expensive lot and made around $500 commission. The most money he had ever had in his life. He went out and bought a 'round the world cruise. He spoke of it often; how he cried as he left a sweetheart on the dock in Honolulu; how he saw a man beheaded in China, etc. Later when he was more established he would travel with my mom and they would buy this and that and have it shipped back home by ship. Sometimes I would go with him down to customs in Long Beach to pick things up. He would look at the ships and say, "Boy, I would love to get on one of those and go somewhere!!" I have been getting on something and going somewhere ever since.

When did you go from casually traveling to making this a full-time goal, and what motivated you to travel to every country?

I had a trip scheduled to the five 'Stans, and at the last minute my wife had to cancel due to her sister falling ill. (As an aside this was the only trip for which I purchased trip insurance — yes, they paid.) It was a great trip. There was a professor from a local college here in Southern California on the trip and one day on the bus he asked me how many countries I had visited. We went over the list and then he told me how many he had visited. He was way ahead. It had never occurred to me to try and go to ALL the countries, but I caught the bug. Soon thereafter I became aware of the Travelers' Century Club (TCC) and an obsession was born.

Do you remember the point where you said to yourself, "I can really accomplish this"?

Whenever I start something I assume that I can accomplish it. The Travelers' Century Club list immediately appeared to be something which was possible; however the Most Traveled People (MTP) list is a completely different animal, because you can actually see where you are on the list, so it is competitive. That was never the case with the Travelers' Century Club. I used to resent those who would start a conversation at the TCC lunches with the question, "How many have you been to?"

But as with all the traveling, *going* is the true quest; *going* is the big adventure; *going* is the wonder book which never fails to amaze.

What have you done over your life to gain the freedom and finances to pursue as much travel as you have?

I grew up in a family where being financially successful was a given. So I had the great advantage of having the idea/goal of becoming financially successful. I didn't want to get a job; I wanted to make *real* money. Along the way, after an ulcer and ventures which were really not me, I added the goal of not tying myself down. Difficult goals, but somehow it all worked out. Certainly my wife has been a big part of my success in many ways.

Was there ever a time you felt like abandoning this goal?

NO! I did adjust my Travelers' Century Club goal of going to all 324 places on their list. Diego Garcia (BIOT) is simply not possible and has not been possible for some time. Also Norwegian and French Antarctica will be terribly expensive (my wife would have to come), and since we have already been to Antarctica three times I have put finishing that list on hold. If I can get to Diego, then I may finish the list. Until that point, I will work on the Most Traveled People list.

What were your worst travel experiences (i.e. detainment, bribes, car accidents, sickness, etc.) and why?

Catching Giardia in Afghanistan; it stayed with me into Nepal. My wife wanted to go to the Everest View Hotel, so we flew up. I was on the "Sudden Death" cure for Giardia; take seven big black pills for x amount of days. Basically they killed everything inside you, including the Giardia. They made you very sick. But she wanted to see Tengboche. It is normally a two day hike but we only had one day to do it. I literally crawled back to the hotel. The hotel had no heat except for the fireplaces. I was not a happy camper. When it came time to fly out, the clouds settled over the tiny air strip. When a small plane took off, it headed directly into a huge wall across the valley. The pilot initially said, "No way." But then he changed his mind and agreed to try it. As we took off, he cursed the ground crew in Kathmandu for never filling up the oxygen. When we took off we quickly lost sight of everything due to the low visibility. He said, "Hang on," and flipped the plane over so he could get a better bearing. We made it, but flying upside down with huge mountains looming all around us and not being able to see anything is not something I care to repeat. Later we found out our Swiss pilot was a local legend; he could fly and land anywhere.

My back has gone out several times on trips. Most recent was on a trek in the Indian Himalayas this year. We had to trek out with big time pain, and that was after downing two Vicodin; and altitude sickness... over and over and over. First time was when we went up Mt. Kilimanjaro. Never been anywhere near that high before so I thought I was just wimping out. We reached the summit (at least what I thought was the summit) and I collapsed. I was in serious pain. But then my wife started kicking me on my foot saying, "Let's go." Turned out the true top, another 500 feet of more altitude to the 19500+ top, was more hiking along the lip of the crater. Oh, and I was constipated with bad stomach cramps.

I had a kidney stone in the Northwest Territories. I was traveling alone and called a late night taxi to take me to the emergency room. I had to stop to throw up on the curb on the way. Almost did a good job but later saw evidence on my right shoe. They hooked me up to an IV, gave me the required doses of morphine, and waited for it to pass. Only other patient was a drunk Indian throwing up in a wastebasket. They mailed me a bill — $87 for everything.

I am prone to Delhi belly so I've endured big time diarrhea in half the countries of the world. Worst was on a trip to Sri Lanka where I not only had diarrhea but also the barfs. Coupled with a sleeping pill, my midnight bathroom visit had all exits in full production. As I tried to move from the toilet to the sink to throw up, I managed to slip on the mat while spraying nasties here and there, break a glass on the counter, and smash my finger on the side of the tub as I hit the floor. I crawled back into bed while my poor wife had to try and clean up after me. The next day my finger was just hanging there. I went to the hospital and had a very interesting experience. Nothing like an emergency to get some local color. The doctor looked at me and said, "You look tough… we won't have to give you any pain medicine." Then he yanked my finger trying to reset it. "Ouch." No movement. Then he wrapped my finger with gauze to get a better grip. Second time did it. Still ouch.

But no car accidents, no robberies, no muggings, and no missed trains, planes, or buses. But once while trying to get home from Myanmar with my wife and girls, we got to the airport and they asked for the credit card with which I had purchased the tickets. My original card number had been in a stolen batch so MasterCard had sent me a new card. They would not accept the replacement card and voided our reservation. We had to buy new tickets for the flight to Bangkok. Once there we found out that our seats were no longer available on the continuing flight to Los Angeles even if we bought new tickets. Once you don't use a leg of a ticket you lose all the subsequent legs. I knew this and asked the people in Rangoon about it, but they assured me that they would not be canceled…

I have had some snakes much closer to me than I would like. Once as we picked up our ground sheet and there were several big ones squirming there. Snakes scare me to death. I also once had a huge spider on my arm in Namibia. We were on the back roads trying to find a farm which took tourists and got more than lost. I got out of the van trying to figure out where we were. My wife suddenly yells, "Look out!" I thought an animal or something was approaching so I jumped back into the van. Her eyes were saucers and she pointed to my arm and I see it and after a BIG SHAKE from me the spider came jumping off my arm, disappearing into the metal work next to my feet. My kids scrambled out and almost refused to get back in the van — a very nervous time, especially for me since I was in sandals. We never saw the spider again. It was BIG, at least three inches across.

I've also been very, very, very cold at times — for instance, in a deep valley in Nepal while trekking, and in the back of an overland truck coming out of the Atlas Mountains in Algeria.

I got out of Uganda into Kenya the day they tried to kill Ida Amin. The border was closed that night. That was a very, very close call.

What do you consider the most adventurous trip you have taken?

We floated the Omo in Ethiopia with Sobek in 1979... There were no lifelines attached to the trip. Almost didn't make it into the country. We had no visas as Ethiopia at that time did not issue them. But Sobek had a deal with in-country people and we were to be met at the Addis Ababa airport by someone from the tourist agency and she would get us in. But when we tried to leave Kenya the immigration guy said we could not get on the plane without a visa. I started to blow, but my wife took over. She very patiently explained to him that it would not be his fault if there were a problem in Addis Ababa. Astoundingly, he just said OK and let us through. It was just us, our boatmen, the rafts, and Africa. If you fell in at the wrong time a crocodile or hippo might crunch you. The Tsetse flies were simply dreadful. Every tenth one or so would feel like someone had jammed a pin into you. At one point, I wore my parka to avoid them, even though it was very hot on the water. The tribes were no-madic; only coming down to the river when it was low so they could plant in the very rich bank soil. At times, they were aggressive in their stealing. They were armed. There was absolutely no authority around within a week of us. The Tsetse flies meant that there were no permanent settlements.

What were your most challenging countries to visit and why?

Africa, because Europeans are a mark; we stand out because of our skin color, and white skin means rich. So every hustler and thief are interested. We have been to Africa over 20+ times and never had any real trouble, but it can be a grind to fend off the constant attempts to gain something from an association with us. That said, we love Africans in general.

One of our most fascinating experiences was going to a night time city dance in Upper Volta (now known as Burkina Faso). It had something to do with the French and the dancers got more and more excited. This was not a hotel show; this was real Africa. Their feelings for the French were not kind and the dance showed that. But the energy and direction of the dance became so intense that it became frightening — after an hour or so we left. In that same town, we went to a dance in a junk yard. It was just dirty dirt. My wife got up and danced when asked with the general mob. But she had a cut on her leg and something got into it and her leg started a serious swelling the next day. Fortunately someone had some very strong anti-whatever and it calmed it down. But the speed with which the infection moved was awful.

When we went through Afghanistan on the overland truck it was often touch and go with the locals. One war had just ended and banditry was a way of life.

What is the strangest thing you've seen/experienced while traveling?

While traveling up a river in Suriname on a zodiac just after dusk with flashlights on looking for eye shine, we suddenly saw hundreds of pairs of little sparkles floating down the river toward us. Turned out to be tiny spiders on leafs which must have been blown off trees by wind further up the river — magic.

While we were going through southern Rhodesia (which is now Zimbabwe) on an overland truck in 1976, a convertible with three girls pulled up beside us. This was Rhodesia, so there was basically no traffic and certainly no convertibles. Earlier that day as we were having lunch by the side of the road an armed jeep came shuddering to a stop in the middle of the road and they shouted, "What the fuck do you people think you are doing!? This is a WAR zone. Cars are ambushed along this stretch regularly. Get out of here!" So we did, and as we were jetting down the road later that day the convertible came up behind us. The girls were European. They waved and then the two not driving lifted their blouses and gave us a very nice *HELLO THERE* with their boobs. Then they were off... stranger than fiction.

Also, on a day trip into Paraguay, we visited the site of a European doctor's place in the forest, a man who had made an impact on local health many, many years before. Out of nowhere a Korean group shows up, looks around, and then starts ballroom dancing. Right there in the middle of nowhere... dance, dance, dance.

Which travel experiences stand out the most and why?

Being surprised. We travel to see and experience *different*. We are seldom disappointed. Off Niue while snorkeling, we came across some sea snakes. Highly poisonous, but they have tiny mouths so it is almost impossible for them to bite you. We followed them for quite a period, observing snake movement under water. Another time we had just broken camp in the Hindu Kush (Afghanistan) when a group of nomads came streaming out of the mountains. It was a National Geographic moment; women with ramrod straight backs, the very small children bundled on top of the camels, the men with rifles slung over their shoulders. Sitting over the Omo River in Ethiopia, watching the play of the water against the far bank and seeing a young boy, complete with body paint, come walking along the trail. Suddenly he saw us and stopped in absolute shock. We must have been "from the moon" for all he knew. At that time

Europeans were virtually unknown along that stretch of the river.

What are the most overrated and underrated countries you've been to in your travels and why?

Arthur Frommer wrote later in his life that "the magic" was going out for many of the most famous tourist points. I've visited Anne Frank's House and being crushed by hundreds of other tourists in the exceptionally small hallways is not magic. Going to the Potata Palace in Tibet was similar. Small passageways filled with Chinese tourists — none of which had any consideration that this was a place of worship. A sacred place made into a Disneyland.

What are the best and worst meals you have ever had traveling and where were they?

Worst are beyond counting... best are forgotten.

What country made you feel most out of your comfort zone and why?

Japan and China have the least amount of English, and that includes signs. So we are the most lost there. That doesn't mean we don't love Japan — it is a place where every part of their culture is an art.

Do you speak any foreign languages? If so, which has been the most useful for you besides English?

No, but my wife picks up portions of a language quickly. If I'm completely frustrated I will simply say in a very loud voice, "Does anyone speak English here?" Fortunately there is almost always someone who does and that someone is universally helpful.

Looking back from when you started traveling to where you are now, in what ways, if any, have travel changed you?

It made me much more tolerant. Made me much more patient and broadened me immensely. I carry the images of a lifetime "out there" within me at all times. It is like the best entertainment in the world — I can draw on it at any time.

What is the longest continuous trip you have ever taken? When was it and where did you travel?

Eight to nine months — London across Africa on an overland truck to Johannesburg; hitchhiking back up from South Africa and eventually seeing the mountain gorillas in Zaire. Then another eight month trip from London to Kathmandu on another overland truck with a month long trek in the Himalayas thereafter. And finally, a seven month long stay in South Africa with our young children.

What is your favorite "off-the-beaten-path" destination and why?

Albania and Yemen because they are singularly unique; almost like strange stories come true.

What are the best and worst places you have ever spent a night?

We once camped directly in the path of the great migration in East Africa with the animals and their associated noise passing around us all night. Another time with our small group crowded into a concrete container for a night in Yemen. It was able to be locked from the inside, which was necessary due to our location. It was more than stuffy and goodness knows what else had slept there previously. Whatever they were, they had left their smells behind. And for a night bathroom break we had to wander into a small field with decades of prior use for that purpose and snarling dogs to top the action.

In your opinion, what country or place in the world feels the most authentic and untouched by tourism?

This is a very difficult question because tourism is moving so fast. Even if we have visited a spot just a couple of years ago it can be overrun today. We visited Mongolia in 1999 and today it has completely changed. But judging from what I read and from the trips I can see offered, I would say Yemen and Albania. We visited Yemen in the early 80's and it felt as if we had fallen back in time. Albania has to be one of the strangest places out there but endlessly fascinating and entertaining. I strongly feel that it is the best largely unvisited destination in the world.

In your opinion, where is the most beautiful place on Earth?

Antarctica.

What do you enjoy most when traveling (cities, nature, people, cultural spots, etc.) and why?

We love the natural stuff, but enjoy just about everything — just as long as there are not too many tourists.

What travel accomplishments are you most proud of?

That we have been willing to go virtually everywhere in the world without prejudice and also be willing to suspend over-whelming negative opinions about going to many places. The most common last words we hear from people before we leave is, "Be safe." We have found the world, outside major cities, to be far safer than here at home.

If you had just one personal travel story to share with someone, what would that be?

Gorillas. We have seen them in Zaire, Gabon, and Rwanda — each time different and each time a very different journey.

Before we left in 1976 for our life-changing, epic overland trip across Africa from London to South Africa in 1976, my father, a devoted traveler but at an age where certain things were no longer possible, told me that there were two things he regretted he had not done in Africa: seeing the Okavango swamp and visiting the mountain gorillas. After completing the almost five month truck trip from London to Johannesburg and then a month long lark into Botswana (but not the swamp) and Namibia with three wild young men, two adventurous young women, and an overloaded Land Rover, we decided to head north from South Africa to find gorillas.

But first the swamp: Hitchhiking up to Botswana from South Africa was a special treat. Among the people who picked us up were an ivory smuggler and a small bird collector. The collector had a Land Rover with a rig with an enclosed mesh attached to its rear. Naturally there were a couple of Africans to do all the physical work — it was Africa in 1976. They would find ravines and put a net across it and then chase the birds into it. The birds would be sold to collectors, etc. It was fine fun except one of the helpers forgot to tighten the lug nuts properly so a wheel came loose, stripping the thread. We had to move on so we were once again on our thumbs. This was the middle of Botswana, so there was just an empty dirt road stretching seemingly forever into the horizon. We were picked up by the next car, maybe three hours later, and taken to Maun — the gateway to the Okavango. At that time Maun, was one saloon and a couple of stores plus a few simple lodges/camp ground which were perhaps five miles from the saloon. We were dropped off at the saloon at dusk and had a quick bite. When we inquired about how to get to the campground, we were met with blank stares. So we stood in the parking lot and asked every person who we saw if we could have a ride. No luck. We were about to drop our sleeping bags in the bush when a very intoxicated black man suddenly appeared and asked if we needed a ride. We said yes and were off on "Mr. Toad's Wild Ride". He was more than drunk and veered crazily across the very wide dirt road which was lined with large trees. He would say, "Whoa Betsy," when his speed took off and then drift down to almost zero. The car was a VW with me squished in the back seat with our backpacks on top of me. Providence shined on us and we made it to Croc Camp. When we woke in the morning, we found that some people we had met in Los Angeles just before leaving for Africa were camped next to us — very small world.

The next morning we asked around to find some way to get into the swamp. People looked at us as if we were damaged children. We could go on a lodge sponsored boat trip but to actually GO INTO THE SWAMP AND CAMP? No way. Undeterred, we wandered into a village and started to try and ask if anyone there would take us in. No one could speak English. Just as we were about to give up a small boy appeared and agreed to be our translator. He found a very old fisherman who agreed to paddle us in using his fishing canoe. I can't remember the fellow's name, so I will call him Al.

The daily price was established using sign language. About seven oar strokes and we were in a water world. Our only problem was that the way we sat in the bottom of the canoe gave us only a look up view of what was around us. But the birds were great and we would periodically stop on one of the many small islands for nature stops and to look around. This was Africa and there were animals around. We could only hear them crashing around but very, very rarely saw them. At night we would camp on an island and put up our small orange tent. Tsetse flies were our constant visitors when we camped. They have very nasty bites. We drank the swamp water unfiltered from the swamp — it was very clean and caused no problems. Al supplied us with fish to supplement the canned food we had brought. It was fun and an adventure, but after four days we were ready to return. But Al had other ideas; he wanted the full seven day's pay. Originally we had said we wanted to visit the swamp for seven days. The language barrier prevented us from quickly communicating that we would pay him for the full seven days, but we wanted out NOW. Finally he understood and we were soon back at Croc Camp. He wanted something else, but we had to find a camp employee to find out what it was. He wanted to have a drink at the camp bar. This was southern Africa in 1976 and blacks were not welcome at bars. But we took him in anyway and overcame the immediate chill in the establishment and bought him a beer.

We had been on the sandy road north from Maun to Chobe on our Mad Tea Party Land Rover trip. It was an exceptionally bad road and was very sparsely used. Hitchhiking did not look promising, so we went to the tiny Maun airfield and hoped. Luck, as usual, was with us and we hopped on a small private plane which was heading to Chobe. Naturally we helped pay for the gas. The unexpected joy was that we got to see the swamp from the air. Landing in Chobe, we once again used our thumbs to get to the Kazungula ferry crossing into Zambia. We did not immediately cross over. Zambia had its share of problems just then and I did not want to be standing on a road there with my thumb out. We waited until we could get a ride all the way to Lusaka. It was not a long wait. A very nice gentleman picked us up and away we went. Turned out he was an ivory smuggler delivering some goods to a contact in Lusaka. Near town, we were pulled over by a motorcycle policeman. This was rare in itself, as in all our time in black Africa we had never seen a motorcycle policeman before. He said that there was not enough tread in the rear tires. Obviously it was payoff time, but our driver was adamant. He would not pay. The policeman, becoming angry, said that this would have to be settled at the police station. Still our driver would not pay. So off we went — very nervously I might add as police stations were not the place one wanted to be. I was going to tell him to drop us off when he finally decided that the cop was deadly serious and came up with the bribe.

We found a campground run by Indians, at which we had stopped on our way south. The Indians were the money changers in those days. We had planned to take the Tanzania-Zambia railroad up to Dar es Salaam, but it was broken, so we flew to Nairobi. Nairobi was the tourist hub for East Africa and hopefully the place where we could find information on how to see the mountain gorillas. In 1976, there was no Internet and communication between and about a place even a very short distance away was seldom available. But there was no information. We went to the fancy outfitters and the animal protection groups. There was a faint sentiment that the gorillas were in Zaire but no one knew how to go see them. I had read George Schaller's *Year of the Gorilla* before beginning the trip and we were determined to find the big apes. Finally we met a traveler who told us that we had to get to Bakavu, next to Lake Kivu in Eastern Zaire.

We booked a flight and landed at the air strip servicing Bakavu. It was just a set of bamboo walls. We got off and looked around. We saw no cars, no taxis, no buses, no nothing. And then the people started to thin out. We asked how to get to Bakavu, but everyone spoke French and we got nowhere. Out of nowhere the pilot of the plane which had flown us in asked us what we were doing. We told him. "There is no real way to get to town, so why don't you guys climb into the back of that truck over there. It takes people here and there but ends up in Bakavu." he said.

It was late afternoon and we set out. It was a very slow journey as we seemed to go up every dirt path off the road to drop someone off at this village or that. After dark we pulled up to a village among some low hills. Everyone else got out. Except for some cooking fires, there was no light. The driver, using sign language, informed us that the truck was broken and we were there for the night. We decided to sleep in the back of the truck, but just as we were getting our sleeping bags out the driver comes back and tells us that the truck was fixed (probably he was finished with his girlfriend) and we could start again. At about 11:00 p.m., we got to town. As we jumped out of the back of the truck the pilot charged up and started apologizing. Where had we been? He was worried about us. To compensate he gave us his airline room at the only working hotel in town. He was leaving the next day and could stay elsewhere. "Stay as long as you like since there isn't another flight for a while."

The room came with bullet holes in the walls. Bakavu was the hot spot in the Katanga succession; a few short years before they had been eating people downstairs. No hot water but we were happy to have a bed. We spent the next two days (three nights) trying to find out how to see the gorillas. There was a little shack which had "Tourist Information" on it, but it was always closed. We bought some baby strawberries from a street vendor who was immediately ambushed by some passing French nuns for overcharging us. Then the hotel manager showed up and told us that enough was enough and we had to either start paying or get out. We got out and moved to a local hotel down the road. ("local" as in they built little fires in the corridor to cook.)

In the morning, we went back to the good hotel for some coffee and a miracle occurred. A group of European tourists were sitting a couple of tables over and we heard the word "gorilla." I sent Susan (my wife) over to investigate. She is of some ability with other languages and has much, much ability with people. Through three languages, she found out that they had two Land Rovers and were off to see the gorillas the next day. Yes, there was room for us but we had to help pay for the guides…

Early the next day we set out. At the entry point, we meet a local guide who speaks French and two pygmy trackers. His French goes through a German who kinda explains to us in English what is happening. Susan and I have been in Africa for over seven months and know when to wear what so we are in shorts as we know how hot and steamy it will be in the jungle. Great idea — except there were stinging needles everywhere. Our legs were on fire for the entire day. We plunge up and down, up and down through the jungle. Most of the time there is a semi path but often we are just blazing a path through the bush. We start to see gorilla scat — large piles of it — and finally some sleeping pads. We are told to hurry as the only time it is safe to see them is while they are eating. Otherwise they are moving and the last thing the guide tells us that we want to do is end up among a moving group — you might get between mom and her little ones. Number one rule with wild animals: don't get between mom and her runts. We plow along awhile further and then the pygmy's stop. They tell us to just go down and wait. They have been smoking marijuana the entire time. Then two baby gorillas are playing in the branches about twenty yards from us. We watch enchanted and they have our entire attention. Daddy silverback mountain gorilla decides to make an entrance by showing his massive head through the thick growth about ten yards from us. He pulls down substantial branches to get a better munch. Later mom shows up. The entire experience is about an hour. No one remembered to notice our blistering legs.

The following day we went to the airline office but they didn't have any flights. "Just go to the airport." Swell. We then decide to take the ferry across the lake up to Goma and hope to catch a ride to Kigali, Rwanda. But the ferry isn't running. No gas, and no gas for cars either as we try to hitch hike out to the bamboo fence airport. But a priest picked us up and we get to the airport near dusk. There is NO ONE there. Zero. So we cook up a little of something and spread our sleeping bags and hope for better luck the next day. Around 9 p.m. we are awakened by God knows who and told, in French, but we got the message, that we could not sleep at the airport. But there was a hotel next door… surely owned by his brother. The hotel was a hut with bamboo partition — but no bugs.

The next day there was a plane and we got a ticket, via Burundi, back to Nairobi.

End of Gorilla story #1

By 2007, Rwanda had become the destination spot for gorillas. Everything was very organized and tourists were almost certain to see them. Arriving at the ranger station the gorilla seekers were arranged by ability to absorb various difficulty levels to see a group of gorillas. Each gorilla family group is constantly monitored by rangers to protect against poachers. Right across the mountain ridges is Zaire and Uganda where lawlessness is the norm. Each night the families move and some settle in fairly close to the staging area and some are at a distance. We were put in a group which had to travel some distance, but the trails were pretty good. When we did get to our family group, they paid us no attention and just went about doing what gorillas do; eating the forest. It was relatively dense there with only narrow trails created by the gorillas. As they were spread out we had to be careful not to get in the way of one who decided to move from one location to another. But one gets tired of having one's head swivel, so stuff happens.

We were both looking at some young gorillas when I noticed a male walking toward us. I started to say something but it was so close I decided not to startle it. I shrank back into the bush, but Susan's elbow remained sticking out into the trail. Mr. Gorilla gently moved her elbow out of the way and continued on. Later we were again concentrating on some young ones when another Mr. Gorilla came by. This time I was closest to him and did not see him coming. Using his forearm to move me, he catapulted me into the bush. It felt like an aircraft carrier had just crashed into me. They allowed us to get VERY close to the gorillas. We were literally within a couple of yards. Great pictures — but almost certainly not a good idea. There can be few wildlife experiences superior to standing this close to these magnificent creatures.

End of Gorilla story #2

In 2008, Gabon was not long a tourist destination for anyone other than the French. Then a rich American decided that he would make something of the tourist infrastructure and started "The Loango Project." It included lodges and a small airline. The travel company, Journeys, had a trip there for which we signed up, but at the last minute we were unable to go. Some friends of ours did go but were unimpressed. But they had a name in the country so we contacted the name and made arrangements direct, just for the two of us. A journey never to forget in many ways, but that is another story… gorillas. We fly into a small air strip with a wind sack and nothing else. A jeep was there to meet us and drive us to the path which would lead us to where we would sleep. They took off at an amazing speed and soon we were crashing through the jungle with various branches, etc., smashing onto the windshield. It felt like a Bond movie during a chase scene. Arriving there we shouldered our packs and trudged up the hill, which was a little steep and very hot. The research camp, with some tourist facilities was set up to study the neighboring bai. A bai is an open spot in the jungle, often with a salt lick, which allows for good viewing of the hard to see jungle animals. The camp was on stone and perhaps the first thing we heard was to watch out for snakes. Great…

After breakfast, a guide took us along a dark jungle path to the bai. There was a raised platform for viewing. He left us there for the next six hours. First day we saw lots of animals, but no lowland gorillas; second day lots of animals, but not gorillas. The third morning, our last scheduled day, Susan informed me that she wasn't leaving until she saw a gorilla. Third day slowly passes. Then Susan says, "Well at least we see one."

"Where!!!!"

And there he was… looked like the gorilla in an Abbott and Costello movie, just lumbering along. He was some distance away, but we were able to bring him in close with our binoculars. On the way back to the camp our guide silently motioned us to stop. His eyes opened wide and he said, "There." We looked and there was nothing… He said again, "THERE!"… we looked and saw nothing. We started to move closer and he almost violently stopped us. We then used our binoculars to look at the ground. Perfectly camouflaged amount the leaves was a Gabon viper — a snake with a bye-bye bite. We hiked down the hill the next day and, viola, the jeep was waiting for us. While on our way out, crashing through the arching over-brush, a family of gorillas ran across the road in front of us.

End of Gorilla story #3

Besides your home country, where do you find yourself returning to over and over and why?

We very, very seldom return to the same place. The world is getting smaller and smaller with more and more impact from tourism. What was unspoiled yesterday will be filled with travelers tomorrow. First love is the best; returning to places almost always disappoints me. We have revisited Paris and Istanbul recently with great success, so this is not entirely true, but generally very much so. Many, many people prefer to return over and over because after their initial visit they begin to feel comfortable. We like the edge of not knowing what to expect; of finding and seeing new things. Within reason, and certainly not when we have a flight to catch, we don't mind getting lost. Something always happens to straighten us out and we see unexpected things. We once missed a couple of turns with the girls in the van and ended up in Soweto. Was a little nerve racking at first but all turned out well.

What is the ideal amount of time you prefer to travel each trip before you are ready for home and a break?

At this stage of life, sometime around three weeks.

If you had an unlimited budget and space and time was no object, what would your perfect travel day look like? (for example: start your morning in Bora Bora; afternoon on a safari in Kenya; night in Australia, etc.)

Wake up in the morning with a map and then follow our first idea.

For those looking to travel to every country, what is the best piece of advice you could offer them?

Start now. Trying to go everywhere is a marathon, not a sprint. And take your time. Some places deserve much more time than others, but we have found unexpected pleasures in places we initially did not want to visit. I often remark that I have visited on average over six places a year for the 50 years since I have been out of college. Try not to get stuck. I have many friends who have decided that Hawaii or Tuscany are the best places in the world and they visit over and over.

For someone that has been almost everywhere, what still gets you excited about packing your bags again?

Knowing that new and unexpected things awaits me.

Do you feel you have missed out on certain aspects of life being away from home so much?

Certainly there has been a disruption in the normal continual presence of normal family life.

Looking ahead, what travel plans and goals are you still pursuing, and what is on your "Bucket List"?

My quest is to see everything. My goals are to visit all the spots on the TCC list, if I can somehow in the future get to Diego Garcia, and to move into the top 20 on the Most Traveled People list by the end of 2016. We take four big trips a year and I add solo short hops to pick up some of the less interesting places.

In 2015 we will do a small ship cruise around islands of the Philippines; I will do a solo trip to Western India; we will do a double trip to Russia: the Russian Caucasus plus South Ossetia and then Trans-Siberian railroad; then an organized trip to Alaska with one of our favorite guides; and end the year with a month in China with lots of high speed rail movement. Yes, I have already started planning 2016.

Bob Bonifas, U.S.A.

(Bob Bonifas in Pakistan)

Where did you grow up and what was your early life like?

I have lived in Aurora, Illinois my entire life. I graduated from Marmion Military Academy, an all-boy's Catholic military high school. I helped my father in my senior year to build a super-market and even welded the roof metal sheeting. Forty-seven years ago, I went into the alarm business. I love this business and I am still actively involved.

When did you go from casually traveling to making this a full-time goal, and what motivated you to travel to every country?

I have no travel goals but I am very competitive and successful. I simply do what I find challenging one day at a time. I traveled quite a bit before I discovered the Travelers' Century Club

(TCC) and MostTraveledPeople.com, two travel clubs. Understand this is not a full-time obsession on travel but one of many interests and involvements I have. I am the busiest man I ever met with all my many focuses and a legend in my own mind (ha, ha, ha). Traveling to every country was not difficult. It just took 15% of my time for seven years. That leaves plenty of time for other focuses.

Do you remember the point where you said to yourself, "I can really accomplish this"?

I never had a goal or set out to accomplish anything, I simply took advantage of travel opportunities, which I love, as they were available and my schedule permitted. I am 77 and still have plenty of energy to travel six or eight major trips a year and still enjoy life in a half dozen other internal focuses.

What have you done over your life to gain the freedom and finances to pursue as much travel as you have?

I worked hard and played hard, and the harder I worked the luckier I got.

I did it for over 50 years. I still have not retired and will not until health prevents work.

Was there ever a time you felt like abandoning this goal?

No, I am traveling to places I have an interest in visiting as opportunities become available. When I lose interest in the remaining destinations on my list, I will stop "new place" travel and continue the many other interests in my life.

What were your worst travel experiences (i.e. detainment, bribes, car accidents, sickness, etc.) and why?

Worst travel experiences have nearly all been chartering small boats on big oceans to reach tiny islands with no civilians and are of little interest. They nearly all are very dangerous to merely reach a destination which offers only the satisfaction of achieving one more destination on a bucket list.

What do you consider the most adventurous trip you have taken?

Without question the most expensive, most adventurous, most challenging and the most suspenseful trip I have ever taken was the December 2014 "White Desert" Antarctica trip starting in Cape Town to their base camp near the Russian Novo airfield in Queen Maud Land, then a further five hour trip to a refueling depot at 83 degrees latitude South in Antarctica and then another two hours to the U.S. Amundson/Scott base at the South Pole, a ten-day trip.

Following a two hour visit to the ceremonial South Pole and 200 yards away, the adjusted actual geographical South Pole which, because of the movement of the several mile deep ice moves about ten feet per year, or now about 200 yards north.

While at the U.S. base we were denied access to the half billion dollar U.S. facility in spite of outside temperatures between -20 and -30 degrees. We then re-boarded the turboprop modified DC-3 (tail-dragger) and flew two hours back to the 83 degree latitude to refuel and camp in an unheated tent overnight with 25 mph winds. The next day we re-boarded the DC-3 for the five hour return flight to Novo airfield and our camp.

The unsaid tension was that with two days for a flight to and from Antarctica to Cape Town we had seven days to achieve the South Pole visit, and in our case, we were down to the last day to begin the two day trip to and from the South Pole and we were extremely concerned that this virtually two week endeavor, including travel to and from the U.S. to Cape Town, would result in no visit as it did last year.

The climatic conclusion was exuberance as we were offered an opportunity the pilots were willing to provide whereby under somewhat marginal weather conditions we would take off on the 7-1/2 hour flight covering 1500 miles each and requiring acceptable weather conditions not only at our base at Novo but also at the refueling/overnight base at 83 degrees latitude and also at the South Pole, and if the weather turned bad, at the pilot's option, they would return.

The end product is the weather cleared and we were successful in completing the visit to the Pole and ultimately returned to Novo airfield and the next day to Cape Town to state that we successfully visited the South Pole. It was the greatest adventure of my life.

What were your most challenging countries to visit and why?

I clearly remember my visit to Upper Mustang in Nepal as extremely challenging. After arriving in Kathmandu, Nepal, we flew to Pokhara and overnighted and then took what I consider a high-risk flight to Jomsom, which had to be done in a three hour window because after 11 a.m. the mountain winds at the destination make direction making landings and take-offs unsafe until the next morning.

Once there, you have a half-day drive each way on a snow-packed, narrow, winding mountain road with 1,000+ foot drops two feet away from the wheel track to reach Upper Mustang.

Evidence of the risk was the sight of a Kamatsu backhoe lying 1,000 feet down in the riverbed as it fell, with unknown harm to the operator, while repairing the high risk road. The trip was a success but the tension was significant for most of the trip.

Also, the trip from Peshawar, Pakistan across the border into the Tribal Area of Pakistan went so well that the border guard who was distracted didn't see or stop us and so our driver and our guide just kept on going down the road about ten miles before the military saw light skinned people and stopped us. The guide was told to follow them back to the border with Peshawar to the military headquarters. They stopped traffic to turn us around and then they were to follow, but the guide was talking to the driver in a language we did not understand and he started driving like crazy, swerving in and out and beat those following us by a bunch and at the border we again were able to keep going because the border guard was distracted while talking to a semi driver.

We had successfully escaped a very dangerous area on the 25 mile long road through the Khyber Pass into Afghanistan. Later that day we visited Abbottabad, Pakistan where a number of months prior the U.S. Seal Team Six had killed Osama Bin Laden. The date of our visit was 9/11/11, the 10th anniversary of the 9/11 attack on the World Trade Center.

What is the strangest thing you've seen/experienced while traveling?

Two come to mind.

The first is the pygmy village an hour and a half from the capital city, Bangui, in the Central Africa Republic where the approximately four feet high pygmies did more than an hour of dancing and ceremony for our benefit. This was done near their homes which looked like igloos made of branches and leaves and were four feet high.

The second was to Vientiane, the capital of Laos on the Mekong River where we visited a village of crude dwellings on poles five feet above the ground so the indigenous snakes did not eat the children while they slept. Also while on this part of the Mekong River, we saw three ten year old's paddling like hell in a dugout canoe and we asked them where they were going so aggressively. The guide said they were paddling from school back to their village for lunch.

Which travel experiences stand out the most and why?

I enjoy seeing the unusual and unexpected better than another big city which is similar to many others except for language and architecture. Examples: the Faroe Islands, the middle of Africa like the Sahrawi refugee people near Tindouf in southern Algeria or the mud houses in Timbuktu, Mali, the wildlife of Botswana or the wonders of Antarctica and South Georgia, or scuba diving with 100 sharks near Socorro Island in the Pacific.

What are the most overrated and underrated countries you've been to in your travels and why?

I never heard of the Faroe Islands until I flew there and I found them beautiful, so they must be underrated. Without a globe I bet most people cannot even tell you where it is. Places which are overrated? Many tropical destinations advertise and do not measure up to their ads, but an ad is not a rating.

What are the best and worst meals you have ever had traveling and where were they?

I find the food of very many cultures nearly inedible. I always travel with packages of M&M Peanuts so if restaurants are closed on arrival or the meals are inedible to someone accustomed to western food, I just eat some M&M's to survive. Many times I would rather pay $100 for a McDonald's meal rather than what third world countries offer. I eat to live another day, not live to eat.

What country made you feel most out of your comfort zone and why?

If the question is, have I ever been scared in a country, or part of one, no, never; but while on a small boat on a big ocean, I have felt uncomfortable many times. Not five good minutes go by on a small boat on a big ocean. On land, I have been in the Tribal Area of Pakistan, North Korea, Kabul, Afghanistan, all over Iran and Saudi Arabia, Mogadishu, Bosaso, Berbera and Hargeisa in Somalia, South Ossetia, and two years ago in Kirkuk, Mosul, Erbil, and Baghdad, Iraq in 2012 and have never been scared. Now, my children have been scared for me as I have traveled to every country on Earth, many where most people would be afraid to visit because of the perceived danger. My five children have made it very clear that they "don't negotiate with terrorists."

Do you speak any foreign languages? If so, which has been the most useful for you besides English?

I only speak one language, English, but I always arrange for an English-speaking guide to accompany me or meet me where English is rarely spoken. It is well worth the cost for destinations where English is almost non-existent.

Looking back from when you started traveling to where you are now, in what ways, if any, have travel changed you?

Travel rounds out my understanding of foreign politics, customs, problems, and dynamics of each country I visit. As good and bad events occur in the world, I better understand the cause and effects that impacted and caused the events to occur.

What is the longest continuous trip you have ever taken? When was it and where did you travel?

One month (approximately) on the MV *Plancius* to Antarctica and ultimately to South Georgia; we were about one hour out of South Georgia heading out on a five day journey to Tristan de Cunha when the single electric propelled prop lost power because the transformer failed. We waited ten days for a rescue boat and traveled about seven days on the rescue ship to Montevideo, Uruguay so we could fly out.

What is your favorite "off-the-beaten-path" destination and why?

The wildlife of the Okavango Delta in Botswana or the pygmy villages in rural Central African Republic, Thailand, Bali, Mauritius, and the Seychelles are wonderful and certainly "off-the-beaten-path."

What are the best and worst places you have ever spent a night?

The worst is easy. On a trip to the disputed Aksai Chin in western China, we were at 17,000 feet (5200 meters) for two days and found a tin lean-to shanty/restaurant. We found out they "rented" dirty bunks located in an attached lean-to with one light bulb, no bathroom, no heat, and ten strangers. The roof was simply corrugated tin held in place with rocks on top (ugh).

As to the best, I have been to hundreds of world class five-star hotels and resorts and all of that class were beautiful. Maybe the villas with privacy and in-villa pools in Mauritius and Bali might be a bit above most.

In your opinion, what country or place in the world feels the most authentic and untouched by tourism?

The Western Sahara refugee camps of the Sahrawi people near Tindouf, Algeria. The native camps on the Mekong River in Laos or the villages on the Brazilian tributaries of the Amazon River or the Upper Sepik in Papua New Guinea.

In your opinion, where is the most beautiful place on Earth?

Cities — Hong Kong, Rio de Janeiro and Dubai

Mountains — Bhutan

Tropical resorts — the villas in Mauritius in the Indian Ocean

Diving — the sea life of the blue corner in Palau and the sting-less jellyfish in the mountain lake nearby

What do you enjoy most when traveling (cities, nature, people, cultural spots, etc.) and why?

Primarily primitive destinations where people live off the earth without modern medicines, with trenches for bathrooms, rooms on stilts to stay above the snakes, and cook outside on a pile of rocks. I can think of 50 such places. I do love the major Asian and European cities, but those are not unusual.

What travel accomplishments are you most proud of?

Getting to Aksai Chin and Upper Mustang in Nepal (both very difficult); also getting to the South Pole, getting through Iraq, Iran, Pakistan, and visiting most of the South Pacific islands.

If you had just one personal travel story to share with someone, what would that be?

This adventure was terrific and disappointing — all wrapped into the same trip. I went on a cruise departing Ushuaia, Argentina and scheduled to visit the South Shetland Islands (my second visit), two destinations on the Antarctic Peninsula, South Orkney, South Georgia, Tristan da Cunha, St. Helena and the other Ascension Islands.

The weather inside the volcanic caldron of Deception Island in South Shetland was very bad so we sailed around inside. Not finding weather that would permit a zodiac to go ashore, we departed. We then visited Brown Bluff and the Spanish Esperanza Base, and got good visits on both. We then headed for South Orkney but the weather went from bad to worse and rapidly deteriorated to Force 11 winds (Force 12 being a hurricane), so the captain ducked back into the Shetland Island for protection which cost us the time needed for the visit to South Orkney.

Twelve hours later we headed for South Georgia, one of the world's finest destinations, for a two-day visit. South Georgia had a "village" named Grytviken in a protected harbor which up to about 1960 processed 100,000 whales a year for whale oil. Some of the old buildings, including the church, remain and all of the huge equipment and storage tanks are still in place that were used to process the whales. This was very interesting.

Ernest Shackleton and his ship *Endurance* departed from this harbor on his ill-fated attempt to cross Antarctica, which is one of the greatest survival stories of all time. It resulted in him saving the lives of all 27 of his crew when the *Endurance* was crushed in the ice. The end of that story is that he rigged a lifeboat with a sail and in 45 days navigated and sailed back to South Georgia and got help to retrieve his crew. (Shackleton later died on a subsequent expedition. His grave is on South Georgia.)

We were scheduled to be in South Georgia for two days to visit penguin colonies, the British scientists, the cemetery, and the Grytviken village. All a great experience. On the third day, we left the harbor and sailed toward a South Georgian area called Salisbury Plains, where I was in the middle of 300,000 King penguins. It doesn't get any better than that. What a thrill! Then we went across a bay to an island with hundreds of big sea birds which were nesting.

We boarded the ship and headed out for a five-day voyage to Tristan da Cunha. About an hour later I noticed that the northbound ship was going south and I told some of the other guests. About a half hour after that the captain announced that we were heading back to the harbor; we had a problem and did not know the ramifications.

Six hours later he said we were not continuing on the last 17 days of the trip. Two days later he announced that a rescue boat would arrive in eight days (ugh). To keep us amused and busy we hiked one route up and down the mountain that Shackleton had taken as he crossed the island from south to north.

Also, I used my satellite phone and called my office and told them to do a press release with a picture of me and my friend, Janice, in the middle of a hundred thousand penguins. The next day all the press wanted to talk to me. I was the only person on the boat with a SAT phone and to the shock of the tour leader used it to talk to eight different Chicago TV stations and several radio and newspaper people. The tour leader did not want publicity. Because this was the fourth boat with a breakdown in 2012, and we were in Antarctica, the press viewed that we were in a dangerous spot and therefore each of the TV networks went national with all of the interviews. Some fun!

Ten day later the rescue ship *Ushuaia* arrived and seven days later we disembarked in Montevideo, Uruguay. Taunted by the other tourists, I got off and kissed the ground as they snapped pictures.

Except for the disappointment of not visiting four planned destinations, in hindsight it was an unexpected adventure. Like Shackleton, we were stranded, but for only 17 days, not a year and a half, and we were in relative luxury.

Besides your home country, where do you find yourself returning to over and over and why?

I visit over and over because I want to, not because I need to connect with a plane through it. Countries and cities such as Hong Kong, Singapore, the upscale islands in the Caribbean, and in the winter U.S. resort areas such as Boca Raton, Florida or Palm Springs, California.

What is the ideal amount of time you prefer to travel each trip before you are ready for home and a break?

Ideally two weeks to 18 days. It is long enough to fly the long flights to get to and from any place on Earth and have time to enjoy the best destinations that far from home.

If you had an unlimited budget and space and time was no object, what would your perfect travel day look like? (for example: start your morning in Bora Bora; afternoon on a safari in Kenya; night in Australia, etc.)

Don't miss Mauritius (magnificent resorts), Bali, the Seychelles, most of the islands in the Caribbean, the Greek Isles, the Roman ruins of the world and the wonderful major cities of Europe and Asia.

For those looking to travel to every country, what is the best piece of advice you could offer them?

If you can afford the time and the cost, go for it. Seeing the "real, whole" world is eye-opening, informative and broadens your understanding of the "real world."

For someone that has been almost everywhere, what still gets you excited about packing your bags again?

The thrill of finding something different from anything found anywhere else on the planet.

Do you feel you have missed out on certain aspects of life being away from home so much?

I do not feel I have missed anything in life. I have a family of five children, 11 grandchildren, and all are close to Aurora. I do not travel in the summer, because we collectively have four summer homes at Powers Lake, Wisconsin that we all enjoy immensely. I have a fantastic business with 225 terrific employees; I have been president of two national associations in the alarm industry and am still involved in numerous important committees in the industry. I am on two company boards of directors, two major charities for 20 to 45 years, still scuba dive, water ski, snow ski, race sailboats in the summer at Powers Lake along with one son and two grandchildren, have a "significant other" that travels with me when she has time (she owns and runs a manufacturing company). I am with my family in my business with four of my children, a brother, sister-in-law, two nephews, and I am with my children almost every holiday and event — so, what am I missing out on? The question seems to assume that travel is mutually exclusive. That is only true if you have a single focus.

Looking ahead, what travel plans and goals are you still pursuing, and what is on your "Bucket List"?

I have, as of February 5, 2015, been to 839 Most Traveled People (MTP) destinations in the world leaving 36 remaining. I have four scheduled before May of 2015, which will leave 32. I may casually attempt ten more after that, but I believe no one will get them all because most of the remaining ones are very difficult and expensive, without civilians, and of very little interest. Many of my remaining places are in Antarctica, where a charter boat qualified to go in that environment is too expensive for just a few people to reasonably finance and simply, in my opinion, not worth the extraordinary expenditure of time and money to achieve.

David Langan, Ireland

(David Langan)

Where did you grow up and what was your early life like?

I grew up in Dublin. I was always full of questions and remember asking my Dad so many questions about what was outside Dublin and was "the countryside bigger than Dublin?" I recall going to the school library and selecting two books. One was on Egypt and the other on money. The teacher was quite interested in my choices. Of course, at that time I felt Egypt was very far away, and if I was lucky I might visit it someday. My parents took me to Spain and the UK on holidays, which was sort of usual growing up. Around 12 or so I started to collect stamps and was very interested in the countries of the world. My favorite subjects in school were Geography and History.

When did you go from casually traveling to making this a full-time goal, and what motivated you to travel to every country?

I left school at 15 in 1977 and went to work. I had a great love of stamps, and still do. I decided to start saving and to visit some of the countries I was collecting. After three years, I made my way to Tuvalu, Fiji, Kiribati, Nauru, and Hawaii. It was a fantastic experience, bearing in mind this was pre-Internet. However, I had spent time in the Commonwealth Institute in London learning all about these small countries. I always had a love of small islands. Well later in life I had my own business and was traveling just occasionally, and then on business to Europe and Asia. I always enjoyed travel but was mostly doing it for work reasons. However, in 2004, I was reading a book by Ben Fogle called, *The Tea Time Islands*. I loved the book and it mentioned the Travelers' Century Club (TCC). It was then I decided I would try to visit as many countries and territories as possible.

Do you remember the point where you said to yourself, "I can really accomplish this"?

In 2004, I had a very successful furniture business and decided over time I would visit every country and territory. In 2008, with the downturn in the economy, my business closed. I felt it may prove difficult to achieve my aim. However, I was lucky that my stamp collection was quite valuable and it has in effect paid for my travel ever since.

What have you done over your life to gain the freedom and finances to pursue as much travel as you have?

I was always a great saver and planned my travel when I was working. I went back to the Pacific in 1983 and loved it again. In 1986, I started my own business and it was a great success. I had about 75 countries up to 2004 through a mix of leisure travel and business. As a single gay man at that time it was easy enough to travel. My commitments were only to business.

Was there ever a time you felt like abandoning this goal?

No, not really. I am a goal-driven guy so it has never occurred to me that I would not achieve this.

What have been your worst travel experiences (such as detainment, bribes, car accidents, sicknesses, etc.) and why?

I have had no "bad" experiences. In 1983, I did get bit on my knee. I was lucky as I was in Nauru and at the time all hospital costs were free. So I got my knee attended to there. I have never been detained. Yes, I've paid a few bribes in Africa, but they were small stuff.

What do you consider one of the most adventurous trips you have taken?

I think my first trip to the Pacific in 1980 will always stand out. I went out a boy and came back a man. In Tuvalu in 1979 the tourist count was less than 60 people for the whole year. There was only one flight per week, and so every day while on this trip I learned a lot about living on an atoll. It was five weeks of pure adventure and learning about the world.

What were your most challenging countries to visit and why?

Pitcairn Island stands out as it was not easy to find a cruise company who had successfully landed passengers there. I spend a lot of time in advance making sure I took the best option to get there with the highest chance of success. Most remote islands are like this. Equatorial Guinea was also a challenge getting a visa for. The embassy in London would not issue tourist visas to anyone from UK or Ireland due to a coup. I ended up organizing a tour with some American friends (who don't need a visa), and got the visa in the United States.

What's the strangest thing you've seen/experienced while traveling?

When in Tuvalu in 2000, I had met the "Prime Minister of Tuvalu." He told me the first white person to land on Funafuti was Irish. Not sure if that is true or "Blarney."

I was also lucky to join an official government approved trip to the British Indian Ocean Territory (BIOT), going there with scientists and eight other tourists. While on the trip we discovered that on one of the islands there were people from Maldives fishing and sleeping. I was walking on this remote island and was shocked to discover clothes on a washing line. This was completely forbidden and the head scientist of our group called the BIOT Marine patrol and they went to the island.

In Tristan da Cunha, I was there for St. Patrick's Day. In the local hall/pub visiting Tristan was a local Elvis Presley impersonator. We had a great night with "The real Elvis" as we called it in Tristan. A night not to forget.

Which travel experiences stand out the most and why?

I have a passion for engaging with people. As a salesman and an Irishman I can talk until the cows come home — so even in countries where there is little to see, I always enjoy talking to the locals. That way you get to see their point of view. This tends to happen even more in less well-off countries in Africa. In Somalia, I wanted to stay longer prior to my visit. So I went to the Somalia Embassy in Djibouti and I was brought in to the ambassadors' office. While waiting I saw a large book on the table — and it was a shopping guide for weapons. It had stickers on certain pages. When I told the ambassador I was visiting Somalia as a tourist, he would not believe me!

What are the most overrated and underrated countries you've been to in your travels and why?

Overrated would be hard to say. I am a positive person and tend to enjoy where I visit regardless. Underrated — Iran. I have just been back for the third time. Iranian's are not Arabs and so it is a very unique country. So much history, and the people stand out as the most friendly I have ever met. On my last trip, one of my American friends came and his view of Iran changed after being there.

What are the best and worst meals you have ever had traveling and where were they?

Some of my worst meals were in Russia. I ended up in the main cities eating McDonald's. My recent trip to Iraq also stands out for poor food. In Baghdad, it was all kebab and more kebab. The last night was great as we went to a restaurant with music and wine and a great night was had. When I came home, I gave up chicken for one month. Some of the best food has to be Italy and France. My other stand-out country for food was New Zealand. Very fresh and great flavors.

What country made you feel most out of your comfort zone and why?

In Guyana. Before I had left, I talked to a good friend of mine who worked in the American Embassy in London. When I told him I was visiting Georgetown he informed me how dangerous it was. The taxi driver bringing me in from the airport even confirmed this as he was held up the previous week and someone was shot dead. So when walking around I had no map, so as not to look like a tourist. There were no police in uniform as they were all in plain clothes.

Do you speak any foreign languages? If so, which has been the most useful for you besides English?

I only speak English. Even my Irish is not great. However, I can pick up some French and Spanish. I have never had issues with languages in different countries. I just smile and find a way to communicate.

Looking back from when you started traveling to where you are now, in what ways, if any, has travel changed you?

Well it has changed me a lot. I call it my university. I had no formal education after 15, so it was the "School of Life" for me. I guess by living on an island (Ireland) we always tend to see the world as an extension of where we live. I learned to really be prepared for many good surprises when you visit a country, and that one may be surprised at the culture and how good natured most people are.

What was the longest continuous trip you have ever taken, when was it, where did you travel?

It was two months traveling in 2006. It started in Buenos Aires and then on to Ushuaia in Argentina. It was the start of my Antarctica adventure and Atlantic islands trip. I was in London in 2004 and just by chance discovered that Oceanwide Expeditions were doing a trip to include Bouvet Island. At that time I did not understand or know how difficult it was to land there. I booked the trip. My first part of the trip visited a number of bases on the Antarctic Peninsula. So I was lucky to visit an Argentine base, as well as Spanish, Chilean, American, and British ones on this trip. The tour leader had told me that they had never visited so many bases on a trip before. Unknown to the tour leader, it was I who requested these stops. I had been in touch and told the cruise company that there would be passengers on this trip from TCC and we would have to stop at the bases. However, there was only me. It was great as I was able to mail postcards back home. That was a ten day trip. The ship then went back to Ushuaia. We started out the following day with new passengers and visited Falklands Islands, South Georgia, Bouvet Island, Tristan da Cunha, St. Helena, Ascension Island, and Cape Verde. A great trip which included a solar eclipse. The bonus is that we landed on all the islands and it was a great success.

What is your favorite "off-the-beaten-path" destination and why?

I like Iran in the Middle East and also Syria before the war. I did enjoy Asmara in Eritrea as it has a much to offer and the Italian food is excellent.

What are the best and worst places you have spent a night?

I spend a great night in Western Sahara in Laayoune under the clouds. It was an "oasis" hotel and I spent the night lying on a blanket looking up at the stars. It was magical. Staying a night on Tristan da Cunha was a dream come true and I remember the crayfish dinner that we had. One of my worst nights I can remember was in Herat in Afghanistan. The hotel was terrible and very basic with a mattress on the ground. I could also say the same for the hotel I had in Tibet, but I changed to a nicer hotel the next day. Everyone in the hotel was Chinese except for me, and no one understood a world I said.

In your opinion, what country or place in the world feels the most authentic and untouched by tourism?

Well, I have to say Iran again. Even in the shops there are no hard sells or people asking you for money like you find in other countries in the region. Bhutan is another standout place.

In your opinion, where is the most beautiful place on Earth?

A very difficult question and depends on the context. One standout place was Nuka Hiva in the Marquesas Islands, part of French Polynesia. I love islands, and my first time there I will never forget. Here you have a mixture of mountains and sea. Very laid back and safe. However, it is a little bit out of the way, and not the cheapest place on the planet.

I would also have to give a mention to New Zealand, which is a wonderful country. Quite relaxing with great food, friendly people, and lots to see.

What do you enjoy most when traveling (cities, nature, people, cultural spots, etc.) and why?

I enjoy people the most. I tend to have this ability to bring the most out in people and enjoy a good laugh. I have a great interest in history and tend to read before I go and do a lot of background research. I do like to see as much as possible, so I will visit UNESCO World Heritage Sites.

What travel accomplishments are you most proud of?

Visiting the remote British Atlantic islands was something I wanted to do for a long time, even before I had planned to visit every country. Getting to Scott Base in NZ Antarctica and visiting the huts which included that of the famous Irishman Sir Ernest Shackleton. And visiting British Indian Ocean Territory — they were pristine, and just walking, watching the crabs, or swimming and diving in the pristine waters, was wonderful.

If you had just one personal travel story to share with someone, what would it be?

I guess some of my best travel experiences have been at sea. In some of the expedition trips you have days at sea between islands. This is a great time to chat and get to know people. I have enjoyed listening to stories of travel and learning from other fellow travelers.

Besides your home country, where do you find yourself returning to over and over and why?

I enjoy Spain a lot. The weather is nicer than here (in Ireland) and it is very good value. I like the culture and the way of life.

What is the ideal amount of time you prefer to travel on each trip before you are ready for home and a break?

Most of my travel are now three or four week trips. I tend to do two of those per year. These are usually to countries I have not been to. Outside that, I take about two one week trips around Europe and a few weekends away. I would not mind longer trips, but I do have to get back to work.

If you had an unlimited budget and space and time was no object, what would your perfect travel day look like? (for example: start your morning in Bora Bora; afternoon on a safari in Kenya; night in Australia, etc.)

I would start in the Indian Ocean somewhere, perhaps the Seychelles or Mauritius. The sand is so soft and the water so warm to swim in. Lunch would be in Italy, perhaps on the island of Sicily. In the afternoon, I could spend time at one of the vineyards near Cape Town and take in the wonderful views and skyline. Finally, I would spend the night in New York City or Sydney.

For those looking to travel to every country, what is the best piece of advice you could offer them?

Plan well in advance. Try and connect with people who in recent years have been to those places you plan to go to and ask for advice on what to see. As a world traveler, you will find some countries that guidebooks are not helpful for. For example, I recently purchased the *Lonely Planet* guide to Africa. Many of the countries they have no current information on. As Christine — one of my great travel friends — told me, "When in West and Central Africa, as soon as you land, make sure you check planes to get back out again." This is sound advice as flights change and you need to go straight to the airline office to confirm your flight is going and you have a seat on it. Also, take your time traveling. Enjoy the moment. Don't have your head stuck in a camera all the time. Take time out to enjoy the country. It is all about travel experiences, not about ticking countries off a list.

For someone that has been almost everywhere, what still gets you excited about packing your bags again?

The very idea of going to somewhere I have never been. My next trip is to Cocos (Keeling) Islands and Christmas Island. I am also spending three weeks in Malaysia. I have been to Malaysia many times but still look forward to it.

Do you ever feel you have missed out on certain aspects of life being away from home so much?

No, I don't think so. For a few years, I was away nearly six months out of every year traveling. But now it is about nine or ten weeks per year. It is spread out through the year.

Looking ahead, what travel plans and goals are you still pursuing, and what is on your "Bucket List"?

I am very much looking forward to getting to Tokelau. I tried to visit a few years ago but the ship I had booked had already left when I got to Samoa. Tokelau is waiting on a new ship to arrive and it is my last country/territory to visit that has no airport. My big aim, though, is to get a postcard from every postal administration in the world. Some people may have a card from every country in the world. However, no one as far as I am aware will have been to every country/territory and sent a postcard back home from each place. It is great, as my postcard collection is now a travel blog.

Stewart Sheppard, Canada

(Stewart Sheppard off Cape Adare at the entrance to the Ross Sea in Antarctica)

Where did you grow up and what was your early life like?

My life began just before WWII in St. Catharines, Ontario, not far from Niagara Falls. Because of the war my parents, my older sister, and I moved to Toronto and then my father went to Ottawa where he was stationed for the duration. My family was an average middle class one and I had a safe and comfortable early life. After the war my father got a job at the British Embassy in Washington, D.C. We spent the next five years in Virginia, first in Manassas and later in a couple of locations in Arlington. In 1950, the family moved to Barbados, where we lived in two different homes for about a year and a half. As a young boy it was a great adventure living in Barbados and I loved my time there. From Barbados, we relocated to Vancouver, B.C. where I attended another couple of schools. I had my last two years of high school in La Jolla, California where, along with my classmate Raquel Welch (nee Tejada), I graduated in 1958. I thoroughly enjoyed my younger years, although in some ways they greatly influenced the rest of my life. Because we moved so frequently and I changed schools so often, I was never close to relatives and hardly knew any of my cousins. Also, by changing schools, I never had any long-term friends from my early years. I did, however, have good friends at the various schools, but it never bothered me to move away and then start over with new friends at the next school. Probably because of my nomadic life I have never felt the need to put down roots and am usually happy wherever I am.

When did you go from casually traveling to making this a full-time goal, and what motivated you to travel to every country?

I have not made the transition and am not particularly motivated to visit every country (I have just under 30 UN countries remaining — almost all in Africa). I have never been a systematic, goal-oriented type of traveler. I do want to see, experience, and learn as much as I possibly could, but that does necessarily involve visiting every country. I travel for the joy of it rather than marking ticks on a list. Repeat visits and non-independent countries are often the most interesting and enjoyable trips.

Do you remember the point where you said to yourself, "I can really accomplish this"?

Because I am not goal-oriented or never planned to visit every country, I have never thought, "I can really accomplish this." I have covered enough of the world already; it would not be difficult to complete the country list. If it was ever my intention to visit every country, I would have done so by now.

What have you done over your life to gain the freedom and finances to pursue as much travel as you have?

Because my primary interest has always been traveling and exploring the world, I have been focused and able to save and put money aside for my passion. My lifestyle is frugal with few needs or wants, so saving has never been a problem. It helped that in the early years my travel was of the budget variety and did not require much money. Once I began working seriously, I made a good wage, much of which was invested. I was fortunate with my advisers and made good gains on my investments. Finally, my finances received a boost with a modest inheritance on the passing of my parents.

Was there ever a time you felt like abandoning this goal?

I have never had travel goals, but my interest in exploring the world has never wavered. I have always had a lot of energy and an insatiable curiosity to explore and discover what is around the next bend or over the next hill. I am not yet ready to surrender my passport, but am sure the day will eventually arrive when the passion to travel will subside. Until then, I will continue to look forward to my next adventure.

What were your worst travel experiences (i.e. detainment, bribes, car accidents, sickness, etc.) and why?

I think my scariest travel experience happened during the summer of 1969. My wife and I were between jobs and thought it would be a good time to explore Central America. After traveling for a while in Mexico, we eventually reached Guatemala City and decided to take the TICA bus to Panama. It turned out not to be the best time to be in the area and we were the only passengers on the bus when they resumed service between El Salvador and Honduras after the "football war." There was no other traffic in either direction and the border area between the two countries was still a war zone with burned out vehicles and smoldering buildings all around. On crossing the bridge into Honduras, we were ordered out of the bus by what looked like a rag-tag group of young guerrilla fighters. I believe they were the Honduran Army, but none looked old enough to be out of high school. Our luggage was placed in the middle of the road and, with the "soldiers" standing behind us poking their rifle barrels into our heads and necks while we were kneeling, we were told to open our bags and spread everything out on to the road. As we had few possessions, and nothing of interest, I guess they decided we were not a threat and allowed us to proceed.

What do you consider the most adventurous trip you have taken?

In 1987 I made one of my more adventurous trips with my mother who, as a traveler, was years ahead of her time. We thought it would be interesting and fun to do the Trans-Siberian railway on our own. This was during the Cold War and before the days of the Internet and easy communications. I don't remember how we found out about a Soviet ship (the *Felix Dzerzhinsky*) that went from Yokohama to Nahodka, but we were able to get on. We did buy our rail tickets before we left Canada. We boarded the train shortly after arriving in Nahodka but, due to it being a closed port, were unable to make our first intended stop in Vladivostok. We were, however, able to make many stops en-route and eventually reached East Berlin almost a month later. Until Moscow we never encountered another westerner and were surprised that our compartments for four on the train were never shared with anyone, although most of the trains were full or close to it. I remember meals on the various trains were a laugh. They had a very good menu on the train and it was even translated into English. The problem was the food that was served consisted of nothing but borscht and black bread. During one our frequent stops in a Siberian village, I discovered the train staff was selling the food out the door on the side of the train not facing the station, leaving nothing available for train passengers to purchase.

What were your most challenging countries to visit and why?

I think of a challenging country mainly (but not exclusively) as one with security and transportation issues. Where possible and practical, I like to travel by ground and if there are difficulties getting around it can be both challenging and disappointing. Uganda, Rwanda, and Burundi were challenging when I visited them in 2010. Yemen and Ethiopia are other examples of places where security and transportation can slow your progress and diminish your enjoyment of a place. My solution to challenging destinations is to arrange for a car/van and driver(s) before entering the country as I did in the above countries (where I had great experiences).

What is the strangest thing you've seen/experienced while traveling?

After many years of travel, I have seen and experienced many weird and wonderful things. One experience I find strange, though very pleasant, is unexpected encounters with people in places where you least expect them. During the winter of 1972/73, I was on a six month work assignment in Oahu. On days off I often made trips to other islands in the Hawaiian chain. On a visit to Lanai, my wife and I were two of only a few guests in what was then the only hotel (12 rooms) on the island. One day while walking alone along the beach at Manale Bay on the southern end of Lanai, I noticed in the distance a lone figure walking towards me — we were the only two people on that long beautiful beach. As we were about to pass, we recognized each other as old friends and fraternity brothers at San Diego State College from many years before. We had not kept in touch, and Jesse (that's my friend's name) had gone off to war in Vietnam and become involved in drugs. He had since turned his life around and was working for the State of Hawaii talking with students and others about the evils of drugs. Being a traveler there is always a possibility of meeting, in an unusual place, someone that you had previously traveled with. I was exploring the ruins of My Son in central Vietnam when I came across the very well-traveled Polish traveler, Wojceich Dabrowski. We had done an expedition cruise together years before but had not been in contact since. As Mr. Disney says, "It's a small, small world."

Which travel experiences stand out the most and why?

The travel experiences that I remember most fondly are usually expedition trips which visit more remote and less touristy destinations. Some examples of memorable expeditions are both the peninsula and Ross Sea sides of Antarctica, the Indian Ocean French sub-Antarctic islands, and the islands of the South Atlantic, Greenland, and Svalbard. I prefer such off-the-beaten track travel because of the often stark and rugged landscapes as well as the variety of wildlife.

Another interesting story was in the Fall of 1988. My wife and I decided we would like some sun and warmth, as it was beginning to get wet and cool in Vancouver. We thought Cuba would make a nice break for a week and booked flights on Cubana Airlines from Toronto to Havana and back. I can't remember if the Cubana aircraft was a Russian built Tupolev 154 or an Ilyushin 62, but it had the engines at the back and was tail-heavy. On the day we left Toronto it was cold and snowy and we boarded the aircraft through the forward entrance on portable stairs from the tarmac rather than through a bridge from the terminal building. To keep the plane from tipping, the boarding procedure was slightly unusual. Passengers who were seated at the front were boarded first and then they had the back passengers loaded last. Once we were all on board they tried to remove the portable stairs — but with the weight of all the passengers the aircraft had come down on the stairs and they were stuck. For about the next hour it was like a comedy skit as they tried to juggle the passengers so they could remove the stairs. First they asked passengers from the front of the plane to disembark to reduce the weight and then change the distribution by moving people up and down the aisle to get balance right. Finally, with about forty people shivering on the tarmac and enough people standing in the aisle towards the back, they were able to free the stairs and position them close enough so the passengers outside could re-board by stepping over the six or eight inch gap. Then, after everybody was re-sorted and re-seated, they were able to close the door and we were on our way to the sun. The rest of the flight was uneventful and we arrived safely in Havana a little over an hour late.

What are the most overrated and underrated countries you've been to in your travels and why?

It seems both Australia and Japan are on many travelers' bucket lists, but I believe both are overrated. In the mid-1960s, I made my first extended visit to Australia and have returned many times since, including within the last few months. I enjoyed every minute of my earlier visits but have noticed a big change in the country in more recent years. I believe Australians now take themselves too seriously and I miss the wild and crazy, fun loving Aussies of old. Since my first trip to Japan in the late 1960s, I have visited many times for both business and pleasure. Originally communications were difficult, but that situation is much improved. Although generally considered a courteous nation, I find Japan to be an inflexible and closed society. Japan seems to accept tourism, but not welcome it. There are many places in the world where most people would not consider visiting. I think of countries like Uganda, Ethiopia, Burma/Myanmar, and the five 'Stans are in this category and are underrated. I find the antiquities, landscapes, and wildlife (like in Uganda) all makes these countries interesting, exciting, and worthwhile destinations.

What are the best and worst meals you have ever had traveling and where were they?

I am not, nor ever have been a foodie and never have been adventurous when it comes to food. I do not eat a lot and take what I do more for necessity rather than pleasure. Give me a cheese sandwich and a bottle of water or canned drink and I'm happy. People frequently tell me that I am missing one of travels best experiences by not sampling local cuisine, but I'll opt for not taking health risks and enjoy problem free travel. I can only recall having one food related problem and that was many years ago in Quito, Ecuador. I was very surprised when the doctor prescribed a laxative but, although I was a little weak, I was ready to move on the next day.

What country made you feel most out of your comfort zone and why?

Probably because of my early nomadic life, I rarely feel culture shock or out of my comfort zone. I am open to new places and experiences and adapt quite easily. I have certainly felt security issues in some countries, but they are generally in certain local areas rather than a country as a whole. Because of the requirement to always be accompanied by a "minder," North Korea would probably be the place I felt most out of sync with my surroundings. In 2008 my wife and I took a train from Dandong, China to Pyongyang, where we were met at the station by our soon to be constant companions. I never felt unsafe or uncomfortable in the country, but it was the lack of freedom of movement that got to me. I have visited many oppressive states but, although being followed on occasion, my movement was never as restricted as it was in North Korea. That being said, I found North Korea to be a unique, interesting, and exciting experience.

Do you speak any foreign languages? If so, which have been the most useful for you besides English?

I have always envied people with linguistic abilities. Unfortunately, languages do not come easily to me. My first two years of university in the late 1950s were at an American institution in Mexico City. The instruction was in English but I did pick up enough Spanish to get by and can still manage the essentials. I am always grateful that my mother tongue is English as it increasingly becomes the international language of travel. My only natural ability when it comes to travel is a good sense of direction.

Looking back from when you started traveling to where you are now, in what ways, if any, have travel changed you?

Since I began traveling at an early age, I don't think my life has changed much because of it. I know my travel has certainly made me more knowledgeable about the world and its people. It has also made me appreciate the good life I have enjoyed and to realize how fortunate I am to have been born when and where I was. My travel experiences have taught me to count my many blessings.

What is the longest continuous trip you have ever taken? When was it and where did you travel?

I have had the pleasure of making a number of extended trips, but the two longest were each about 18 months long. The first was a backpacking trip through Europe and North Africa in 1962/63. During that time, I visited all the major countries of the continent including western USSR. The second trip was to Australia/New Zealand and some islands in the South Pacific in 1965/66. Both trips were low budget ventures and involved brief periods of doing menial work en-route to get funds to continue my wandering ways. In Europe, I employed every inexpensive mode of transport possible and spent nights under the stars, in various vehicles, or cheap hostels. In Australia, I managed to purchase an old car which held together long enough for me to get around and complete my journey. Crossing the Pacific back to Canada, I mostly flew between islands but also utilized small inter-island supply vessels. Some of the island groups visited on this crossing of the Pacific were New Caledonia, Fiji, Tonga, Western and American Samoa, Tahiti, and Hawaii. I was lucky to have made these trips when I did as I think it would be very difficult or impossible to make them in the same way today.

What is your favorite "off-the-beaten-path" destination and why?

I have many favorite "off-the-beaten-path" destinations that are special to me. South Georgia, Kerguelen Island, southern Greenland and Svalbard all stand out for the same reasons. All have beautiful natural settings with fabulous scenery, wonderful wildlife, and are not heavily populated.

What are the best and worst places you have ever spent a night?

My overnight accommodations have covered the complete range of places to spend a night. I have enjoyed the fanciest of luxury hotels and resorts at one end of the scale and slept in parks, on beaches, and in the cheapest of hostels at the other end. Once, near Sorrento, I went to sleep in a tunnel which was under construction and had a rude awakening when, in the morning, they started blasting at the other end of it. I have stayed in a jail in Algeria, slept under the stars with the statues in Rano Raraku, Easter Island, and spent three nights on sacks of potatoes on the deck of a rusty old coastal ship crossing the Gulf of Mexico from Veracruz to Progresso. In the end, no one place stands out as the best or worst place I have spent a night but many were good experiences, and most were even by choice.

In your opinion, what country or place in the world feels the most authentic and untouched by tourism?

I think of Yemen as a living museum, particularly as you journey out of Sana'a. The architecture and local inhabitants both combine to make Yemen seem to jump off the pages of history. During my visit in 2008, tourism did exist but it was limited and did not affect the old world authenticity of the place. I have had the opportunity to visit many seldom visited and un-touched places (mainly islands in various parts of the world), but few destinations have the impact of Yemen.

In your opinion, where is the most beautiful place on Earth?

The list of places of great natural beauty is very long and is enough to satisfy every taste. A few of my favorites are: Bora Bora, French Polynesia; Rock Islands of Palau; Li River, Guilin, China; Valley of the Ten Peaks, Moraine Lake, Alberta, Canada; the Grand Canyon; Machu Picchu, Peru; Torres del Paine, Chile; Gold Harbour, South Georgia; Paradise Bay and Lemair Chanel, Antarctica, and what I consider to be the most spec-tacular sight on the planet, Iguazu Falls on the border between Brazil and Argentina.

What do you enjoy most when traveling (cities, nature, people, cultural spots, etc.) and why?

I am definitely a nature/landscape type of traveler. On the cul-tural side, I do like antiquities and always search out historic and archaeological sites. Locations which include a combina-tion of the above, such as Machu Picchu, Petra, Hier-apolis/Pamukkale, and the Tiger's Nest, are very special places to me. For natural scenic attractions, I have found waterfalls like Niagara, Kaieteur, Angel, Murchison, Blue Nile, Victoria, and Iguazu all to be incredible locations worth a visit. I also very much enjoying seeing a wide variety of wildlife around the world. Few thrills are greater than seeing wild animals in their natural environment. The power and emotion of witnessing the beauty of nature keep me searching different locations for more.

What travel accomplishments are you most proud of?

I cannot say I am particularly "proud" of any of my travel "ac-complishments". I am certainly pleased and feel fortunate to have been able to see so much of the world but, although my experiences are special to me, I do not think "proud" is an appropriate word to describe anything I have done. Given the time and the inclination anyone could do what I have done.

If you had just one personal travel story to share with someone, what would that be?

Every traveler has stories to tell; most are best related spontaneously over a few drinks. This story is about the March 2006 landing on what many travelers consider to be the ultimate destination: Bouvet Island.

Our trip was a 39-day long expedition cruise which began in Ushuaia, Argentina and ended in Sal in the Cape Verde islands. Our ship was the 2,000 tonnes, 66 meters long *Aleksey Maryshev* which was built in Finland in 1990, crewed by Russians, and at that time was operated by Oceanwide Expeditions.

The capacity of the ship was 46 passengers, but our complement was a little less. The group on board was a diverse bunch with a wide range of ages and representing a number of different nationalities. The passengers' interests were almost as varied as their ages and nationalities. We had a number of nature lovers, some bird watchers, and, as there was to be a total eclipse of the sun during the voyage, a few people were onboard for that experience. Among the group, however, were a bunch of serious, very well-seasoned, hardcore travelers. I expect a number of people doing this book were on that expedition.

For the uninitiated, Bouvet Island is a sub-Antarctic island located in the middle of the South Atlantic and is regarded as the most isolated spot on the planet. And, to make it more challenging, it is not easy to land if you do get there. From satellite photos it is known that Bouvet does not enjoy a very pleasant climate and is, in fact, usually covered in cloud and sea mist and is not visible at all.

The morning we arrived was clear and sunny and the island looked spectacular. Because of potential weather conditions and the difficulty to land, the original expedition itinerary called for two days at Bouvet. Due to a last minute change to a slower ship, however, we were not going to be allowed the full two days at the island. The itinerary change added to the pressure because Bouvet is an ice covered volcanic mountain rising out of the sea where there are few possible landing locations. Our plan was to land on a narrow rocky "beach" on the northwest side of the island near to the site of the Norwegian automated meteorological station. Initially, landing conditions did not seem ideal but the staff was hopeful; preparations were made, and the zodiacs were placed in the water. The first three boats were able to put people ashore, but then, although the weather was perfect, the wave activity increased and landings were canceled because it had become dangerous. Because of Bouvet's geography, there was nowhere else to go from the rocky beach on which we landed. The problem now was how to get people off the island. While the expedition staff and crew pondered the problem, we spent our time enjoying the spectacular scenery and being entertained by some seals and a few penguins.

The first attempt to evacuate the island resulted in the zodiac being tossed in the air and its occupants were dumped onto either the beach or into the cold sea. One of the fit and healthy, though more elderly ladies, was shaken up, but some on shore quickly came to her aid and after being dried and warmed she was game for another go at getting off Bouvet. The method devised to make escape possible was to tie a rope from a zodiac positioned beyond the waves to the zodiac making the pick-up on shore. When the timing was right, we would run down the beach and dive into the zodiac as the one off shore rapidly pulled away.

I was the only one in the zodiac I dove into and it was full of water because of the nasty shore break. Others were luckier and somehow managed to get away with barely getting wet. The crew and expedition staff did an incredible job but were thoroughly drenched and exhausted when the operation ended. We were not long on the island and, depending when you got hauled off, the average time was probably about two and a half hours. Very early the next morning, before we sailed north for Tristan da Cunha, a second easier but shorter landing was made at Kap Circoncision for those determined travelers unable to land on the first day. For a number of reasons, including safety and lack of interest, a number of passengers elected to remain on the ship and skip the excitement of one of the most unusual wet landings I have ever made. In the end, a total of about 27 passengers, expedition staff, and crew made it ashore, including the entire hardcore travel bunch. I understand that our landings over those two days put the most people on Bouvet to that date.

Besides your home country, where do you find yourself returning to over and over and why?

There is not any one special place where I return to over and over again. There are many countries or areas I have visited numerous times such as Hawaii, Mexico, and various islands in the Caribbean. Most of my "comfort" places have sun and warmth in common. One place that always makes me feel good is Easter Island. Since my first visit in the late 1960s, I have been back three more times — the last being in 2008. I find Easter Island to be a good mix of an interesting destination with great land and seascapes combined with a nice climate, relaxed atmosphere, and not too many tourists.

What is the ideal amount of time you prefer to travel each trip before you are ready for home and a break?

If it were possible, I would continue on forever with occasional short breaks en-route to regroup and digest what I had most recently experienced. As this approach is not practical, I prefer frequent trips of three to five weeks. I am always happiest on the road and go home mostly because of commitments and not to take a break.

If you had an unlimited budget and space and time was no object, what would your perfect travel day look like? (for example: start your morning in Bora Bora; afternoon on a safari in Kenya; night in Australia, etc.)

With an unlimited budget, I would chose the ultimate destination and spend a day in space watching multiple sunrises and sunsets and marveling at the interesting and diverse planet we inhabit. I would love to be able to look down from space and see the world I've spent so much time exploring closer to the surface.

For those looking to travel to every country, what is the best piece of advice you could offer them?

My advice would be to take it slowly. Do not treat your quest as a race, competition, or a scavenger hunt. Take it easy, smell the roses and enjoy your experiences. I would also advise not to just concentrate on individual UN countries but take a broader approach and also visit places that are not independent countries. On the suggestion of some traveling friends, in January 1990 I joined the Travelers' Century Club (TCC) with a total of 140 locations at that time. I think the TCC approach, or the broader Most Traveled People website, give a better indication of your travel accomplishments. Finally I would say travel for interest, enjoyment, and to learn rather than to collect meaningless ticks on a map. There is no prize for visiting every country, but there can be an endless amount of pleasure in enhancing your life's experiences.

For someone that has been almost everywhere, what still gets you excited about packing your bags again?

The thrill of exploring and discovery always keeps me coming back for more. No one has or ever will see and do everything so there is always something more to experience. My love of adventure and insatiable curiosity keeps me looking forward to getting back on the road.

Do you feel you have missed out on certain aspects of life being away from home so much?

I am sure I have missed out on some aspects of life by being away so much. Maybe it has been easier for me because my immediate family, although being close, have always led independent lives. Although we stayed in touch, and tried to be together for important dates, we still lived separate lives. My best friend and closest companion is my wife and she has shared most of my journeys. Close friends understand, and some share, my passion for travel. It is not difficult to keep in touch with family and friends, particularly in these days of the Internet. There is also always the pleasure of meeting new friends while on the go; some of these people are now best friends.

Although some aspects of my life may not have been ideal, it is still a great life and I have few regrets.

Looking ahead, what travel plans and goals are you still pursuing, and what is on your "Bucket List"?

I do not have a "bucket list" or specific travel goals but look forward to many more years of enjoyable travel. There is much more of the world for me to see so there is a never ending list of travel options. Among possible future destinations are areas of northwestern India, I would like to visit and there are still parts of Africa that interest me. You never know what lies ahead; I only hope my desire to travel leaves me before my good health.

Wolfgang Stoephasius, Germany

(**Wolfgang Stoephasius realizing his boyhood dream in Timbuktu, Mali**)

Where did you grow up and what was your early life like?

I was born in 1941 in Landeshut/Silesia, former Eastern Germany, which now belongs to Poland. I made my first trip attempt at traveling at the age of just five years old, to the last stop at the train station in Landeshut, as I wanted to visit my father, who was an English POW. The travel was financed in the form of Polish zloty I obtained through the sale of porcelain figurines, which I'd found in attics. In 1947, I left Silesia and made a new home in Passau, where I would start school in the same year. I was a terribly bad pupil, because I really wanted to be an American Indian (Sioux).

When did you go from casually traveling to making this a full-time goal, and what motivated you to travel to every country?

As a young police officer, I did not earn too much money, but it was just enough for a car. The first was an old banger, a Renault Dauphine that always broke down. My wife and I then scraped our savings together; it was enough for a new Renault R4, the legendary car with the strange handle circuit. It cost 4400 marks. With a roof rack added and taking a tent along, we went across Europe in it.

Do you remember the point where you said to yourself, "I can really accomplish this"?

It was in the year 2003. In the spring, my wife Renate and I were finally granted a visa in Guyana to visit the country of Suriname. In the state capital, Paramaribo, it is striking that Christians, Muslims, Jews, and Hindus live there easily together. The Friday Mosque is completely peaceful beside the unguarded synagogue. Hundreds of Muslims in traditional Javanese clothes, with men wearing round white caps, and the women in white robes, demonstrate for peace. The American flag on the Space Center remains untouched. We looked into the Saint Peter and Paul Basilica with the beautiful, little-too-heroic-shown-for-our-taste, woodcarvings of the Passion of Christ. Afterwards, we noticed a Toyota Land Cruiser with Swiss license plates. The car was driven by a gentleman with a gray beard. We talked to him and arranged to meet for the evening at the waterfront with its many small restaurants on the wide Suriname River. There we met him and his wife, Liliana. Emil Schmid and his wife have been on the road for seventeen and a half years with this car, traveled through 136 UN member states and are in the Guinness Book of Records. It would be an exciting evening with many stories from the adventurous life of these two. As Renate and I crawled into bed late that evening in our small pension, she asks me how many countries I had been to, and I answer, "I do not know?" Back in Munich, I begin to research and had come up with about 150. "The other approximately 40 countries I will also travel to," I think to myself. There were nearly 190 UN member states at this time. My career as a "country collector" had begun.

What have you done over your life to gain the freedom and finances to pursue as much travel as you have?

During my professional time I traveled as much as possible. I am now able to really indulge as pensioner in my travel passion.

How to finance such a travel life anyway? This is easier than you think: Give up a car, look at your time and what you earn in your professional life together with your wife. Travel by public transport, even if they are sometimes uncomfortable (e.g Sub-Saharan Africa), eat and sleep where the locals do, then you not only save, but have human contact, which is the most important thing.

Was there ever a time you felt like abandoning this goal?

Never!

What have been your worst travel experiences (such as detainment, bribes, car accidents, sicknesses, etc.) and why?

I've had no real problems besides some small pocket-thieves and sometimes, perhaps every ten years, a case of diarrhea.

What do you consider one of the most adventurous trips you have taken?

In Peshawar (Pakistan, Waziristan) I made friends with a Pashtu Prince. He knew all the tricks and ways to travel in the region. So he clothed me with a white skull cap and shawl that the Pashtun people wore and I grew a beard. Waziristan is considered a refuge for Al-Qaeda and the Taliban. In the town of Darra Adam Khel they produce weapons, which are man-made there in small factories, and they will make you a copy of any desired handgun, which takes about a day, and each additional copy is then finished in three to four days. A Kalashnikov costs about 60 euros. Also there are all kinds of pistols, revolvers, submachine guns, shotguns, and assault rifles from Beretta's to Uzi's. In general, these things cost a tenth of the normal price. There are a lot of these small workshops that manufacture with machines using primitive devices. Pashtu showed me the artisans in a shack and all the details of the production. At one of the machines, a device is rotated in a barrel and out comes precision work that is amazing. An older man was inside sitting on the floor and there were magazines for the Kalashnikov automatic rifles he was putting some finishing touches to. I now realize how easy it is for terrorists and bandits to get guns for little money. There are more than 18 million unregistered firearms in Pakistan, many of them in the hands of Taliban fighters.

What were your most challenging countries to visit and why?

Somalia in 2008. After a long journey to the border with Kenya, I was back in Addis Ababa and ready for my trip to Somalia. Somalia in Europe has a bad reputation — and it is also justified. Now you must know that Somalia is a de facto country divided into three parts. The real heartland around Mogadishu in the south and Puntland in the north area are extremely dangerous. There is fighting with Islamic fundamentalists and warlords with their claims against each other completely irrational. The Ethiopian army is also in the country. And there's Somaliland, incomprehensibly a haven of relative peace in this desolate environment. However, there had been a series of bombings there a few weeks before my trip, which obviously was also directed against Ethiopia because the consulate was destroyed in the capital, Hargeisa. There were 24 dead and many injured. I think in Europe it was not even reported. If there are 500 dead black people in Africa, the message is not worth the media anyway. Somaliland has an embassy in Addis Ababa and the friendly people there were able to get my visa within half a day.

I started out towards Somaliland traveling in stages to the holy Muslim city of Harar, a Muslim enclave, but most Ethiopians are Christians. From there, I was early to the bus station to travel to the nearest major city in the border area, namely by Jijiga. From Jijiga, I took another bus to the border. Along the way, there were some checkpoints where I was treated very politely. Each of my traveling companions assured me how safe Somaliland is in contrast to the rest of Somalia. The people are very friendly and approachable. It is obvious that there were members of the same clan living on both sides of the border, so the transition runs just as smoothly as it did before the opening of the border between Bavaria and Austria, for instance. The problem is further transport. The taxis are in fact kind of like traveling sardine cans. I was actually stowed along with three other people in the station wagon's trunk. At the first stop a young man offered me his place and squeezed himself back to where I was before. Then I had a clear view of the vast desert landscape, which is covered by loose bushes. Camels were everywhere. Again, we had to overcome several checkpoints everywhere, where I was treated friendly and they gave a quick glance in my passport with the visa entry and that was it. Nobody wanted any bribes. The militiamen ensure that no bandits or terrorists come from neighboring provinces into that area. The taxi driver took me straight to the Oriental Hotel, in the provincial capital of Hargeisa. At the entrance, I was greeted by the friendly manager who had lived for many years in the United States. When he saw my German passport, he reduced room rate from $20 to $15 US dollars and I was well placed in a clean room with all the comforts and was even provided with a working hot shower. The hotel was quietly situated in the heart of the densely populated city.

Papua New Guinea: Early in the morning my wife and I set off in the direction of Minj (the capital of Jiwaka province) to find a minibus to Goroka, another town in the highlands. At an intersection, we get off and waited for a bus connection. To our right there were warriors sitting on loading platforms of trucks, smeared with clay, faces painted colorfully, grass tufts on their rears, armed with spears, axes, and wooden shields, with partially constructed helmets on their heads. Later a pickup stops and takes us to Minj, a small town in a valley, surrounded by green hills, with a collection of tin houses, a police station, and a small hospital. In a tropical park lies the small resort named Tribal Tops Inn. There were no guests there that day, but a lovable buxom black allowed us to leave our luggage there. She spoke excellent English and told us that there had been a bloody tribal war between the Konobuka and the Kondika tribes due to unresolved land rights. In addition to countless casualties, there had hundreds of houses burnt, and a large number of raped women. Through the missionaries, a peace treaty was to be signed between the warring tribes that day.

On a walk we see on every side of the village warriors with spears and shields, followed by stronger fighters with sticks and axes swinging and some with simple guns in the hands. Their faces were painted in frightening ways. Some also wore colorful headdresses. We walked to a huge open space on which a wooden podium with rough-hewn wooden benches had been constructed. In the middle of the surface, a cable was tensioned. Men drug gigantic pieces of pork and beef and placed it before the temporary grandstand. A friendly white man in an ill-fitting suit introduces himself to us. He is a missionary and significantly involved in the peace negotiations. He invited us to his VIP box. His wife, clad in a simple gray cotton dress, was already there, sitting next two old native men. Some white people in suits were present too. All of them give us a friendly handshake. It has escaped our attention that suddenly no warrior can be seen with their families anymore and soon we know why. They obviously had pulled back up onto the hill.

Suddenly we hear bloodcurdling war cries. From two sides the warriors stormed towards the square and swing threatening their weapons. More and more groups storm the hill towards us, with the threatening spears in their arms. The blood seems to clot in my body. The place is filled with creepy characters. There are several thousand. The hostile tribes are separated by a rope in the middle of the square. This limit is obviously only symbolic. The enemies roared against one another. The day before they even fought against each other. Slowly a break occurs and the warriors sit on the floor, looking grim. From each side a stately figure comes on the platform on which we sit with the other guests of honor, each holding a spear in their hand. They are the leaders of the two clans. An endless discussion begins, and many different men talk on the podium, screaming in a language we do not understand. Then the two chiefs shake hands. They all go throw their weapons in a heap. Old men look at the pile and put iron weapons, such as gun barrels, to the side. Many wooden spears, lances, and shields are left on the heap. The old men ignite the wood pile. Young warriors clamp the iron weapons under their arms and go away with them. From the bushes, the women come and get the meat. They bring it to their villages. We had feared that we must participate as guests of honor at a feasting meal. The dirty meat had not made a particularly trustworthy impression on us.

Southern Ethiopia: We traveled through the fascinating green cultivated landscape of high mountains, as the Toyota we were in makes its way through large herds of cattle, many of them well-fed zebu, and the river crossings we must traverse. Roadside bushes bloom white. In the village of Key Afer market live the Banna-People. Many of them bare half calabashes on their heads. The men are adorned with colored ribbons and feathers. In the small town of Jinka, a young man who has apparently never seen a white man laughs at the sight of us. The next morning we arranged a guide and started very early, so that we are on the road ahead of the other tourists. The drive leads through the Mago National Park. A pack of wild dogs disappear in the bush, baboons cross the road in front of us, guinea fowl flutter on. Even from a distance we see a group of men with Kalashnikov's. They belong to the people of the Mursi, a minority of about 10,000 people. The women are known for their lip plates. We continued and reached a village where we are asked to photograph the tribes. Each photo taken there costs 2 birr (of course we had to shell out a large amount to the village elders first). The people there stand very close to you and we were constantly touched and asked to photograph them. The women wear huge lip plates, sometimes hanging far down on their lips cut down like thin cloth. At the end of puberty, the girl's lips are cut and the front lower incisors are knocked out and they use a clay plate, which get progressively bigger over the years, to stretch out the lower lip. Often their earlobes are decorated in the same manner. Supposedly this body jewelry is a symbol of beauty. It was also once invented to make the women unattractive to slave hunters. The body of men and women are scarified and adorned with attached wide scars. Some men are painted white and almost all of them carry Kalashnikov's.

Which travel experiences stand out the most and why?

Timbuktu. It was the first journey after my retirement. Before that my longest journey was only eight weeks.

The road to Timbuktu: There are things that stay with a man since his childhood — and will eventually become an obsession. In the 40s and 50s of the last century it was known as cigarette cards, which you could collect and store in thematic albums. On one of these prints a signpost is shown in the Arabic and French language, which had a nomadic Bedouin camel rider and the inscription in front of desert sand dunes that said, "The stuff that dreams are made of. Tombouctou 52 Jours."

Eventually I knew that I had to follow the footsteps of the caravans in this mysterious city one day.

When I started my life as a retired police officer on September 01, 2001, I saw it come at the right time: The fixed idea was for real projects. I knew long ago that strange sign was somewhere in Morocco and that for the traveler the way to Timbuktu is denied on the classic route over Algeria. I put three fixed points for my trip: the sign, Timbuktu, and Saly in Senegal, because I wanted to meet my wife there for Christmas. It was a four-month long journey!

What are the most overrated and underrated countries you've been to in your travels and why?

The most overrated for nearly nothing to see was Equatorial Guinea and because of all the expensive papers I needed for the visa. The cheapest was Brazil in 1989 because the Brazilian money was nearly worthless.

What are the best and worst meals you have ever had traveling and where were they?

The best is Thai food, especially Tom Yum Goong.

The worst was sheep testicles in Samarkand, Uzbekistan.

What country made you feel most out of your comfort zone and why?

Transnistria (a breakaway state located in eastern Moldova) because of the rude former Soviets with ruined houses and a lot of stretch limousines for the Mafia bosses.

Do you speak any foreign languages? If so, which has been the most useful for you besides English?

I speak only English, German and Bavarian Dialect, a little bit French, Spanish, and Italian. The best language is the language of the heart.

Looking back from when you started traveling to where you are now, in what ways, if any, has travel changed you?

You learn to be tolerant.

What was the longest continuous trip you have ever taken, when was it where did you travel?

Four months from Munich to Istanbul, then Ladakh and Kashmir, across India to Bangladesh and on to Malaysia and Vietnam.

What is your favorite "off-the-beaten-path" destination and why?

The hyena man of Harar: "Do you need a guide?" asks the young man in green t-shirt. On the way to Somalia in 2008, I stayed for a few days in the Muslim holy city of Harar, Ethiopia, which lies at an altitude of 1850 meters. It was not only the boy but numerous other guides offering their services to me. Since I had a lot of time and preferred to wander alone through the streets, so I told them simply that I was with a guide the day before and I knew the place now quite well (although this was a white lie, but works wonders). The narrow streets wind their way through an intricate maze of shallow corrugated iron covered mud houses. People jostle seemingly aimlessly through the chaos, women in colorful robes sell qat, men sluggishly lie in front of the houses with their chubby cheeks filled with qat, the blind are led by children, cripples and lepers raise their hands (or the leftover stub), pleading in my direction. Happy school girls with head-scarves talk cheerfully to me, brave boys politely ask, "What is your name?" Madrasas (Koran schools) and mosques announce the fact that I am in a holy city of Islam. In a small hidden restaurant, I eat a huge serving of goat meat stew, before I make my way to the city wall. I then visit the hyena man. The hyena man I went to was a frail boy of perhaps

18 years. His name was Abbas and he has learned the custom of hyena feeding from his father and it is then passed on for generations. The food is made within a metal bucket, which is filled with sliced strips of donkey and camel meat. To feed the hyenas, I didn't put the stick between my teeth, but I took it gently in my hand, and as one of the animals snuck over to me, the beast took the meat and silently disappeared.

What are the best and worst places you have spent a night?

The best: Cinnamon Grand in Colombo, Sri Lanka.

The worst: A pension in Bora Bora with thousands of cockroaches.

In your opinion, what country or place in the world feels the most authentic and untouched by tourism?

Tana Toraja in Indonesia with its eerie cult of the dead.

In your opinion, where is the most beautiful place on Earth?

1) The Viktualienmarkt in Munich: It takes place in the center of this German city of 1.3 million people where you sit with people from all over the world if it is not too cold and talk with a glass of the best beer in the world, surrounded by stalls with products from all over the globe such as vegetables from Bavarian farmers, cheese from France, tropical fruit from Southeast Asia, and wine from Chile or South Africa.

2) Disko Bay in Greenland: Seeing the sparkling glaciers golden in the midsummer night and remembering that there will be no more within a few years due to global warming.

3) Gangtok, capital of Sikkim, at the foot of the Himalayas: When the sun rises, the Himalayan giant Kanjenjunga turns purple.

And 1000 more places!

What do you enjoy the most when traveling (cities, nature, people, cultural spots, etc.)?

People, people, people — because you can learn so much from other cultures!

What travel accomplishments are you most proud of?

None. I'm so happy that I have such a privileged life in a wealthy country.

If you had just one personal travel story to share with someone, what would that be?

Below the Vesuvius: The intercity train is on time at Roma Termini Station, in Rome. It turned out to be a good idea that we reserved seats. After two hours my wife Renate and I arrive in Naples. We had to walk a few hundred meters through a tunnel to the station of the "Circumvesuviana," a commuter train. The approaching train is a collection of very old, rattling coaches. As we entered the train with our backpacks, a well-dressed man in his fifties partially blocks the door from the hallway to the compartment. Normally in such a situation my inner alarm bells would be ringing, but they did not. Renate and I push past him and take the only two free seats left. The train leaves the station. After a while the train stops at a station and I see a man in ragged clothes and he has a small leather bag in his hands, looking at it quizzically. This case looks like an elongated purse that belongs to me. There is no money in it, only cheap sunglasses. In this moment I learn instantly that the well-dressed "gentlemen" pulled the bag out from the outside pocket of my trousers, closed with a hook and loop fastener, in the moment when he provoked me and my wife when we entered the train, and then passed the purse to his companion. The duo had quite evidently such a different outfit so that one does not make a connection between the two. I stood from my seat, walked up to the guy, and took the bag out of his hand.

Besides your home country, where do you find yourself returning to over and over and why?

New York City, because it is *the city*; Jerusalem to see what happens with religion; Vienna with its own charm.

What is the ideal amount of time you prefer to travel on each trip before you are ready for home and a break?

Now because I'm older, two months is the ideal time.

If you had an unlimited budget, and space and time was no object, what would your perfect travel day look like? (For example: start your morning in Bora Bora, afternoon on a safari in Kenya, night in Australia, etc.)

A journey to space to see our Blue Planet from above.

For those looking to travel to every country, what is the best piece of advice you could offer them?

Meet people, talk to them and learn from them.

For someone that has been almost everywhere, what still gets you excited about packing your bags again?

Even though I've spent 17 years of my life traveling, of course I have seen only a tiny part of our planet. I need a lot of lives to see every angle, every island. But actually I'm satisfied. In the future, I will go with my wife to some corners of the world I liked very much. There are a few travel goals that I would like to achieve, such as Fernando de Noronha, Lampedusa, and maybe some regions in Russia. But I am happy that I have seen so much of the world.

Do you ever feel you have missed out on certain aspects of life being away from home so much?

Nearly nothing, but sometimes German bread!

Looking ahead, what travel plans and goals are you still pursuing and what is on your "Bucket List"?

I'm nearly satisfied.

Harry Mitsidis, Greece

(Harry Mitsidis)

Where did you grow up and what was your early life like?

I was born in London, England but grew up in Athens, Greece. I had quite a typical middle-class early life, with a couple of notable twists — my mother is South African so I grew up speaking English at home, which from the start set me apart from everybody else. Also, as an only child of a father who was also an only child, I grew up without any larger family ties, which I suppose made me very independent. I liked playing games on my own. One of my favorites was spending a whole day, which I would call "Big Day," playing with my large airplane collection by creating an airport.

When did you go from casually traveling to making this a full-time goal, and what motivated you to travel to every country?

There were various stages. In 2000 I opted to go to Moldova and Odessa for a few days; that could be considered my first truly "way out" trip, and very quickly I found myself wanting to see more and more. Initially I only planned on doing all European countries, but they were already finished in June 2001 (Belarus was the last). So I then went forward for them all. I guess, being a big geography fan, I wanted to have the full set.

Do you remember the point where you said to yourself, "I can really accomplish this"?

Afghanistan was always the no-go zone and, unlike some other travelers or clubs who count putting half your toe across a borderline as "visiting" a place, I only count a place as "visited" if I really go, and truly seeing it seemed impossible. Then the Taliban were ousted and it became a distinct possibility, and I was there in October 2003 — it was my 100th country, possibly not accidental. After that I knew this could be done, as the other "difficult" countries were not that hard. Once I ticked off Saudi Arabia (not by transit, but by successfully getting a business visa) in 2006, I knew I was there.

What have you done over your life to gain the freedom and finances to pursue as much travel as you have?

I think freedom is a choice. It's a matter of priorities. For me, as a typical Aquarius, freedom has always been a priority anyway, and I have always gone my own way, usually in the opposite direction of the masses.

In terms of finances, I have to admit I've been lucky. I'm an only child of middle-class parents who have always been overindulgent. I owe it all to them in that sense.

Was there ever a time you felt like abandoning this goal?

I remember once sitting on an Air Zimbabwe plane in Dar es Salaam, and there was a technical problem and we didn't know if we would be going. It had been a long trip through Africa and I was exhausted, and I truly thought, "Why I am here? Why am I doing this?" The plane did make it in the end, and soon I had "conquered" Zimbabwe and those thoughts were gone.

I have had many mishaps in more recent years. Twice I didn't make it to Tokelau and was stranded in Samoa. As a result of a canceled flight in Lord Howe Island, I missed my connection and didn't make the Torres Islands. I was also stranded on Ascension Island for five days, which resulted in me having to do the Falklands on another trip at considerable expense. However, all these setbacks have probably just strengthened my resolve rather than weakened it. I want to see it all.

What were your worst travel experiences (i.e. detainment, bribes, car accidents, sickness, etc.) and why?

I am tempted to say my detainment in eastern Yemen for illegally entering the country (without a visa), but in retrospect that experience, while scary and horrible at the time, is not only nuts but makes a wonderful travel story. Not to mention becoming friends with one of the officers on Facebook!

I think my worst experience was my five days on Ascension Island. I don't like small islands anyway, and that is a particularly boring and rather unfriendly place. I hadn't taken my computer with me, quickly finished my supply of 3 books, and I was losing my mind. Not knowing when the plane to take me to the Falklands would arrive (due to the "Big Freeze" in the UK) made the whole experience unnerving. But, if you think about it, this was not so terrible anyway. I believe once you travel you need to take the good with the bad and always enjoy it. That's the point of the trip anyway.

What do you consider the most adventurous trip you have taken?

Every trip is an adventure. It's true that the "developed" countries of the world offer far more predictable chances of true adventure. They are too safe perhaps, but it all depends on your point of view and there are plenty of opportunities for confusion and misunderstanding even in your own home country. The most adventurous day was a very long transfer between Freetown and Monrovia. The condition of the road itself, the huts and the villages passed, the inevitable small bribes here and there, plus the excitement of a border truly in the middle of nowhere make that day especially memorable. I won't forget a whole village rejoicing when I gave them $1. I hope they are alive now, poor people.

What were your most challenging countries to visit and why?

It's clearly the ones where the visa was problematic. In my case, the only really tough visa was the one to my final independent country — Equatorial Guinea. That place doesn't grant tourist visas and despite efforts in Douala, Paris, and even Luanda, nothing seemed to work. In the end, my parents found an acquaintance who ran a business with lots of dealings there and it became the easiest of visas to secure given that contact. I was even met at the airport and had one of the smoothest stays once there.

What is the strangest thing you've seen/experienced while traveling?

Seeing two grown men wearing leather peeing on each other in the middle of the street in Amsterdam left a mark on the 22-year-old me that nothing has ever quite surpassed.

Which travel experiences stand out the most and why?

The ones that stand out tend to be people-related, that is, the times when I met new people who, ultimately, have also become my strongest memory of a place. No matter what monuments, great landscapes, temples or food one may have, in the end it is the people who always make the difference. In that sense, my one truly memorable experience was on the small Japanese island of Daito, where I happened to meet a man named Satoshi when I was walking out of the airport. He was a really nice young guy, who spoke English as he had spent time in Australia, and he ultimately showed me around his island, taking me to local houses, lunch, and to all the sites of this magnificent, and truly off the radar, small dot in the Pacific. I cannot forget how the local people whose home we went to, who were in their 60s, had never had a foreigner in their house, and the amazing honor they felt. The woman told me, "You are rich," implying the spiritual riches that come from travel. At that moment I truly did feel rich. It's only people who can give you that gift.

What are the most overrated and underrated countries you've been to in your travels and why?

This assessment has mainly to do with expectations, as well as the image of each country globally. Personally, I find the United States very overrated. With the exception of some truly wonderful natural sites (Grand Canyon, Yellowstone…), many others are purely money-making machines with little substance. I will never forget driving through southern Indiana and bothering to see the "big sight" of the area, the Marengo Caves. I left feeling so cheated. Caves I had seen in Abkhazia, Lebanon and even in Daito were far superior…

There are many unknown gems still, which make us true adventurers happy. Sierra Leone was one of them, but I don't know what it's like now with the Ebola virus. I also feel somewhat "off the beaten track" places like Ecuador, Rwanda, Laos, and especially Romania, are incredibly interesting and should be top destinations.

What are the best and worst meals you have ever had traveling and where were they?

Food is very important for me, but I'll admit that you can buy me off with a good cake and I'll be such a happy camper. I had the best lemon meringue pie in Swakopmund, Namibia. I plan to return just for that! I recently had a marvelous afternoon tea in Quito's exquisite Casa Gangotena hotel. It was worth every penny. I remember a really good meal in Vilnius too, including a mushroom soup in a round bread loaf. Anything in Turkey is amazing, especially their full "village" breakfast, which is enough for two days of calories.

I've had many a lousy meal in poorer countries. A fly-infested, bland rice with chicken on Gorée Island kind of stands out, mainly because of the flies. I recently had the worst spaghetti bolognese in the world somewhere in Asia (can't remember where) — it serves me right for ordering a western dish in Asia. One should always go local.

What country made you feel most out of your comfort zone and why?

Believe it or not, my own country, Greece. I had been away for almost seven years, studying and working abroad, from 1993 to the end of 1999. Returning, I found a completely different place. Its social fabric had changed. Credit cards, which had been unknown before, were suddenly the norm, and people's lives and habits had gone from being a backwater on the fringes of Europe to so-called high sophistication. I think I still haven't recovered from the shock, and long for the Greece of my childhood which, alas, is no longer to be found. Suffice it to say I was the least surprised when the crisis hit. A country can't change so suddenly and not undergo a deep economic — and also social — fractures.

Do you speak any foreign languages? If so, which have been the most useful for you besides English?

One of the great travelers, Jorge Sanchez, has called me "the polyglot traveler." I am entirely fluent in English and Greek, and almost fluent in Serbian, which I learned alone out of spite when NATO bombed Yugoslavia. I speak above average Spanish and French, average Romanian and Dutch, and can "survive" in Russian, German, Portuguese, and some basic Turkish and Bahasa Indonesia. I can also read the newspaper in Italian and Bulgarian.

I think French, Spanish, and Russian have all been equally useful. I cannot imagine traveling in French-speaking Africa on my own with no French, neither in South America (or even Spain) without Spanish. As for Russian, I am very lucky I can read everything in Cyrillic, this has really helped understanding the environment, and having conversations with Russian taxi drivers is among the greatest highlights of my travel career!

Looking back from when you started traveling to where you are now, in what ways, if any, have travel changed you?

Probably the main change is that now I am addicted to traveling. If I stay put for two weeks without a border crossing, I start getting nervous. In the last 12 years, the longest I have gone without a border crossing is 54 days. Having said this, I haven't changed so much. I am still quite a shy loner, still as curious about the world as I was when I was two, and still try to treat everybody with humanity.

What is the longest continuous trip you have ever taken? When was it and where did you travel?

I don't do really long trips for a variety of reasons. I travel with a tiny piece of hand-luggage and get my clothes washed every week or so. Some trips get quite lonely, no matter how many people I meet, and I tend to miss the "comforts" of Europe as well as the people in my environment. My longest trip, in the sense of not being a move for work out of my base, was a seven-week one back in 2010, which started in Azerbaijan (and Nakhchivan), then took in Abkhazia and parts of Russia, moving on from Novosibirsk to Urumqi and spending three weeks in China, and then a few days in the Philippines with another few in Kuwait and Lebanon on the way back.

What is your favorite "off-the-beaten-path" destination and why?

It's a contest between Laos and Romania. If pushed I will choose Romania. The country is nuts. It's fascinating, and if you go to regions in the north like Maramure?, you forget you are in the 21st century. They have incredible eco-stays for almost nothing and you can experience family life. I guess Romania isn't the only place that has this, but its quirky language which is a mix of unmixable elements of Latin and Slavic, along with its rather diverse populations and geographical regions, add to make an unusual, intriguing place. I go almost every year for around a week of driving on its perilous, but always appealing, country roads.

What are the best and worst places you have ever spent a night?

If you're talking about hotels, one of my best was Hotel Gmachl in Bergheim, near Salzburg in Austria. I also had a wonderful stay in a very inexpensive ($25) place called Hue Serene Palace Hotel (in Hue, Vietnam). However, spending the night in a hotel can never be "best" — I think the home of my

Aunt Vivien in Milton Keynes (near Luton, England) is always the "best place." It feels so homey.

I've stayed in some very lousy places. When I first went to Astana in 2001, I stayed in a real cheapo which was full of Tajik refugees. On the "cruise" to Pitcairn, which was anything but, we were all subjected to an awfully uncomfortable boat in really rudimentary conditions without a real bathroom. But, in the end, the jail cell in Al Ghaydah, Yemen, has to take the "Oscar" in this category — if only for the zillion mosquito bites I suffered.

In your opinion, what country or place in the world feels the most authentic and untouched by tourism?

I certainly don't think one can talk about a "country" level because almost every country's main cities are somewhat touched by tourism. Still, there are plenty of places where tourists would not dare to tread and so there is no effort at all to cater to their needs, which is great for us travelers. The minute you see a Starbucks-like cafe, the place is "lost." I think it's not always only tourism, but the needs of aid workers, etc., that can also transform a place. In that sense, finding a top-notch sushi restaurant in Monrovia was a big surprise (I was starving and welcomed every piece of it, I admit). There are many places in Africa that are untouched, but to be a bit less predictable, I would say that some places in Iran (outside the main circuit) seem incredibly authentic. Try Sanandaj or Rasht. There isn't really a trace of anything geared to the foreigner there.

In your opinion, where is the most beautiful place on Earth?

This is the hardest question of them all, because beauty is so many different things at once. There's landscape, architecture, cultural artifacts, the people themselves, food, way of life, and attitudes… Putting all of these in an equation to come up with a final answer is impossible, and in my opinion rather pointless. My final answer is "everywhere," as long as there is peace and no disease or hunger. Earth is beautiful everywhere if you have the eyes to find its beauty. It depends on how you see it, not what you see.

What do you enjoy most when traveling (cities, nature, people, cultural spots, etc.) and why?

The people. Do I really need to explain why? People are always the most interesting, colorful, mysterious, and amazing finds. (OK, almost always.)

What travel accomplishments are you most proud of?

To the best of my calculations, there are only 100 people or so who have been to every country in the world. And this is not just today, but across the whole of human civilization. Belonging to this club is a supreme achievement for everybody who has done it, and I don't think there can be any other achievement that tops that in terms of travel, or even otherwise. I am possibly the best traveled civilian (non-diplomat or army) whose work is not related to tourism under the age of 45, so this, too, is a big achievement.

If you had just one personal travel story to share with someone, what would that be?

This one is really difficult to answer. I'm completing a book with 60 stories from my travels, some funny, some tragic, which should be ready by mid-2015, precisely because there are so many. One that always makes me smile happened on the island of Canouan in the Grenadines. This is one of those exclusive destinations for the super-rich. I spent a few hours on the island, walking all the way to the main settlement from the airport, which took over an hour. On the way back, after a sudden downpour, I managed to hitch a ride with a lorry going to the airport. The driver and I chatted a little about the island and how they were upgrading the airport. Then, once we got close and the tarmac was in view, full of private jets, he casually asked me, "So, which plane is yours?" I thought his question was hilarious. For this local driver, any white guy on the island would naturally have their own jet.

Besides your home country, where do you find yourself returning to over and over and why?

I keep on returning to Serbia. I guess since I learned the language this is an obvious choice. I have many contacts there, and it's only a short hop from Greece. The country reminds me somewhat of a time-warp, maybe of my childhood in a way, as it's very 70s in a lot of things because of the complete lack of progress from 1990 to recently. It's familiar in terms of mentality, but still extremely exotic in my eyes, and the differences between the more European north and the more Balkan south are remarkable. I have been through Belgrade airport almost as many times as Heathrow.

What is the ideal amount of time you prefer to travel each trip before you are ready for home and a break?

I like three week trips. This is just enough to feel the freedom and the pace of a destination without getting lonely or tired of it. Additionally, it allows me to have more trips a year to very different regions.

If you had an unlimited budget and space and time was no object, what would your perfect travel day look like? (for example: start your morning in Bora Bora; afternoon on a safari in Kenya; night in Australia, etc.)

Morning with breakfast somewhere in Turkey just to savor that incredible meal and a late morning spent walking somewhere in China for the fun of getting completely lost, and for the noise, chaos, and smells. Lunch in Pécs or Szeged in Hungary, both of which are architectural jewels — and Hungarian food is amazing. Following lunch, an adrenalin-filled ride through Mogadishu to remember the destruction and the ruins that got me all excited when I was there in 2011. Afternoon tea in the UK, as it is part of who I am and I miss it often. Later on, a walk down to La Boca in Buenos Aires and other parts of this amazing city as well. A quick stroll in the evening market of Luang Prabang, followed by a pre-dinner walk by the sea somewhere in Italy (maybe Portofino), then an evening dinner in a taverna in Athens, preferably with local music, followed by late night outing first in Belgrade and then somewhere in Vietnam, ideally with a ride on a motorbike included. Finally, the day would conclude with me going to sleep in my own bed. What a wonderful day!

For those looking to travel to every country, what is the best piece of advice you could offer them?

How many people really want to do this, I wonder? I think all they need is the will. Everything else will fall into place as long as you really want it. And don't let anybody tell you it's impossible or that you're crazy!

For someone that has been almost everywhere, what still gets you excited about packing your bags again?

I always get very excited when a trip is around the corner. In that sense, I am lucky to be able to tap into the child within, like the days when I was going to visit my grandparents in London and looking forward to flying the Trident or the Lockheed TriStar on British Airways. Everything about the trip gets me excited — the flight itself, the destination, whether known (it's like revisiting an old friend) or unknown (there is a mystery ahead of going there). I also think that all of us world travelers are very conscious of the fact we have hardly been anywhere! A little like Socrates' comment, "I know one thing: that I know nothing," you realize how enormous the world is and that it is never possible to really go everywhere…

Do you feel you have missed out on certain aspects of life being away from home so much?

Absolutely. In fact, I am torn between staying and leaving, and keeping a balance between these two has always been problematic. I really love the theatre and the cinema. Such simple things, and have missed out on a lot by never being home. I'm often guilt-ridden for not spending enough time with my parents, and though I have loads of friends, often the thread of a continued contact is lacking. Additionally, any sort of intimate relationship becomes very difficult to keep, and I have a deeply romantic and dreamy side that is wasted. Many of the top travelers are single or divorced, and there are reasons for this. And of course, professionally, things get messy too. You can't travel all the time and have a normal job. In the end, life is about priorities. When you're a travel addict, the addiction chooses for you.

Looking ahead, what travel plans and goals are you still pursuing, and what is on your "Bucket List"?

My ultimate goal is to visit every country of the world twice. Out of the 193, I've been to 127 at least twice, so there's 66 to go. No rush here, I'll take it slowly. I would also like to reach 1000 points (out of 1281) on the increasingly popular traveler's site that I have founded, The Best Travelled. I think that will be reached by early 2016, so it's certainly doable. I should know Europe better. I've never been to Florence, believe it or not, and there's amazing sites in France, Spain, Portugal, and areas of Poland I'd like to explore more. It always seems these places are near and can be done any time, but I do feel I've often ignored Europe in favor of more distant places. Last but not least, I have explored the two countries of my citizenship, Greece and the UK, shockingly little. They say, "There's no place like home," and I need to check that out for myself!

Charalampos "Babis" Bizas, Greece

(**Charalampos "Babis" Bizas**)

Where did you grow up and what was your early life like?

I was born in 1954 and grew up in Arta, a small provincial town in northwest Greece. Nothing special happened until I was 18 years of age when I left for Thessaloniki in northern Greece for university studies.

When did you go from casually traveling to making this a full-time goal, and what motivated you to travel to every country?

I started traveling to the nearby countries in Europe and the Middle East. After I graduated from university, I started working as a tour escort for a major Greek tour operator. Eventually, I traveled to all of the mainstream tourist destinations of that time. Then I became the Planning Manager of the company and I started planning new tours never offered by the global travel market, like Nigeria, Guinea Bissau, Saudi Arabia, etc. By 2000 I had visited, either through those tours above or individually, approximately 170 countries. Only then did I realize that it was possible to travel to the 25 remaining countries. By 2004, I had visited Mogadishu in Somalia, Liberia, and Sierra Leone, East Timor, and a few years later, South Sudan, completing the list of the "official" countries. In 2010, I met some great travelers during the Pitcairn expedition cruise and I learned of the various "clubs".

Do you remember the point where you said to yourself, "I can really accomplish this"?

I cannot say exactly when it happened, but I believe it was when I visited the most difficult places to get visas (Saudi Arabia and Equatorial Guinea) around the year 2000.

What have you done over your life to gain the freedom and finances to pursue as much travel as you have?

Mostly I worked in the tourist industry and I organized — with total freedom from my company — tours for pioneer travelers. During my annual leave I visited those other places I could not propose for tourist traveling. I also enjoyed travel industry airfares and concessions for my private trips.

Was there ever a time you felt like abandoning this goal?

No, never. I only have postponed certain itineraries or chosen other goals instead of what I had originally set.

What were your worst travel experiences (i.e. detainment, bribes, car accidents, sickness, etc.) and why?

I am rather lucky in my trips. I have been jailed in Libya, though, for a day. In Rio de Janeiro, I have been jailed for an hour until I had agreed to pay a $100 USD bribe to the duty officer of the Copacabana police station. I was deported for the first time from Equatorial Guinea (but I returned the next day). No major sicknesses (sunburn was the worst thing I have dealt with).

Which travel experiences stand out the most and why?

My first visit to Antarctica. It was something I couldn't expect to happen to me. The grandiose scenery and silence had a tremendous impact on my senses.

What are the most overrated and underrated countries you've been to in your travels and why?

Zambia is the most overrated. Too expensive for similar things you get easily in other African countries. The most underrated is Bangladesh. It is a superb country with magnificent scenery, people, and unexpected sights. Overrated is also Upper Mustang (Lo Manthang). Interesting place, but not worth the trouble to get there for what you get.

What are the best and worst meals you have ever had traveling and where were they?

I don't remember the meals I eat — especially the worst. Recently, I had a very bad experience in Yellowstone National Park when I decided to try the 'Buffalo Burger'. Three days sick. The best I had was in Azerbaijan, in the Baku central market. The Uzbek Plov in Tashkent, and Ethiopian food — even here in Athens!!

What country made you feel most out of your comfort zone and why?

None. Probably because I easily adapt myself to the situations and I obey the rules. I don't try to change the world.

Do you speak any foreign languages? If so, which has been the most useful for you besides English?

I speak Russian, French, and Spanish. Each of them is territorial and you cannot survive easily in West Africa without French, or Latin America with Spanish, and in the former Soviet Union countries (except the Baltics) without Russian.

Looking back from when you started traveling to where you are now, in what ways, if any, has travel changed you?

It made me more tolerant of other people, increased my interests, and I learned a lot and I feel more complete as a personality.

What was the longest continuous trip you have ever taken, when was it, and where did you travel?

It was a trip overland from Greece to Iran and Afghanistan, then to India, Nepal, Bangladesh, and Sri Lanka. There I decided to work as a seaman on a Greek ship and I traveled to Mozambique, South Africa, Cape Verde, and the United States. After five months, I returned from New Orleans with some money, ready to pass my last exams for the Constitutional Law in my university (Political Sciences).

What is your favorite "off-the-beaten-path" destination and why?

South Ethiopia. The tribes of Omo River valley. Now they are somewhat spoiled by tourism, but they are always gorgeous.

What are the best and worst places you have ever spent a night?

The worst night was in Tubuai Island in the Austral Islands of French Polynesia. Too many mosquitoes.

My best night — or one of the best — was in a lodge in the Orinoco Delta in Venezuela.

In your opinion, what country or place in the world feels the most authentic and untouched by tourism?

São Tomé and Príncipe as countries; as a place, the town of Ayoru in Niger during the Sunday markets; it is a dream to see the people of the Sahara and Sahel gathering there.

In your opinion, where is the most beautiful place on Earth?

Antarctica. The feelings of sailing slowly in iced surroundings, the tranquility, the absence of humans.

What do you enjoy most when traveling (cities, nature, people, cultural spots, etc.) and why?

People by far. I travel for meeting and interacting with people. Then there are the great monuments of those peoples and, finally, there are the natural wonders.

What travel accomplishments are you most proud of?

Visiting all the 90 inhabited Greek Islands! I could not suffer to hear from friends, "OK, you traveled to Wrangel Island and Franz Josef Land, but have you been to Donousa? (a little Greek Island)." So I decided to respond with, "YES!" to this question. In about four months I visited all the remaining ones.

If you had just one personal travel story to share with someone, what would it be?

My visit to Somalia in 2003. It was a very different way to visit this place from the moment I arrived till my departure. I had to arrange a personal bodyguard team of eight Kalashnikov wielding militiamen, one escort, and a driver. I enjoyed very much my stay there and was even invited to a wedding party! (Yes, I had to refuse the invitation of a pretty lady to spend the night together).

Besides your home country, where do you find yourself returning to over and over and why?

Moscow, New York, London, and Sydney. These places have an appeal to me and I try to find an excuse to stop there even if they are not exactly on my itinerary. I visit Moscow for the cultural life, Sydney for the beauty of its natural setting, New York for the energy that it transmits, and finally London, because I love to spend hours in bookstores there.

What is the ideal amount of time you prefer to travel on each trip before you are ready for home and a break?

I don't need a break. I can travel continuously. I have to return to my base for routine obligations: to change a passport, to pay my bills, and to arrange some part-time work. Also recently, I have been joining expedition cruises one after the other departing from different parts of the world. Every time I have to return home and start a new one. Typically my trips last for three weeks. But also I make short ones like one week. I love to stay four-five months on the road.

If you had an unlimited budget and space and time was no object, what would your perfect travel day look like? (for example: start your morning in Bora Bora; afternoon on a safari in Kenya; night in Australia, etc.)

I like to explore the places in-depth. If money and time were not a problem, I would rather stay two months in Polynesia visiting every single island rather than move from continent to continent.

For those looking to travel to every country, what is the best piece of advice you could offer them?

To divide them in groups of neighboring countries. You can visit six or seven of them in one trip of three weeks. In every continent, there is always a group of such countries.

Do you ever feel you have missed out on certain aspects of life being away from home so much?

Of course. I don't have close friends. I am not there when a friend needs me. I am somewhere in the world. We exchange messages on Facebook or SMS, but that's all.

Looking ahead, what travel plans and goals are you still pursuing, and what is on your "Bucket List"?

A lot of places. I just now "started" really traveling. Places that I didn't know existed. Islands, small towns, beautiful corners of countries I visited previously. Every day I am a beginner.

Lee Abbamonte, U.S.A.

(Lee Abbamonte **arriving into Mangareva, French Polynesia after an epic week-long trip to Pitcairn Island, one of
the world's most remote islands, April 2012**)

Where did you grow up and what was your early life like?

I grew up in Trumbull, Connecticut in the United States. My
life was pretty normal with great family and friends. I was/am
really into playing sports and that was pretty much what I focused on through high school.

**When did you go from casually traveling to making this a
full-time goal, and what motivated you to travel to every
country?**

In 2006, after I had been to some 100+ countries just by
chance (aka: traveling for fun), I got an email that there was a
record to be the youngest to visit every country. I am pretty
competitive, and that was a big motivation for me. I have to

also say that living through the 9/11 tragedy was a massive motivating factor in deciding to live my life to the fullest.

Do you remember the point where you said to yourself, "I can really accomplish this"?

I never doubted that I could accomplish it. I've never failed at anything I set my mind to, but I think the moment I really knew I'd do it was when Libya was the only country I had left. I had to wait a few months for the Arab Spring to pass — or should I say, until the rebels took eastern Libya — to get in, but I knew I would do it, so that's when I said it for sure!

What have you done over your life to gain the freedom and finances to pursue as much travel as you have?

I have worked my entire life and have always been well disciplined with money. I am an entrepreneur and also worked on Wall Street for eight years.

Was there ever a time you felt like abandoning this goal?

No, there was never a time I wanted to abandon the goal. There were some places I wasn't thrilled to visit, but I knew that they were all part of the bigger picture and I was always good at managing expectations by setting none so I was never disappointed and I never got disheartened — plus I learned a ton and saw things I never dreamed of seeing. Not everywhere can be like the U.S., France, Australia, or the Maldives!

What have been your worst travel experiences (such as detainment, bribes, car accidents, sicknesses, etc.) and why?

If you've traveled as much as I have then you've pretty much dealt with every annoying situation possible. Delays, bribes, car accidents, theft, etc., happen. But for me, I have always been pretty vigilant and I am also a pretty big guy, so I have never really been physically threatened. My worst experiences have been illness in some places you really don't want to get ill. I had my worst experience in Turkmenistan and Iran. I have never been so sick in my life from eating something bad — I think it was lettuce in a salad I had, but I'm still not sure to this day. Let's just say it was awful, and I was worried that Iran wouldn't let me into the country and I would be stranded in no man's land as I had already left Turkmenistan, which ended the validity of my visa. Luckily they let me in, but the whole time I was beyond sick. I think I lost 20 pounds in five days — that's not good!

What do you consider one of the most adventurous trips you have taken?

Adventure is kind of my thing, so I have taken dozens of trips based on doing adventurous things like skydiving, bungee jumping, shark diving, etc. But what I really love is accomplishing things — I like goals. That said, I love climbing things or hiking things. After all that I've done, I still think my most adventurous trip was back in 2006 when I climbed Mount Kilimanjaro with my friend Jake. That was an adventure in and of itself because of the experience, the weather, and the unknown in an unknown place. Then we camped in the Serengeti and the Ngorongoro Crater for another two weeks before ending in Zanzibar. At the time, I thought it was the most adventurous trip I could think of, and to this day, it was still the most adventurous because of the great unknown — nothing beats your first time!

What were your most challenging countries to visit and why?

For me, my three most challenging countries to visit were Angola, Pakistan, and Libya. Angola is simply the most difficult place to get a visa to as an American. Pakistan is not far behind it and I actually had to convince a Pakistani citizen I've never met before to send me his national ID to sponsor my visa. I met the guy on the Internet. Talk about trusting in others — I couldn't believe it, but I am eternally grateful! Libya, I've talked about at length in other questions, but all the factors including war, no government, no fly zones and the fact that I crossed at a remote border between Egypt and Libya, made it tremendously tough to visit but also the most rewarding as it was my last of the 193!

What's the strangest thing you've seen/experienced while traveling?

This is a tough question because I have seen so many strange things I could write a whole book just on that alone! I will go with the fetish market in Lome, Togo. I am not a fetish guy to say the least and seeing all the dead things like animal heads and corpses and other witchcraft type things for sale at an open market was really weird to me. It may be normal in Togo, but it pretty much blew my mind! The other thing that blew my mind about was I saw other travelers actually buying animal skulls… for what reason I'll never know!

What stand out as your most memorable travel experiences and why?

This is a very difficult question because I've had so many memorable and wonderful experiences traveling around the world. However, I must say that my first trip abroad was my most memorable because it changed my life completely. I studied abroad in London in 1998; which was the first time I had ever left the country. That experience in London and traveling around Europe that year led me to do so many things I never thought I would ever do. It was the best experience of my life and led to many other amazing and memorable experiences. Not to mention I did just about all of it with one of my best friends, whom I credit with convincing me to go in the first place.

What is the most overrated and underrated country you've been to in your travels and why?

For me personally, I find China to be the most overrated country in the world. I have been several times and traveled much of the country, but I find it difficult to really "get it." I think China has beautiful places and amazing sites, but I find the experience overrated every time I go there and I always go with an open mind. I look forward to my next trip to China and hope it changes, but as of now that's it.

I think so many places are underrated and because I feel strongly about so many places, I am going to take the cheap way out and give two really broad answers! I feel that Africa is the most underrated place and the place that gets neglected by travelers the most. I am not talking about the triangle countries; meaning Egypt, Morocco, and South (all of Southern) Africa or the very touristy countries of Kenya and Tanzania. I mean the real Africa where you never know what's going to happen — to me, that's why I love Africa. You see the best and worst of humanity and it's all gorgeous.

What is the best and worst meals you have ever had traveling and where were they?

I consider myself to be a foodie and I have had so many amazing meals that I cannot name one. However, I will say this: if I had to choose one meal in the world before the world ends, it would be pizza in Naples, Italy at Da Michele. I cannot pick a worst meal but I will say I hated any meal that ever made me really sick — that's quite a few!

What country made you feel most out of your comfort zone and why?

Nigeria made me feel the most out of my comfort zone. Normally I love that feeling, but on my one and only (thus far) visit to Nigeria, I was threatened by police on multiple occasions that they would put me in jail if I did not bribe them. That doesn't even include the shakedowns at the border entering overland from Benin. Additionally, my friend and I used the ATM three times in Lagos and all three times, we got the wrong amount of money — always less.

Do you speak any foreign languages? If so, which has been the most useful for you besides English?

I speak Spanish fluently and that has been a massive help in the Americas and random other places around the world. However, teaching myself to read Cyrillic has been an even bigger help to get around much of Eastern Europe, Russia, and the former Soviet republics. I don't know what all the words mean, but I can pronounce them and read signs, which is more helpful than you realize.

Looking back from when you started traveling to where you are now, in what ways, if any, has travel changed you?

Travel has changed my life completely. The desire to see, experience and learn has taken over my life. Without travel, I would be a typical working Wall Street guy. Now I see the world differently and have made travel my business. It's never working if you do what you love, and (knock on wood), I have done that!

What was the longest continuous trip you have ever taken, when was it, and where did you travel?

My longest consecutive trip was about nine months around Australia, New Zealand, and Fiji in 2003. I traveled a lot from 2002 to 2004, but that was the longest I was away consecutively. I almost didn't come home I loved it so much!

What is your favorite "off-the-beaten-path" destination and why?

Pitcairn Island is my favorite off-the-beaten-path destination because Pitcairn is the epitome of that! Few people have ever been there and there are only 50 residents. What's amazing about Pitcairn isn't the sites, it is the people and hearing their stories and getting to know them and their history. Of course the island is beautiful, but it's the people, and the remote location, that make it awesome.

What is the best and worst place you have spent a night?

It's really hard to beat the overwater bungalows in French Polynesia and the Maldives. They are the epitome of luxury and are as cool as you dream them to be.

I have spent horrible nights in bus stations, train stations, airports, parks, random grass and dirt patches, churches with no roof, psychiatric institutions (unknowingly), and just about every awful kind of guest house, hostel, and any other kind of rat hole you can think of. However, my worst sleeping experience I've ever dealt with was on a small boat in the Pacific en route to Tokelau. The boat was disgusting, the sleeping conditions were abominable, and the entire situation sucked. It was five days of pure torture...

In your opinion, what country or place in the world feels the most authentic and untouched by tourism?

I think Sub-Saharan Africa is the salt of the earth. It is what it is and hasn't been touched by tourism because tourists don't go there.

What do you enjoy most when traveling (cities, nature, people, cultural spots, etc.) and why?

I like it all. That's what travel teaches you; to appreciate everything. However, I do love cities and beaches and am drawn to both in countries I visit.

What travel accomplishments are you most proud of?

This is an interesting question as I've never thought about it as being proud of anything; it was just something I did and still love to do. Obviously, I am quite proud of being one of a small fraternity of people who have traveled to every country in the world. There really is something to that and it shouldn't be minimized.

If you had just one personal travel story to share with someone, what would it be?

I would share my well documented entry into Libya from the Egypt land border. I was shot at and caught in cross fire. It was quite an exciting way to finish the UN list of visiting every country in the world!

Besides your home country, where do you find yourself returning to over and over and why?

I am American and I have been to both England and Canada over 50 times each. I have also been double digit times to most countries in Western Europe plus Australia, Mexico, Costa Rica, South Africa, China, and Fiji.

What is the ideal amount of time you prefer to travel on each trip before you are ready for home and a break?

At this point in my life, three weeks is a good number for me. Obviously some of my trips last longer than three weeks, but I like being home and like to feel like I have a normal(ish) life!

If you had an unlimited budget and space and time was no object, what would your perfect travel day look like? (for example: start your morning in Bora Bora; afternoon on a safari in Kenya; night in Australia, etc.)

Waking up in an overwater bungalow in Bora Bora is a nice way to start the day followed by a morning snorkel trip in Palau and a late morning walk along Bondi Beach in Sydney, Australia. I'd do a street food lunch in Bangkok, Thailand, followed by a quick hike in Bhutan and an afternoon game drive in the Ngorongoro Crater in Tanzania. I would have dinner in Naples, Italy, then dessert in Paris followed by a night out in Las Vegas. I would end the night perfectly, as I have thousands of times, with a late night slice of pizza home in New York City and falling asleep in my own apartment to SportsCenter on TV. That's a hell of a day!

For those looking to travel to every country, what is the best piece of advice you could offer them?

Save your money! True story! Yes, you can travel cheaply in places and cut back where necessary, but anyone who tells you it's cheap to travel to every country and get a real worthwhile experience is full of it.

For someone that has been almost everywhere, what still gets you excited about packing your bags again?

I still get excited because every experience is different. I can go to London or Paris or the middle of the desert in Egypt or Mali and it will always be a different experience. For me, it's all about experiences. Experience can come from the place you're visiting, the people you meet or the people you go with. If you travel long enough, you'll most likely travel with different people and I take joy in watching others see amazing places for the first time. The look in their eye makes me feel like it's my first time again. Travel is like golf: it's a hobby you can do your whole life and it's always different even if you play the same course (i.e., country).

Do you ever feel you have missed out on certain aspects of life being away from home so much?

I feel like I have done as good a job as possible to maintain my home life with friends and family. I also always make sure to be at events like weddings, holidays, etc. You have to make an effort if you want others to do the same if you're away a lot.

Looking ahead, what travel plans and goals are you still pursuing, and what is on your "Bucket List"?

I plan to go to the North Pole in spring of 2015 if all goes according to plan, one cannot go to the South Pole and not the North Pole, and then hopefully space in 2016!

Pekka Suonio, Malaysia

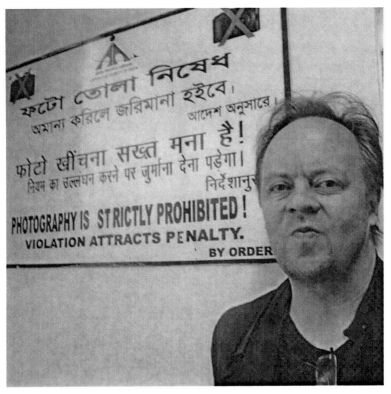

**(Pekka Suonio at Bagdogra Airport,
Northeast India, April 2014)**

Where did you grow up and what was your early life like?

I was born in Finland and spent most of my childhood there without much travel at all. However, my family lived in Turkey when I was aged one to four, and we made the trip back from Turkey to Finland by car, covering Greece, Italy, France, Belgium, Netherlands, and Germany on one trip over about three weeks, which clearly left a lasting impression on me.

I vaguely remember giving a presentation very early in primary school with a slide projector, telling about the cities we saw on the way, and how Italian gelato tastes different from the ice cream in Finland. I'm not sure if other kids were impressed or thought I was making it all up, since overseas traveling from Finland in the '70's was not that common at all. I don't think I ever left Finland again until I was 12 years old, except to cross over to Sweden in Haparanda to buy cheap butter while my family was based in Oulu.

Apart from a couple of ski trips to Austria with my family and one summer exchange to the U.S. through CISV, there was not much travel in my teenage years either, until at 17, when I made my first Inter-Rail trip with a friend. I felt very comfortable with the idea of traveling in general and excited about entering new countries for the first time. On the second Inter-Rail trip the following summer, I made an effort to visit countries like Andorra, Monaco, Luxembourg, and Liechtenstein, hoping to eventually visit all the countries in Europe.

When did you go from casually traveling to making this a full-time goal, and what motivated you to travel to every country?

I was running a project in Delhi, India, and became friends with the client's managing director, a Romanian-born French-man called Norbert Aleco. After dinner and a couple of bottles of wine at his residence, he asked if I was planning to visit more places in India after the project.

"No, but I am planning to visit Bhutan, which is quite close by."

"You probably need to start arranging your visa quite soon, it may be difficult."

"Yes, it takes two weeks but it should be quite straightforward. At least it should not be more difficult than going to North Korea which I did last year."

"Oh, so you have been to North Korea. Congratulations. By the way, I have also been to North Korea. In fact, I have been to every other independent country in the world as well."

I thought, "I am not worthy, I am not worthy," but then asked the obvious question:

"How old are you?"

Mr. Aleco was 43 then and had finished his project two years earlier, at 41. I was 31 at the time and started to think that it might not be unrealistic to actually go everywhere within the next ten years, if this guy had done it.

Back in London I went to my boss, Greg Ernest, who I knew was a keen traveler as well.

"Greg, we have a really interesting client. He has been to every independent country in the world!"

"Well, how many have you been to?"

I did not know, as back then I was not fully clear on what counted as a country, like whether Hong Kong would qualify, but I guessed that I had maybe 60 countries under my belt.

"What? You are over ten years younger than me and have been to almost as many countries as I have," said Greg. "Let's check our lists properly so we know where we are."

It turned out that at that point I had been to 65 countries and Greg to 75. It was quite clear to us that only independent countries would count, as we had not heard about TCC (Travelers' Century Club) back then. Eventually, I left the company, and being my own boss at my own shop I had time and flexibility to travel so that I reached my goal much sooner than initially expected. Greg is still working on his, but he is missing only about 15 countries and plans to finish within the next couple of years.

Do you remember the point where you said to yourself, "I can really accomplish this"?

There were three inflection points in my travel. The first was at the railway station in Milan, Italy, at the age of 17, when I realized that I can take an overnight train, and choose the country where I want to wake up the next morning, practically anywhere in Europe. God bless the person who came up with the idea of the Inter-Rail pass.

The second was a similar experience on my first, improvised RTW (Round the World) trip at the age of 32. I was looking at the departing flights schedules at Hong Kong Airport Express station, and suddenly realized that I could be almost anywhere in the world in about 24 hours — and by now I had enough money in my bank account so that I could do exactly that if I liked.

After that, doing new countries felt quite easy (some visas, of course, posing a challenge). When the going got serious, the point where I felt I would have this in the bag quite soon was on a flight from Windhoek to Luanda, having secured the Angolan and DRC visas, which were countries 168 and 169 for me. From then on, it only took six months to visit the remaining 26.

What have you done over your life to gain the freedom and finances to pursue as much travel as you have?

I studied diligently and have worked hard since I graduated, and have always earned a decent professional services senior-level income. I once took three months of unpaid leave from work to travel (approved by Greg), but returned to the same company so my CV had no gaps.

I was quite lucky to pick a company after my MBA where I learned a set of skills that are marketable globally. I was able to set up my own shop and earn enough money from projects, so that I could afford all the travel that I wanted during the downtime. My job was, and still is, helping my clients sell more drugs (i.e. advising pharmaceutical companies on sales, marketing, and market access issues). I have worked with Pfizer to plan how to sell more Viagra, in more than one country.

Was there ever a time you felt like abandoning this goal?

I had contacted Charles Veley and found out that he had finished his independent countries at the age of 37 years and four months, and it was looking like I could have a shot at finishing younger than him. (I eventually did, at 36 years and nine months). However, when I was at about 135 countries, I found out that Maurizio Giuliano had finished all countries by the age of 29, which meant that I would not break any records. For about a week I thought about slowing down the travel rate, but then I saw a very attractive airfare to Cuba, and travel went on as usual.

What were your worst travel experiences (i.e. detainment, bribes, car accidents, sickness, etc.) and why?

I had never paid a bribe in my life until I arrived at the border between Tajikistan and Uzbekistan, which were not officially open for foreigners, but shortened the journey a great deal. There were three border posts on each side: customs, immigration, and the interior ministry, and after crossing this border, I had paid bribes six times in my life! It was not a big loss at about $10 USD for two persons with maybe 10-20 minutes of haggling at each stop, and overall was more a humorous than scary experience.

Also, the only time I ever got mugged, in Kinshasa, DRC, was more funny than scary. I was jogging on a wide main street around noon in broad daylight, when a white car drove next to me with four men inside waving handcuffs and asking me to jump in, as they were the police and wanted to check my passport. Of course I knew they were not policemen, but I had no choice, and like in a game of chess, I clearly knew what the next moves would be. My passport was back at the hotel, but these guys did not care and proceeded to relieve me from my stash of about $50 USD cash and a mobile phone. They even gave my SIM card back after stealing the phone!

I believe that I was specifically targeted, since the previous night I had a long (and probably unnecessary) argument with a taxi driver about the fare from the airport which had left him quite pissed off. I generally believe that with normal precautions, one's chances of getting in trouble without one's own fault are extremely slim regardless of the reputation of the country. In Asmara, Eritrea, I once got beaten up by the police and spent a night in a police cell (actually a container), but it was because of my own stupidity as I had got a bit "tired and emotional." That one was not much fun since I needed a couple of stitches in my head, but I never felt that my life was in danger.

I rarely get sick, as I drink local beer instead of water and take doxycycline as a precaution for malaria whenever I travel to dodgy places. Doxycycline also kills other germs one may come across and protects you from diarrhea, and yes, I am a licensed pharmacist, so that helps too (obviously).

What do you consider the most adventurous trip you have taken?

Flying to Cape Town and trying to get to Lagos and all countries in between in 2.5 weeks was quite challenging, such as finding connections and getting all the notoriously difficult visas sorted on time. In Libreville, I was incredibly lucky to get a São Tomé visa in a day and the last seat on the weekly flight there on that same day. Probably several others were sold the "last seat" as well, since there were about 20 passengers on a 12-seater plane, plus a few live chickens and goats. I was squeezed next to the U.S. Ambassador in Gabon who was on his way to monitor the general election in São Tomé.

I made it to Lagos just in time, and had an incredible time joining a group of London Business School students on their study trip. I loved Lagos. It is the most chaotic place in the world — really the other end of the spectrum. (The opposite end is probably Singapore.)

Physically, the most challenging thing I ever tried was to climb Mount Wilhelm in Papua New Guinea in the rainy season. The trip from Kundiawa to Kegsugl next to the mountain, on the road that looked impossible to traverse, suddenly became more exciting after the driver and his friend opened their first beers about two minutes after leaving Kundiawa, sharing with me that they, "…have to drink in the car since this is a dry province."

The beer case was empty by the time we eventually made it to Kegsugl just before dusk. All happily inebriated but in one piece. I found a guide, although I was told I was the only climber that month, and started the climb the following morning. However, in torrential rain, it was not the best idea to try to summit, so I never made it to the top, and made a mental note to be realistic about the weather in my next destinations.

What were your most challenging countries to visit and why?

Probably the only independent country that may be physically difficult to get to is Nauru, given the unpredictability of the airline flying there, and clearly, it is the difficulty of getting a visa that makes some countries a challenge. For me, Sudan and Equatorial Guinea took a few embassies to try my luck, and Nauru took a lot of correspondence.

London is a great base for getting visas, since there are not many countries in the world that do not have an embassy in London. Sometimes, however, it is easier to get a visa from a neighboring country, and optimizing itineraries in Africa in this respect took a great deal of effort from me. Holding a refundable onward ticket is the trick that secured me (and probably many other keen travelers) transit visas to many really difficult countries, including Angola and Saudi Arabia.

What is the strangest thing you've seen/experienced while traveling?

Without going into details, an underground club in Tokyo that I visited with the legendary Finnish rock band, Hanoi Rocks.

Which travel experiences stand out the most and why?

Meeting interesting people and having interesting experiences with them always stands out. Seeing some places of breathtaking natural beauty for the first time is also amazing.

What are the most overrated and underrated countries you've been to in your travels and why?

The most overrated country is Canada. It combines the worst aspects of Finland and the U.S.A. — cold, long distances, strict with alcohol and many other regulations. The fact that the immigration grilled me, a neatly dressed guy with a Finnish passport and hotel reservations for the entire length of stay and a business class onward ticket to London, for over an hour before letting me in the country did not help getting a good first impression. I have not been back ever since.

West Balkan, from Albania to Slovenia, is a region that I rate consistently higher than most people. Also, the English-speaking southeast African countries are really easy to enjoy and probably not appreciated enough.

What are the best and worst meals you have ever had traveling and where were they?

I have had my share of Michelin starred foods, but the Kobe beef, at restaurant Misono in Kobe, Japan, was like from another planet.

Food in Mongolia and Africa in general do not stand out, but probably the most overrated food destination is Singapore, which is ironic because Singaporeans like to think of themselves as real "foodies". To my taste, the local fare at hawker centers is just plain awful.

What country made you feel most out of your comfort zone and why?

Living and working in South Korea was not a very positive experience for many reasons. Koreans have one of the lowest levels of English comprehension in the world, and their culture, especially at the workplace, is very difficult for an outsider to adapt to.

I'm not surprised that in many recent movies the villains are Korean, without necessarily being North Korean. The bad guys used to be Russians speaking heavily accented English. Now they are Korean, speaking no English.

Do you speak any foreign languages? If so, which have been the most useful for you besides English?

As a Finn, I learned fairly fluent Swedish and German at school but they are not a big help in traveling globally. I can speak decent French if necessary, and to get by in many parts of Africa it is absolutely necessary. Also, I used to speak survival level Russian which was pretty useful anywhere between Germany and China.

I regret not learning any Spanish when I was at the age when languages actually stick in your head. I must have spent thousands of hours trying to learn Chinese over the past ten years, but quite frankly, I cannot even order food in Mandarin. At least in Cantonese, I can tell the taxi driver where to go in Hong Kong.

Looking back from when you started traveling to where you are now, in what ways, if any, has travel changed you?

What completely changed my view of the world was doing my two-year full-time MBA at London Business School (LBS) with classmates from all over the world. I am pretty sure I would have remained quite Euro-centric, had I gone to INSEAD (in France) or IMD for a year instead, but the LBS experience, especially the second year, really opened my eyes to realize that there are brilliant people from all corners of the world.

Traveling the world, big time, for six-seven years after graduation just reinforced what I had learned at LBS. In every other way I still feel like the 17-year-old guy at the Milan railway station who just figured out he can travel anywhere he likes, but without going to London Business School I would still live in Europe and not Malaysia. I even met my wife there for the first time at a party we both attended a couple of years after I graduated.

What is the longest continuous trip you have ever taken? When was it and where did you travel?

I never "left everything behind to become a traveler," and my longest trip is the first round-the-world trip in August-October 2002, which was just six weeks, and even that was a bit of an accident. For this trip the only things that I had arranged in advance were the Pakistani and Chinese visas on my passport, hotel bookings in Kuwait and Qatar, and a one-way ticket from London to Kuwait City.

I had missed Pakistan on my trip to Afghanistan earlier that summer, as local fixers were asking journo prices for crossing the Khyber Pass from Kabul to Peshawar, but now I spent 1.5 weeks there, well looked after by my client's (Mr. Aleco) local agents. Eventually, I took the Karakoram Highway by bus, from Islamabad to Kashgar, and then flew to Beijing to see one of my MBA classmates there. She told me she was going to

Boston to see her sister in a week's time, and asked if I would like to join.

I had not planned to go to America, but why the heck not? I visited a couple of more countries in Asia, had that "aha" experience looking at flight board in Hong Kong, joined my friend on a long flight to the U.S., spent a few days with her in Boston, and then some time island-hopping in the Caribbean before returning to London.

On the other hand, one could say that I started the longest trip when I left my native Finland over 18 years ago, and have not returned. After completing the intensive country-collecting phase, I am now living in my fifth Asian country since leaving London in 2008.

What is your favorite "off-the-beaten-path" destination and why?

My favorite destination in the world is Montenegro, which is still not quite on the beaten path. I am undecided whether I am a mountain person or a sea person, and in Montenegro you can have both in the same view.

There are also a couple of rarely visited Pacific Islands that stand above the rest: Palau was so nice on my first visit that I chose it as our honeymoon destination, and Vanuatu is great as well, combining the best elements of both British and French colonial history.

What are the best and worst places you have ever spent a night?

My best memories are from Banyan Tree Phuket, with my current wife. We first had our own pool villa, which we enjoyed a lot, and then for the last night we got an upgrade to a double pool villa. It was absolutely massive, could have hosted a party of at least 50 people, and had a dedicated butler and amazing beds which we took full advantage of. Upgrade to the E-Wow suite at W Leicester Square, rack rate 6,000 GBP, was not bad either.

The worst one was on a business trip from Delhi to Jaipur, where I stayed in a local "three-star" hotel, booked by the client. Without going to the exact methods that I perfected, I killed over 50 cockroaches in my room in one night. I gave my employer some feedback about that place when I got back to Delhi.

In your opinion, what country or place in the world feels the most authentic and untouched by tourism?

Myanmar in 2002 was quite nice, although it probably has changed by now. Iran in 2000 was fantastic, and probably still untouched by tourism. I also, surprisingly, quite liked the 'Stans in spite of all the bureaucratic hassle.

Interestingly, all these places were among my first 100, or actually first 75 countries — initially I wanted to visit the quirky countries that most people do not visit, rather than all the countries.

In your opinion, where is the most beautiful place on Earth?

Kotor Bay in Montenegro or Rock Islands in Palau.

What do you enjoy most when traveling (cities, nature, people, cultural spots, etc.) and why?

I like meeting people, and got a deeper understanding of some countries by getting to know closely a local person of the opposite sex. Options for this are obviously a lot more varied when you still travel with own hair and teeth, so I chose to see the world mostly as a young, single man, and thankfully managed to visit all the countries before it was time to settle down and eventually get married.

I never deliberately attempted to collect "flags" like the PUA (pick-up artist) community, though, but recently, one female (!) friend from a faraway country confessed to me that getting a flag from every country in the world is on her bucket list.

I do study the history of each place I go to quite carefully, but once there, I rarely visit museums. If there is a musical or sports e6vent typical of the country when I am there, I try to attend.

I don't really care for the UNESCO World Heritage sites, but visiting all the Michelin three-star restaurants, which I recently read someone had done, is a commendable achievement. I may be tempted to do the same one day as I like fine dining. That list changes every year like the UNESCO list, but not so much that it would be an impossible moving target.

What travel accomplishments are you most proud of?

I am most proud of the fact that I made it to all the independent countries legally, with proper documentation, and never even had to make up a cover story to get a business visa.

For example, in July 2002, there were not many people applying for visas at the Embassy of Afghanistan in Delhi with "tourism" as the purpose of visit, but I got one after some persistence. Neither have I ever paid an outright bribe to get a visa. Sometimes a special fee is charged for "express processing", but that is done officially by many countries as well.

If you had just one personal travel story to share with someone, what would that be?

I'm not really a storytelling type of person, so I don't have one story at hand that I would always tell people about my travels. Neither did I ever come across something so touching on my travels that I would feel compelled to share it with the world.

Also, I never outright share the fact that I have visited to all the countries in the world unless someone specifically asks, except of course in the first TCC London chapter meeting which was right after I had finished my travels. Some of my friends introduce me to new people by mentioning this achievement and I find it embarrassing.

Besides your home country, where do you find yourself returning to over and over and why?

I do not return to my original home country very often. I have visited Finland on average less than once a year in the past ten years. Instead, I keep going back, and will eventually return to my adopted new home country, the United Kingdom, to live in the greatest city in the world, which is London.

In Asia, I feel like making a trip to Hong Kong, specifically South Lantau, every couple of months, and to Bali and Japan every year or every other year. My retirement home is in Montenegro and I keep going there once or twice a year.

What is the ideal amount of time you prefer to travel each trip before you are ready for home and a break?

I found trips of about two, maybe three weeks, covering about five-six countries quite comfortable. Visiting multiple countries on one trip to a region like Indochina, Central America, or the Caribbean, gives a good perspective.

Funnily enough, after my first RTW, on which I visited five Caribbean island nations including St. Lucia in ten days, I learned that my brother had been in St. Lucia with his fiancé at the same time. They had left their all-inclusive couples resort only once, to play golf, during their two-week stay.

If you had an unlimited budget and space and time was no object, what would your perfect travel day look like? (for example: start your morning in Bora Bora; afternoon on a safari in Kenya; night in Australia, etc.)

By now I appreciate that it is more comfortable to stay in one place the whole day, so I have really not thought about things from this perspective. In Hong Kong, you can probably get closest to doing all the nice things you could ever imagine in one day, using only local public transport.

Instead, the question that I have been trying answer since my first RTW is, "Which two or three residences would you share your time between in a year, to optimize the weather and to maximize comfort?"

For those looking to travel to every country, what is the best piece of advice you could offer them?

Study the loyalty programs of airlines and hotels carefully. Flyertalk.com is a great resource for that. If traveling on business, keep your expenses above board and your dick in your trousers.

For someone that has been almost everywhere, what still gets you excited about packing your bags again?

Pathetic as it may sound, I still get a kick from designing "neat" travel itineraries that optimize the destinations covered, level of comfort, and time and money spent. I like good deals but avoid package tours like the plague.

At Amex UK Travel Services, who I used a lot around 2002-2005, there was a guy called Tim who was really good at this, but I have not come across a perfect travel agent since. Amex did not do the Indian Ocean, so I remember walking to STA Travel at Piccadilly Circus and asking a young trainee if she could help me book a trip to Mauritius.

" Sure, which level of hotel would you prefer?"

"Well, actually I would just like you to book these flights for me MRU-TNR-HAH-SEY-MRU-DEL, as I cannot book all of them online myself, please."

"Excuse me?"

Combine a good deal with a place that I have never been to before and I am game.

Do you feel you have missed out on certain aspects of life being away from home so much?

I could have started a family 10-20 years earlier like most of my peers did, and probably could have progressed faster and higher in my career, but I am glad I balanced things the way I did.

Looking ahead, what travel plans and goals are you still pursuing, and what is on your "Bucket List"?

I am picking destinations leisurely from the TCC list, and may eventually just about hit 300 destinations up from my current count of 245. For example, when I was recently working based in Mumbai, I made trips to Kashmir, Sikkim, and the Andaman Islands.

However, I am not planning to cover the entire TCC list, or any of the longer lists either. "Every country in the world" means to me (and most people) every independent country, rather than slices of Antarctica (not done by me) or cantons of Switzerland (done by me), and since September 02, 2006, I have 'Been there, done that'.

If a new, independent country is born, I will be among the first to visit. Also, there are about half a dozen countries where I was unable to stay overnight on my visit, and I guess I will re-visit them at some point.

I may be tempted to try to break some funny travel records though. I am working with my ex-colleague, Marc Gawley, a Guinness World Record holder for visiting all the London Underground stations in the shortest time, to out-geek the Norwegian guy who visited 18 countries and Kosovo in 24 hours last year and beat his record.

Most importantly, right now I am trying to figure out the best possible environment for my four-month old daughter, and possibly other offspring, to grow up in. Through international parents, our daughter is eligible for no less than four citizenships at birth, and has the world open for her!

Don Parrish, U.S.A.

(Don Parrish on Conway Reef, November 2, 2013. With this visit, he became the #1 traveler on MostTraveledPeople.com)

Where did you grow up and what was your early life like?

I was born in Washington, D.C. At age one, my family returned to Des Moines, Iowa where my brother was born. A few months before my 4th birthday, we moved to Dallas, where I grew up in the typical circumstances and values of the 1950s.

Looking back, there were events that prepared me for a life of travel. In the first grade, my father got me started on a stamp collection with a cigar box of loose stamps. By third grade, I could recognize the country of origin of almost any stamp. A Reunion stamp initially confused me because it is also a French stamp, and I did not know about colonialism at that age.

Sixty years later, when I visited Reunion for the first time, it had a special meaning for me. I became familiar with many places growing up. So, for example, a visit in 2009 to Corsica meant, of course, I would visit Napoleon's birthplace. In 1971, I viewed his magnificent tomb in Paris (Les Invalides) and in 2014 I visited Longwood House, where he died on St Helena. And, yes, I visited Waterloo.

In the fifth grade, I made my first trip by myself flying from Dallas to Chicago to visit an old family friend. Chicago was an exciting place. I visited museums that had a German submarine, Egyptian mummies, European paintings, a simulated coal mine, etc. My father explained to me that the return flight would land in Fort Worth and that I should take a limo to meet my parents at the Adolphus Hotel in Dallas.

When the plane landed, I asked the pilot (or co-pilot) where to get a limo to the Adolphus Hotel. He was surprised and asked me where my parents were. I explained they were waiting for me at the hotel. He then led me through a door labeled "Authorized Personnel Only" to the limos. My life as an independent traveler was launched!

Two months later, for my 11th birthday, the old family friend in Chicago gave me Richard Halliburton's book, *The Complete Book of Marvels*. This book captured my imagination with his tales of climbing the Great Pyramid of Egypt, swimming the entire length of the Panama Canal for a toll of 36 cents, and so on. It made a profound impression on my young mind.

During high school in 1960, I started corresponding with a pen pal in East Berlin, and I have visited him several times over the years. I remain in contact with him. In 1961, I started my 50 plus years of subscribing to the *National Geographic* magazine. Before the Internet, it was one of my sources for detailed travel information.

I attended the University of Texas graduating with honors in Mathematics in 1966. Between my junior and senior years, I spent the summer working in Germany as an unskilled worker in a metal factory. This was a unique experience for a native-born American, so it is worth explaining at some length.

In 1965, I was one of 60 students from the University of Texas who flew to Germany to work in summer jobs. On arrival, we took trains to our job locations all over the country. I went alone. I saw my friends at the airport three months later.

I was employed as an unskilled worker in a metal factory in Hanau, near Frankfurt. I bought an old motorcycle and lived in a room in the home of a German family with three children. I did not speak a word of English in Germany that summer. Even coming back to the U.S. on the plane, I spoke mainly German.

I visited my pen pal in East Berlin. We had written letters in English since 1960, but spoke only German when we met. We always debated politics since he was a Communist party member. Seeing the general conditions in East Berlin was a shock, and the wind could blow their aluminum coins out of your hand.

Near the end of the summer I made a nine-day trip with a dozen Germans on motorcycles to rural France. One day we camped by a lake and the French came running up to us, looking very upset. I guessed that someone was drowning and ordered the Germans into the water. In less than a minute, they found a teenage boy, but were unable to resuscitate him. He was the first dead person I had seen.

Also, I will never forget visiting Fort Douaumont in Verdun and seeing the results of WWI carnage. Hanau, where I worked, was an example of WWII carnage. It was 85% destroyed in a bombing raid just weeks before the end of WWII.

This was a formative experience in my life. I grew up. I learned what it took to live successfully as a foreigner. Later in my career, at AT&T Bell Labs, I was very successful in communicating in English with non-native speakers of English.

When I returned for my senior year at the University of Texas a week after returning from Germany, I showed up at the initial meeting of the German Club wearing lederhosen and speaking German. I was elected President.

During a job interview at Bell Labs in 1966, when one of the technical interviewers noticed that I had been President of the German Club, he switched to German for about ten minutes. Other interviewers recommended me too. I got the job. I spent my whole career at Bell Labs, the world's top R&D organization at that time.

When did you go from casually traveling to making this a full-time goal, and what motivated you to travel to every country?

This was a lifelong process. One thing led to another. Looking back, it all seems obvious. I loved to travel. I loved discovery. I loved seeing places that I had read about. History has always been a hobby of mine. So it was a matter of at what point was I free to pursue full-time travel. That was 2007.

When I started working in 1966, I used my two-week vacations to travel overseas as much as I could. In 1969, for example, I visited Russia and Eastern Europe. My coup was making a six-week circumnavigation in 1971 by "merging" vacations for two years and negotiating for two additional weeks. This was a real achievement in corporate America in that period, and my contemporaries were amazed that I was able to pull this off — a six week vacation around the world!

In 1977 when AT&T decided to sell its Electronic (telephone) Switching Systems (ESS) overseas, I volunteered and was made the planning manager for the International Switching development organization. It grew in size and complexity over the next 25 years.

This role, which I created, required intensive international travel, often with short fuses when opportunities popped up out of the blue. I was always a key member of a small team in-country sizing up major opportunities. I was the technical guy who knew the product and who could explain the product to different levels of customer management. Because of my life-long traveling, I was culturally sensitive. Customers trusted me with their vital technical information enabling us to understand their real needs.

My group analyzed technical specs, determined the detailed features that would need to be developed in both software and hardware, and then decided on the subset of this work to be committed in a complex technical proposal that might involve 1500 paragraphs.

I negotiated technical details balancing customer wants, competitive pressures, and development organization capabilities. This leadership role required a person with a wide range of skill sets who could deal with murky unstructured situations.

It required enormous creativity to win these multi-million dollar projects. In some cases, the customer selected us even though we were the highest bidder because they perceived our value as higher. I believed in our product and organization and I figured how to explain this to customers in understandable terms. I was a kind of a legend in winning or helping to win projects.

When I was working in International Switching development for AT&T Bell Labs, I took many international trip business trips. For example, I visited Japan 60 times, the Netherlands 18 times, Saudi Arabia 13 times, about five times each in Costa Rica, Egypt, Korea, Singapore, Switzerland, and China. There were more than a dozen other countries where I made business trips.

Ironically, although I spent about four years of my life working overseas on business trips in International Switching, the number of countries I visited was less than if I had remained working on domestic projects. Out of the 840 locations I have visited on MTP (Most Traveled People), less than 25 are due to work.

After I retired in 2001, my travel was limited for five years because I need to help my elderly father. He needed increasing amounts of help and I spent a lot of time in Texas.

Starting in 2007, I had no restrictions on my time and I began my travel quest, spending half my time overseas.

Do you remember the point where you said to yourself, "I can really accomplish this"?

No. Certainly my trips to Cuba in 2001, Libya in 2004, and North Korea in 2005 were major milestones on the quest to visit all 193 UN members.

As I traveled to more and more countries, I developed the contacts, experience, and confidence that I would be able to visit all of the countries.

To accomplish any big project, you must have the implicit belief that you will be able to do it even though you cannot explain exactly how until near the finish line.

What have you done over your life to gain the freedom and finances to pursue as much travel as you have?

These comments are going to seem obvious to some readers. For others, it is a matter of understanding the power of compound interest, which Einstein famously explained was the most powerful force in the universe. And one needs to have the discipline to follow through month after month and year after year.

I was raised to save money. In elementary school, I would deposit one dollar every Tuesday on "banking day." Later in life, using spreadsheets, I calculated the increased amount needed every month for savings/investment that would allow me to retire earlier.

You can save a lot of money by not smoking and buying a new car only every 10 to 15 years. If you don't have a taste for a daily double latte, the savings add up.

I got personal finance software to track my expenses when I got my first Mac in 1986, and I was amazed at how I was spending my income. I made adjustments. Psychologically saving more did not mean that I was denying myself, but I was advancing my personal 'Financial Independence Day'.

In the United States, there are all sorts of mutual funds to help you invest money. So a normal salaried person who lives below their means and invests regularly can achieve financial independence. Every American should have a Roth IRA.

So now I am spending my life savings on travel. Flying economy means I can afford to travel more. I'm turning money into memories.

Was there ever a time you felt like abandoning this goal?

Not really. I completed my visits to all UN countries in 2011 with Mongolia. On November 2, 2013, I became #1 on MTP with 830 locations. At the end of 2014, I had visited 840 locations and was still ranked #1. By April 2014, I had visited all but one of the countries on the TCC list.

I have been visiting UNESCO World Heritage Sites before they created their list, e.g. seeing the Taj Mahal and climbing the Great Pyramid of Egypt in 1971. By 2014, I achieved the Hall of Fame level (400 WH Sites) on MTP and I was also on the top 25 list of WHS enthusiasts on World Heritage Site (worldheritagesite.org) by visiting 414 World Heritage Sites. My goal is not to complete that list, but certainly I would like to visit at least 500 sites. Then I will set myself another goal.

I was recruited for TheBestTravelled.com in 2012. At the end of 2014, I was ranked #5 and was ranked ahead of its founder. I would like to visit at least 1000 of its 1281 sub-regions.

Travel is its own reward. It is fun to keep track of where you have visited. In my case, I cherish the memories, the stories, and the linkages I've figured out.

What were your worst travel experiences (i.e. detainment, bribes, car accidents, sickness, etc.) and why?

When I consider that I have spent about ten years of my life working or traveling outside of the United States, I have been fairly lucky. Remember, I've traveled on small ships in rough seas, been driven 1,000's of kilometers on poor highways, flown dicey airlines in old Russian planes with bald tires, etc. I've traveled in politically unstable places with armed guards and in extreme weather conditions.

Adventures have included 62 scuba dives in the oceans, para-sailing, windsurfing, etc. I've flown in gliders, hot air balloons, hang gliders, an ultralight over Victoria Falls, many helicopter flights over oceans, many single engine planes in remote places. I have had many animal interactions. I've ridden horses, camels, elephants — even an ostrich in South Africa. I've touched li-ons, cheetahs, stingrays, etc. I've had safe close encounters with walruses, polar bears, sharks. So I have taken more than aver-age risks over my 50 years of international travel.

In 1995, when Albania was in the early days of opening up to tourists, I hired a taxi for three days to drive me around the southern part of the country. I was very careful what I ate, but I still got very sick. It was coming out of both ends. Periodically, I signaled the driver, who stopped quickly and I would do my double suffering in public in a ditch. I left Albania walking 300 meters through the border in a mountain pass into Macedonia where I got antibiotics. In 12 hours, I was fine.

My most dangerous near-death experience was in Nepal. My driver, my guide, and I were returning to Kathmandu from a visit to Buddha's birthplace. It was late at night on a two-lane mountain highway when a large truck passed another large truck. My driver had no choice but to veer off the highway on-to an unknown "shoulder" to avoid a head on collision at 100 kph. Very scary. Less than 30 minutes later, there was a repeat of the same potential head-on collision!

I have been officially detained six times over the years, from 1965 in East Berlin by the communist authorities to 2014 by the Jamaican Coast Guard. In each case, I was able to explain the situation or wait it out. I never was arrested, nor did I have any money taken from me. I felt in all cases that I had done nothing wrong. My approach was to assume the officials in-volved were doing their job and to explain my situation patient-ly. I treated them respectfully and always was willing to wait them out. What could have been unhappy experiences are nice stories.

In 2011, when I was in Iceland, I went pony riding at the same stable I did back in 1977. The weather was clear and crisp. There were two Icelandic guides, four guests from Sweden, and me. My pony was named Siby. This was going to be a two-hour ride across the fields. About 30 minutes into the ride, and after we had crossed a stony creek, Siby stumbled on his left front leg and fell. I was thrown on the ground, did a somersault and survived with no serious injuries. I had cuts on my hands. This was first time in my life that I had been thrown from a horse. I was directed to wash my hands in the creek, was given band aids, and we mounted up to continue the ride. Twenty minutes later Siby stumbled again on his left leg and fell. Damn! I was thrown again and got more cuts! I called a halt to my ride and the owner came to get me. We had a good chat for an hour about some of his celebrity guests and ancient Egypt. Then he drove me back to my hotel.

Frankly, this was a scary experience, and I realized how lucky I was not to have suffered a disaster like Christopher Reeve's. From the hotel, I walked a kilometer or so to the local pharmacy where a nice older lady recommended a special alcohol "scrubber" and an antibiotic cream. In a week, I was all healed up. When I recounted this story to some of my friends, they were scandalized to hear that the stable did not offer to refund the riding fee. My thinking was different. I had survived and was grateful that I was not seriously injured.

What do you consider the most adventurous trip you have taken?

There are several candidates. My visit to North Korea in 2005 was an adventure. I was part of a group of five Americans. The first allowed in two or three years. The story of our five days there merited an article on the front page of the *Los Angeles Times*.

My trip to the South Pole in 2011, to celebrate the 100th anniversary of Amundsen's achievement of making the first visit to the South Pole and beating the British Empire by three days, was a true adventure. Extreme weather conditions delayed my arrival and departure via small plane. I spent three nights in an unheated tent at the South Pole. The toilet was even unheated. Since I am a member of the Circumnavigators Club, I made 100 circumnavigations around the pole to honor Amundsen's achievement. I also spoke to the Norwegian Prime Minister.

Making a visit to Puntland in Somalia was a true adventure. No one knew how to get government permission. My travel agent refused to help me and another traveler because he was convinced that we would be kidnapped. At that point (2010), 500 people and 25 ships were being held for ransom in Somalia. It took luck and skill to negotiate a visit with the help of the station chief of Jubba Airlines in Bosaso. The result was a visit using two SUVs, four uniformed armed guards with AK-47s, and a government inspector. This was a kind of VIP visit without crowds or paparazzi. When we walked into the university, we saw anything we wanted. Departing the airport the next day, there was no standing in line or security checks. To my surprise, armed guards didn't mean cowering in fear, but that you were important. Two Somali Americans at the hotel, in separate conversations, explained the city was run by business people and there were no pirates there. These conversations, the construction I saw and the general spirit of the place left me profoundly optimistic for the future of Bosaso in spite of its unpaved roads, unpaved landing strip and significant illiteracy.

What were your most challenging countries to visit and why?

The common theme is getting government permission.

1) Cuba in 2001 — the U.S. Government opened the window to make a legal visit as a tourist. I had joined the Travelers' Century Club the year before and they had obtained a State Department license. We flew in a chartered 737 from Miami to Havana in 47 minutes. I was part of a group of 11 travelers who spent 11 days there visiting all parts of the island. TCC had arranged a discussion with the woman who was the de facto U.S. ambassador. I traveled with TCC many times after this fabulous visit.

2) Libya in 2004 — I had to wait like other American travelers for the 28-year embargo by the Libyan government to end. The local people were excited to see American tourists and they saw us as harbingers of better times and a general normalization between their country and the outside world. The Roman ruins in Leptis Magna are some of the best anywhere.

3) North Korea in 2005 — When the six-party agreement was signed, DPRK let in a few tourists in as a signaling method to the U.S. government. I had waited for over two years to get permission to enter.

4) South Sudan in 2010 — I had to fly to Addis Ababa, Ethiopia to be interviewed in person to get travel authorization at the GOSS office. Hotels in Juba were iffy in those days. They were expensive and cash only. It was an exciting time to visit because of the tremendous anticipation of the vote for independence in less than 2 months — there was a large countdown clock on the main street.

5) Angola in 2011 — That was another case of figuring out how to get permission to visit. Luanda looked better than I expected. Clearly the government is spending money to improve the highways.

What is the strangest thing you've seen/experienced while traveling?

Here are some examples, nothing too dramatic:

1) In Leningrad in 1969, I was talking to people on the street. One of them told me he was a heroin addict. I found that hard to believe, and he rolled up his sleeve to show the needle marks. Communism did not end drug addiction.

2) In Moscow at the Science and Technology exhibit in 1969, I saw a globe of the moon marked to show where the United States had landed the previous month. Looking back, I can see that when the U.S. landed men on the moon it was the beginning of the end of communism in Russia because it dashed their hope of overtaking the United States.

3) Seeing a fully automated gas station in Sweden in 1977. There was no one there. Another customer drove in while I was wondering what to do, and he "trained" me in the simple procedure.

4) In 1978, seeing the religious police (*mutawa*) in Riyadh, Saudi Arabia, switch the legs of foreign women whose dresses did not cover their ankles. The mutawa without comment would switch their legs repeatedly. It wasn't painful, but annoying, and the

women were herded like animals out of the public square. In 1998, attending an embassy party in Riyadh with an open bar was a shock. Liquor is strictly forbidden in Saudi Arabia.

5) Visiting Zambia in 2009, I started to offer to take a photo for a couple in the blue jump suits who had just completed their ultralight flight when I exclaimed, "John!" He was a former colleague I had not seen in 15 years. I had lost contact with him. This is a touching story that I wrote up for the *Circumnavigators Log*. This man, a beloved manager, retired early to help his wife, who was dying of cancer. But she beat the odds and told me proudly that day, "I am alive."

Which travel experiences stand out the most and why?

Meeting a Russian my age in Leningrad (now St. Petersburg) in 1969. This was the height of the Cold War, and I was the first foreigner he had ever met. At the Hermitage Museum, I noticed that he was looking at me because of my foreign clothes. I struck up a conversation in my very limited Russian. He had studied German. So we used a mixture of these two languages to communicate during the next ten hours.

In spite of the tremendous effort it took for us to communicate with each other, we both realized what a special opportunity it was to meet. I don't remember his name, so I'll call him Ivan. Ivan was a college student from Stalingrad (now Volgograd). His father was a member of the Communist Party. We were both visiting Leningrad for the first time, so we combined forces to see its impressive attractions like the Peter and Paul Cathedral, the burial site of almost all of the Russian czars from Peter the Great until the last. We spent hours as tourists seeing all of the major sites in this famous city.

When it came time for dinner, Ivan wanted to treat me. In this period, Russians who randomly shared a taxi ride with me insisted on paying for it when they found out that I was an American. Thinking back over my travels, I believe that Russia in this period was the most pro-American place I have ever visited. The fact that I could speak a bit of Russian enhanced my positive treatment, but the fundamentally positive fascination with Americans was deep during the Cold War.

Ivan and I checked out a number of restaurants, but he wasn't satisfied with any of them. I guess the restaurants he could afford weren't what he wanted me to see. So I came up with the obvious idea. We were already on the Nevsky Prospect. I suggested that we join my tourist group. So we walked a couple of blocks, and the tour leader was happy to let Ivan join the group for dinner.

Ivan and I were sitting on the edge of a private room at a table for eight, and everyone trying to make him feel welcome with a few words in German. I could see that Ivan was a bit uncomfortable. That day he had met me, his first foreigner, and now he was with 25 foreigners in a private room.

Later, while we were eating, Ivan asked me if they were still there. At first, I didn't understand what he was talking about and then I remembered that there had been a couple of policemen near the doorway. When I looked over to answer him, he was pouring sweat. He could not eat any more. It was time to go.

He had not smoked a cigarette that day, but now he needed a pack of cigarettes. We had to go to a second shop because he would only smoke Cuban cigarettes. The basic situation was clear. He perceived it was dangerous for him, who lived in a city closed to foreigners and with a father in the Communist Party, to be in a group of foreigners. I don't know Ivan's exact concern, but the big picture is clear to me. I'll never forget the sweat on his face.

In the last six years, I have visited Perm 36, a gulag site in Siberia now turned into a museum. I've seen the monuments to the victims of brutal repression above the Arctic Circle in Norilsk and the memorials outside of Chelyabinsk to people killed in the woods during Stalin's purges in the 1930s. So I understand why people could be fearful in 1969.

A companion story will show the progress. In 2009, 40 years later, I was in a remote place in Siberia on a fairly full second-class train. I sat down on a wooden seat across from a Russian man who was about my age. It turned out that I was the first

American he had met in his life. He was so excited. The purity of his excitement gave me a flashback to 1969.

I invited one member of our small group who spoke good Russian so I could have a nice chat with this man. I felt an emotional bonding with him. He looked older than his years. He had bad teeth with bad dentistry. I could image the suffering he had experienced during his life. I have a photo with him and you can see the bond between us. He couldn't wait to tell his daughter that he had met an American.

What are the most overrated and underrated countries you've been to in your travels and why?

The earlier questions triggered more Russian memories from 1969…

I was shocked when I visited Russia in 1969. They were the number two superpower, and I had studied Russian for a year because of their prominence. Although I had read about the poor conditions in Russia, I was still amazed at the reality because the actual conditions were worse than the media reported.

Russians stood in two lines to buy milk: one line to pay and get a receipt and a second line to turn the receipt in for the bottle of milk. Russians did not make ball point pens, and an abacus and cash box were commonly used in place of a cash register. The toilet paper was unbelievably bad. Shoes were terrible.

All of the construction in the Soviet period was shoddy. Signs on elevators and other places would frequently have signs that said in Russian: "No Work." One man my size struck up a conversation and negotiated for 30 or 45 minutes to buy my shoes and any blue jeans I would sell. Finally it became obvious to him that there was nothing in Russia that I wanted to trade for my clothes.

On the plane to Moscow on that 1969 trip, I met a Costa Rican student who was attending medical school in Russia. I visited the apartment where he and his Russian girlfriend lived. It was a three-bedroom apartment. They had one bedroom and shared the kitchen and bathroom with two other unrelated couples who had their own bedrooms. This was the arrangement for about 40% of the population in Moscow in 1969.

For me, it is thrilling to see the changes in Russia since the collapse of communism. Now I think it is an underrated country to visit, and has much to offer travelers. Toilets have greatly improved, although there still are examples of toilets that are the worst in the world. I don't have problems eating anywhere in Russia. It is one of my favorite countries to visit.

There are other countries that are better than you might imagine. Recent visits to Bulgaria, Romania, Chechnya, Namibia, and Botswana were better than I expected.

In general, all over the world people have mobile phones and they are working on their roads. Water quality is much better than 30 or 40 years ago. So travel conditions have improved. Still, highway safety is still an issue. My advice is that if you want to visit a country, go for it. You may be positively surprised.

What are the best and worst meals you have ever had traveling and where were they?

I have no comments on the worst meals. In general, food quality has improved over the years. So I generally do not have problems traveling.

In Japan, I like shabu-shabu. And my favorite food is Peking duck, which I have eaten in China and the U.S.

Thinking about a major meal, what came to mind was a dinner in Wuhan in 1985. In the 1950s, I was told, as were many American children, to "clean up your plate because children are starving in China." I cleaned up my plate although I could not figure out how that was going to help children in China.

Those memories were in my mind when I was at a business banquet in Wuhan, China in 1985. They were our first customer in China for AT&T's 5ESS digital telephone switch. There were two circular tables of eight people, half American and half Chinese perfectly intermixed. It was formal seating with name cards.

I lost count of the courses — various kinds of meat would be served one by one: chicken, beef, pork, duck, shrimp, different kinds of fish, lobster, abalone, etc.

The dish would be put on a Lazy Susan, and the Chinese host on your right would serve you, not the wait staff. In between courses, you would toast colleagues. These were formal toasts to educate the other side on how you were connected to your colleagues. Then there would be another course. Repeat!

So you were standing up and down a lot. Later I assumed this was a proven technique from antiquity that would allow you to eat more.

This dinner took hours. I did not want to make a mistake that could damage this key project that I had been working on for a year, so I watched carefully for clues on proper etiquette.

After a couple of hours, I saw a dish placed on the Lazy Susan that looked bad to me. It was green and slimy looking. I did not know what it was until later. Then the Lazy Susan was rotated person by person until I was the next one to be served. One of these green lumps was placed on my plate by the host on my right.

To avoid offending my hosts, I figured I had to eat the green lump (a sea slug) and did it quickly. That was a mistake. The host on my left assumed I liked it so he put two more sea slugs on my plate. And yes, I ate both of them. (Sigh.)

Incidentally, this initial Wuhan project started sales for over 20 years, serving millions of telephone customers all over China.

What country made you feel most out of your comfort zone and why?

My comfort zone must be fairly robust after so much travel. I would say that the most unusual country I have visited is the Democratic People's Republic of Korea. Visiting there in 2005 was a bit like being in an alternate reality.

We were the first group of Americans permitted in North Korea in several years. Bill Altaffer was our group leader. There was a front-page story in the *Los Angeles Times* quoting our individual observations.

To start our trip, we had to line up and bow to the statue of Kim Il-Sung. All five of us did it because we did not want to ruin the visa chances for other Americans by being disrespectful. This was not out of my comfort zone, but you have to wonder what is motivating this felt need to force public obeisance. A few days later, I was selected by the group to put flowers at the grave of the wife of Kim Il Sung. And after placing the flowers I dramatically backed up without turning around. I wasn't told to do this, but thought my extra efforts might be noticed.

I think the general point here is that countries that are out of your comfort zone are very interesting places to visit.

Do you speak any foreign languages? If so, which have been the most useful for you besides English?

At the University of Texas, I studied German for two years, Russian for one year, and French for one semester. After I retired, I studied Spanish for two years at a community college. I taught myself 300 to 400 Chinese characters in the 1990s, but have forgotten many of them.

Traveling, I have had a chance to use everything that I could remember. These days the only language that I can speak is German and my vocabulary is fairly limited. Survival Russian, French, and Spanish comes in handy all the time.

Also, I know several alphabets at different proficiencies: Korean, Greek, and Arabic. My memory of the Korean alphabet and the capital letters in Greek is good enough to still sound out words. I remember about half of the Arabic letters. Alphabets often help me to figure out signs. In a museum in Sparta, Greece, in 2012, I was studying a mosaic over 2,000 years old when I blurted out "Alcibiades." My guide said "Bravo!" Alcibiades was a major figure in the Peloponnesian War.

What I can do is speak English slowly and clearly and simply. I can speak English without slang. This means that people who have studied English feel more comfortable speaking English to me than to many other Americans. This is a big advantage. Sometimes I have been an English to English interpreter because I could understand the English spoken by two different nationalities, who could not understand each other. I helped by just repeating what they were saying in English.

The other factor that adds to the communications is if you can speak some words in a person's language, they may feel comfortable trying out their minimal English.

I believe that many Americans do not appreciate what a terrible mistake it is not to know and use metric units when traveling. Many educated people have never studied the English measurement system. There is really no need to do so.

So if you haven't studied metric, here are some roughly correct conversions. Say "meter" instead of "yard." Say "liter" instead of "quart." Say "kilometer" instead of half a mile. Say "half a kilogram" instead of a pound. Or better yet, learn metrics.

Looking back from when you started traveling to where you are now, in what ways, if any, have travel changed you?

I've gained knowledge, confidence, and perspective. I can appreciate the "logic" of history, and understand various cause and effect relationships.

As all travelers know, travel is a tremendous education. It broadens your horizons and changes your perspective on things. So I find myself more tolerant because I have seen there are many ways to accomplish the same thing.

But I now am less tolerant of people who live in countries with tremendous opportunities but like to complain about minor things.

I've seen enough unspeakable poverty to want to kiss the ground when I return home after some trips. I count my blessings that I was not born in some third world country where regardless of how hard you work, your options are limited.

The sheer number of data points gained from travel has made it possible to figure out many connections and interrelationships.

I am a much more informed reader of history, and the daily newspaper.

As I have traveled to the level where I have almost visited everywhere by some measures, I find a sense of wonder that our world works as well as it does.

I also have an astronaut-like awe of the beauty of our planet.

One thing that I have gained is an appreciation for the animals on planet Earth. As a child you see animals in the zoo. Then the first trip to Africa is a revelation to see herbivores mix freely. Over the decades, I've visited many of the famous animal reserves in Africa. I've seen lions and cheetahs in the wild many times, and I have touched lions and cheetahs under controlled conditions.

I'm crazy about lemurs and penguins, and I love elephants.

Now in the last three years, after five and soon six trips to the polar regions, it has been a privilege to have interactions with polar bears, walruses, and penguins. I had a "bonding experience" with a royal penguin on Australia's Macquarie Island. He must have liked my bright blue coat. He waddled up to me, looked up at my face, put a small pebble at my feet, looked up at me, and put a second pebble at my feet.

Traveling with birders, who watch patiently for hours, has deepened my lifelong enjoyment of birds. Seeing an albatross soar is a sublime experience every time.

What is the longest continuous trip you have ever taken? When was it and where did you travel?

My first circumnavigation in 1971 was my longest trip. It was six weeks from August 5th to September 18th.

I took Pan Am's Flight 1 most of the way. The "round the world" ticket was a bargain at $1341, including the tax of $3.00.

My flights were: Chicago to San Francisco to Tokyo to Hong Kong to Bangkok to New Delhi to Tehran to Beirut to Cairo to Nicosia to Tel Aviv to Istanbul to Athens to Rome to Paris to London to Chicago. I was seeing all of these places for the first time!

There were wonders of the worlds, and discoveries and/or adventures every day. I saw virtually all of the major tourist attractions in these places. So here are some scattered memories of that journey of a lifetime at age 26.

In Japan, I climbed Mount Fuji and then mailed my boots home to save weight.

In Hong Kong, I bought custom made suits and shoes. I learned my first Chinese characters. I took the hydrofoil to see Macau. The massive cigarette smoking in the casino drove me out in 30 seconds.

In Thailand, I saw the temples, transited the canals, and rode my first elephant.

In India, I saw the Taj Mahal and got on my hands and knees to feel the quality of the stone inlays. The advice for success was: "No hurry, no worry, and no curry." I subsequently rode my second elephant.

In Iran, tourists could visit the vault of the Treasury to see dishes of jewels and jeweled thrones. The clothing and haircuts were influenced by French fashion. I watched my step so as not to break an ankle in the open water ditches in Tehran.

In Lebanon, there were trips to Baalbek, Byblos, and the Casino. It was like a movie set in a James Bond movie with well-dressed people gambling in French. The show at the casino was a wonder of the world with camels, motorcycles, a simulated volcano, and rain. There was a gutter in the floor to catch the "rain." It concluded with almost nude young men and women painted silver and gold suspended from the ceiling on wires, moved overhead and lowered on the stage. Three years later, the civil war started, and the country has never fully recovered.

In Egypt, immediately after checking in, I went to the pyramids at night. There were men in native dress who took you part way into the Great Pyramid with a flaming torch. I met a guide there and arranged to climb the pyramid in the morning at 6 a.m. All of the arrangements cost $13.

We climbed back and forth across one the edge of the pyramid. My 19-year-old guide was fast and I could keep up with him. So he went faster and so did I. It became a race. In less than ten minutes we were at the top of the Great Pyramid of Egypt completely out of breath. It was a boyhood dream achieved. The overcast weather did not diminish the joy. We got down before the tourists arrived.

I also took the overnight train to visit Luxor, Thebes, and Karnak. Saw King Tut's tomb. Took a felucca on the Nile; the captain had two wives living in separate houses in the local village. In Cairo's National Museum, I was alone in the room with the mummies of the Pharaohs of Egypt. I noticed Ramses II had red hair.

Since Egypt and Israel had no diplomatic relations, there was no direct route in 1971. Cyprus was the best way to travel between them. It was ironic. The top tourist attraction in Nicosia for me was the "Green Line" which divided the Greek part from the Turkish part of Cyprus. There was a chain in the street that could be pulled up to stop cars. The UN policed this division. Cyprus is still divided.

In Israel, there were trips to Jerusalem, Bethlehem, Masada, the Jordan River, the Sinai, the Sea of Galilee, the Dead Sea, etc. I saw a 17-year-old asphalt road in perfect condition (the first and only time I ever saw natural asphalt).

In Istanbul, I saw the wonders of the Haga Sophia, the Blue Mosque, and the Topkapi Palace. In a high-ceilinged hama, I experienced my first Turkish bath.

In Athens, the Parthenon was open and you could wander around unrestricted. I did all of the standard tourist things. Poet Edgar Allen Poe captured my emotions: "The glory that was Greece, and the grandeur that was Rome."

To see Rome immediately after Athens was to see the whole foundation of the West in a week. This is really overpowering. In Rome, I saw the Vatican, marveled at the Pantheon, climbed into the catacombs, walked Apian way for two straight hours and even saw a spot where the asphalt was worn away revealing the original Roman road, etc. I visited the Coliseum, the most complex building of antiquity.

In Paris, three French guys, who I met in the U.S. in 1970, took pride in showing me their beloved city. I did not have a camera at this time. So I have only 27 photos of this incredible journey, and 22 of them are candid photos taken as we walked around Paris. Naturally I visited the Louvre, full of more treasures than any other museum, the Eiffel Tower, and saw the majestic tomb of Napoleon at Les Invalides.

In London, the former imperial city of the world's greatest empire, I saw the Tower of London, the crown jewels, the changing of the guard at Buckingham Palace, the British Museum, where I touched the Rosetta Stone, the National Gallery, Trafalgar Square, etc. I was shocked because all of the wait staff at restaurants I could afford were foreigners.

What is your favorite "off-the-beaten-path" destination and why?

This is the category that extreme travelers get excited about! My favorite is Tristan da Cunha because its unique culture has sustained it against the odds for over two centuries. The same can be said for Pitcairn Island. Other places that are virtually unknown that quicken my pulse are Socotra with its fantastic 'dragon blood trees'. I felt a lot of optimism for Bosaso in Puntland in Somalia, which seems counter intuitive because I had to hire armed guards to visit. I was thrilled by a recent visit to Grozny, Chechnya because it is completely rebuilt after the war and the city has no graffiti. There are many others.

What are the best and worst places you have ever spent a night?

The absolute worst was in a small charter boat in the middle of the Pacific after a rogue wave had crashed down on top of the boat causing an on and off leak above my double bed. There was no pan that could prevent the leak from wetting my bed randomly and in random amounts as the ship was tossed about by rough seas. I toughed it out by sleeping in a U shape the first night to avoid the wet spot in the bed. The next night it had grown, and I learned that your body heat will warm a wet spot. The third night I was miserable sleeping in a wet bed on rough seas. After that I had to "sleep" propped up to keep part of my body dry. The moral of the story is to travel with duct tape.

I have been upgraded to luxury status a few times. For example, a peacock suite in India. But my best experiences will be in some small hotels. One that comes to mind, but is now gone, was Noah's motel in Adelaide. I stayed there three nights in 1974 during a two-week fly/drive to Australia. It had a mixture of brick and wooden walls with built-in furniture. There were 17 different kinds of wood used. The first night I liked it, the second night I thought it was truly special, and by the third night I was convinced it was the best place I had stayed.

Another atmospheric hotel is Dwarika's Hotel in Kathmandu. It preserves Nepalese culture by incorporating old wood carvings and various objets d'art all over the hotel. The rooms have external locks like you would put on a trunk. There are many other touches like flowers floating in water. I walked around the main courtyard in one direction and then the other and saw more things.

In your opinion, what country or place in the world feels the most authentic and untouched by tourism?

Here is sampling over time: Point Barrow, Alaska in 1975; Syria in 1978; Bhutan in 2006; Bosaso, Puntland, Somalia in 2010; Umm Ruwaba, Sudan in 2014.

In recent years, I have occasionally selected off-the-beaten-path cities to see places without tourists to get a sense of the real conditions in a country.

In your opinion, where is the most beautiful place on Earth?

The most beautiful place is the place we call home. There is external beauty — and I have seen it all over the world and even under the sea. Like every traveler, I can tick off dozens of places. It is a joy to see.

But there is also inner beauty that appeals to our core values. There is no place like home. It is the place we always return to regardless of what inspirations we have seen on our travels.

The more of our planet I see and experience, the more I appreciate the place called home. And lest we forget, it is also the place where we plan our next trip.

What do you enjoy most when traveling (cities, nature, people, cultural spots, etc.) and why?

I don't travel for one thing! I'm a generalist who enjoys a wide range of things. My peak experiences are moments when I experience an "emotional bonding" with a person in another country. That's when I tune into something that is genuine and represents some deep, shared value.

What travel accomplishments are you most proud of?

Spending the summer of 1965 in Germany, speaking only German to the Germans. Native-born Americans rarely experience living for a sustained period without English. It was a life-changing experience for me.

Professionally, I'm extremely proud of my work, including my business travels that helped countries like Korea, Egypt, China, Singapore, and Japan, make major improvements in their telecommunications. I helped many other countries in telecommunications.

Then there was the joy of helping Norway honor Amundsen on the 100th anniversary of his arrival at the South Pole, by making 100 circumnavigations around the South Pole. During the two hours it took me, I thought about my grandfather, born in Norway, who turned 17 on the boat coming to America.

My first achieved travel objective was visiting all 50 U.S. states in 1983.

Then in 2011, I finished my visits to all of the countries that are now members of the United Nations.

On November 2, 2013, I became the sole #1 ranked traveler on MostTraveledPeople.com. At this point, only two others have achieved that same distinction: Charles Veley and Bill Altaffer.

On February 7, 2015, I became the 4th person to have their sub-regions certified by TheBestTravelled.com (TBT). They selected 60 sub-regions at random from my list of 942 which had to be proven using passport stamps, photos and/or other documentation. This was a grueling process. I had previously passed their 193-UN-member certification by providing passport stamps for 20 countries they picked at random. TBT is the only travel club that certifies their top travelers.

If you had just one personal travel story to share with someone, what would that be?

Of course, the story would depend on the person, their interests and the circumstances. For this book, a fun story seems right.

In 1976, I made a fly/drive trip to South Africa. I drove to an ostrich farm in Oudtshoorn (between Cape Town and Port Elizabeth) that I read about in a guidebook. During the tour I learned all sorts of facts and figure on ostriches, like how an ostrich egg equals 24 chicken eggs. And how male ostriches fight for females by intertwining their necks and kicking each other until one gives up.

My guidebook explained this farm would ask for volunteers to ride an ostrich. I was looking forward to giving it a try — and it was free.

At the end of the tour, there were about 25 of us seated in the stands in front of an oval ring. They asked for volunteers. I was the only one who raised my hand.

So I came down from the stands, and they brought over the ostrich with its head covered. There was a small step stool. So I got up on the bird. There was no saddle. The bird's back is not horizontal; it slopes down toward the neck. It is uncomfortable. I was having some doubts about this.

I was told to hold onto the wings and to steer by covering the bird's opposite eye. I thought "I am not going to release these wings!" Then they took the sock off the ostrich which twisted around and stared at me with its huge eyes. Without any more clues to me, they released the bird.

Immediately, the bird was off running around the oval like it was crazy. There were other ostriches without riders also running around the oval. These birds are fast. This was not what I was expecting. This was the Wild West.

As this bird was running around at high speed, I realized that I had not been told how this ride was going to end. This was a major oversight!

At the end of the second lap, my ostrich finally slowed down in front of the stands and I had the sudden inspiration that I could just push myself off the back of the animal. So I did a flying dismount. It worked. I landed on my feet. Everyone in the stands stood up and clapped. This is the only standing ovation I have received in my life.

Besides your home country, where do you find yourself returning to over and over and why?

In addition to my trips for personal travel, I made 60 trips to Japan on business spending a total of almost two years there in the 1990s. It was a tremendous learning experience. I appreciate the Japanese and their accomplishments.

I've been to Russia 12 or 13 times since my first visit in 1969. This has been mainly for travel. One reason is to see the evolution of the place since the communist system collapsed. I like the people, the landscape and its vastness. And it took a lot of time to visit all 83 of its political subdivisions — a real travel achievement.

What is the ideal amount of time you prefer to travel each trip before you are ready for home and a break?

Three weeks.

If you had an unlimited budget and space and time was no object, what would your perfect travel day look like? (for example: start your morning in Bora Bora; afternoon on a safari in Kenya; night in Australia, etc.)

My thinking is different. I would think about a perfect travel day qualitatively. I love to visit historical places, to enjoy art, to see where famous people lived, to walk the battlefields, etc.

I get charged up by making discoveries and figuring out connections.

Thinking about this question carefully, I realize that learning something that changed my point of view would occur on a perfect day.

As I mentioned earlier, some peak travel experiences are moments when I experience an "emotional bonding" with a person in another country. That's when I tune into something that is genuine and represents some deep value.

And I enjoy a bit of adventure — scuba diving with sharks, swimming with dolphins, walking with lions, wind surfing, zip lining, flying in gliders, riding in hot air balloon, hang gliding, sliding down the "banisters" in a salt mine, etc. I've done those already so some new adventure that is not too threatening for my age would be ideal. (Bungee jumping is probably not on my list anymore.)

And at the end of the day, I'd like a glass of red wine, a reasonable meal, and a good conversation.

For those looking to travel to every country, what is the best piece of advice you could offer them?

1) Plan trips to visit all or most of the countries in a region on the same trip. This saves time and money and gives you insights into those countries. You hear different sides of the story.

2) Take trips with small groups initially to save money and learn tips from experienced travelers. Start conversations with them and make notes.

3) Join travel clubs to learn about trips and to meet serious travelers.

4) Seize your opportunities even if the timing/price isn't perfect. To visit all of the countries is tough and requires determination. Keep that old car a few more years and spend the savings on travel.

5) Take care of your health. You don't want to miss an expensive and carefully planned trip due to sickness or accidents. And frankly, you need to be healthy to visit remote places.

6) Pack your pillow. It will prevent neck pain. When traveling in coach, strap the pillow over your body and rest your arms on it. This helps you sleep on the plane in economy.

For someone that has been almost everywhere, what still gets you excited about packing your bags again?

The thrill of discovery. I cherish seeing things first-hand.

Do you feel you have missed out on certain aspects of life being away from home so much?

Yes, but life is about making choices. Often a major choice precludes others. I am very happy with my life choices, and feel blessed.

Looking ahead, what travel plans and goals are you still pursuing, and what is on your "Bucket List"?

I don't have a "bucket list" where you should see certain places or do certain things before you die. I have an open, ongoing, and adaptive process.

In addition to the various travel lists, I listen to recommendations from people. These could be explicit or implicit travel ideas. I get ideas from reading history or news stories. Potential places to visit are greater than I have time or money to pursue. So I'm opportunistic and work in as much as I can when planning a trip.

I cannot emphasize enough that when you are traveling to keep your eyes and ears open. You may discover something on the spot that is wonderful, interesting, and memorable — and better than what you had planned.

One place I would like to visit is the North Pole.

Gunnar Garfors, Norway

(Gunnar Garfors by Linda Cartridge ©)

Where did you grow up, and what was your early life like?

I was born in Hammerfest, the world's northernmost city, as my parents lived in Havøysund, a tiny village even further north than that. We moved to Naustdal on the Norwegian west coast a few years later, and I still consider that village home. I am the eldest of seven siblings, so I cannot remember being alone as a child. That has probably contributed to me being relatively social, and to take responsibility. We all had to help around the house. I remember being rather annoyed for having to babysit my three sisters when my friends were playing football, but in retrospect being given responsibility at an early age has really taught me a lot. My mom and dad are both well-educated and well-traveled. They saw the value of showing their kids large parts of Norway and of foreign countries, to open our eyes to the diversity of the world. Mom, in particular, also believed in letting us find things out for ourselves. Her attitude was, "If you fall down from that tree, you might learn to be more careful next time." I might be slightly biased, but I'd say that was great parenting — and much better than just telling curious kids what to do and what not to do, and to be over protective. I see too many parents not letting their kids make mistakes these days. That is probably the biggest mistake they can do.

When did you go from casually traveling to making this a full-time goal, and what motivated you to travel to every country?

Traveling has never been a full-time activity for me. I have of course always been researching, planning, and dreaming about my future journeys, but they have always been undertaken during normal holidays and weekends. That means that I am the youngest "hobby traveler" to have been to all 198 countries in the world. It all started in 2004. My brother Øystein and I were at our mom's house in Naustdal. I was visiting for the weekend from Oslo, where I work. In the local newspaper, *Firda*, there was a story about a group of Kyrgyz engineers who had come to the region to learn about hydroelectricity. The story itself wasn't very exciting, but Kyrgyzstan certainly was. Øystein and I had already discussed going somewhere off the beaten track together. He's a teacher and gets time off for the autumn holidays, and I had some vacation days saved up. I shouted to Øystein, and showed him the article. Neither of us had ever even heard of this former Soviet Union republic until now. We quickly found an atlas and an encyclopedia and looked it up. We even threw in a few Internet searches on Mom's awfully slow dial-up connection. What we found out excited us, and we did indeed go there and to Kazakhstan several weeks later. We were so well received in a virtually tourist free area, and I loved the entire travel experience so much that I promised myself to visit every "Stan" country (the seven countries ending with 'stan'). In 2008, I needed another challenge, and having visited around 85 countries by then, I decided to go for all of them.

Do you remember the point where you said to yourself, "I can really accomplish this"?

The moment I decided to go for it was in 2008. I am stubborn as hell, and I always go all in when it comes to the goals I set for myself. And, of course, a bet always helps. I was hosting a party at my place when I told Ola Akselberg, a very good friend of mine, "I will visit every country in the world."

"Every country? How many countries are there?" he asked.

"197," I replied. It was 2009 and two years before South Sudan was welcomed as a member of the United Nations and the number increased to 198.

"Ha! There is no chance in hell that you will make it!" he assured me.

"Oh no?" I asked, offering him my hand. "You wanna bet?"

"OK, but you have to finish by the time you are forty," he stipulated.

My hand was still there. Ola grabbed it and we shared a long handshake. The bet was official. We even had witnesses. There wasn't too much at stake, though — only honor, glory, and beer; one for every country. I had 112 countries left, and I had to visit them within six years to win. He gave in and surrendered the beers live on national Norwegian radio on May 7, 2013, the day before I was heading to my last country, Cape Verde.

What have you done over your life to gain the freedom and finances to pursue as much travel as you have?

Well, not too much, except for always working full-time. It helped that I purchased my own flat in Oslo, where I still live, back in 2000, something that has guaranteed me a cheap place to live, especially after the outrageous hikes in real estate prices since then. I don't have any wives, kids, cars, dogs or other costly "hobbies", either. It has always been about priorities, about spending my money on jet fuel, bus tickets, hostel beds, and mosquito nets — and not much else. Let me just say that I don't have any expensive art on my walls at home.

Was there ever a time you felt like abandoning this goal?

Never — although I was always looking for options when embassies declined to give me visas. I even contemplated swimming into Eritrea, until I discovered that it is a police state where a third of the adult population works in the police or military. It wouldn't have been a very smart move. I luckily got a visa on my second attempt.

What were your worst travel experiences (i.e. detainment, bribes, car accidents, sickness, etc.) and why?

It is quite funny, but I have never really had awful experiences, whereas friends of mine who hardly ever travel often run into troubles when abroad. I assume that experience has something to do about it, and probably a fair deal of luck too. I have, of course, been food poisoned in India (I mean, who hasn't?), and almost been involved in fights in Somalia and Central African Republic, but nothing major. I guess traveling it is a little like passing a dog. If the dog senses that you are afraid, it is more likely to attack. You just have to show that you know what you are doing, even if you don't. And ask politely for assistance if needed when you feel confident with the people around you. And of course, smile a lot! It's the best travel trick in the world, and it is even free.

What do you consider one of the most adventurous trips you have taken?

I had planned to fly to São Tomé and Príncipe from Gabon, but the plane had been canceled due to Easter and I did not have time to wait for a week until the next one would go. I therefore haggled my way onto a cargo ship. The journey was supposed to take 15 hours, but it ended up taking 40, which meant that my water and oranges had run out almost before we started. Sleeping on deck was amazing, though, with no lights and only a billion stars.

What were your most challenging countries to visit and why?

Eritrea was by far the hardest to get into. My first visa application was returned without any explanation. Well, unless you count the Post-it note that was attached to my passport, saying: "Hello! Visa denied", as an explanation. Angola and Equatorial Guinea were also hard and I really needed my press card to enter Libya and Afghanistan.

What's the strangest thing you've seen/experienced while traveling?

Being invited to a wedding in Afghanistan, just to have the invitation withdrawn the next day was strange. Upon asking about it, we learned that the mother of the bride had been killed, so the wedding was postponed and replaced with a funeral. Such a sad story that we only experienced very much on the sideline.

Which travel experiences stand out the most and why?

The "Door to Hell" in the Karakum Desert; it is the most underrated tourist attraction ever. Except that there are no tourists. Which is all the better. It is a crater, 70 meters wide, that was allegedly created by an explosion in the '70s. It also ignited the gas sifting up from the ground, something that created the fire which has been burning ever since. To be there in the middle of nowhere in the middle of the night is just magic. We stayed in a tent near the crater, and our guide made us a meal to remember, served to us where we sat on an Afghan carpet spread on the sand.

What are the most overrated and underrated countries you've been to in your travels and why?

I'd say that the seven "Stan" countries are the most underrated countries out there. The amazing scenery, the hospitality, the lack of tourists, their no bullshit attitude, their ability to party, their vodka, the chilled out atmosphere, the Silk Road. Need I say more?

I am clearly not going for the audience award for the next one. The United States of America is the most overrated country in the world. We have been indoctrinated by Hollywood films and American TV series for years and years about how great the U.S. is. When you go there you notice that the average American is superficial, arrogant, extremely tip oriented, not very interested in anything outside the country. The U.S. is of course diverse, but there are so many other much more exciting countries out there — countries that feel much more real; countries with a history; countries with an identity. The U.S. feels fake in many ways. It might be easy and convenient to travel to, but I feel that it is cold and lacks a soul. There are so many much more amazing, appealing, and less unknown countries out there.

And just for the record: I have lived in the U.S. twice in addition to have visited it at least a dozen of times. I should also say that I have some great U.S. friends that have nothing in common with what I have described, and I am sure they can stomach such comments about their country.

What are the best and worst meals you have ever had traveling and where were they?

I have had some incredible meals in amazing restaurants in many countries in the world. The most memorable ones are however very much context dependent. Who I am with, where we are, and of course, what we eat, is essential. Food alone won't make memorable meals for me. Street food in India, Vietnam, and São Tomé and Príncipe can beat most other posh experiences.

I had eminent street food, meat and corn that were prepared over coal on old car wheels in a dark street under a starlit sky in São Tomé.

"What are you doing here?"

A local English-speaking man in his 50s sat down next to me to eat his skewers.

"I am just visiting. As a tourist."

"A tourist? But why are you eating here with us? Why aren't you in one of the posh hotels?"

"I wouldn't have met you there, would I?"

He agreed with my logic. We continued discussing world problems, even solving a few.

The worst meal was in Mumbai, India. I was there with my ex-girlfriend, and we both had some curry-like dish in a restaurant near the train station. We both started puking less than an hour later. Eruptions the other way soon followed. We were destroyed for days, if not weeks after. And I don't even know why we went into that restaurant in the first place. It was not particularly cozy.

What country made you feel most out of your comfort zone and why?

I don't ever feel out of my comfort zone in any country. Not anymore. Traveling so much has made me realize that we are all the same, despite our differences in religion, beliefs, cultures, customs, and traditions. I try to tell other people to expand their own comfort zones, but I think this is something that can only be done properly through their own experiences, their own travels. Everyone should challenge their comfort zones, I am sure that would create less war, more love.

Do you speak any foreign languages? If so, which has been the most useful for you besides English?

I obviously speak Norwegian. In addition a fair amount of German, some Spanish, and a tiny bit of Chinese (Mandarin). English has always been my traveling language. Even if the people I meet don't speak it, there is always someone who does. Typically a girl or a boy aged 13 or 14 eventually appears and steps in as a translator. That really is an ice breaker. I have still, on occasion, had to use my notebook to communicate. In Iran, I drew two sheep, a cow, chicken and four breads on a napkin in a restaurant. There were four of us there, and we got what we wanted. And then some! The meals were amazing.

Looking back from when you started traveling to where you are now, in what ways, if any, has travel changed you?

Traveling so much has taught me to be humble, to be contact seeking, to listen and to ask questions. I have learned to appreciate the small things, and I am now able to realize that we live in a little spoiled bubble in the Western world, that the world isn't only about us. I can also, to a certain degree, see the bubble from outside and, in a slightly better manner, understand the world from other perspectives.

What is the longest continuous trip you have ever taken? When was it and where did you travel?

I have never traveled for longer than five weeks in one go. Since I have always traveled while maintaining a full-time job, that has been my limit (although I could, of course, have taken five weeks at the end of one year and five weeks in the beginning of the next — but that would have left me with travel withdrawal symptoms for the remainder of those two calendar years). One five week trip in 2003 took me to China, Australia, New Zealand (to meet my sister who was studying there), Chile (to meet my ex-girlfriend from the country), Argentina, and Brazil. Another one in January and February 2014 took me to Georgia, Brazil, South Africa, Namibia, the Philippines, and Japan. That was a book writing trip, on which I finished writing my book about my travels to every country in the world. I could, naturally, not sit at home in snow-filled Oslo to write a book about traveling.

What is your favorite "off-the-beaten-path" destination and why?

Answering this question might ultimately ruin it, don't you think? "Off-the-beaten-path" kinds of chapters in guidebooks are self-contradictory. You can find such places in almost every country as long as you go away from the big cities and the most famous sites. There is usually a village, an island, a mountain or a forest where you can find authentic experiences, and be at total peace with yourself. Rest assured that you are in a tourist-free area.

What are the best and worst places you have ever spent a night?

This is also context dependent. I could, of course, answer with, "an amazing hotel in the sun," but I spend very little time in hotels, except for sleeping, as I'd rather be out exploring. I also rarely stay in posh hotels as I rather use my money on traveling and food.

For one of the best, I will have to say a little hotel on the beach south of Mombasa in Kenya. My ex-girlfriend and I had our own simple cabin; fishermen worked from the beach and provided super fresh seafood for our meals that were served on the patio of the hotel, overlooking the ocean. Diving was also incredible, and yet the town wasn't too far away, so we could explore that as well without much hassle.

It was also very memorable when I got to stay in the guestroom of the mayor of a little town in Somalia. There were no hotels there, and I walked from shack to shack. The bed wasn't much to write home about, but it was a bed. No luxury at all, but a great experience nevertheless. The same applies to a night on the deck of a cargo ship taking me from Gabon to São Tomé and Príncipe. To sleep under the stars on my towel, which was spread on the metal deck, wasn't all that comfortable, but still out of this world for other reasons.

The worst place I have stayed was in a police station in Niger. I got to stay in a filthy old room next to the guards' office (although they did actually offer me a mosquito net).

In your opinion, what country or place in the world feels the most authentic and untouched by tourism?

You can find such places in almost every country. Just leave the big cities and avoid the most famous sites, and there will almost always be a little village, mountain, forest, or island where you feel at peace, far away from any tourists. The great thing about tourists is that they usually act like sheep: they all go where everyone else goes. That leaves a lot of "untouched" oases around the world.

In your opinion, where is the most beautiful place on Earth?

I am, of course, biased, but I will have to also answer the Sunnfjord region on the Norwegian west coast and around Narvik in northern Norway.

The rugged coast of Iceland is also fantastic. So are the mountains in Kyrgyzstan and Patagonia in Argentina. I am (as you probably get) a big fan of spectacular scenery.

What do you enjoy most when traveling (cities, nature, people, cultural spots, etc.) and why?

I totally adore nature's wonders and breathtaking scenery. But I do prefer trips where I also get to meet people, have incredible meals, and just feel the energy of towns or cities. Where I can discuss what I have seen, share it, and find out more from good friends. I prefer combined trips where all my senses are stimulated, where there is a variation of impulses and impressions.

What travel accomplishments are you most proud of?

That I have actually visited all 198 countries in the world, in my spare time, is by far my biggest travel accomplishment. But visiting five continents in just one day with Adrian Butterworth from the UK, something that was acknowledged as a Guinness World Record, is also high up on the list. Not far behind is the Recordsetters listing I achieved when visiting 19 countries in 24 hours with Norwegian friends Øystein Djupvik and Tay-young Pak. And I will of course also have to mention visiting all 19 counties in Norway in 24 hours, a world-first which I did together with my brother, Øystein.

If you had just one personal travel story to share with someone, what would that be?

I have told this story from Turkmenistan loads of times.

Four of us, all guys, had organized the trip through a local agency and drove in to the border by taxi from Mashad, Iran. After having walked across and sorted out formalities, we were met by our guide, Oleg. He turned out to be quite a character.

"Welcome to Turkmenistan! Are you here for drinks or for girls?"

"Hehe…I am sure we will have some drinks, but we have girlfriends at home."

"So?"

"But Oleg, do you not believe in love?"

"Love was invented by the French. They were too cheap to pay for prostitutes."

This mother of ultimate responses came without hesitation.

Besides your home country, where do you find yourself returning to over and over and why?

I studied and lived for three years in Falmouth in Cornwall. The UK is therefore in many ways my second home country, and I regularly get an urge to go back. I have on occasion jumped on a plane on a few hours' notice just to go back and suck in the culture, the sense of humor, the atmosphere. Korea is also on my list, and I have been there 15 times. The never-ending action in Seoul just gets to me. It is a truly underestimated city.

What is the ideal amount of time you prefer to travel on each trip before you are ready for home and a break?

I have never actually traveled for longer than five weeks in one go, but I seem to have virtually unlimited amounts of energy, so I cannot really see that I would ever need a break from traveling. Then again, maybe five weeks is perfect as that enables me to see my family and friends, to soak up and really let in my experiences at home.

If you had an unlimited budget, and space and time was no object, what would your perfect travel day look like? (For example: start your morning in Bora Bora, afternoon on a safari in Kenya, night in Australia, etc.)

Well, being in five continents in one day (June 8, 2012) was an incredible experience; having a night meal in Istanbul, almost being thrown in jail in Casablanca for filming the big mosque at night, experiencing the truly stereotypical arrogant French train conductor in Paris, testing the waters of the Caribbean in Dominican Republic, and partying the night away in a jazz club in Caracas. The experiences were perfect, although I would certainly have preferred a much faster plane to get more time to enjoy actually being on the ground.

For those looking to travel to every country, what is the best piece of advice you could offer them?

Travel with hand-luggage only, don't plan too much, and be open to impulses. Too many people plan their trips to death, thus eliminating any possibility of real, non-choreographed experiences which you will not know existed before you are actually there, being offered the possibility.

For someone that has been almost everywhere, what still gets you excited about packing your bags again?

Any potential trip, be it in Norway or abroad. The mere thought of the sense of freedom and the possibility of more exploring gets me excited.

Do you ever feel you have missed out on certain aspects of life being away from home so much?

Not really. Maybe I should have been home with my family more often, or spent more time with my friends, but I have never ignored them or pushed them out of my life, and I have always been at home to visit my parents and my six siblings at least three or four times a year, even during the most hectic traveling periods. I have had so many amazing experiences, met so many inspiring people, that I would not have missed out for the world.

Looking ahead, what travel plans and goals are you still pursuing, and what is on your "Bucket List"?

I have actually never had a bucket list, although I guess visiting 198 countries is pretty damn close. Traveling to me is about random experiences. I prefer to be impulsive and see what happens. Having a bucket list sort of defeats the purpose of travel. I will of course never stop traveling, and I am still looking forward to my next trip as much as I have ever before. There are so many new places I want to see, so many places I want to return to in order to meet old friends, notice changes, and discover more of.

I have some work trips coming up. My next private trips will be to Antarctica, Saudi Arabia, and Iran. And I am very much looking forward to them all, of course.

Andre Brugrioux, France

(**Andre Brugrioux**)

Where did you grow up and what was your early life like?

I grew up in Brunoy (in the suburbs of Paris), close to a forest (Forêt de Sénart). My activities with the Boy Scouts in this forest gave me the best training for my future life of an adventurous globetrotter. As I was born before WWII, I also spent years as a kid in Langeac, a town of Auvergne in the farm where my father was born. With my aunts, for food, and security! Later during my three months school vacations, I also stayed there each year until 16. I loved the mountainous countryside there and the life on the farm. So I received both countryside and big city (with Paris nearby) influences. My father was a peasant at heart. He had to leave his father's farm because they were too many children. He finally landed in the Parisian region working in a railway depot. He never left his garden and never traveled. My mother, also from Auvergne, traveled before marriage. We were three brothers and did not have much money in the house. From youth, I learned to live on little. This was precious for my future life on the road: to be happy with little. My first trip happened at the age of seven — to Switzerland during the war in order to buy some food missing in Paris! Then as a Boy Scout I went camping to Germany, Luxembourg, and Belgium at the age of 13.

When did you go from casually traveling to making this a full-time goal, and what motivated you to travel to every country?

I left France at the age of 17 and came back after 18 years of absence. During the last six years (1967-1973), I hitch-hiked 340,000 kilometers round the world non-stop with my savings from Canada. My dream to see the world was powerful. I never thought it would last so long and that I could do so much, because when I left in 1955 I had no money in my pocket, we had no travel information, nobody was roaming around like today, and we were still rebuilding France from the war! I did not want to come back, but I was sick from dysentery. I was furious because I was still missing a lot of countries. From 1975 until 2005, I left France steadily every year, six to eight months at a time, in order to fulfill my dream of visiting all countries and territories of the world (250 different entities). This is now done. Since 2005, I keep on traveling to see things I missed because there was no information at the time. Today is the opposite: I can prepare any trip at home and follow my plan to the hour and to the euro thanks to Google and TV. So, for me, traveling has been a full-time job from the start!

What motivated me to visit every country? Pure curiosity of the mind and the desire to learn and understand. The truth is that what I have done is not a tour of the world but a tour of mankind. Deep down, I wanted to meet all people to find out, following my childhood in the war, if men one day will be able to bring about peace. You cannot bounce around all your life on a dream. You must be strongly motivated: finding out about peace has been my true motivation. In fact, my life on the road was not my choice, but destiny. I obeyed unconsciously to something pulling me forward. And to sum it up, I am not a real traveler. I am rather a student on a grand scale.

Do you remember the point where you said to yourself, "I can really accomplish this"?

I had nothing else in mind from the start except for seeing the whole world. I never thought I could do it, but the hand of God, as I've said, was directing me apparently! My life, in other words, was a kind of spiritual quest. I have found the answers to the establishment of peace with the discovery of the Baha'i plan for mankind. Then keeping on traveling so I could check that this plan was on its way!

What have you done over your life to gain the freedom and finances to pursue as much travel as you have?

When I left France I had two dollars in my pocket. I had to work abroad right away; I did any kind of jobs; first in order to learn languages. I was later able to save money during my three years in Canada working as a translator. On my return to France, I managed to get money from writing books and giving lectures. You have to understand that my travels never cost a lot as I never sleep in hotels, never eat in restaurants, or take taxis.

Was there ever a time you felt like abandoning this goal?

No.

What have been your worst travel experiences (such as detainment, bribes, car accidents, sicknesses, etc.) and why?

The list would be too long, but to sum it up, I was put in jail seven times, deported three times, nearly got shot ten times, and survived other great dangers half a dozen times. Like a U.S. F-16 airplane exploding 50 meters in front of me, or a buffalo herd charging me in the Congolese night. It is a miracle I am alive. I left Angkor Wat ruins, for example, during the war in Cambodia on June 7, 1970. The next day they were taken: 120 people got killed… Luck is a very feeble word for me. As a matter of fact, I think no word in the dictionary fits me for my survival. Like a cat thrown in the air, I always land back on my paws!

What do you consider one of the most adventurous trips you have taken?

None. I am not looking for adventure. But adventure seems to be looking for me! I find no fun, for example, in having six Kalashnikov's stuck in my ribs or a bayonet between the eyes!

What were your most challenging countries to visit and why?

Saudi Arabia was one. This country is the only one not issuing individual tourist visas. It took me 37 years of searching to get an invitation from a Saudi man in order to receive a "business" visa. Some places out of the way are also hard to reach like Pitcairn, Tristan da Cunha, Tromelin, etc. At one time, China was the most challenging: Mao had closed the shop! And Burma also was closed at one time. The art of traveling today is to enter before or after the revolution.

What's the strangest thing you've seen/experienced while traveling?

A custom officers looking at my passport in reverse. Instead of looking at my passport normally, he looked at it upside down! And very seriously, as if he could read it!

Which travel experiences stand out the most and why?

Hitchhiking six weeks in winter in Alaska. In 1969, it was the coldest winter of the last century. Why: - 45° C or Fahrenheit (same temperature). Hitching in winter is even against the law in Alaska. I was even risking my life as, remember, I never go to hotels.

What are the most overrated and underrated countries you've been to in your travels and why?

Funny question. I am not a tourist "buying" countries like slices of ham at tourist agencies. All countries enriched me to a different degree with their differences. Beauty is everywhere. You just have to open your eyes. And I have personally met beautiful people everywhere. The trick is to travel with an open mind and heart.

What are the best and worst meals you have ever had traveling and where were they?

Wherever he goes, a Frenchman will suffer from the quality of the food. Nevertheless, you can find a dish you like in every country. Even in England! To me nevertheless, two countries have brought cooking to an art: China and France. When I had to rush to brush my teeth, I guess the meal was not to my taste. In Vietnam, I could not swallow boiled chicks in their shells, although it is a delicacy there. Food is a matter of habit. The best one is my mum's, because she trained us to seek a type of food we'll be looking for all of our life.

What country made you feel most out of your comfort zone and why?

The United States! I cannot feel good in a society based, according to me, on the theories of Darwin: the survival of the fittest. Its rodeo atmosphere is unfortunately not my cup of tea. And Russia! Every time I come out of this huge territory, I feel like I'm coming out of jail!

Do you speak any foreign languages? If so, which has been the most useful for you besides English?

I speak, read, and write fluently in English, Spanish, German, Italian, and French (my mother tongue). I worked ten years in the corresponding countries to learn those various languages properly. I also manage more or less in Portuguese. Let me tell you that the most useful language in South America is not English but Spanish (if you don't want to be spit at!) and in West Africa it is French. To me a man that cannot manage with English, French, and Spanish is not a real traveler. Russian is also useful today (15 countries speak it). I wanted to learn it when young but the USSR did not allow foreign workers like me to enter. Chinese, the most spoken language, concerns only one country, and Swahili only a small part of Africa. Arabic people don't understand each other. All having been colonized. English and French will suffice when passing. I have also learned a few words of many languages to roam around. But knowing a few words is not speaking a language. Vive l'Esperanto!

Looking back from when you started traveling to where you are now, in what ways, if any, has travel changed you?

Traveling will open your eyes, but only if you are ready to look. What has changed me during my life on the road is not the traveling in itself, although this has helped widen my horizon, but the discovery of the Baha'i writings. They totally changed my perception of man and made clear to me the world and its history. I have made mine their motto: The Earth is but one country.

What was the longest continuous trip you have ever taken, when was it where did you travel?

The first one: 18 year-longs (between 1955 and 1973) during which I visited 135 countries on the five continents (and hitch-hiked 340,000km) between the age of 17 and 35.

What is your favorite "off-the-beaten-path" destination and why?

None! Once I have seen a thing, "beaten path" or not, I don't want to see it again. The first impression is the one that I want to keep. And my ambition is to see the maximum. So I have no time to go back to any place, although this happened inevitably, crisscrossing the world.

What are the best and worst places you have spent a night?

How do you want me to answer that question? After 60 years on the road, without paying for a hotel, every night is memorable. There are so many of them outstanding but, let us say perhaps, the most romantic, is in a Chinese pavilion on the Sun Moon Lake in Taiwan by moonlight and warm breeze. One of the most terrible: my head stuck under the farting arse of a fat, drunken Mexican snoring in a hammock above me in a very narrow hut!

In your opinion, what country or place in the world feels the most authentic and untouched by tourism?

Those are hard to find nowadays.

In your opinion, where is the most beautiful place on Earth?

The most beautiful place on Earth, according to me, is the one where you feel happy; in other words, where you feel in total harmony with yourself, with the environment and the cosmos.

What do you enjoy most when traveling (cities, nature, people, cultural spots, etc.) and why?

The heart of man. Everything surrounding man interests me because those surroundings are shaping his heart, from food to philosophy. Also, my curiosity has no end. To discover the diversity of our planet is the most motivating factor to me. What makes me "fly" is to discover something for the first time. Whatever. Any "first" is heaven to me.

What travel accomplishments are you most proud of?

Entering Saudi Arabia after 37 years of research on an invitation (this country does not issue individual tourist visas); getting a free lift with the Pacific French Naval Forces to reach Pitcairn (from Tahiti); reaching Tristan da Cunha after waiting nine years for a cargo boat leaving Cape Town; entering Tajikistan in August 2000 after a terrible fight for the visa that nearly brought me a heart attack; and reaching by their unique public boat the islands of Tokelau after a nightmarish flight from Europe.

If you had just one personal travel story to share with someone, what would it be?

Sorry, but mission impossible to me. So many come to my mind at once!

Besides your home country, where do you find yourself returning to over and over and why?

I carefully avoid returning to any place or country I have seen, if possible, for two reasons:

1) The first impression is the strongest.

2) I want to see the maximum of the world, so next is the best!

What is the ideal amount of time you prefer to travel on each trip before you are ready for home and a break?

The necessary time to get to know the place well, if possible. Can vary, of course!

If you had an unlimited budget and space and time was no object, what would your perfect travel day look like? (for example: start your morning in Bora Bora; afternoon on a safari in Kenya; night in Australia, etc.)

A perfect travel day for me is when I meet marvelous people or enjoy most beautiful scenery, or even when I discover something new and baffling for the first time. Wherever!

For those looking to travel to every country, what is the best piece of advice you could offer them?

Traveling depends on the traveler. So, love people, they'll answer. And if you like the sea, don't go to Switzerland!

For someone that has been almost everywhere, what still gets you excited about packing your bags again?

Seeing something I have not seen before. A "first" is the top excitement for me.

Do you ever feel you have missed out on certain aspects of life being away from home so much?

No, I have missed nothing away from home (but camembert and baguettes!). The road has been a wonderful companion. I even managed mixing family life and steady travels at the end, thanks to a unique and understanding wife.

Looking ahead, what travel plans and goals are you still pursuing, and what is on your "Bucket List"?

After 60 years of roaming around, I have fulfilled my childhood dream beyond my wildest expectations: to visit all the countries and territories of the world. Nevertheless, I could still fill up a notebook of things I would still like to see. But I must take into account that I just celebrated my 77th birthday, so all depends on my knee: as long as they are following I'll be keeping on, even if it is at a different speed. I still keep sleeping on a dustbin plastic bag anywhere when traveling. I have noticed that we don't move any longer in the tomb. So I would rather move before!

Johnny Ward, Ireland

(Johnny Ward at a bar in Cuba, 2015)

Where did you grow up and what was your early life like?

I was born in Galway, Republic of Ireland and grew up in Northern Ireland. Life was fun but pretty simple — my early life was pretty poor. I had a single parent with two children, no central heating, no car, no washing machine, etc. It was a small family full of love, but no material goods — no Nintendo, etc. As we got older, things improved slightly, but growing up with no money on a small island always meant that I wanted to be financially independent and be able to travel freely.

When did you go from casually traveling to making this a full-time goal, and what motivated you to travel to every country?

I'm a little different from a lot of the country counters in that I travel extensively through these countries on epic land journeys — Cape Town to Cairo; Japan to Australia; Beijing to Ireland, etc. So I racked up about 90 countries before I fully admitted my goal. Initially I couldn't afford it so I never told anyone about my goal, but as I approached 100, and my online stuff was generating good money, I knew I could do it — that was about three years ago. Now it's just a matter of time before I finish. I'm a goal-orientated person so this is a perfect long-term goal for me.

Do you remember the point where you said to yourself, "I can really accomplish this"?

I do — I was on about 50 countries, and I had my first five-figure online month and I thought, "Wow, this is seriously do-able."

What have you done over your life to gain the freedom and finances to pursue as much travel as you have?

Cracking the online money game — initially with a travel blog, then an SEO company (which is heavily outsourced), and now recently with an education start-up in Hong Kong. Coming from a poor family meant I didn't have the head start lots of others have, but excuses get us nowhere, so I did it myself. Also, I spent my whole twenties traveling, teaching English, etc., which, in my opinion, was an awesome lifestyle choice as opposed to people who spend their twenties and thirties grinding out the corporate life, scrambling together money so they can travel as they get older. That's not for me at all.

Was there ever a time you felt like abandoning this goal?

There are points during the nine or ten months each year I'm traveling that I think, "Aaaag, fuck this — I'm so tired, I wanna go back to Thailand and recover before I hit the road again." But I set my goal at the start of the year, so realistically I know I won't quit.

What were your worst travel experiences (i.e. detainment, bribes, car accidents, sickness, etc.) and why?

Like everyone here, I've had so, so many. Once in Odessa, Ukraine, for example, I was partying in a bar during the day on the Black Sea — awesome vibe. My buddy and I decided to run back to our hotel, get changed, and then come back and carry on all night. It was only about two in the afternoon. Outside the bar, strangely, a frail old woman with a battered cart offers us a beer. "One for the road mate?" I say to my buddy. Sure, we plan to drink it as we go back to the hotel. Ksssssht. We open the cans and two policemen arrest us before I even tasted the stuff. Straight to the cells, locked up, demanding five hundred euro. We didn't budge, so we waited in the cells for hours. To cut a long story short, a fake student ID allowed us to barter down to fifty euro each. They handed us our beers back and off we went, hours later.

We come back to the bar to party, it's around 8pm — we had drunk a bottle of vodka reminiscing about the corrupt cops, and the old lady, as we got ready. So we're pretty toasted when we get back to the bar. As soon as we arrive — we're arrested again for being drunk and disorderly! You gotta be kidding! Back sitting in the cells, another barter situation, another 50 euro.

My buddy is pretty drunk by the end of the night, the police arrest him for a THIRD time that day when they see him again, recognize him, and thankfully think they've given us a hard enough time that day. Wow.

Also a broken knee cap, fibia and tibia in Thailand, dengue in China, car crashes in Sudan, bribes all the way through Africa — I could talk about this stuff forever.

What do you consider the most adventurous trip you have taken?

It's gotta be back in my English teaching days in Thailand. I had dreamed of visiting China, but on $700 USD per month and a three week "Christmas" break, it wasn't financially viable. I took a local bus to a part of the Mekong River where it enters Thailand, negotiated through my Irish Thai and his Chinese

Thai to hitch a ride on his cargo boat to Kunming in China. I was told the journey would be less than a day. I paid my $30 USD and jumped on board. Five days later, after an illegal two days in a hooker town in Burma, locked in a cupboard as Chinese customs boarded, and another illegal night in Laos, I was dropped off in the middle of nowhere in China — mental experience.

What were your most challenging countries to visit and why?

I guess Somalia or Somaliland was tough. Having an armed guard escort you outside the cities is a bit disconcerting. Haiti was pretty tough, too. So many people have literally nothing after the earthquake — there's lots of destitute locals begging and committing robberies and actually, for the first time in my life, I can understand why. Really sad. Other than that, I live my life on the road, so it's never too tough.

What is the strangest thing you've seen/experienced while traveling?

A constant stream of naked Indian men pleasuring themselves on street corners across the country. Strange but true. I have a few awesome experiences like watching a sing-sing when I stayed with a local tribe in Papua New Guinea. Oh, and I watched a coming-of-age exorcism when I was sleeping on the floor of a nomadic tribe in the Gobi Desert in Mongolia — throwing up all over the place, insane.

Which travel experiences stand out the most and why?

It's probably the first step I took towards living this life. After graduating from university, I left Ireland to teach English in Thailand. I was living in Chiang Mai for a year, and that really taught me that living a different lifestyle was possible. To this day, I don't think I would have achieved such a fun lifestyle had it not been for making that step at 23 years old.

Riding a scooter to work, studying Thai, every day being an adventure. It was one of the most exciting times of my life. I was broke, but so, so happy.

What are the most overrated and underrated countries you've been to in your travels and why?

It's tough to say that a whole country is overrated, because everywhere has its sweet spots. That being said, if pushed, I'd say Costa Rica. So battered by tourism and located amongst so many other awesome countries like Nicaragua and Guatemala. It's such a polished touristic product in Costa Rica that you have to work hard to see the real country.

Underrated, for me, is most places in the Middle East. Western media have people terrified of Iran and all the 'Stans — all of which are unbelievable travel spots. Uzbekistan is so beautiful, and the history with the old Silk Route, means you really get transported back in time. And Iranian people have to be the friendliest on the planet. Unreal.

What are the best and worst meals you have ever had traveling and where were they?

Being based in Thailand for two or three months a year means I can never get enough of Som Tam and Gai Yang — spicy papaya salad and grilled chicken. Aaaagh, even thinking about makes my mouth water. So delicious, but if you can't handle your spice, steer clear — you have been warned.

Worst meals — I could write a book about that. From pigs testicles in Beijing, to dog soup in North Korea, and everything else in between. I'm up for trying pretty much everything, so that's got me into a few tricky situations.

What country made you feel most out of your comfort zone and why?

I'm on the road almost full-time, so ironically being on the road is my comfort zone these days. It's when I'm stationary that I get agitated and uncomfortable.

Do you speak any foreign languages? If so, which have been the most useful for you besides English?

I'm Irish, so English is my mother tongue. I own a place in Thailand to recover from my epic trips, so my Thai is pretty good. I studied French all the way through to university, so I can get by if pushed, although pretty badly. I studied Spanish in Medellin, Colombia for a month last year, so I have basic Spanish now too. I'm certainly no polyglot, but I try my best.

Looking back from when you started traveling to where you are now, in what ways, if any, has travel changed you?

Traveling has changed me more than I ever could have imagined. One of the major changes is the level of appreciation I have for my life. I grew up "poor" in Ireland, but that's so relative — free health care, free education, food in my belly almost any time I needed it. Traveling showed me just how fortunate a hand I had been dealt.

It's also taught me a lot about life choices and opportunities. I have met so many inspirational people along the way, and the one thing that binds them all is an ambition to better themselves. I hope that's rubbed off on me. Sitting around bemoaning aspects of society changes nothing, we have to do it ourselves.

What is the longest continuous trip you have ever taken? When was it and where did you travel?

Realistically, I'm on one long trip. I have traveled nine to ten months out of every year for the last seven years apart from a year in Australia. Then, as I mentioned before, I moved to Thailand to recover from each journey, which I guess could still be considered "traveling" to some.

I did a fourteen month trip from Japan to East Timor overland, a ten month trip from China to Ireland, a ten month trip from Mexico to Antarctica, and a few other trips similar in length in Africa, Central Asia, etc.

What is your favorite "off-the-beaten-path" destination and why?

I visited Harar in eastern Ethiopia, on the border with Somalia, and it blew my mind. It's the oldest Islamic city in the whole of Africa. I had heard a rumor that the city was home to some wild hyenas which, over generations, had become 'friendly' with a local family. The elder of the family fed them red meat each night. I hunted him down at dusk and ended up feeding the hyenas mouth to mouth with red meat on a stick. Scary but amazing experience.

What are the best and worst places you have ever spent a night?

The worst — wow. Before I made money online my travels were SUPER low-budget, initially around $500 USD per month for everything — accommodation, food, transport, sites, etc. So my accommodation was often the worst imaginable. I'll never forget sleeping on a bed in Khartoum, Sudan which turned out to have a rat's nest underneath it; or the room in Agra, India with a locust infestation; or staying in an open-air, crumbled building in Old Dhaka, Bangladesh. All ridiculously bad, but all amazing experiences.

The best? One of two for sure. Either Niyama Resort and Spa in the Maldives — accessible only by a sexy James Bond-esque sea plane, and a favorite of Jay Z and David Beckham. Bungalows on the water with the clearest water I've ever seen — it's pricey, but I was celebrating my 100th country so it was well worth it.

Also in the running would be Sri Panwa in Phuket, Thailand. Two room villas with private pools overlooking the ocean. ABSOLUTE luxury. Still mesmerizes me looking back at the pics.

In your opinion, what country or place in the world feels the most authentic and untouched by tourism?

There are still a lot of places untouched by tourism. You just have to be a little brave and explore. Vast swathes of Africa are untouched, as is much of Central Asia and the beautiful Pacific Island nations are hard to beat for authentic cultural experiences combined with the most stunning beaches you've ever seen, and often not a hotel/resort in sight.

In your opinion, where is the most beautiful place on Earth?

You know, this is always a tough question, and having traveled a fair bit, it's one I get asked all the time. Personally speaking, in terms of living in a country, the people, food, culture and beautiful sites and scenery than Thailand, as an ex-pat, is awesome. You can live a crazy big city life, which carries its own beauty for me, especially coming from a small town in Ireland. You can also hike in the mountains, sit on the most breathtaking beaches, and explore a culture so different to your own.

Traveling, though, I'd have to say Ethiopia. There are few regions in the world that you really feel like, "Wow, I'm really off the beaten track here," and backpacking around Ethiopia offered me that all the time; the Rift Valley, the amazing Lalibela, Africa's oldest Islamic town in Harar and the center of Rastafarianism (Shashamane) — they're all unreal. East Africa, as a whole, is amazing, but Ethiopia is a real gem. I hope to go back sooner rather than later.

What do you enjoy most when traveling (cities, nature, people, cultural spots, etc.) and why?

'Real' experiences. Ones where I don't felt like I've flown to the capital, stayed a night or two, and flown out with the country box ticked. That's not my style at all. I loved to overland from one side of a country to the next, so it's often the culture I loved to feel the most. Although, that being said, I'm still a huge sucker for world famous sites, despite the crowds.

What travel accomplishments are you most proud of?

It's more the lifestyle that I've created that I'm proud of. And that I've tried to really explore the countries around the world, as opposed to stepping one foot in them and moving onto the next. I'm proud that I've given almost every country a real chance, and I've been rewarded a thousand times over for that.

If you had just one personal travel story to share with someone, what would that be?

Lots of them wouldn't be safe for work, so I'll leave those for bar stool chats. I had a great experience one time on Christmas Day. I was flying from Bangkok, Thailand to Seoul, South Korea on Christmas Eve, due to arrive a few hours into Christmas Day, visit some friends there and celebrate Christmas together in Asia. I was too submerged in my "*Sopranos*" addiction and missed my connection from Malaysia to Korea, despite sitting at the gate four hours early — my earphones, and not changing time zones were to blame, and my serious stupidity.

Anyway, I spent all Christmas Day in Kuala Lumpur airport, and got the next flight eighteen hours later. I arrived in Korea on Boxing Day morning, took the train to the city, then onto a bus for two hours, then onto another bus for two hours. On my final bus I was so tired from a night in the airport, then a night on a flight, I suddenly realized I hadn't taken my back-pack from the first bus, I had just left it and connected onto my next bus without it. Idiot.

I got off the bus in a random town and tried to explain to the staff in the bus station — my Korean is terrible, and generally speaking, South Koreans don't speak great English either. Sud-denly an old woman hands me her cell phone. Confused, I pick it up and the girl on the other end speaks English. The old lady had called her grand-daughter in Switzerland who speaks Eng-lish. Angel! The next thirty minutes entailed lots of translations, phone calls, stress, but they found my bag in the station two hours behind me. I then tried to buy a ticket back to the sta-tion.

"No," the old women said abruptly.

"Sorry, I'm so, so, so grateful for your help, but I really need to go and find my bag".

"NO."

She beckons me outside.

We get in her car, she drives me two hours back to the other station, finds my bag, drives me two hours to the original sta-tion, then asks where I was going anyway, and drives me an hour to my actual final destination, bag in hand. SUPERSTAR. A quick hug, smile, and bow and I'll never see her again. The kindness of strangers is so, so beautiful.

Besides your home country, where do you find yourself returning to over and over and why?

Thailand, as it's my base, to the extent that as soon as I could afford the cash to buy a place, I bought a condo immediately.

As a travel destination, I often find myself back in China. It has so much to offer real travelers.

What is the ideal amount of time you prefer to travel each trip before you are ready for home and a break?

I travel almost indefinitely, but ten months are about my limit before I need a few weeks off — then the next ten months starts again.

If you had an unlimited budget and space and time was no object, what would your perfect travel day look like? (for example: start your morning in Bora Bora; afternoon on a safari in Kenya; night in Australia, etc.)

I would love to wake up in the Maldives, breakfast on a private balcony with my partner followed by a spot of snorkeling and fly-boarding. Then I'd go for a Thai massage and lunch at Huay Thung Tao Lake outside Chiang Mai in the north of Thailand. An afternoon spent watching River Plate play football against Boca Juniors in Buenos Aires, Argentina followed by dinner in Santorini, Greece overlooking the amazing sunset in Oia, followed by a night of some serious partying in London with my Irish and English friends. Perfection.

For those looking to travel to every country, what is the best piece of advice you could offer them?

I see traveling to every country as two different things. Either travel is your lifestyle and you travel full-time, or you work hard, make money and travel far and wide when you can, knocking off countries as and when it's possible.

I can't speak for the second group, but if you want to be part of the first group you need to work out how to sustain yourself. So assuming you're not from a wealthy family, like myself, you need to crack making money on the Internet. If you can do that, then you're free to do anything.

For someone that has been almost everywhere, what still gets you excited about packing your bags again?

I love landing in a new continent — new currency, new food, and new atmosphere. I honestly can't get enough of it. Walking in a new country at dusk, sun setting, eating some cheap street food, grabbing a coffee and watching how people in every corner of the world live their life — it's so exciting.

Do you feel you have missed out on certain aspects of life being away from home so much?

For the first five years of my adult life, I was worried that I had missed out on building a career. I was entering my late twenties and had zero office work experience. I had been away too long, on the road, so I didn't think anyone would give me a job. Knowing that, I started something myself, and it worked out. So now, aside from seeing my friends and family a bit more, I don't think I've missed out on much at all to be honest.

Looking ahead, what travel plans and goals are you still pursuing, and what is on your "Bucket List"?

I think it's going to take another eighteen months for me to finish my journey, which means I'll have spent nine years of almost constant travel to reach my goal. I'm doing Cape Town to Casablanca in 2016 by land and then I'm almost done.

In terms of Bucket List stuff, it's hitting my final country. I've been to all the places I dreamt of as a poor kid, and done almost all the activities I've ever thought of, but there's always more. Carnival in Trinidad, the tomato festival in Spain, Holi in India, and maybe Christmas or New Years in New York are all high on my list. As is cycling across the USA from San Francisco to New York and, time, health and finances permitting, I'd love a crack at Mount Everest before my time is up.

Endnotes

I would like to thank all the travelers who were kind enough to give me so much of their time as this book was compiled over a nearly nine-month span of time from late summer of 2014 to spring of 2015. Without you people, none of this would have been possible.

I would also like to thank Ryan Scheife of Mayfly Design for his help in crafting a great cover, and the superstar team at Ebook Launch for their fast services formatting the ebook and paperback.

To the readers, we hope this book inspires you to see more of the world and live your life to the fullest!

Ryan Trapp

CPSIA information can be obtained at www.ICGtesting.com
Printed in the USA
LVOW08s1448170716

496677LV00003B/84/P